CW00394494

DISPUTE RESOLUTION IN TRANSNATIONAL SECURITIES TRANSACTIONS

This book explores the transnational legal infrastructure for dispute resolution in transnational securities transactions. It discusses the role of law and dispute resolution in securities transactions, the types of disputes arising from them, and the institutional and legal aspects of dispute resolution, both generally and regarding aggregate litigation. It illustrates different dispute resolution systems and aggregate litigation methods, and examines the legal issues of dispute resolution arising from transnational securities transactions. In addition, the book proposes two systems of dispute resolution for transnational securities transactions depending on the type of dispute: collective redress through arbitration and a network of alternative dispute resolution systems.

Dispute Resolution in Transnational Securities Transactions

Tiago Andreotti

·HART·

OXFORD · LONDON · NEW YORK · NEW DELHI · SYDNEY

HART PUBLISHING
Bloomsbury Publishing Plc
Kemp House, Chawley Park, Cumnor Hill, Oxford, OX2 9PH, UK

HART PUBLISHING, the Hart/Stag logo, BLOOMSBURY and the Diana logo are
trademarks of Bloomsbury Publishing Plc
First published in Great Britain 2017

First published in hardback, 2017
Paperback edition, 2020

Copyright © Tiago Andreotti 2017

Tiago Andreotti has asserted his right under the Copyright, Designs and Patents Act
1988 to be identified as Author of this work.

All rights reserved. No part of this publication may be reproduced or transmitted in any form or by
any means, electronic or mechanical, including photocopying, recording, or any information
storage or retrieval system, without prior permission in writing from the publishers.

While every care has been taken to ensure the accuracy of this work, no responsibility for loss or
damage occasioned to any person acting or refraining from action as a result of any statement in it
can be accepted by the authors, editors or publishers.

All UK Government legislation and other public sector information used in the work is Crown
Copyright ©. All House of Lords and House of Commons information used in the work is
Parliamentary Copyright ©. This information is reused under the terms of the Open Government
Licence v3.0 (http:// www.nationalarchives.gov.uk/doc/open-government-licence/ version/3)
except where otherwise stated.

All Eur- lex material used in the work is © European Union,
http://eur-lex.europa.eu/, 1998-2020.

A catalogue record for this book is available from the British Library.

Library of Congress Cataloging- in- Publication Data

Names: Andreotti, Tiago, author.

Title: Dispute resolution in transnational securities transactions /
Tiago Andreotti.

Description: Oxford ; Portland, Oregon : Hart Publishing, an imprint of
Bloomsbury Publishing Plc, 2017. | Based on author's thesis
(doctoral - European University Institute, 2014). |
Includes bibliographical references and index.

Identifiers: LCCN 2017031270 (print) | LCCN 2017031540 (ebook) |

ISBN 9781509908486 (Epub) | ISBN 9781509908462 (hardback)

Subjects: LCSH: Securities. | Dispute resolution (Law)

Classifi cation: LCC K1114.3 (ebook) | LCC K1114.3 .A96 2917 (print) | DDC 346/.0666–dc23
LC record available at https://lccn.loc.gov/2017031270

ISBN: HB: 978-1-50990-846-2
PB: 978-1-50993-747-9
ePDF: 978-1-50990-847-9
ePub: 978-1-50990-848-6

Typeset by Newgen KnowledgeWorks Pvt. Ltd., Chennai, India

To find out more about our authors and books visit www.hartpublishing.co.uk. Here you will find
extracts, author information, details of forthcoming events and the option to sign up for our newsletters.

ACKNOWLEDGMENTS

This book is the culmination of the research I developed at the European University Institute and is a reviewed and updated version of my PhD thesis defended in 2014. This has been a long and fulfilling journey and I am delighted and honoured to present it to you through Hart Publishing.

There were many people that were by my side during this process, from the days when I only planned to enrol in a PhD programme through the revision of the work for this book; they were essential for this achievement.

Dennis Patterson and David Ramos Muñoz, my PhD supervisors, guided me brilliantly and stimulated my thoughts through the research process. Thank you for the support and patience during these years; it has been a pleasure working with you.

The LLM programme at NYU allowed me to develop the background to prepare a research proposal for the EUI PhD programme. From this period, I would like to thank my father, Renato Andreotti, for instilling in me the drive to persist, and my friend Rafael Alves, for the early discussions and suggestions about my project.

During the research I was privileged to attend seminars, present papers and have discussions with Professors Antonio Nicita, Claire Cutler, Ernst-Ulrich Petersmann, Fabrizio Cafaggi, Geoffrey Miller, Giovanni Sartor, Giorgio Monti, Hans-W Micklitz, Miguel Maduro, Mattias Kumm, Marco Lamandini, Nehal Bhuta, Neil Komesar and Stefan Grundmann, among others, whose inputs and insights enriched my work and contributed to my professional development.

While developing my thesis I had the opportunity to intern at the Wilmer Hale International Arbitration Group, where I had some real-life experience of arbitration. For this I am grateful to Gary Born and the Wilmer Hale International Arbitration Group.

The Spanish government provided the funding for the research, allowing me to spend four years in Florence conducting my work.

Sinead Moloney, Roberta Bassi, Tom Adams and Carolyn Fox helped me through the process of reviewing my thesis and transforming it into this book.

I am glad I met Adriana Bessa, Agnieszka Janczuk, Alba Ruibal, Alexis Galan, Alice Margaria, Ana Morales, Andrea Talarico, Annarita Zacchi, Antonio Marcaci, Barbara Warwas, Benedict Wray, Berenika Drazewska, Boris Rigod, Carolina Costa, Christopher Serke, Constantin von der Groeben, Cristina Blasi, Danielle Borges, Daphne Letizia, Edurne Iraizoz, Elisa Novic, Eric Ng, Eugenia Macchiavello, Fabiano Correa, Farah Haidar, Federica Casarosa, Fennie Weng, Filippo Fontanelli, Greg Lourie, Jacob Oberg, Javier Habib, Kasia Granat, Kevin Huber, Luana Swensson, Lucila Almeida, Marija Scekic, Maciej Borowicz,

Marina Aksenova, Mario Viola, Niels Baeten, Noam Zamir, Paolo Saguato, Philipp Hempel, Rebecca Schmidt, Ricardo Garcia, Samantha Ribeiro, Sandro Masseli, Shakeel Sameja, Shalaka Patil, Sonja Sreckovic, Stephanie Law, Stephen Coutts, Társis Gonçalves, Wojtek Mucha and many other people in Europe during these years, with whom I was able to share part of my life, either through work or leisure. This journey would not have been the same without you.

I also wish to thank my friends and family, Adalto Felix, Álvaro Maravieski, Antônio Parron, Antônio Teixeira, Caio Costa, Cauli Costa, Cynara Okuhira, Diego Lerner, Edmir Rodrigues, Elaine Araújo, Eliane Félix, Eurize Pessanha, Fagner Bezerra, Francisco Carvalho, Gabriela Lopes, Giovanna Araújo, Gislaine Machado, Jackelyne Silva, Jenny Andreotti, Jessica Rosa, Letícia Gutierres, Margareth Araújo, Paula Araújo, Pedro Ivo, Renan Peralta, Renato Andreotti, Rodrigo Araújo, Silvia Rodrigues, Tathiany Parron, Thalia Araújo, Vivian Ribeiro, Viviane Araújo and Yvanil Araújo, for their presence in my life and making it as great as it is.

I also would like to mention and thank Professor Clélio Chiesa, who inspired me to get into academia while I was pursuing my undergraduate studies in law.

I dedicate this book to my family: Elaine, Eurize, Renato, Rodrigo and Viviane. Thank you for all the love through these years.

Tiago Andreotti
Campo Grande/MS, Brazil,
April 2017

CONTENTS

Acknowledgements v
Table of Cases xiii
List of Abbreviations xix

1   Introduction: Transnational Securities Disputes and
    Legal Pluralism 1
    I.   Setting the Scene 2
    II. The Objective of This Book 5
    III. Outline of the Argument 7
    IV. Scope and Limitations 8

2   States, Law and Dispute Resolution 11
    I.   The Development of the Modern State 12
    II. The Modern State, the Rule of Law and the Judiciary 16
    III. The Economic Function of Law on Private Matters and Dispute
         Resolution 17
         A.   Basic Structure: Property and Contract Rights 18
         B.   Imperfect Markets and Regulatory Law 20
         C.   The Role of Dispute Resolution Mechanisms 21
    IV. States and Transnational Disputes 22

3   Securities Regulation Theory and the Importance of Private
    Enforcement 24
    I.   Financial Markets 25
         A.   The Mechanics of Price Accuracy 27
         B.   Consequences of Price Inaccuracy 29
              i.   Non-optimal Capital Allocation 29
              ii.   Market Liquidity 30
              iii. Corporate Governance Failures 30
    II. Securities Regulation 31
         A.   Rationale for Securities Regulation: Disclosure 32
         B.   Securities Regulation in the European Union 36
    III. Institutional Aspects of Securities Regulation and the
         Importance of Private Enforcement 37
         A.   The Regulatory Regime—Institutional Aspects 38
              i.   The Regulatory Mix for Securities Regulation 39

      ii.   Standards for Private Enforcement: the Interplay
            Between Public Law and Private Law 40
    B. The Importance of Private Enforcement in Securities
        Regulation 41

4   The Liability Regime for Securities Disputes 45
   I.   Transacting Securities and Disputes 46
      A. Issuing Securities 46
      B. Types of Disputes 47
      C. Transacting Transnationally 49
   II. Legal Framework for Securities Liability—Issuers 50
      A. The United States 51
         i. The Securities Act of 1933 51
         ii. Claims under the Securities and Exchange Act
            of 1934 54
      B. European Union 58
         i. The European Perspective 59
         ii. Implementation in Domestic Systems: the
            Case of Spain 60
         iii. Other Liability Regimes 62
      C. Brazil 63
      D. Disclosure Liability Standards: Similar But Not Equal 66
   III. Legal Framework for Securities Liability—Financial
       Intermediaries 66
   IV. Legal Framework for Securities Liability—Informational
       Intermediaries 71
      A. Compensation 72
      B. The Liability Regime 74
   V.   Concluding Remarks 77

5   Building a Transnational Securities Dispute Resolution System 79
   I.   Problems with Transnational Dispute Resolution of
       Securities Transactions 80
   II. Dispute Resolution Systems in Transnational Securities
       Transactions—Institutional Considerations 81
      A. Investor–Issuer 81
         i. Setting the Incentives 82
         ii. Overcoming the Prohibition of Opt-Out Aggregate
            Litigation 83
         iii. Transnational Aspects 84
         iv. System Design and Rule of Law 84
         v. Implementation Aspects 85
      B. Investor–Financial Intermediary 85
         i. Transnational Aspects 86
         ii. Implementation Aspects 87

C. Investor–Informational Intermediary..88
III. Two Systems for Transnational Dispute Resolution of Securities
Transactions...90
A. Aggregate Litigation Through Arbitration.....................................91
i. Seat of Arbitration and Arbitrability................................91
ii. Arbitration Clauses..92
iii. Importance of the Arbitral Institution................................94
iv. Possible Problems Remaining...95
B. A Network of ADR Systems...96
IV. Concluding Remarks..97

6 Institutional Aspects of Dispute Resolution..99
I. Legal Aspects of the Institutional Framework..................................99
A. The Legal Basis of the Dispute Resolution System......................100
i. Direct Jurisdictional Basis...100
ii. Consent Jurisdictional Basis: Arbitration.........................101
iii. Considerations of the Legal Basis of a Dispute
Resolution System..106
B. The Decision Maker's Independence and Accountability...........106
i. Public Officials...108
ii. Private Decision Makers...109
C. The Reasoning and Publicity of Decisions...................................110
II. Economic Aspects of the Institutional Framework...........................112
A. Costs of Maintaining a Dispute Resolution System....................113
B. Costs of Engaging in a Dispute Resolution Procedure...............113
i. Costs of Access...114
ii. Costs of Evidence and Representation..............................115
III. Implications of the Institutional Framework for a Dispute
Resolution System..115

7 Alternative Models of Dispute Resolution Systems..................................118
I. National Models..118
A. Small Claims Court Model..118
B. The Financial Ombudsman Service Model...................................120
C. Self-Regulation Model..123
D. Arbitration..124
i. State-supervised Model..124
ii. Private Arbitration Model..126
II. International Models...128
A. International Courts..128
B. International Arbitral Institutions..130
C. The European Cross-Border Mechanism for Financial
Disputes: a Network of Dispute Resolution Bodies.....................130
III. Implications..132
A. General Implications..132

    B.   EU Implications 133

8 Aggregate Litigation Design 134
    I.   Aggregate Litigation Design: a Framework for Analysis 135
        A.   Conflicts in Aggregate Litigation... 137
            i.   Conflicts Between Plaintiffs and Lawyer 137
            ii.   Conflicts Between Group Members 138
            iii. Third-Party Financiers 139
            iv.   Conflicts in an Opt-out Procedure 140
        B.   Ethical Limitations 144
        C.   Preclusion Principles and Limits on Choosing an
             Opt-in or Opt-out Mechanism 145
            i.   The Operation of Preclusion – General Aspects................. 145
            ii.   Types and Scope of Preclusion 149
            iii. Preclusion and Non-Mutual Parties: Possibility
                  of the Opt-out Procedure.. 151
            iv.   Preclusion in Arbitration: What Law Will Govern Its
                  Operation? 156
        D.   Final Considerations on Aggregate Litigation Design 158
    II. Aggregate Dispute Resolution and Securities Disputes 158

9 Aggregate Litigation Models 162
    I.   The American Class Action 162
        A.   A Brief History of the Class Action... 162
        B.   Types of Class Action and Their Prerequisites 165
        C.   Class Certification 166
        D.   Class Action and Securities Litigation... 168
    II. Representative Actions: Brazil and Spain... 170
    III. The Dutch Act on Collective Settlement of Mass Damages 173
    IV. The English Group Litigation Order.. 174
    V.   The German Capital Market Model Claims Act 175
    VI. Aggregate Litigation and the European Union 176
    VII. Class Arbitration 179
        A.   Historical Development of Class Arbitration 179
        B.   Class Action Waivers... 181
        C.   The Types of Class Arbitration 182
            i.   The Hybrid Model 182
            ii.   The Provider-created Model... 183
        D.   Class Arbitration Outside the United States 184
        E.   Class Arbitration and the European Union 185
    VIII. Concluding Remarks 185

10 Transnational Aspects of Dispute Resolution 187
    I.   Jurisdiction and Enforcement.. 188
        A.   Jurisdiction 188

    i. The Relationship Between Courts and Parties
      to the Disputes.. 190
    ii. The Relationship Between the Forum Court and Other
      Courts 191
  B. Recognition and Enforcement of Foreign Judgments 197
    i. Integrated Recognition and Enforcement Systems:
      the EU Example 198
    ii. Unilateral Recognition Systems 200
  C. An Attempt at a Global Convention on Jurisdiction 201
  D. Arbitration... 202
  E. Jurisdiction and Enforcement Aspects of Aggregate
    Litigation... 203
 II. Applicable Law.. 204
  A. Contract 206
  B. Tort 208
  C. Applicable Law in Arbitration 209
  D. Applicable Law in Aggregate Litigation with Transnational
    Elements 210
 III. The Public Policy Question... 212
  A. Public Policy and Securities Disputes... 212
  B. Public Policy and Notice in Aggregate Litigation 214
  C. Public Policy and Arbitrability of Securities Disputes................. 216
  D. Public Policy and Arbitration Based on Corporate Charters 218
 IV. Implications for Securities Disputes 220
  A. Investor–Issuer Disputes.. 220
    i. Exchange-based 220
    ii. Open Market 223
  B. Investor–Financial Intermediary Disputes 224
    i. Investor Acts Towards Financial Intermediary......................... 225
    ii. Financial Intermediary Acts Towards Investor......................... 226
  C. Investor–Informational Intermediary Disputes 227
 V. Concluding Remarks on the Transnational Aspects of Securities
  Disputes 228

Bibliography... 229
Index 243

TABLE OF CASES

Australia

Bathurst Regional Council v Local Government Financial Services
Pty Ltd (No 5) [2012] FCA 1200 75

Brazil

American Home Assurance Company v Braspetro Oil Services
Company (STJ, 4th Chamber, REsp 251438 / RJ) (2000) 197
Asa Administradora de Bens v ABN Amro Bank (TJSP, 5th Private Law
Chamber, Civil Appeal n 9247433-87.2005.8.26.000) (2011) 64–65
CZ6 Empreendimentos Comerciais Ltda v Lúcio Maciel (TJRJ,
15th Chamber, Civil Appeal n. 2008.001.30250) (2008) 212
Defensoria Pública da União v Caixa Econômica Federal (4th Federal
Court of Porto Alegre, Statement of Claim Acceptance in Public
Civil Action no 5008379-42.2014.404.7100, 04 February 2014) 172
General Eletric Company v Varig SA (STJ, Special Chamber,
SEC 646/US) (2008) 225
Instituto Brasileiro de Defesa do Consumidor v Caixa Econômica
Federal (STJ, Special Court, EResp 1134957/SP) (2016) 172
Luiz Gonzaga Murat Junior v Justiça Pública (TRF3, 5th Chamber,
Criminal Appeal 45484) (2013) 172
MBV Commercial and Export Management Establishment v Resil
Industria e Comercio Ltda (STF, SE 5206 AgR) (2004) 103
Ministério Público do Estado de São Paulo v Comind Empreendimentos
SA (STJ, 3rd Chamber, REsp 8878 / SP) (2002) 172
Queensland Cotton Corporation Ltd v Agropastoril Jotabasso Ltda
(STJ, Special Chamber, SEC 6753/EX) (2013) 216
RS Components Limited v RS do Brasil Comércio Importação
Exportação Ltda (STJ, 3rd Chamber, REsp 804306 / SP) (2008) 197
Telebrás SA v Ministério Público Federal (TRF1, 2nd Chamber,
Civil Appeal 93.01.04391-2/DF) (1995) 172

Telesp v Ministério Público (TJSP, 7th Private Law Chamber,
    Instrument Appeal 0013965-80.2002.8.26.0000) (2002) 172
Usiminas v Donaldo Armelin (TRF3, 6th Chamber, Civil
    Appeal 1275780) (2008) 172
Usiminas v Ministério Público Federal (TRF3, 6th Chamber,
    Instrumental Appeal 212476 (2004) 172
Walter Appel v Ministério Público (TJSP, 8th Private Law Chamber,
    Instrument Appeal 9034921-85.2007.8.26.0000) (2007) 172
World Company Dance Show v Patrícia Chélida de Lima Santos
    (STJ, 4th Chamber, REsp 1168547 / RJ) (2010) 197

Court of Justice of the European Union

Case Asturcom Telecomunicaciones v Cristina Rodríguez (C-40/08)
    [2009] ECR I-09579 216
Bier v Mines de Potasse d'Alsace [1976] (C-21/76) ECR 01735 221
Eco Swiss China Time Ltd v Benetton International NV (C-126/97)
    [1999] ECR I-3055 150
Gambazzi v DaimlerChrysler (C-394/07) [2009] ECR I-02563 215
Gasser v MISAT (C-116/02) [2003] ECR I-14693 193
Genil 48 SL v Bankinter (C-604/11) (30 May 2013) 70
Hirmann v Immofinanz AG (C-174/12) (19 December 2013) 60
Josi v UGIC (C-412/98) [2000] ECR I-05925 194
Köbler v Republik Österreich (C-224/01) [2003] ECR I-10239 149
Krombach v Bamberski (C-7/98) [2000] ECR I-1395 199
Kronhofer v Maier (C-168/02) [2004] ECR I-06009 ....187, 221, 224
Mostaza Claro v Centro Móvil (C-168/05) [2006] ECR I-10421 216
Oceano Editorial v Roció Quintero (C-240/98) [2000] ECR I-04941 ... 212
Owusu v Jackson (C-281/02) [2005] ECR I-01383 194
Pubblico Ministerio v Ratti (C-148/78) [1979] ECR 1629 60
Renault v Maxicar SpA (C-38/98) [2000] ECR I-02973 199
Réunion Européennee SA v Spliethoff's Becrachtingskantoor BV
    (C-51/97) [1998] ECR I-6534 227
Rewe-Zentral AG v Bundesmonopolverwaltung für Branntwein
    (Cassis de Dijon) (C-120/78) [1979] ECR 649 .... 36, 50
Roche v Primus (C-539/03) [2006] ECR I-06535 211
Rosmarie Kapferer v Schlank & Schick GmbH (C-234/04) [2006]
    ECR I-2585 149
Turner v Grovit (C-159/02) [2004] ECR I-03565 193
Van Duyn v Home Office (C-41/74) [1974] ECR 1337 60

European Courts of Human Rights

Ashingdane v the United Kingdom (1985) Series A no 93 146
Lithgow and Others v the United Kingdom (1986) Series A no 102 214
Tinnelly & Sons Ltd and Others and McElduff and Others v the
   United Kingdom ECHR 1998-IV 146

France

Minister of the Interior v Cohn-Bendit [1980] 1 CMLR 543 60

The Netherlands

Converium Settlement, NJ 2010, 683, NIPR 2011, 85 (Court of
   Appeal Amsterdam 12 November 2010) 203
Converium Settlement, no. 200.070.039/01, LJN: BV1026 (Court of
   Appeal Amsterdam 17 January 2012) 203
Shell Petroleum NV Settlement, LJN: BI 5744, NIPR 2010, 71
   (Court of Appeal Amsterdam 29 May 2009) 203

Spain

AP Madrid (Sección 20a), Sentencia 427/2013 (AC 2014/156) 86
Tribunal Supremo, Sentencia 244/2013 (RJ 2013/3387) 86

United Kingdom

Al Saudi Banque v Clarke Pixley [1990] Ch 313 76
Belmont Park Investments v BNY Corporate Trustee [2011] UKSC 38 4
Bigge v Parkinson [1862] 7 H & N 955 20
Brown v Vermuden (22 Eng Rep 796 (Ch 1676) 163
Caparo Industries v Dickman [1990] 1 All ER 568 76

FOS DRN 1570597 86
FOS DRN 191087 86
FOS DRN 2604832 86
FOS DRN 3727359 86
FOS DRN 3824818 86
James McNaughton Papers v Hicks Anderson Court [1991] 1 All ER 134 76
Jones v Just [1868] LR 3 QB 197 20

United States

American Express Co v Italian Colors Restaurant, 133 S Ct 2304 (2013) 182
APA Excelsior III LP v Premiere Technologies Inc, 476 F 3d 1261
    (11th Cir 2007) 52
AT&T Mobility v Concepcion, 536 US 321 (2011) 212
Baesler v Cont'l Grain Co, 900 F 2d 1193 (8th Cir 1990) 180
Baker v General Motors Corp, 522 US 222 (1998) 149
Basic Inc v Levinson, 485 US 224 (1988) 52,57
Berner v British Commonwealth Pac Airlines, 346 F 2d 532 (2nd Cir 1965) 152
Birnbaum v Newport Steel Corp, 193 F 2d 461 (2nd Cir 1952) 54
Blonder-Tongue Laboratories, Inc v University of Illinois Foundation,
    402 US 313 (1971) 152
Blue Chip Stamps v Manor Drug Stores, 421 US 723 (1975) 54
Bonny v Society of Lloyd's, 3 F 3d 156 (8th Cir 1993) 214
Brown v Ticor Title Insurance Co, 982 F 2d 386 (9th Cir 1992) 166
Burke v Kleiman, 277 Ill App 519 (1934) 165
Burnham v Superior Court of California, 495 US 604 (1990) 190–91
Central Bank of Denver, NA v First Interstate Bank of Denver, NA,
    511 US 164 (1994) 55, 57
Champ v Siegel Trading Co, 55 F 3d 269 (7th Cir 1995) 180
Cheng v Oxford Health Plans, Inc, 2005 WL 5359732 (NY Sup Ct 2006) 181
Cheng v Oxford Health Plans, Inc, 45 App Div 3d 356 (NY App Div 2007) 181
City of Pontiac v UBS AG, No 12-4355-cv (2nd Cir, May 2014) 223
Dabit v Merrill Lynch, 547 US 71 (2006) 170
Dominium Austin Partners, LLC v Emerson, 248 F 3d 720 (8th Cir 2001) 180
Dun & Bradstreet, Inc v Greenmoss Builders, 472 US 749 (1985) 74
Dura Pharmaceuticals, Inc v Broudo, 544 US 336 (2005) 56
Eisen v Carlisle & Jacquelin, 417 US 156 (1974) 167
Erie Railroad Co v Tompkins, 304 US 64 (1938) 200
F Hoffmann-La Roche Ltd v Empagran, 542 US 155 (2004) 195
Farmers High Line Canal v City of Golden, 975 P 2d 189 (1999) 147
General Telephone Co v Falcon, 457 US 147 (1982) 165, 167

Green Tree v Bazzle, 539 US 444 (2003) 180
Gulf Oil Corp v Gilbert, 330 US 501 (1947) 194–95
Halliburton v Erica P John Fund, 573 US ___ (2014) 58
Hansberry v Lee, 311 US 32 (1940) 146, 165–66
Hartford Fire Insurance Co v California, 509 US 764 (1993) 195–96
Haynsworth v The Corp, 121 F 3d 956 (5th Cir 1997) 214
Herman & MacLean v Huddleston, 459 US 375 (1983) 52
Hilton v Guyot, 159 US 113 (1895) 200–01
Huddleston v Herman & Maclean, 640 F 2d 534 (5th Cir 1981) 57
In re AOL Time Warner, Inc Sec and ERISA Litigation, 381 F Supp 2d
    192 (SDNY 2004) 76
In re Enron Corp, Sec, Derivative & ERISA Litigation, 511 F Supp 2d 742
    (SD Tex 2005) 74
In re Merck & Co, Inc Securities Litigation, 432 F 3d 261 (3rd Cir 2005) 53
In re Scottish Re Group Securities Litigation, 524 F Supp 2d 370 (SDNY 2007) 76
Initial Public Offerings Securities Litigation, 471 f 3d 24 (2nd Cir 2006) 167
International Shoe Co v Washington, 326 US 310 (1945) 190–91
JSC Surgutneftegaz v President and Fellows of Harvard College, 2007 WL
    3019234 (SDNY 11 October 2007) 180
Kardon v National Gypsum Co, 69 F Supp 512 (DC Pa 1946) 55
Kasper Wire Works, Inc v Leco Eng'g & Mach, Inc, 575 F 2d 530
    (5th Cir 1978) 149
Keating v Superior Court, 645 P 2d 1192 (Cal 1982) 179, 182
Koster v (American) Lumbermens Mutual Casualty Co, 330 US 518 (1947) 194
Kremer v Chem Constr Corp, 456 US 461 (1982) 149
Laker Airways Ltd v Sabena, Belgian World Airlines, 731 F 2d 909 (1984) 195
Lee v Hansberry, 24 NE 2d 37 (1939) 165
Lehman Brothers v BNY Corporate Trustee, 422 BR 407 (SDNY 2010) 4
Lewis v Circuit City Stores, Inc, 500 F 3d 1140 (10th Cir 2007) 157
Mace v Van Ru Credit Corp, 109 F3d 338 (7th Cir 1997) 141
Martin v Wilks, 490 US 755 (1989) 140, 151
Mitsubishi v Soler Chrysler-Plymouth Inc, 473 US 614 (1985) 212, 217
Montana v United States, 440 US 147 (1979) 151
Morrison v National Australia Bank, 561 US 247 (2010) 2, 85, 196, 221–22
NY Times v Sullivan, 376 US 245 (1964) 74
O'Brien v City of Syracuse, 429 NE 2d 1158 (NY 1981) 147
Oxford Health Plans LLC v Sutter, 133 S Ct 2064 (2013) 182
Parklane Hosiery Co v Shore 439 US 322 (1979) 152
Perkins v Benguet Consolidated Mining Co, 342 US 437 (1952) 191
Perry v Thomas, 107 S Ct 2520 (1987) 219
Phillips Petroleum Co v Shutts, 472 US 797 (1985) 141, 166
Pinter v Dahl, 486 US 622 (1988) 54
Piper Aircraft v Reyno, 454 US 235 (1981) 195
Richards v Jefferson County, 517 US 793 (1996) 146

Richards v Lloyd's of London, 135 F 3d 1289 (9th Cir 1998) 214
Roby v Corporation of Lloyd's, 996 F 2d 1353 (1993) 213–14
Rothman v Gregor, 220 F 3d 81 (2nd Cir 2000) 76
Scherk v Alberto Culver, 417 US 506 (1974) 217
Seagate Technology II Securities Litigation, 843 F Supp 1341 (ND Cal 1994) .. 139
SEC v Capital Gains Research Bureau, Inc, 375 US 180 (1963) 67
SEC v Goldman Sachs and Fabrice Tourre, WL 2305988 (SDNY 2011) 2
Smith v Swormstedt, 57 US 288 (1853) 163
Stolt-Nielsen SA v Animalfeeds Int'l Corp, 435 F Supp 2d 382 (SDNY 2006) ... 180
Superintendent of Insurance of State of New York v Bankers
    Life and Casualty Co, 404 US 6 (1971) 55
Supreme Tribe of Ben-Hur v Cauble, 255 US 356 (1921) 164
Taylor v Sturgell, 553 US 880 (2008) 151
Tellabs Inc v Makor Issues & Rights Ltd, 551 US 308 (2007) 56
Triplett v Lowell, 297 US 638 (1936) 152
United States v Aluminum Co of America, 148 F 2d 416 (2d Cir 1945) 195
Vernon v Drexel Burnham & Company, 52 Cal App 3d 706 (Cal 1975) 179
Weaver, Bennett & Bland, PA v Speedy Bucks, Inc, 162 F Supp 2d 448
    (WDNC 2001) 140
Wilko v Swan, 346 US 427 (1953) 217
World-Wide Volkswagen v Woodson, 444 US 286 (1980) 189

ABBREVIATIONS

AAA	American Arbitration Association
ADR	Alternative Dispute Resolution
ADS	American Depositary Share
AIFM	Alternative Investment Fund Manager
BSM	BM&F Bovespa Supervisão de Mercados (Brazil)
CAM	Câmara de Arbitragem do Mercado (Brazil)
CDS	Credit Default Swap
CFR	Code of Federal Regulations (US)
CJEU	Court of Justice of the European Union
CNMV	Comisión Nacional del Mercado de Valores (Spain)
CRA	Credit Rating Agency
CVM	Comissão de Valores Mobiliários (Brazil)
DSB	Dispute Settlement Body (WTO)
EEA	European Economic Area
ECHR	European Court of Human Rights
EEC	European Economic Community
EU	European Union
FAA	Federal Arbitration Act (US)
FASB	Financial Accounting Standards Board
FCA	Financial Conduct Authority (UK)
FINRA	Financial Industry Regulatory Authority
FOS	Financial Ombudsman Service (UK)
GAAP	Generally Accepted Accounting Principles
GAAS	Generally Accepted Auditing Standards
GLO	Group Litigation Order
HCCH	Hague Conference on Private International Law
IASB	International Accounting Standards Board
ICC	International Chamber of Commerce
ICJ	International Court of Justice
ICSID	International Centre for Settlement of Investment Disputes
IPO	Initial Public Offering
MiFID	Markets in Financial Instruments Directive
NASAA	North American Securities Administrators Association
NASD	National Association of Securities Dealers
NRSRO	Nationally Recognized Statistical Rating Organization
NY	New York

NYSE	New York Stock Exchange
ODR	Online Dispute Resolution
PCA	Permanent Court of Arbitration
PSLRA	Private Securities Litigation Reform Act of 1995 (US)
SEC	Securities and Exchange Commission (US)
SLUSA	Securities Litigation Uniform Standards Act of 1998 (US)
SPV	Special Purpose Vehicle
STF	Supremo Tribunal Federal (Brazil)
STJ	Superior Tribunal de Justiça (Brazil)
TEU	Treaty on European Union
TFEU	Treaty on the Functioning of the European Union
TJMS	Tribunal de Justiça do Estado de Mato Grosso do Sul (Brazil)
TJSP	Tribunal de Justiça do Estado de São Paulo (Brazil)
UCITS	Undertakings for the Collective Investment of Transferable Securities
UK	United Kingdom
UN	United Nations
US	United States
WTO	World Trade Organization

1

Introduction: Transnational Securities Disputes and Legal Pluralism

[C]ross-border problems call for cross-border solutions.[1]

This book explores the dispute resolution systems for securities transactions in a transnational environment. The argument is that a transnational legal infrastructure for transnational securities transactions, especially regarding dispute resolution, is still lacking, undermining the emergence of stronger transnational financial markets. It attempts to identify the problems of transnational securities disputes and to propose a solution to improve the legal infrastructure that addresses them.

Globalisation results in a higher number of cross-border financial transactions, many of which involve securities transactions, which are regulated predominantly at the local level. While the flows of capital are becoming more and more global, the markets, from a legal perspective, are highly local, as are the regulatory systems and dispute resolution mechanisms available to investors. Since financial markets are legal constructs,[2] the rule of law is essential to their proper functioning and therefore this situation may pose serious problems, especially to small and medium-sized investors, who may not be able to seek legal relief due to transaction cost constraints in pursuing a lawsuit against an entity in which they have made an investment.

The problem becomes even more acute in an environment in which, notwithstanding the existence of multiple jurisdictions, there are political and legal processes in development which aim to facilitate a common internal market, such as the European Union. Solving it would create the scope for a higher number of transnational financial transactions as a wider pool of capital would be available for investment, enhancing the benefits of the free flow of capital[3] and guaranteeing that investors' rights would be protected.

---

[1] T Bingham, *The Rule of Law* (Allen Lane 2010) 115.
[2] K Pistor, 'A Legal Theory of Finance' (2013) Columbia Public Law Research Paper No 13–348.
[3] For the benefits and risks of an increased flow of capital, see International Monetary Fund, 'The Liberalization and Management of Capital Flows: an Institutional View' (2012) 10–14.

I. Setting the Scene

The world is a different place than it was 100 years ago. Technology has changed it completely, generating greater interconnectivity than ever before; financial transactions are not an exception. Two recent financial transactions with dire consequences for their investors can illustrate this point:

1. Paulson & Co, a New York-based hedge fund, requested that Goldman Sachs structure a synthetic financial product based on Residential Mortgage Backed Securities[4] to be sold to qualified institutional buyers under Securities and Exchange Commission (SEC) Rule 144A[5] and to foreigners outside the United States under SEC Regulation S.[6] Thereafter two different legal entities, one based in the Cayman Islands[7] and another based in the State of Delaware in the United States were set up as Special Purpose Vehicles (SPVs) to issue such securities. To increase their marketability, ACA Management LLC, a portfolio selection agent, was chosen to select the underlying mortgages. During the selection process Paulson & Co helped ACA Management but the hedge fund had—since the beginning—been betting against the residential mortgage market without disclosing such information. The deal was closed on 26 April 2007, the securities were sold, including to foreign investors,[8] and by 29 January 2008 those investors had already lost more than US$1 billion on the product, while the hedge fund that helped to choose the underlying mortgages was profiting by a figure of around the same amount, i.e. US$1 billion.[9]
2. In another case, National Australia Bank, an Australian bank with shares not traded on an American exchange, but traded on various foreign exchanges and also having American Depository Receipts traded on a US exchange, purchased HomeSide Lending, a company headquartered in Florida that was in the business of servicing mortgages. The purchase was made in 1998 and until 2001 National's annual reports touted the success of HomeSide.[10] On 5 July 2001 National Australia Bank wrote down HomeSide Lending assets by US$450 million and did the same again on 3 September, this time by US$1.75 billion, heavily impacting a multitude of Australian and other non-US investors.

The transnationality of these transactions is evident. Capital flows across borders and parties engage in commercial relationships that are anchored in many different legal systems. Globalisation brings many advantages but it also poses

---

[4] This product is the ABACUS 2007-AC1 created by Goldman Sachs.
[5] 17 CFR § 200.144a (1992).
[6] 17 CFR § 200.901–§ 200.905 (1998).
[7] Abacus 2007-AC1 Indicative terms.
[8] eg, IKB Deutsche Industriebank AG.
[9] See Complaint, *SEC v Goldman Sachs and Fabrice Tourre*, WL 2305988 (SDNY 2011).
[10] *Morrison v National Australia Bank*, 561 US 247, 251 (2010).

serious risks, especially when it comes to finance.[11] As the pace of globalisation increases, the number of financial transactions with a transnational character also tends to increase, posing serious legal problems to the existing state-based legal framework.[12]

The problem is one of a plurality of legal systems governing the same transactional scheme without any consistent mechanism of coordination. The rule of law and different legal concepts of national legal systems, which are essential to the successful functioning of markets, become increasingly difficult to manage when they are tied to different sources of legal authority that apply either to the specific parts of the transaction or to the transaction as a whole, often failing or being insufficient to address market failures that are essential to the development of healthy markets.

Law, when applied to commercial and financial transactions, provides a background in which transactions can be made and disputes can be peacefully resolved in cases of disagreement between the parties. It provides a level of certainty that allows parties to engage in transactions and to avoid the necessity of the private deployment of force. Trust solely in the counterparty is substituted, at least in part, for trust in the legal system. An investor living in a country with a robust legal system can invest in a company without having to worry if the information provided to him is true; if he has been misled he can summon his lawyer and recover the money that has been lost in the transaction.

Now imagine this investor is in the United States, a country considered to have a robust legal system and strong securities regulation. Make him invest in China. If the businessman invests in a Chinese company and that company's shares lose value because of fraudulent information, the investor may be left penniless, even though the whole strength of the US Securities Regulation system may be on his side, simply because the Chinese company has its assets in China.[13]

There are additional questions in relation to transactions that are transnational as opposed to merely national: Where can the dispute be entertained? Which law is applicable? Where and how is the decision enforceable? These questions bring new factors that have to be weighed in deciding whether to invest abroad; the decision will depend on how developed the legal infrastructures are of the place in which the transaction is anchored. When it comes to finance, another wrinkle

---

[11] HS Scott, *International Finance: Transactions, Policy, and Regulation* (Foundation Press 2010) 20–22.

[12] Randall Kroszner claims that 'many international financial transactions occur in a realm that is close to anarchy'; see RS Kroszner, 'The Role of Private Regulation in Maintaining Global Financial Stability' (1999) 18 *Cato Journal* 355, 355.

[13] Cultural, language and legal barriers raise the costs of pursuing litigation in a case like this, since either the case is pursued in the US and the judgment has to be enforced in China or the whole case has to be litigated in China. The small settlement amounts that have been reached in securities cases with Chinese companies listed in the US are indicative of these possible hurdles. See K LaCroix, 'The Modest Early Settlements of Securities Suits Involving US-Listed Chinese Companies' (*The D&O Diary*, 22 June 22) www.dandodiary.com/2012/06/articles/securities-litigation/the-modest-early-settlements-of-securities-suits-involving-u-s-listed-chinese-companies/.

emerges in conceptualising the problem: many of the transactions involve the use of securities, which are heavily regulated by national states. National mandatory law defines what securities are, the duties of the issuer and the range of action that brokers and market players are afforded when transacting these instruments, even though these transactions, considering the bigger picture, are often in fact transnational.

The transnational character, embedded in the legal pluralism that is inherent in transactions occurring across borders, increases the complexity of legal problems that need to be managed. Due to the size of many transnational securities transactions and the amount of trading that is done, there is a lot at stake.[14] The health of financial markets is tied to the legal and technological infrastructures underpinning them, and a decision of a national court can completely change expectations, sometimes risking billions of dollars that are based on transactions similar to the one on the basis of which the decision was made.[15]

At a more individual level, the question arises to what extent investors are able to rely on the legal infrastructure in place. The free flow of capital is good for economic efficiency but the aperture of the system can also bring fraudsters to the market, who may harm investors in places far away from where they actually operate. A robust transnational legal system for dispute resolution could ease these concerns, as it would allow investors to obtain redress.

---

[14] There has been an increase in the number of securities transactions in recent years. The US and Brazil can be seen as good examples of the increase of foreign positions on securities. In the US there has been a significant increase in foreign private securities assets in the last 40 years, from US$44,157 million in 1976 to US$6,222,864 million in 2010. Brazil also experienced an increase; on December 2001 Brazil's international position regarding foreign securities assets was US$6,402 million and 11 years later the amount increased to US$25,759 million. In Spain the increase in foreign positions in private securities investments was not so impressive; it went from €78,053 million in 2004 to €89,494 million in 2012. Before the crisis, Spain reached €132,954 million in foreign securities assets, but evidenced a strong decrease following it. Nonetheless, the foreign position in securities remains substantial and it has been recovering. See Banco Central do Brasil, 'Série Histórica da Posição Internacional de Investimento', www.bcb.gov.br/?SERIEPIIH; Bureau of Economic Analysis, 'International Investment Position of the United States at Yearend, 1976–2010', www.bea.gov/international/xls/intinv10_t2.xls; Banco de España, 'Boletín Estadístico 12/2012' (2013).

[15] Interesting examples are two cases involving the same transaction in the Lehman Brothers bankruptcy: *Lehman Brothers v BNY Corporate Trustee*, 422 BR 407 (SDNY 2010) and *Belmont Park Investments v BNY Corporate Trustee* [2011] UKSC 38. The transaction in these two cases was composed of a series of credit swap transactions through the use of various SPVs incorporated in jurisdictions chosen for tax purposes. In the specific transaction under consideration involving the SPV Saphir Finance plc, which was incorporated in Ireland, English law was chosen. The SPV had a credit default swap (CDS) with Lehman Brothers Special Financing. The transaction was collateralised, and the trustee for the collateral was BNY Corporate Trustee Services Ltd. There was a provision in the transaction documents that the priority of the collateral would shift in case there was an event of default by Lehman Brothers Special Financing, which occurred when Lehman Brothers Special Financing went bankrupt. Even though there was an expectation of the parties ex ante that this was a possible transaction, the US decision in 2010 signalled otherwise, creating an uncertain environment for all similar transactions where the CDS counterparty is American. Later, the UK Supreme Court confirmed that the transaction was valid under English law. The American case settled in 2010, without a decision of a higher court, and new litigation on the same subject has started again. See T Alloway, 'The Lehman flip-clause flap gets settled – sort of' (*FT Alphaville*, 27 July 2011) ftalphaville.ft.com/2011/07/27/634976/the-lehman-flip-clause-flap-gets-settled-sort-of/.

The existence of multiple legal orders to which a single economic transaction can be attached is a legal risk that can become problematic to the development of global securities markets. Legal instability due to the competing sources of norm creation, decision making and enforcement mechanisms affects the predictability of results, which in turn affect the costs of doing business. The development of complementary mechanisms of dispute resolution and coordination among different legal systems can be a valuable instrument to improve the costs of transacting in a globalised world.

II. The Objective of This Book

The instability of legal relations arising from the tension of the transnational being regulated nationally is the starting point of this book. While capital mobility is deemed to be easier today than it was 100 years ago, be it due to the increasing interlinkage between the different corners of the world or the technological developments that have been made in recent decades, moving capital and goods across borders is not yet as easy as moving them within a country. Notwithstanding claims as to the loss of power of the nation state, its power is still substantial in regulating economic activity under its area of influence.[16] There is no vacuum; the nation state is still present with its entire institutional framework, remaining relevant to every aspect of everyday business life, either by exercising power through direct regulation or by setting the background environment for business.[17]

The role of the legal system in the operation of a market is threefold: first, it provides the background framework so economic transactions can be entered into; secondly, it regulates behaviour that should not be allowed due to the negative effects that it may have; and finally, it provides avenues for redress for those who have been harmed by a party that does not comply with what has been promised or that does not behave according to the rules of the market.

In contract law, an example of the first role of the legal system is the possibility to recover damages from a broken contract in a court of law.[18] In the securities area, the example of the second role and third role of the legal system is the

---

[16] For a discussion of the nation state in a globalised era, see V Cable, 'The Diminished Nation-State: a Study in the Loss of Economic Power' (1995) 124 *Daedalus* 23.

[17] It is true that illegal activities fall outside the direct control of the state, but this is not the focus of this work. In every other activity the state is deeply present. Think about a business that operates according to the legal rules, obtaining the necessary permits and paying all the required taxes. The entrepreneur may decide to avoid such rules and taxes and move to another nation state, but he will have to abide by the rules and pay the taxes imposed by the second state. Contracting around one nation state is possible, but this means not doing business in it and invariably being subject to another state.

[18] Specific performance is not the usual method for compensation in the US. See J Calamari and J Perillo, *The Law of Contracts* (4th edn, West Group 1998) 611–13.

following: if A is obliged to disclose information and fails to do so, A will be liable to B for the loss of value in stock when the information is subsequently discovered.

The framework of a given legal system affects the way in which people behave. This is true not only in respect of the identification of the substantive rules and the expected outcome given the occurrence of a legal fact, but also with regard to the costs of engaging the state in the dispute, by solving it and enforcing the outcome. In each legal system the architecture is defined by policy choices that have been made throughout history, creating different substantive rules and enforcement mechanisms depending on the jurisdiction that is analysed. These are aspects that have to be taken into consideration. It is clear that given a breach of a legal rule in a country where the legal system is effective, it is less likely that the party harmed will need other guarantees for the transaction since the legal system will be available to solve the problem. Where the legal infrastructure is weak, for example with high costs of litigation and trials that are too long, the parties would use other means of protection, such as demanding collateral in an escrow account or the guarantee of a trustworthy person, before engaging in a transaction. This is important for the development of a local financial market as high legal costs and uncertainty as to the rules operating at a given time, or the enforcement of those rules, may discourage investment.

The transnational aspect brings new considerations that have to be taken into account. In this environment, there is no longer only one legal system that has to be considered, but rather, as many as the different jurisdictions that may be involved in the transaction. The *BNY* case cited above involved Australian investors purchasing securities from an Australian SPV that purchased securities from an Irish SPV, which in turn had a swap transaction governed by English law with an American company, with England being the chosen forum for any disputes. There were at least four different jurisdictions involved in this single case.

The legal uncertainty arising from this scenario undermines the safety that law can provide for securities transactions. The problem of legal uncertainty is even stronger in this field as finance is a legal construction.[19] Legal uncertainties create risk, but the fewer legal risks that are present, the better it is for the parties to engage in transactions.[20]

The answer to any question arising out of these considerations has to include both the national and the international legal framework, substantively and procedurally. Depending on the legal question being decided, the answers can differ widely across different jurisdictions, even if the substantive rules of behaviour are similar. In addition, even if the rules are the same, the enforcement of a decision from one jurisdiction is not always enforceable in a second one, where the assets of the person liable for the harm caused to the investor may be located. This is due to the public policy aspect of securities regulation, and more generally financial

---

[19] See Pistor (n 2).
[20] For an overview on legal risk, see R McCormick, *Legal Risk in the Financial Markets* (2nd edn, Oxford University Press 2010) 13.

regulation, especially in the so-called public markets, where the general population can purchase securities. Business and investment decisions are, consciously or not, embedded in this social reality.

The stability of the legal infrastructure upon which a transnational transaction is anchored matters because it allows for the enforceability of the parties' rights when duties are breached, being related to the costs of doing business. As the legal structures in place to address these concerns are far from being perfect, the objective of this book is to propose mechanisms to improve the legal infrastructure for transnational securities transactions disputes.

To achieve this objective it is first necessary to assess the current problems present in the transnational framework for dispute resolution in securities disputes and then to provide options to strengthen the procedural efficiency of the legal framework used to resolve transnational securities disputes, improving investor protection and creating a background for the development of a more robust global financial market.

Notwithstanding that all countries do indeed have securities regulation and are interested in investor protection, the level of protection is a matter of public policy, which can be a barrier to the effective transnationalisation of securities transactions, or at least to the enforcement of decisions related to them. Therefore, in reaching the objective of this book, it is also necessary to consider the extent to which public policy considerations of securities transactions influence private (national and international) law.

The book proceeds in the following way: in Chapter 2, I analyse how the state and the legal system relate to markets; in Chapter 3, I establish the purpose of and importance of securities regulation and enforcement and the policy choices behind it; in Chapter 4, I analyse the private liability regimes arising out of securities regulation in order to define the scope of disputes that are relevant in this field; in Chapter 5, I propose two systems for dispute resolution of transnational securities transactions; in Chapters 6 and 8, I provide a framework to analyse the important aspects of a dispute resolution system, generally and regarding aggregate dispute resolution; in Chapters 7 and 9, I survey certain frameworks that can be used in securities disputes, justifying the choices made for the two proposed systems in Chapter 5; finally, in Chapter 10, I analyse the private international law regime and the legal problems arising therefrom, related to securities disputes.

III. Outline of the Argument

The book is premised on the following thesis: 'Considering that private enforcement is a crucial mechanism for the application of securities laws, investor protection and the construction of efficient capital markets, a more stable system of dispute resolution for transnational securities transactions is necessary for a better functioning of the transnational securities market.'

The main claims that I make throughout the next chapters can be briefly summarised as follows:

1. As financial markets are legal constructs, the rule of law is necessary for their development (Chapters 2 and 3).
2. The role of law for financial markets is twofold: to provide protection for property and to enforce promises and to regulate market failures in order to protect investors and avoid the 'lemons problem' (Chapters 2 and 3).
3. These two goals run together: the regulatory aspect creates expectations; breaches of these expectations are better addressed through private rights of action as a starting point, both from an economic as well as a social point of view (Chapter 3).
4. Therefore, the enforcement of these expectations becomes a problem of access to justice, where the investor needs to be able to enforce both the rights arising out of the security itself as well as the rights related to the regulatory background within which the transaction was embedded (Chapters 6, 7, 8 and 9).
5. The adequacy of a dispute resolution method for securities transactions depends on the type of dispute at stake, since their specific characteristics may warrant different types of schemes (Chapter 4).
6. Collective redress is adequate for disputes involving a multitude of claimants based on the same underlying facts, but not for transactions made with financial intermediaries (Chapters 6, 7, 8 and 9).
7. At the transnational level, the transnational infrastructure of private law enforcement does not yet provide a proper solution for the problem as the rules of private international law remain too uncertain to be relied upon due to the underdevelopment of its rules concerning securities transactions and due to public policy considerations (Chapter 10).

Based on these claims and the analysis undertaken throughout the rest of this work, which shows that there is no one-size-fits-all solution, I propose in Chapter 5 two dispute resolution system designs to increase legal certainty and to provide better access/protection to investors in transnational securities transactions.

IV. Scope and Limitations

The volume of literature on transnational litigation and securities regulation is quite dense, but the discussion of transnational securities litigation is still in its infancy. While a few studies have already been undertaken, a systematic understanding of the problems involved in these kinds of disputes is still lacking.

The importance of this book is based on the use of securities as a method of financing the most varied types of economic activities. The process allows corporations to raise equity or to issue debt in order to pursue their business as well as to structure different investment vehicles through the securitisation process,[21] which is backed by the legal system in creating duties and liabilities for the parties involved. The breach of a duty is corrected through litigation or another form of dispute resolution, either public or private.[22] Both types of enforcement form part of the regulatory architecture but the private one plays a crucial role in stabilising the expectations of the parties in a securities transaction and providing confidence for engaging therein, contributing to the integrity of a securities market.

As the legal systems involved in securities regulation and the disputes in this area of law are grounded in state structures, the research is comparative in nature, which imposes a limitation on the current work. Its main focus is on the United States, the European Union and Brazil; however, some consideration will be given to important developments occurring in other jurisdictions. The choices have been made on the basis of determinations pertaining to relevance and practicality.

The United States is the crib of securities regulation and securities disputes; discussing transnational securities dispute resolution without discussing the American literature would lead to a failure to grasp some important questions in this area. The European Union was chosen due to its internal transnational aspect and its federalist structure, which is interesting both from a securities regulation perspective and in light of the legal infrastructure for transnational dispute resolution. Finally, with its growing importance in the international arena and being a developing country, Brazil was the third jurisdiction chosen for this study. Moreover, the different aspects of the dispute resolution structure and the practice involving securities litigation in these countries were deemed relevant to this decision. The United States has a predominantly dual structure, with the possibility of class actions against issuers and a highly institutionalised arbitration system against broker-dealers; The European Union has seen some litigation against financial intermediaries, particularly following the demise of Lehman Brothers, generating a good source of material to analyse dispute resolution in practice, while at the same time bringing to the fore relevant legislation as well as interesting mechanisms underpinning the creation of alternative methods of dispute resolution in this area. Finally, Brazil presents an obscure arbitration system that is mandatory for corporations listed within the two higher corporate governance levels in the Brazilian stock exchange; at the same time, there is almost no court litigation on securities matters, despite specific legislation for aggregate litigation in this area.

---

[21] For an overview of the securitisation process, see DR Muñoz, *The Law of Transnational Securitization* (Oxford University Press 2010).

[22] Public litigation in this work is understood as litigation initiated by governmental bodies, such as securities and exchange commissions or public attorneys' offices, while private litigation is understood as that initiated by a party due to its capacity as an investor, or as an investor's representative, be the litigant a private party or a state.

The peculiarities of these systems provide ample material for the analysis of the problems in dispute resolution systems for securities transactions, giving foundation to a deeper reflection on how to improve the transnational infrastructure for dispute resolution in securities transactions.

2

States, Law and Dispute Resolution

The overarching problem that this book tries to address is one of economic transactions being grounded in different legal structures and how disputes arising out of these transactions are resolved. Legality is dependent on legal systems, which are in turn dependent on socio-political structures.

Legal systems have arisen out of the interaction between men and their political organisations in states or state-like structures. States rise from human interaction. As long as there is a group of men engaging in everyday activities among themselves for an extended period of time, states are bound to appear. Historically they exist at least as far back as the first agricultural societies, 10,000 years ago in Mesopotamia.[1] In the Weberian sense of the term, the 'state' can be defined as 'a human community that (successfully) claims the *monopoly of the legitimate use of physical force* within a given territory',[2] which means that the state's essence is nothing more than power of enforcement.[3] More specifically, the state can be defined in the following manner:

> A compulsory political organization with continuous operations (*politischer Anstaltsbetrieb*) will be called a 'state' insofar as its administrative staff successfully upholds the claim to the monopoly of the legitimate use of physical force in the enforcement of its order.[4]

This essence of the state underpins the whole judicial structure and its effective use by private parties via litigation—and consequently securities litigation. As securities transactions become globalised, different states and their legal structures will increasingly be involved in resolving disputes that may arise out of them. The analysis of the possible interactions of different legal systems in dispute resolution must begin with the understanding of the bases of legal systems and their role in regulating private relationships. This is the objective of this chapter.

---

[1] F Fukuyama, *State-Building: Governance and World Order in the 21st Century* (Cornell University Press 2004) 1.
[2] M Weber, *From Max Weber: Essays in Sociology* (Routledge 1991) 78.
[3] Fukuyama (n 1) 6.
[4] M Weber, *Economy and Society* (University of California Press 1978) 54.

I. The Development of the Modern State

The modern state has the following basic characteristics:

> [I]t possesses an administrative and legal order subject to change by legislation, to which the organized activities of the administrative staff, which are also controlled by regulations, are oriented. This system of order claims binding authority, not only over the members of the state, … but also to a very large extent over all action taking place in the area of its jurisdiction. … Furthermore, today, the use of force is regarded as legitimate only so far as it is either permitted by the state or prescribed by it.[5]

The formation of the modern state has come a long way, and there are different theories as to how the state, as a political entity, came into existence. A convincing one is based on ecological factors of particular regions of the world[6] and its consequence in the organisation of social groups.[7] As far as the ecological theory goes, there are three factors that were relevant to the rise of the state:[8] environmental circumscription, resource concentration and social circumscription.

According to the theory, the organisation of humans began with small autonomous farming communities that did not interact with each other, but were bound territorially by environmental characteristics, such as mountains, valleys and rivers.[9] With the growth of these farming communities, not only in size but also in quantity through the creation of new distinct ones, the available land for farming was soon depleted and the human pressure on the land began to increase, leading to physical disputes between villages.[10] Since they were circumscribed territorially, those who lost could not flee, and to be able to stay on the land they became subordinated to the winners and obliged to pay taxes. This also involved the loss of political autonomy on the part of those who were defeated, as they were incorporated into the political unit of the winner.[11] The process would repeat itself, transforming villages into chiefdoms and chiefdoms into kingdoms. Meanwhile, internally, these newly formed kingdoms had to administer those new areas as they were conquered, leading to social divisions through the empowerment of persons loyal to the winning side of those disputes (the upper class) and the employment of the losers as servants and slaves (the lower class).[12] Finally, those who were made landless but not enslaved tended to go to the towns and cities that were being spawned

---

[5] ibid 56.

[6] RL Carneiro, 'A Theory of the Origin of the State: Traditional Theories of State Origins are Considered and Rejected in Favor of a New Ecological Hypothesis' in JA Hall (ed), *The State: Critical Concepts*, vol I (Routlegde 1994).

[7] This theory will be used to illustrate the initial evolution of the state up to its current model.

[8] The author defines state as 'an autonomous political unit, encompassing many communities within its territory and having a centralized government with the power to collect taxes, draft men for work or war, and decree and enforce laws' Carneiro (n 6) 433.

[9] The example used in the text was the Peruvian coastal valley, ibid 437.

[10] ibid 437–38.

[11] ibid 439.

[12] ibid.

at the time, earning a living through working for the upper class and financed by the surplus taken from village farmers.[13]

The resource concentration and the social circumscription facets of the ecological theory of state creation explain the exceptions of the environmental circumscription factor: states were created not only on the basis of circumscribed agricultural land, but also from more open areas. A small area with a high resource concentration would play a similar concentrating role as environmental barriers, leading to a concentration of different autonomous groups of people that would end up fighting for these resources, ultimately generating similar processes of warfare and political integration.[14] Finally, another factor that may have played a role in political integration in the first days of state formation in the history of mankind may have been social circumscription. Research on the Yanomamo Indians of Venezuela shows that villages that were surrounded by other villages tended to be larger, possibly due to the higher probability of warfare with neighbouring villages and the consequent political integration resulting therefrom, due to the fact that the villages in the centre of an area might have been more prone to attacks and outside influence than those at the periphery.[15] If this theory is correct, the initial formation of states is due to the consolidation and systematisation of the exercise of power through a delimited geographical space, confirming Weber's definition of statehood.

As previously mentioned, the definition of state comprises a claim to a monopoly on the legitimate use of physical force within a given territory,[16] in other words, the exercise of legitimate authority.[17] At the beginning the conquered group may resist the commands of its new master, but over time, acceptance of the new status quo becomes embedded in the resisting social group. At some point, absent revolution, it is likely that the new master will be seen as a legitimate source of command by the group or by the successors of the group that had been conquered, who will acknowledge and obey the master's commands as legitimate authority. As long as there is a belief that those commands are legitimate, the ruled population will follow them without resistance.[18]

This idea of legitimacy constitutes an important aspect of the exercise of power of a given state since it determines the binding nature of its rules and the likelihood of its survival in respect of its internal aspects. Legitimacy creates authority, the right to command and to be obeyed, as acknowledged by the general population.[19] The grounds for the legitimacy of a source of power can be categorised,

---

[13] ibid.

[14] ibid 440–41.

[15] ibid 441–43.

[16] Or over a certain population. RP Wolff, *In Defense of Anarchism* (Harper & Row 1998) 3.

[17] The concept of legitimate authority used here is not the morally justified legitimate authority, but the sociologically accepted one. To this extent, legitimacy within this context is the obedience by a group of people to the commands of a given source. See M Weber, *The Theory of Social and Economic Organization* (The Free Press 1947) 124–32.

[18] See ibid 324–29.

[19] Wolff (n 16) 4–5.

according to Weber, into three different groups: rational grounds,[20] traditional grounds[21] and charismatic grounds.[22]

Until recently the idea of the state and the exercise of power and authority was strongly linked to the ruler as a person, who was considered to possess and even embody the institutions of the state personally.[23] From the old monarchical state to the more modern one based on popular sovereignty, this concept has changed, having attributed to it a double impersonal character; the state authority is distinguishable both from the rulers entrusted with the exercise of such authority as well as the authority of the society over which the power of the state is exercised.[24] As the state is seen as having its own authority, there is a fundamental change in the source of its legitimacy, that is, a shift from the traditional and charismatic grounds to the rational one.[25] This idea of impersonal power brings with it the necessity of the articulation of the rules and processes that will govern the polity through objective determinations. The 'subjective and arbitrary will of particular men' is excluded and those wielding power may even suffer sanctions if they decide to follow the path of arbitrariness, in disconformity with the general rules that are deemed to govern the state.[26] This is what is known as the rule of law, and it is usually attributable to a core of rights attributed to the population of a given state, guaranteeing them minimum political rights.[27]

One important aspect for the exercise of legitimate power is the existence of a theory on the source of the state's power that is justifiable, at least to the extent that

---

[20] Weber (n 17) 328 ('resting on a belief in the "legality" of patterns of normative rules and the right of those elevated to authority under such rules to issue commands (legal authority)').

[21] ibid ('resting on an established belief in the sanctity of immemorial traditions and the legitimacy of the status of those exercising authority under them (traditional authority)').

[22] ibid 328–29 ('resting on devotion to the specific and exceptional sanctity, heroism or exemplary character of an individual person, and of the normative patterns or order revealed or ordained by him (charismatic authority)').

[23] Q Skinner, 'The State' in Robert Goodin and Philip Pettit (eds), *Contemporary Political Philosophy: An Anthology* (Blackwell Publishing 2006) 9.

[24] ibid 13.

[25] Not that the charismatic and traditional grounds are meaningless; just the weight that they have in the justification of the exercise of power by the state is reduced, while the weight given to the rational ground is increased.

[26] C Pierson, *The Modern State* (Routledge 2011) 15–16.

[27] Tom Bingham translates the rule of law through a few principles: '(1) [t]he law must be accessible and so far as possible intelligible, clear and predictable[;] (2) [q]uestions of legal right and liability should ordinarily be resolved by application of the law and not the exercise of discretion[;] (3) [t]he laws of the land should apply equally to all, save to the extent that objective differences justify differentiation[;] (4) [m]inisters and public officers at all levels must exercise the powers conferred on them in good faith, fairly, for the purpose for which the powers were conferred, without exceeding the limits of such powers and not unreasonably[;] (5) [t]he law must afford adequate protection of fundamental human rights[;] (6) [m]eans must be provided for resolving, without prohibitive cost or inordinate delay, bona fide civil disputes which the parties themselves are unable to resolve[;] (7) [a]djudicative procedures provided by the state should be fair[;] (8) [t]he rule of law requires compliance by the state with its obligations in international law as in national law' (T Bingham, *The Rule of Law* (Allen Lane 2010) 37, 48, 55, 60, 66, 85, 90 and 110).

the justification is accepted by the majority of the general population governed by such state.[28] The theory of choice in the Western world is that of democracy.

Notwithstanding the various types of democracy,[29] the overarching idea behind the theory is seductive to justify the exercise of power by the state over its population. Democracy's basic framework consists of treating each person equally and requiring a majority for a decision that will bind others. This is a very simplistic concept of democracy[30] but it is intuitive and provides an easy explanation that can be engaged by the population, namely that the system of rules by which they are bound has in fact, as its source of power, the population themselves, since they legitimise the exercise of power through their vote. As a legitimating mechanism for states, democracy is so important that even manifestly autocratic governments try to engage its convincing attributes, even if merely rhetorically, to advance their image as legitimate wielders of power.[31]

Democracy and the rule of law tend to go together in modern states. The exercise of the state's power is based on a legal infrastructure, which is anchored to a constitution that guarantees minimum rights to the population for the exercise of political rights, preventing the demise of democracy.[32] These rights have to be preserved by institutional mechanisms that offer effective protection; the concept of the rule of law is suited to the task. Having an impersonal state, with decision makers and mechanisms to balance the exercise of power within the state structure, the rule of law has to be built around institutional mechanisms that arbitrate the exercise of power within the state itself, guaranteeing democracy through a prearranged set of rules[33] and preventing the takeover of the state structure by a tyrant.

The importance of the rule of law also goes beyond the political question of justifying the exercise of power, touching upon various economic problems, as will be explained below. The economic benefits that legal rules can bring to the

---

[28] The minority who disagree with the exercise of power by the state will nonetheless be subject to it, having the order imposed on them. Weber (n 17) 132.

[29] For a brief overview of the different types of democracy, see A Gutmann, 'Democracy' in Robert E Goodin, P Pettit and T Pogge (eds), *A Companion to Contemporary Political Philosophy*, vol 2 (Blackwell Publishing 2007).

[30] Robert Talisse called it the *schoolyard view* of democracy. RB Talisse, 'Democracy' in G Gaus and F D'Agostino (eds), *The Routledge Companion to Social and Political Philosophy* (Routledge 2013) 608.

[31] The example that jumps to mind is the 1964 military coup in Brazil, characterised as the 'Democratic Revolution of 1964' by the dictatorship. For an account of the military dictatorship in Brazil, see E Gaspari, *A Ditadura Envergonhada*, vol 1 (Companhia das Letras 2002); E Gaspari, *A Ditadura Escancarada*, vol 2 (Companhia das Letras 2002); E Gaspari, *A Ditadura Derrotada*, vol 3 (Companhia das Letras 2003); E Gaspari, *A Ditadura Encurralada*, vol 4 (Companhia das Letras 2004).

[32] Not all modern societies have a Constitution to limit the sovereign's power. For example, in the UK the Parliament is seen as sovereign, having the power to change any rules that exist in the political system. See AV Dicey, *The Law of the Constitution* (Oxford University Press 2013) 27–49.

[33] The questions posed in such a political system will have to be decided by a human, since the exercise of power presupposes the human will. A rational basis for the interpretation and application of the rules guaranteeing democracy is, to a great extent, also a mechanism guaranteeing legitimacy, since well-articulated decisions are more convincing than arbitrary ones. As long as there is a belief that the decisions within society have a rational basis and can be traced back to its democratic source and the norms guaranteeing it, legitimacy is more likely to be guaranteed.

organisation of society and to the functioning of markets is an essential theme underlying this work.

II. The Modern State, the Rule of Law and the Judiciary

The last section concluded with the assertion that democracy and the rule of law tend to go together in modern states. This is a question of the distribution of power within the inner political workings of the state and its authority over those who are ruled. Law is, by essence, rationally justified, legitimate commands from the state over those being ruled.

However, legal systems are not a given in every single political society. As mentioned above, many states were merely the extension of the power of a specific person or a group of persons; these persons would do what they wanted and as they pleased. At some point during its development, a state might have been legalised. Legalisation is nothing more than the application of the rule of law ideal to the governance of the state and the exercise of the state's power, in the sense that the rulers will be bound by rules not deriving exclusively from their own will; the exercise of the state's power will only be legitimate if such rules are followed.

Within the rule of law ideal, rules form the constraints of the political system,[34] but their legitimisation is only operational to the extent that they are justifiable; it is here that the democratic ideal comes into play.

In democracies, the democratic aspect of the state is what, from a power and authority perspective, backs and sustains the legal system anchored to a rule of recognition. This is a rule 'for conclusive identification of the primary rules of obligation',[35] those that bind the population in a certain way. The rule of recognition lays the parameters for identification of the validity of a given rule within the legal system; one of them being the identification of the political body of the state that is authorised to promulgate rules, which can thus be considered the ruler of the population.[36] The problem is that if the population is not satisfied with the rulers that are embedded in this system, they may launch a revolution and destroy the political system in place, together with the rule of recognition and the legal system established by it. Revolutions do not tend to constitute easy paths, bringing violence, waste of resources and social paralysis that are better being avoided. Democracy, as an ideal, is an adequate concept to avoid these results since it is the exercise of power by the people. By institutionalising democracy within the legal system—and in consequence, also in the political system—the people do not

---

[34] The foundational rule of a political system is its Constitution.

[35] HLA Hart, *The Concept of Law* (Oxford University Press 1994) 95.

[36] Not all rules of recognition need to identify the body that promulgates rules, but it is hard to envision a modern state that possesses a rule of recognition without this characteristic since the rules would then be completely static.

need to engage in a messy revolution in order to change the rulers, but need only to decide, through an orderly process, that new rulers should assume the place of those with whom they have come to be discontented, ensuring the legitimacy and continuity of the state and its legal system.[37] Revolution still is possible, but as long as the majority supports the system in place, the revolutionary activity will most likely be unsuccessful.[38] Since rule through democracy is highly justifiable and acceptable by the general population, the duo of the rule of law and democracy is a good combination for the provision of stability to a political system that decides to adopt it.

The characteristics that have been presented thus far for a modern legal system are the existence of a rule recognising the rules that are binding on the population and the rules that are binding on the population, backed by a democratic system of empowerment. These rules regulate not only the relationship between the sovereign and subject, but also the relationships between subjects. The role of the rule of law and the rules on private transactions is also important for economic development, as it provides the foundations for people to transact without having to use significant resources to ensure their own protection.

In this scenario, there still is something missing; this consideration relates to the institutions that, when a conflict arises, will decide on the particular case, that is, on who has broken a rule of the system. This role falls to the judiciary,[39] which has a double function within society: first, acting as a buffer between the rulers and the ruled and guaranteeing that the rules of the legal system are observed; and secondly, acting as the umpire of the legal rules applicable to private relationships.

The rationale and importance of this second role of legal institutions in the economic area is the next topic of discussion.

III. The Economic Function of Law on Private Matters and Dispute Resolution

Economically, legal institutions are important for two main reasons: they create rules which economic actors can use to protect their investment and plan their economic activity and they reduce market inefficiencies in specific markets through regulation. In addition, a third reason in support of the two mentioned above is that legal institutions also provide a mechanism to resolve disputes arising out of failure to observe such rules and regulations.

---

[37] A good discussion on this idea of democracy as a system for revolution can be found in J Hampton, 'Democracy and the Rule of Law' in I Shapiro (ed), *The Rule of Law: Nomos XXXVI* (New York University Press 1994) 32–38.

[38] ibid 37.

[39] Hart (n 35) 96–98.

A. Basic Structure: Property and Contract Rights

Property and contract rights are important mechanisms for the economic organisation of private matters,[40] being the basic legal instruments that allow for the planning and execution of economic activities.

The same logic for the appearance of states is also that underpinning the appearance of property rights within the state. States appeared as the consequence of power disputes for the control of scarce resources. Within a more stable set of social relationships, the more the population grew the more people had to organise themselves in terms of undertaking economic activity,[41] distributing land and allowing for the use of the natural structure available in an orderly manner.[42]

There are at least three main problems that property rights are designed to address: the overuse of resources leading to their depletion;[43] the avoidance of disputes on the use of a resource; and the incentive to invest.

These three objectives are all tied together and are based on the same source of concern, which is scarcity. If everyone can have access to a scarce good, such as fish in a pond, their capture will soon deplete the reserve available if there is no means to control the rate of extraction compared to the rate of reproduction. The second point is that scarce goods that have value will lead to disputes among people that want to use them, creating a waste of energy that could be focused on other, more productive, activities.[44] Finally, people will only invest energy in a given enterprise, be it the construction of a house or the farming of land, if there is some sort of guarantee that they will be able to enjoy the proceeds of their investment.

---

[40] Private matters are understood as the relationships between individuals or individuals and governments acting in their private capacity, and not in a governmental or regulatory role.

[41] The relationship between the size of the population and the scarcity of resources is essential to understanding the genesis of property rights. It is interesting to quote the statement of Blackstone, back in 18th-century England: 'But when mankind increased in number, craft, and ambition, it became necessary to entertain conceptions of more permanent dominion; and to appropriate to individuals not the immediate *use* only, but the very substance of the thing to be used. Otherwise innumerable tumults must have arisen, and the good order of the world been continually broken and disturbed, while a variety of persons were striving to get the first occupation of the same thing, or disputing which of them had actually gained it' (W Blackstone, *Commentaries on the Law of England* 4 (1766) cited in RA Epstein (ed), *Economics of Property Law* (Edward Elgar 2007) x).

[42] After property rights are established, the actual contours of the institute and the specific types of division of property in a given society, thinking on a scale from commonly held property to individually held property, will be a function of the relationship between transaction costs and exclusion costs. See BC Field, 'The Evolution of Property Rights' (1989) 42 *Kyklos* 319. An ancient system that has been widely studied is the Roman Legal System, which had a well-developed body of property law. See A Borkowski, *Borkowski's Textbook on Roman Law* (Oxford University Press 2010) 151–204.

[43] This is known as the tragedy of the commons. See G Hardin, 'The Tragedy of the Commons' (1968) 162 *Science* 1243.

[44] On the tragedy of the commons problem, there are arguably three solutions: one is privatisation, the attachment of property rights to common property and its division among its users, with a dispute resolution system to back it up as we are discussing here; the second is centralisation, in other words regulation through the state; and finally, self-regulation through binding contracts, with the necessity for an external actor for enforcement. See E Ostrom, *Governing the Commons: The Evolution of Institutions for Collective Action* (Cambridge University Press 1990) 1–28.

Property rights and an efficient legal system would diminish these costs. By having clearly defined rights and a centralised dispute resolution system, people would not need to engage in arguments and/or physical power disputes to settle who has the right to a given property/resource, since they would be able to use the dispute resolution system for the decision, which would then be enforced through the state mechanisms designed for such purpose.

In economic terms, a primary function of property rights is to internalise externalities.[45] Research has shown that strong property rights and efficient enforcement mechanisms can be an important catalyst for the development of economic activities.[46] These studies have demonstrated that property rights can play a crucial role in economic activity and economic development but poorly designed property rights may actually have the reverse effect, pushing a given economy into a 'tragedy of the anticommons', where 'multiple owners are each endowed with the right to exclude others from a scarce resource, and no one has an effective privilege of use',[47] leading to its underuse.[48] In any event, when properly designed, property rights are an important mechanism for the development of capitalist societies, being used for the distribution and control of scarce resources and the channelling of energy into economically productive activities.

Parallel to property rights, contract law also has an important economic function in enhancing economic outputs in a given society, as they are also designed to internalise externalities.[49] The difference of contract law compared with property law is the object of regulation; instead of regulating a bundle of rights opposable to a group of people, contract law focuses on promises made by individual parties to each other. The operation of contract law makes these promises binding, and the normative justification for the legal enforcement of promises is the belief that the enforcement of promises is more beneficial than it is harmful to society, therefore creating a net social gain.[50]

---

[45] See H Demsetz, 'Towards a Theory of Property Rights' (1967) 57 *American Economic Review, Papers and Proceedings* 347, 348 ('What converts a harmful or beneficial effect into an externality is that the cost of bringing the effect to bear on the decisions of one or more of the interacting persons is too high to make it worthwhile ... "Internalizing" such effects refers to a process, usually a change in property rights, that enables these effects to bear ... on all interacting persons').

[46] See H Soto, *The Mystery of Capital: Why Capitalism Triumphs in the West and Fails Everywhere Else* (Bantam Press 2000); on the importance of strong investor protection, see R LaPorta, F Lopez-de-Silanes, A Shleifer and R Vishny, 'Legal Determinants of External Finance' (1997) 52 *The Journal of Finance* 1131; R LaPorta, F Lopez-de-Silanes, A Shleifer and R Vishny, 'Investor Protection and Corporate Valuation' (2002) 57 *The Journal of Finance* 1147.

[47] MA Heller, 'The Tragedy of the Anticommons: Property in the Transition from Marx to Markets' (1988) 111 *Harvard Law Review* 621, 624.

[48] This was a common outcome in the transition from socialism to capitalism in Eastern European societies. See ibid.

[49] CJ Goetz and RE Scott, 'Enforcing Promises: An Examination of the Basis of Contract' (1980) 89 *Yale Law Journal* 1261, 1276.

[50] ibid 1286.

B. Imperfect Markets and Regulatory Law

Due to power imbalances, the basic framework for private ordering may become inadequate, as those with more power may be able to exploit those with whom they engage in transactions. This is true in many different markets where one party has an advantage over the other, such as the labour market, securities market and consumer market, among others. Exploitation and power imbalances can lead to inequitable situations, which can create market inefficiency and/or social unrest.

The second goal of the state and the use of legal institutions is to create substantive rules and standards to avoid such situations, prohibiting behaviour that is unfair and creating mechanisms that can diminish market imperfections in the relationship of private parties.[51] The need for regulatory law was understood even in nineteenth-century England, when freedom of contract was deemed an important principle to be upheld,[52] both in the judiciary[53] and the legislative branches of government.[54] In this sense, regulatory law is a mechanism that is used to achieve social justice.[55]

As these rules influence the private ordering of the parties they must be justified,[56] be it on collective interest grounds or moral grounds.[57] The justifications for regulation tend to be market specific; in general, in the securities field, regulation is justified on the broad grounds of market inefficiency and investor protection. A deeper analysis of the topic is undertaken in Chapter 3.

Often regulatory rules are aimed at correcting problems that have an effect on the economy, diminishing transaction costs and enhancing economic outputs when designed and deployed in an efficient manner. Enforcement mechanisms are essential to their success.

---

[51] Hence the regulatory character they assume.

[52] See generally PS Atiyah, *The Rise and Fall of Freedom of Contract* (Clarendon Press 1979) 219–570.

[53] For example, by the 1860s the *caveat emptor* doctrine was weakened with cases such as *Bigge v Parkinson* [1862] 7 H & N 955, 158 ER 758 and *Jones v Just* [1868] LR 3 QB 197. After these cases, *caveat emptor* was only to be applied in situations where the buyer had examined the goods sold, which had to be specific, and had exercised judgement. On generic goods the seller was responsible for their merchantability. This is clearly a 'consumer common law', which displaces the 'freedom of contract' formerly available. See Atiyah (n 52) 474–75.

[54] In the legislative branch, there were many statutes that limited freedom of contract and regulated private relationships, such as the Trade Union Act of 1871, the Truck Act of 1818 and the modifications that came with the Poor Law of 1795, the Trade Union Act of 1871, the Anti-Truck Act of 1818 and the Passengers Act of 1803, among others. For an overview of the legislation on the period that influenced freedom of contract, see Atiyah (n 52).

[55] On different concepts of social justice, see HW Micklitz, *The Many Concepts of Social Justice in European Private Law* (Edward Elgar 2011) 3–57.

[56] Even in 19th-century England freedom of contract was viewed as the starting point and any interference with it had to be justified. See Atiyah (n 52) 386.

[57] See R Brownsword, 'The Theoretical Foundations of European Private Law: A Time to Stand and Stare' in R Brownsword, Hans-W Micklitz, Leone Niglia and Stephen Weatherill (eds), *The Foundations of European Private Law* (Hart Publishing 2011) 161–64.

C. The Role of Dispute Resolution Mechanisms

As shown in the previous sections, legal rules are designed to diminish transaction costs among parties, creating certainty for future behaviour, allowing parties to plan and invest in activities that they know will be protected, while at the same time correcting imbalances that exist in specific markets. Since these rules need to be effective, an enforcement system has to be in place. Within modern society where states exist and claim a monopoly on the use of force, the legal enforcement system, since it is a system that if necessary can use force to achieve its ends, will have to be anchored to the power of the state, with institutions designed to facilitate enforcement. In practical terms, this means a wide array of mechanisms, from police officers who will protect property to technological systems that may block bank accounts with a simple order from a judge.

Enforcement can be initiated by public institutions or by private parties, either before the harmful event occurs or afterwards. Generally speaking, public enforcement emphasises deterrence while private enforcement emphasises compensation and the fulfilment of private interests.[58] While this is the classical distinction, private parties also have a role in enforcing regulatory rules, either on an individual basis or by becoming private attorneys general to defend the interests of a collective.[59]

Private legal enforcement is the second step to the problem of a dispute arising within a social context. Before any rule can be enforced, it is necessary to first establish what the rule is in the specific dispute and to then apply it.[60] For the execution of these two functions, modern Western states have institutions and rules shaping the development and solution of the disputes and the enforcement of the outcomes. Through adjudication, 'the legal process of deciding a dispute',[61] courts produce two outcomes: the resolution of a dispute, which is beneficial to the parties to the dispute since it solves their problem with finality without resorting to aggression; and rule making, which in clarifying a certain aspect of the rules governing economic activities attributes a higher degree of certainty to future cases and is therefore socially beneficial.[62]

The creation and maintenance of these systems of law and dispute resolution, as well as these enforcement institutions, have a cost attached to them and are only worthwhile as long as there is a critical mass of people and transactions in which the aggregate costs of self-dealing would be higher than having them mediated

---

[58] C Hodges, 'Public and Private Enforcement: The Practical Implications for Policy Architecture' in R Brownsword, Hans-W Micklitz, Leone Niglia and Stephen Weatherill (eds), *The Foundations of European Private Law* (Hart Publishing 2011).

[59] WB Rubenstein, 'On What a "Private Attorney General" Is—and Why It Matters' (2004) 57 *Vanderbilt Law Review* 2129.

[60] Many times when rules are clear and information asymmetry is low disputes will not arise because it will be clear who will prevail.

[61] See 'adjudication', BA Garner, *Black's Law Dictionary* (9th edn, West 2009).

[62] R Cooter and DL Rubinfeld, 'Economic Analysis of Legal Disputes and Their Resolution' (1989) XXVII *Journal of Economic Literature* 1067, 1092–93.

and resolved through the alternative legal channel. In simpler terms, the social benefits of the existence of laws and courts have to be higher than the costs of maintaining them.

One character of these institutions is that they have been formed by human beings who possess their own incentives to act in a certain way. Judges have to be well remunerated and immune from political influence to be able to exercise their duty of deciding disputes according to the rule of law. Otherwise corrupt pressures might be too strong to be resisted and the essence of the rule of law would itself be compromised, transforming the court into just another political forum and destroying any economic benefits that the legal system might attribute to private relationships.

IV. States and Transnational Disputes

This chapter showed the relationship between states, law and dispute resolution, assessing it with a view to the economic utility of these institutions.

The state is a creature of political organisation that has arisen out of long-lasting disputes among different human groups. Within the state, the legal system serves economic purposes by giving rights to people and allowing them to engage in binding commitments to exchange resources, as well as correcting market failures when they appear and where they operate to undermine the economic health of a given market.

When there are disagreements regarding the rights or commitments that people have towards each other or the state, an available forum is necessary to effectively resolve these disputes; this is a role that has normally been performed by the state through its court system. The role of the state is to function as a source of trust; the state becomes the guarantor that the counterparty in a transaction will behave according to the rules, either imposed by the state or agreed upon between the parties. This allows for people to plan and make investments based only on the guarantee that rules will govern their relationships with other parties. This is especially important in the context of regulated markets such as financial markets, as the identities of the counterparties to a transaction are often unknown.

As different states have different sources legitimating their power, each legal system is often closed within itself,[63] operating through its own internal logic and having few mechanisms to communicate with other states. Therefore, in the transnational context, legal mechanisms have to be built as bridges between different legal systems in order to give transnational transactions the economic benefits that a legal system can provide.

---

[63] On the autopoietic nature of legal systems, see G Teubner, *Law as an Autopoietic System* (Blackwell Publishers 1993).

Chapters 6–9 will analyse the institutional framework of dispute resolution systems, identify the characteristics that they should have in order to perform this role in society and discuss the different designs that can be used to achieve such an objective.

3

Securities Regulation Theory and the Importance of Private Enforcement

The concept of securities is an important one to financial markets. A 'security' is a legal mechanism used at the heart of many financial transactions. The underlying idea is of an 'an investment pooled with others and managed by third parties with whom the investors participate in the economic fate of a common enterprise'.[1] Through its formal materialisation, a security becomes a product and can be sold like anything else.

Securities are used both to raise capital through traditional bond and equity issuance and to transfer risk through the process of securitisation. Securities represent a bundle of rights in a company, be it a property stake on the assets of a company or the right to claim repayment of a sum in the future.[2]

The consistent buying and selling of securities creates a market for these products. Like any other market, its proper functioning is dependent on the relationship of the parties that form part of it. In the absence of other mechanisms, trust and the fear of reputational harm are the cornerstones of their functioning. Since these mechanisms are not perfect, market failures may arise, compromising market efficiency.[3] As with any other markets, there is a legitimate interest that securities markets work efficiently. Efficient markets avoid waste of resources. In some aspects, especially where securities markets are well developed, its efficiency is crucial for the economy of a country.

The use of securities is only useful to the extent that companies can obtain funding or shift risks without much expense, or at least without having greater expense than would have been necessary through other financing mechanisms. This is only possible when strong securities markets are in place, but as with any other type of market, securities markets may be prone to failures, which may be remedied by regulation.

---

[1] GW Arnett, *Global Securities Markets: Navigating the World's Exchanges and OTC Markets* (John Wiley & Sons, Inc 2011) 1030.

[2] ibid.

[3] Usually the more impersonal markets are, the less these personal mechanisms are efficient. Highly personal markets tend to use more reputational and trust mechanisms, as can be seen from Lisa Bernstein's research on the diamonds industry and the cotton market in Memphis. See L Bernstein, 'Opting Out of the Legal System: Extralegal Contractual Relations in the Diamond Industry' (1992) 21 *Journal of Legal Studies* 115; L Bernstein, 'Private Commercial Law in the Cotton Industry: Creating Cooperation through Rules, Norms, and Institutions' (2000–2001) 99 *Michigan Law Review* 1724.

The concept of securities as a legal tool is embedded in the regulatory regimes governing the rights of the parties that are issuing, selling, buying and overseeing the whole process. The legal operation of these regimes is tied to national jurisdictions. The rules and norms by which a firm issuing securities will be bound depends on where the securities will be sold, the actors selling or advising on these securities and the possible overreach of distinct jurisdictions. Thus, while a Brazilian company may sell securities in the American market, the rules that that company will have to abide by are those of the United States.

The framework of different securities regulatory regimes has been a consequence of the failures that have led to many serious financial crises in this last century, especially in the United States. Reforms have been aimed at addressing the specific problems recognised as the sources of these crises, and in many instances they have been harshly criticised as creating more harm than benefits or not promoting enough change.

The strength of securities markets is therefore dependent on the institutional framework surrounding the activity of securities issuance and commercialisation, from prudential supervision by government agencies and self-regulatory organisations to the redress mechanisms available to investors.

Before engaging in any discussion concerning the actual dispute resolution mechanisms in this area of law, it is first important to understand the theoretical underpinnings of these regulatory mechanisms and their substantive legal aspects, the black-letter law that purports to regulate actors' behaviour within these regimes and the grounds for redress.

This chapter provides an overview of the literature on securities markets structures and the institutional mix in securities regulation, to then finally establish the importance of private enforcement in this area, while Chapter 4 discusses the legal framework of securities regulation in the United States, Brazil and the European Union.

I. Financial Markets

A market is where the exchange of goods or services takes place, regardless of whether it is a physical location or not.[4] The level of supply and demand determines the price of a given good on the market. For example, if the world's coffee production is reduced in a year due to adverse weather conditions and the demand stays relatively constant, the price of coffee will rise due to the smaller supply until it reaches its equilibrium level for the new situation.[5] The equilibrium

---

[4] See 'market', J Law and J Smullen, *A Dictionary of Finance and Banking* (Oxford University Press 2008).

[5] The 'equilibrium quantity and price' is the level of price and quantity of a given product where both buyers and sellers are satisfied. See R Frank, *Microeconomics and Behavior* (McGraw-Hill Irwin 2010) 29–32.

level is achieved through price adjustment due to the new conditions of supply and demand. In this example, the price rises because coffee consumers do not have as much coffee available to them as before, and those who value coffee will be willing to pay a higher amount to get the same quantity of coffee. The price ceases to rise when buyers reach the threshold of what they will accept to pay for a given quantity of coffee.

Markets are not entities that pre-exist trade. Individuals engaging in transactions make markets, each with their own personalities, preferences and tastes. The importance attached to a given product depends on individual opinions about it. This is an important aspect of a market; it is not a structure that adjusts automatically to a change, but any change is dependent on the individual decisions of every single person transacting in it.

The understanding of a market as a place where transactions are made brings further implications. Transactions, in the real world, have costs. Even if parties had complete knowledge about a product, they would either have to get together to close the deal or ask someone to do it for them; in either case, time and energy would be spent. Complete knowledge is also an assumption that does not hold true in the real world, as parties have to obtain information about the product they want to purchase. A person buying a used car will want to know about the quality of the car, the problems it has and the adversities it was put through before the deal. Everything else being equal, a car in bad shape is less desirable than a car that has been given proper care. Knowledge acquisition is also a cost that is pervasive in any type of market and its absence may lead to market failures.[6]

Developing rules and institutions for a market has the objective of diminishing these costs, therefore increasing its efficiency and avoiding market failures. An economically efficient market should provide for the lowest possible transaction cost. Of course, each market has its own characteristics and weaknesses that may warrant different types of rules.

Financial markets are a specific type of market with the function of allocating economic resources efficiently. In a very simplistic representation, there are two sides to a financial market structure: the savers and the entrepreneurs. The savers want to defer their expenses and not use their capital at the present time, while the entrepreneurs want to use capital now to create value in the future.[7] The decision to make an investment through third-party financing is based on the price of a given security. The transaction depends on what the saver believes a given security

---

[6] A well-known market failure is the 'lemons' problem. When there is informational asymmetry regarding products in the same class and the purchasers are not able to differentiate between a good product and a medium one, the tendency is for the purchasers to discount prices to compensate for the risk of buying a product of medium quality. Since the price will not reflect the real quality of the good product, their owners might no longer be willing to sell them. The same process then happens with the medium and the bad product, pushing it into a downward spiral that may lead to the extinction of the market. See GA Akerlof, 'The Market for "Lemons": Quality Uncertainty and the Market Mechanism' (1970) 84 *The Quarterly Journal of Economics* 488.

[7] See JN Gordon and LA Kornhauser, 'Efficient Markets, Costly Information, and Securities Research' (1985) 60 *New York University Law Journal* 761, 767–70.

is worth trading his money for and whether the entrepreneur is willing to accept such value in comparison with the future income streams that he may be willing to forgo given the value creation possibilities of the project.[8] If their expectations are similar, the transaction will take place and the saver will be able to have his savings remunerated for future spending while the entrepreneur will be able to execute a project that will create value and generate future income streams.

Efficient resource allocation maximises the welfare of the population as a whole, avoiding unnecessary costs. The more developed capital markets are, the more efficient the economy and its growth will be.[9] The question here is not whether financial markets are beneficial. Any social structure that diminishes transaction costs and is able to increase the availability of goods to the population is welcome. The question is whether the regulation of these markets makes them more or less efficient.

To address this question, it is first necessary to understand the inner mechanics of financial markets and the link between economic efficiency and market efficiency, which are distinct concepts in the literature. A market is more economically efficient if, all else being equal, its transaction costs are lower than in a comparable market. The concept of market efficiency is different: a market is efficient if it reflects all available information.[10] The central concept of an efficient market is 'price accuracy'.[11] Markets where prices are inaccurate create unnecessary economic costs.[12] Therefore, market inefficiency creates economic inefficiency for a given market. The next two sections address the mechanics of price accuracy and the costs of price inaccuracy.

A. The Mechanics of Price Accuracy

Price accuracy is dependent on the information available to the market regarding a certain security and its incorporation into the security's price. The premise of an

---

[8] For example, if the interest rate of borrowed money in the market is 10%, a project will only be executed through debt financing if it can provide a higher income than that.

[9] RG King and R Levine, 'Finance and Growth: Schumpeter Might be Right' (1993) 108 *The Quarterly Journal of Economics* 717; R Levine and S Zervos, 'Stock Markets, Banks and Economic Growth' (1998) 88 *The American Economic Review* 537.

[10] There is a theoretical distinction between fundamental efficiency and informational efficiency. Fundamental efficiency is the ability of a market to reflect the best estimate of the future income of an asset, while informational efficiency is the inability to profit from available information because it is already reflected in the securities price. This distinction is only relevant to the extent that there are mechanisms to predict securities price more accurately than the market, given the same set of available information. Since this is an unlikely proposition, the distinction is not relevant for the purposes of this work, and the underlying concept used here for market efficiency will be informational efficiency. See RJ Gilson and R Kraakman, 'The Mechanisms of Market Efficiency Twenty Years Later: The Hindsight Bias', 446 Harvard Law School John M Olin Center for Law, Economics and Business Discussion Paper Series 1, 2.

[11] Gordon and Kornhauser (n 7) 768. If the price is not accurate the decisions made by investors and savers will not be optimal.

[12] Therefore, there is also a link between market efficiency and economic efficiency.

efficient market is that it 'fully reflects' all available information.[13] The 'reflection of available information' is dependent on two factors: how information is incorporated into prices and how information is made available.

The incorporation of information into prices can be framed as a two-step process. First, it depends on the number of potential investors that have access to a piece of information. Secondly, it depends on how these persons transmit this information to the market price of a security. The price adjustment is a function of the initial number of persons possessing the information and the number of transactions that are made based on such information; the greater the number of initial persons possessing the information and the bigger the number and size of transactions made based on it, the faster the information is incorporated into prices.[14]

The availability of information can be thought of as a continuum that goes from publicly available information to restricted information. Information requires effort to be gathered; this is reflected by the use of personal time or by hiring researchers. Even if it is publicly available, its pieces can be raw data that must be organised to be understood. The costs of organising information coherently in such a manner that some use might be made of it may be high. Moreover, it may be necessary to check whether the information provided is true, an activity that also has a cost.[15] Therefore, the level of availability of a piece of information can be translated in terms of the cost to acquire, organise and reasonably rely upon it.

Due to the costs of obtaining, processing and verifying information, many different mechanisms have emerged to diminish these costs through economies of scale and scope. The press, financial intermediaries and individual networks are some of the avenues that are used for this purpose. Such mechanisms increase the initial availability of information to market participants. By diminishing information costs, they enhance price accuracy in financial markets by increasing the distribution of reliable information while also contributing to economic efficiency, both directly, through the reduction of informational costs, and indirectly, through a more efficient capital market.[16]

The second moment of price formation is the incorporation of available information into the prices of a product. In any given market this 'reflection' occurs

---

[13] EF Fama, 'Efficient Capital Markets: a Review of Theory and Empirical Work' (1970) 25 *The Journal of Finance* 383, 383.

[14] Liquidity is therefore an important aspect for market price efficiency: the more liquid the market, the faster the price adjustment is.

[15] In sum, information costs can be divided into three categories: acquisition costs, processing costs and verification costs. For a more in-depth overview, see RJ Gilson and R Kraakman, 'The Mechanisms of Market Efficiency' (1984) 70 *Virginia Law Review* 549, 597–609.

[16] There is an apparent paradox in the relationship between the cost of obtaining information and market efficiency. The premise of an efficient market is that any available information is 'fully reflected' in stock prices at any time. Therefore, if the market is efficient, any information that becomes available is fully reflected in the stock prices, and the costs of acquiring new information will not be worthwhile, pushing the market to inefficiency again. The paradox is just apparent. Since price systems are not perfectly efficient there is always an opportunity to make a profit from arbitraging, justifying the existence of information providers and arbitrageurs. See S Grossman and J Stiglitz, 'On the Impossibility of Informationally Efficient Markets' (1980) 70 *The American Economic Review* 393.

through different mechanisms.[17] In the long run, prices tend to adjust to equilibrium by incorporating new available information; the important question regarding price accuracy is how fast the information is incorporated into prices.[18] The incorporation of information is basically done through transactions that are based on the new information. Actors using the information will evaluate and act on it, pushing securities prices up or down.

These mechanisms are shaped and limited by the institutional complexities surrounding the activities related to gathering, processing and verifying market information, as well as by the legal framework surrounding these processes.[19]

B. Consequences of Price Inaccuracy

Price inaccuracy in financial markets can bring different harmful effects to the efficiency of an economy. As discussed above, an inefficient economy wastes resources that could otherwise be used to maximise the well-being of the population. Identifying the social costs of price inaccuracy is important to further the discussion about the legal mechanisms that can be used to address them. The three main categories of social costs arising out of price inaccuracies are non-optimal capital allocation, market liquidity and corporate governance failures.

i. Non-optimal Capital Allocation

The investment decisions of a company based on inaccurate stock prices may be socially suboptimal. Both the overvaluation and the undervaluation of a company raising money in the primary market through equity offerings may lead to social costs. If the stock price is overvalued, the company may invest in projects that are suffering loss because selling new shares will overcompensate older shareholders; on the other hand, if the stock price is undervalued, projects that could be socially valuable might be put aside if the stock price discount is higher than the expected added value of the investment.[20]

Under this specific problem, price accuracy is important to the extent that it is present at the period when the company is going through the process of issuing new shares. The investment decision is made taking into consideration the amount of capital that can be obtained during an offer in the primary market: it is meaningless, at least as a direct consideration of an investment decision, whether the security price is accurate before or after the process is undertaken.[21]

---

[17] There are four mechanisms of information incorporation into prices: 'universally informed trading', 'professionally informed trading', 'derivatively informed trading' and 'uninformed trading', which have a parallel in the cost structure mentioned above. See Gilson and Kraakman (n 15).

[18] ibid 559–60.

[19] See Gilson and Kraakman (n 10) 35–37.

[20] See M Kahan, 'Securities Laws and the Social Costs of "Inaccurate" Stock Prices' (1992) 41 *Duke Law Journal* 977, 1005–08.

[21] ibid 1012–16.

ii. Market Liquidity

Liquidity[22] is both a cause and a consequence of price accuracy. As explained above, the higher the number of transactions in a market, the faster the incorporation of information into market prices, enhancing price accuracy. Liquid markets are markets where securities can be promptly transformed into cash, meaning that there is plenty of supply and demand for any person to buy or sell a given security.

Apart from the fairness argument of accurate prices for securities transactions, price inaccuracies affect investor confidence, which in turn affects market liquidity. Price inaccuracies are mainly caused by informational asymmetry. When this is the case and there is a consistent practice in the market of trading on non-public information, the individual uninformed investor will be more likely to lose on his transactions and eventually will become aware that the market is rigged against him. Since such a transaction represents a higher risk of loss, the investor may become wary of trading in such an unfair environment.[23] The withdrawal of investors who perceive the market as unfair to them will diminish the amount of trading, which translates into diminished liquidity. Since investors value liquid securities more than illiquid ones, the first consequence of an illiquid market is the higher cost of raising capital that arises out of it.[24]

The second cost arising out of diminished liquidity relates to the cost of transactions within the market. Transactions in illiquid markets tend to be costlier than in liquid ones due to higher brokerage fees.[25] Since a decrease in liquidity means a lower level of trade, brokers and market makers earn less from their activities, notwithstanding that they still have fixed costs that they must bear to provide their services. The consequence is that they have to widen the bid–ask spread to compensate for the loss of business.[26]

iii. Corporate Governance Failures

Price inaccuracy can also have harmful social effects linked to the behaviour of firm managers. Their behaviour can be attached to securities prices in many different ways, ranging from direct ownership of stocks to a sense of duty to shareholders and the assumption that higher stock prices will be in their interests.[27] Unless

---

[22] Market liquidity can be either the opportunity of finding a trade partner with which a large amount of trading can be done without causing market impact, or the possibility of converting securities into cash. For the first definition see Deutsche Bundesbank, 'Securities Market Regulation: International Approaches' (Monthly Report January, 2006) www.bundesbank.de/Redaktion/EN/Downloads/Publications/Monthly_Report_Articles/2006/2006_01_securities_market.pdf?__blob=publicationFile, 37.

[23] Kahan (n 20) 1018–19.

[24] For a model on how informational asymmetry, liquidity and cost of capital are related see D Diamond and R Verrecchia, 'Disclosure, Liquidity, and the Cost of Capital' (1991) 46 *The Journal of Finance* 1325.

[25] Kahan (n 20) 1020.

[26] *See* HR Stoll, 'Market Microstructure' in GM Constantinides, M Harris and RM Stulz (eds), *Handbook of the Economics of Finance*, vol 1A (Elsevier 2003) 562–67.

[27] Kahan (n 20) 1029.

managers are shorting the stock of their company, their incentive structure will be to increase the value of the company's securities prices, either because they own stocks or options or for shareholders' satisfaction.

If the price is accurate, the only way in which managers will be able to change the value of the company's securities will be through the improvement of its fundamental value.[28] In perfectly efficient markets, managers, basing their decisions on stock prices, will not be able to cause socially harmful effects.

Within this context, inaccurate prices raise two issues: the first is, similarly to the social costs arising out of equity funding as discussed above, the decision to invest in non-optimal enterprises due to incentives accruing from management interest in focusing on a higher priced company; the second is the use of signalling techniques.

The logic behind the first issue is the same as the one discussed in respect of the decision to offer securities to the public. If the company has some available capital and different options for investment, it may decide to opt for the choice that is less profitable but more valuable in the eyes of the market. The opportunity to pursue a more socially efficient option would be abandoned due to price inaccuracies.[29]

The second issue is one of transaction costs rather than of allocative efficiency. Signalling is the transmission of information to the market.[30] The practice of signalling is undertaken to inform the market that the price of stock is undervalued. The practice of signalling has costs, and if the security price were accurate, management would not need to engage in signalling. Accuracy prevents the necessity of the company's use of signalling mechanisms to transmit information to the market.

II. Securities Regulation

Inefficient markets have consequences for the real economy; as such, increasing their efficiency is an important task. The economic efficiency of markets can be developed through institutional design. There are different overlapping mechanisms that may be used for this purpose but the creation of an institutional market framework must be made with the specific market in mind. The main objective of securities regulation is to diminish market inefficiency but regulation may also have other objectives. This section briefly analyses the general rationale for securities regulation, and the specific objectives of securities regulation in the European Union.

---

[28] ibid 1030.
[29] The inaccuracy here is not as to the price of the manager's firm, but as to where the investment is going to be made, even though the decision is made based upon the expected share price increase of the manager's firm.
[30] For an overview of 'signalling', see M Spence, 'Signaling in Retrospect and the Informational Structure of Markets' (2002) 92 *The American Economic Review* 434.

A. Rationale for Securities Regulation: Disclosure

The economic efficiency of markets is a by-product of transaction costs, availability of information and its incorporation into prices. In the securities field, outside the domain of the market microstructure, which is concerned with the nuts and bolts of trading, the underpinning concept of securities regulation is 'information disclosure'. Narrowing informational asymmetry creates an environment for better-informed investors, who in turn then become more confident in engaging in financial transactions, contributing to market efficiency.

While financial markets are regulated everywhere, the idea of imposing disclosure duties on actors involved in securities transactions is not shared by everyone. The securities market and its regulation has been a heavily discussed topic since the introduction of the federal securities law in the United States. Initially its detractors criticised only specific provisions of the securities acts that were thought to impede capital formation, and none of these was aimed at disclosure.[31] It was in the 1960s that a new wave of criticism emerged against the mandatory disclosure system.[32]

The initial criticisms were based on the costs for corporations and the lack of evidence that mandatory disclosure was in fact necessary, as corporations were already disclosing some information before the securities system reform.[33] Moreover, insider trading was seen as something beneficial that could be used as a means of rewarding entrepreneurs, therefore leading some commentators to argue that the prohibition of using inside information for trading could be harmful.[34] Securities regulation, these studies preached, accrued few benefits for its costs. These arguments and the evidence used to reach these conclusions, were severely disputed,[35] and since then much has been written on the subject.

Much of the new criticism is based on the assumptions arising out of the efficient market hypothesis, the efficiency of market mechanisms to promote the proper functioning of capital markets and the inefficiency and costs of mandatory disclosure systems.[36] Theoretically, if a firm were issuing securities to fund a project that was expected to be profitable, it would optimally disclose information to convince investors to buy those securities[37] as the lack of disclosure by the

---

[31] J Seligman, 'The Historical Need for a Mandatory Corporate Disclosure System' (1983) 9 *The Journal of Corporation Law* 1, 2.

[32] See GJ Stigler, 'Public Regulation of the Securities Markets' (1964) 37 *The Journal of Business* 117; HG Manne, *Insider Trading and the Stock Market* (The Free Press 1966); GJ Benston, 'The Value of the SEC's Accounting Disclosure Requirements' (1969) 44 *The Accounting Review* 515.

[33] Benston (n 32) 531.

[34] ibid 139–41.

[35] For an overview, see Seligman (n 31).

[36] See FH Easterbrook and DR Fischel, 'Mandatory Disclosure and the Protection of Investors' (1984) 70 *Virginia Law Review* 669; LA Stout, 'The Unimportance of Being Efficient: An Economic Analysis of Stock Market Pricing and Securities Regulation' (1988) 87 *Michigan Law Review* 613.

[37] See S Grossman and OD Hart, 'Disclosure Laws and Takeover Bids' (1980) 35 *The Journal of Finance* 323, 323–27.

firm would lead investors to think that they had only bad information about the project. This would imply that after it started disclosing information, a firm would not be able to stop disclosing new information without triggering investors' concerns. To guarantee that the optimal amount of information were disclosed, the firm would then utilise market mechanisms, such as verification and certification, to 'borrow' financial intermediaries' reputations.[38]

Informational intermediaries would also be used to signal to the market that there are other types of information that, due to competitive advantages, it is better not to directly disclose at that particular moment, such as a new technology.[39] By disclosing information to specific intermediaries that have the possibility of buying enough securities to influence its market price, issuers would be signalling to the market that they have beneficial information that cannot be publicly disclosed.[40]

Another criticism, focused more on the specifics of securities regulation in the United States, is about the quality of information provided. It advances that the focus of disclosure should be less on historical data but more on future projections, since stock prices are calculated on the basis of projected future income.[41]

Currently there is also a discussion in the literature regarding whether mandatory disclosure may make markets more prone to the effects of external shocks due to herding behaviour, making price movements more unstable and inefficient.[42] This is a behavioural aspect of market movement, and it is not clear whether the absence of regulation would in fact be beneficial, as it would impose other transaction costs on the market.

Most of these criticisms assume that markets, as a matter of principle, will always do better if left untouched than if regulatory mechanisms are imposed on them. This is, of course, not always true, as history has demonstrated repeatedly.

The opposing view is that a mandatory disclosure system for securities regulation does matter for share price accuracy and that its costs are lower than the benefits that accrue to society. This position can be generally based on the public goods character of information, the advantages of providing subsidy to informed traders, the standardisation of information, the inefficiencies in the absence of a mandatory disclosure system and the flaws of the self-induced disclosure theory.[43]

Information is a public good because it is indivisible and unexcludable.[44]

---

[38] Easterbrook and Fischel (n 36). The authors frame this idea as the principle of 'self-induced disclosure'.

[39] ibid 688.

[40] This would fall within the insider-trading category.

[41] H Kripke, 'The SEC, the Accountants, Some Myths and Some Realities' (1970) 45 *New York University Law Review* 1151, 1197–201.

[42] See S Deaking, 'The Evolution of Theory and Method in Law and Finance' in N Moloney, E Ferran and J Payne (eds), *The Oxford Handbook of Financial Regulation* (Oxford University Press 2015) 21–22.

[43] JC Coffee, 'Market Failure and the Economic Case for a Mandatory Disclosure System' (1984) 70 *Virginia Law Review* 717, 722–23; L Enriques and S Gilotta, 'Disclosure and Financial Market Regulation' in N Moloney, E Ferran and J Payne (eds), *The Oxford Handbook of Financial Regulation* (Oxford University Press 2015) 520–25.

[44] For an overview of 'public goods', see R Cornes and T Sandler, *The Theory of Externalities, Public Goods and Club Goods* (Cambridge University Press 1996).

A piece of information does not exhaust itself with its use; it will still be available to any other person who may want to use it. This allows persons that have not contributed to the costs of obtaining the information to use it for free.[45] Since researchers will not be able to sell the information to all of its users, they will be under-compensated, and the consequence is that information will tend to be under-provided. This under-provision of information is suboptimal because the fewer informed traders that are available to trade, the higher the amount of time necessary for the information to become incorporated into prices, that which directly affects market efficiency. A mandatory disclosure system would not only address this problem, but would also cut the duplication efforts that are made in collecting and processing information. Absent a mandatory disclosure system, many different analysts would engage in obtaining, processing and verifying the same set of information about a company, wasting unnecessary resources.[46]

This justification for a mandatory disclosure system is aligned with the idea underpinning the mechanisms incorporating information into market prices: it provides both for market efficiency through a wider base of information that reaches different persons more quickly (therefore providing subsidy to informed traders) and also for economic efficiency by diminishing duplicative efforts. In addition, regulation may require that the disclosed information is standardised, allowing for easier comparability of different firms.

Another line of argument defending mandatory disclosure goes against the theory that firms would disclose all beneficial information by themselves. The self-induced disclosure theory can be empirically demonstrated in the market through the various financial institutions and gatekeepers that provide 'reputation' for companies that wish to signal the market. The question though is not whether these mechanisms exist, but to what extent they are sufficient to provide proper and sufficient information to the market. Conflicts of interest between ownership and control in the firm prevent an optimal self-induced disclosure. Even though the logic in the theory is sound, the premises of it are not. The lack of ongoing disclosures after a firm has started with the practice may signal to the market that there is bad news, and therefore the firm, as an institution, would disclose the information. The problem is that lack of disclosure does not show how bad the information is, creating informational asymmetry. In addition, managers do not always have their interests aligned with those of the shareholders, and they might use this market response to pursue their own agenda.[47]

The theoretical case in favour of mandatory disclosure seems to be stronger than against it. In addition, a body of literature demonstrates that securities law

---

[45] This is known as the 'free-rider problem'. See Stanford Encyclopedia of Philosophy, 'The Free Rider Problem' (*Stanford Encyclopedia of Philosophy*, 21 May 2003), https://plato.stanford.edu/entries/free-rider/.

[46] Coffee (n 43) 733–34.

[47] ibid 737–47.

and more generally, corporate law, do matter to protect investors and to strengthen capital markets. The quality of legal rules and enforcement reflects on the size of capital markets.[48] For example, shareholder protection is a determinant of the dispersion of shares ownership, influencing the ability of a firm to obtain external finance.[49] The argument is that a developed legal system of investor protection, by guaranteeing the rights of investors and preventing expropriation, will incentivise investors to pay more for a firm's security since interest or profit will be more likely to come back to them than if such protection did not exist.[50] This not only raises the value of the companies in general, but it also allows investors to consider companies that would not have been considered absent good legal protection.[51] A particular study has illustrated that firms that cross-list in the United States, which is known to have strong investor protection rules, have experienced an increase of up to 37 per cent on their Tobin's q ratio[52] compared with firms that are not cross-listed.[53]

Another argument that strong securities regulation is beneficial arises from the analysis of the costs of raising capital. The literature also demonstrates that 'firms in countries with more extensive disclosure requirements and stronger securities regulation' have a lower cost of equity capital, even after other risk variables were controlled.[54] Another article, also focused on the benefits to the economy of share price accuracy and the importance that mandatory disclosure systems have in accurate prices, reached similar results.[55] Through the use of the R^2 methodology, the study indicated that share price accuracy is important to capital allocation,[56] while specific enhanced disclosure requirements—introduced in the United States in the 1980s—showed an increase of information reflection in share prices.[57]

Empirical evidence indicates that there is an important relationship between developed financial markets and their regulation. It seems clear that securities regulation has a role in addressing market failures and diminishing transaction costs, being beneficial to the development of capital markets. The contours of the

[48] See R LaPorta, F Lopez-de-Silanes, A Shleifer and R Vishny, 'Legal Determinants of External Finance' (1997) 52 *The Journal of Finance* 1131.

[49] See A Shleifer and D Wolfenzon, 'Investor Protection and Equity Markets' (2002) 66 *Journal of Financial Economics* 3.

[50] R LaPorta, F Lopez-de-Silanes and A Shleifer, 'Corporate Ownership around the World' (1999) 54 *The Journal of Finance* 471.

[51] See generally LaPorta et al (n 48) 1147.

[52] The Tobin's q ratio is the value of the firm divided by the replacement value of the firm's assets. See ibid.

[53] See AM Chisholm, *An Introduction to International Capital Markets* (2nd edn, John Wiley & Sons 2009) 165–66.

[54] See C Doidge, GA Karolyi and RM Stulz, 'Why are Foreign Firms Listed in the US Worth More?' (2004) 71 *Journal of Financial Economics* 205.

[55] MB Fox, A Durnev, R Morck and BY Yeung, 'Law, Share Price Accuracy, and Economic Performance: the New Evidence' (2003) 102 *Michigan Law Review* 331.

[56] ibid 366; see also J Wurgler, 'Financial Markets and the Allocation of Capital' (2000) 58 *Journal of Financial Economics* 187.

[57] Fox et al (n 55) 368–80.

regulatory framework must, however, be developed carefully to avoid unnecessary mandatory disclosure costs and drawbacks.[58]

B. Securities Regulation in the European Union

The idea of economic integration remains one of the central aspects of the EU project, the goal of a single market being one of its most pressing objectives.[59] In the Treaty on the Functioning of the European Union (TFEU) the basis of the single market is reflected in the four freedoms: free movement of goods, workers, establishment and the provision of services, and capital.[60] This logic is also applicable to securities regulation, focusing on the construction of an integrated EU securities and investment services market,[61] with the consequence that any EU securities regulation has to be justified as a means towards the construction of the single market.

Primarily, the approach to this area of regulation was based on maximum harmonisation, attempting to equalise the different regulatory regimes in Member States in order to remove the barriers arising from them.[62] Due to negotiation difficulties and the implementation discretion that was given to Member States, this first attempt failed.[63]

The next regulatory approach was based on the 'mutual recognition' principle established in the *Cassis de Dijon*[64] judgment, establishing a minimum harmonisation framework where supervision is delegated to the home country of the service provider/issuer and the host country is obliged to accept such regulation, without imposing any additional burdens.[65] This approach also failed because there was still much power with the host Member State regarding issuer disclosure and investment services, inhibiting the development of an integrated market.[66]

These deficiencies were acknowledged, and in 1998 a Financial Services Action Plan with 42 measures was devised and implemented to address these problems and to change the framework of the EU financial and securities regulation.[67] Today the European Union is becoming the 'monopoly supplier of financial market

---

[58] See Enriques and Gilotta (n 43) 525–33.

[59] For a brief overview of the economic aspects of economic integration, see A El-Agraa, 'The Theory of Economic Integration' in A El-Agraa (ed), *The European Union: Economics and Policies* (9th edn, Cambridge University Press 2011).

[60] Consolidated Version of the Treaty on the Functioning of the European Union [2012] OJ C326/47 (TFEU), art 26; See PP Craig and G De Búrca, *EU Law Text, Cases, and Materials* (Oxford University Press 2011) 581–82.

[61] N Moloney, *EC Securities Regulation* (2nd edn, Oxford University Press 2008) 6.

[62] ibid 9.

[63] ibid.

[64] Case 120/78 *Rewe-Zentral AG v Bundesmonopolverwaltung für Branntwein (Cassis de Dijon)* [1979] ECR 649.

[65] Moloney (n 61) 9–10.

[66] ibid 10.

[67] See ibid.

regulation',[68] creating a regulatory level playing field among EU Member States and enabling market integration.

Therefore, in addition to the importance of securities regulation as a means to address the market failures discussed in this chapter, there is also a more important objective, at least under the EU logic, which is the creation of a single market for securities and investment services. This is relevant because the rules on securities regulation at EU level have to be enacted based on this principle, due to the limitations of EU regulatory competence.

III. Institutional Aspects of Securities Regulation and the Importance of Private Enforcement

Assuming the premise that regulation is beneficial, as demonstrated throughout this chapter, a whole new set of questions becomes relevant. The design of the regulatory regime has to take into account many different aspects. What is the regulatory body in charge of the regime? What are its powers? How will the people in charge of the regime be hired? Who will finance it? What are the standards that need to be followed and how are they developed? What might be the punishment for non-compliance? Who will enforce this punishment?

These questions are a small sample of the wider considerations that should be engaged while deciding on the main dimensions of a regulatory system. The two spheres of regulation are the public, where the government designs and deploys a regulatory system, and the private, where private parties create a regulatory system to provide for their own needs. In many instances, these two different spheres become intertwined, each in charge of specific functions.[69] The moment where this interplay occurs is at the norm-setting stage and at the enforcement stage. Both public and private actors might set the standards and both might also enforce rules made by themselves or by other actors. The division of power between public and private, however, is of extreme importance to align the interests of the different parties in a manner to ensure that the regime will achieve optimal efficiency in respect of its proposed goals. Badly designed regulatory systems may fail, leading to unnecessary costs.[70]

The goals of this section are first to set out the basic general framework of the regulatory regime in securities regulation and then to establish the importance of private enforcement in satisfying its policy objectives.

---

[68] ibid 37.

[69] For an overview of developments regarding the private and the public regulatory sphere see F Cafaggi, 'Rethinking Private Regulation in the European Regulatory Space' (2006) EUI Working Papers 13.

[70] For an overview of regulatory failure, see R Baldwin, M Cave and M Lodge, *Understanding Regulation: Theory, Strategy, and Practice* (2nd edn, Oxford University Press 2012) 68–82.

A. The Regulatory Regime—Institutional Aspects

The design of a regulatory regime can be divided into three different parts: the first is the determination of who should be empowered to create the rules of the regime; the second is the rules with which compliance should be required, that is, what the regime expects the regulatees to do; finally, it must be determined how these rules will be enforced to guarantee that the right incentives are in place so that the regulatees comply with the rules.

In respect of the enforcement aspect, which is 'the process by which a regulatory authority or a person who has suffered harm takes action to punish or remedy a contravention of regulatory rules',[71] the system can be further subdivided into ex ante and ex post mechanisms.[72] Ex ante mechanisms are those where compliance with the rules are checked before a harm arises,[73] while ex post mechanisms are those that can be deployed after the harm took place.[74] Since a regulatory regime will be embedded in a given social reality, the surrounding environment must be analysed so that the best design may be drafted. In other words, the regulatory process has to take into account the institutional background available to assess the possible success of a regulatory scheme.[75]

When designing regulatory systems it is necessary to identify at each stage of the process the potential regulators, regulatees, addressees and enforcers of the rules. Rule-making may be seen as illegitimate if it is done by private actors[76] but on other occasions the involvement of private actors might be the only solution for a specific problem, even if in the public interest.[77]

---

[71] I MacNeil, 'Enforcement and Sanctioning' in N Moloney, E Ferran and J Payne (eds), *The Oxford Handbook of Financial Regulation* (Oxford 2015) 281.

[72] For a brief discussion of the subject, see S Issacharoff and I Samuel, 'New Frontiers of Consumer Protection: the Interplay Between Private and Public Enforcement' in F Cafaggi and HW Micklitz (eds), *New Frontiers of Consumer Protection: the Interplay Between Private and Public Enforcement* (Intersentia 2009).

[73] An example of an ex ante mechanism is the Food and Drugs Administration process of approving a drug for consumption. See J Paradise, A Tisdale, R Hall and E Kokkoli, 'Evaluating Oversight of Human Drugs and Medical Devices: a Case Study of the FDA and Implications for Nanobiotechnology' (2009) 37 *Journal of Law, Medicine & Ethics* 598.

[74] The classic example is tort law.

[75] See Issacharoff and Samuel (n 72).

[76] One example that has been widely discussed is the International Accounting Standards Board, the standard setter for accounting standards that has taken a major role in the world today. For a discussion on the legitimacy of private accounting standard-setting boards, see E Chiapello and K Medjad, 'An Unprecedented Privatisation of Mandatory Standard-Setting: the Case of European Accounting Policy' (2009) 20 *Critical Perspectives on Accounting* 448; AM Fleckner, 'FASB and IASB: Dependence Despite Independence' (2008) 3 *Virginia Law & Business Review* 275.

[77] This is the case with the international accounting standards regime. Due to the lack of a proper organisation in place to create accounting standards that had sufficient quality to be used across countries in the EU while at the same time capable of accommodating different political interests, the International Accounting Standards Board (IASB), a private organisation in existence since the 1970s, was chosen to perform this role. See T Andreotti, 'The Legitimacy and Accountability of the IASB as an International Standard Setter' in F Cafaggi and G Miller (eds), *Private Regulation and Enforcement in Financial Institutions* (Edward Elgar 2013).

The same is true for regulatory enforcement. If compliance control is to be implemented before an action is taken, such as before the authorisation of the issuance of a security, the regulators should guarantee that institutions overseeing the process have the necessary skills to do so, otherwise the regulatory scheme may overburden the economy with unnecessary costs and difficulty in compliance.[78] On the other hand, if the enforcement mechanisms are engaged ex post, for example through lawsuits, it is important to survey the environment to see if the decision makers are independent and if claimants will have sufficient incentives to pursue their claims.

i. The Regulatory Mix for Securities Regulation

The regulatory system for securities is a diverse mix of the public and private sphere, tending more to the public side. Usually the rules of the game are set by government agencies created specifically for the task of regulating and supervising securities markets; with the rule-making power they also receive extensive enforcement powers.

Within their supervisory domain, they may also delegate some of their functions to private institutions. For example, rule-making authority regarding accounting standards—the language of financial disclosure—has long been delegated by the Securities and Exchange Commission (SEC) in the United States to private standard-setting bodies.[79]

At the same time, private regulatory entities are allowed to co-exist with securities and exchange commissions, playing an important role in drafting and applying rules that are in compliance with the objectives of the underlying regulatory regime.[80] In the securities markets, two important examples are the organised markets, such as the New York Stock Exchange (NYSE) and BM&FBovespa, and private regulatory authorities, such as the Financial Industry Regulatory Authority (FINRA). Organised exchanges require compliance with rules of disclosure and corporate governance to admit companies to list, while private regulatory authorities regulate the behaviour of the members of the profession, such as brokers and dealers, through delegated government power.

These private entities also have their own enforcement mechanisms; they can deny access to the regime, which in most cases means denial of market access, and

---

[78] One example of unnecessary costs created by badly designed regulation and lack of close scrutiny by regulators is the effects that Regulation NMS had on the American financial market by incentivising high-frequency trading. See M Lewis, *Flash Boys: A Wall Street Revolt* (WW Norton & Company Inc 2014).

[79] For an overview of the development of the accounting profession in the United States, see SA Zeff, 'How the US Accounting Profession Got Where It Is Today: Part I' (2003) 17 *Accounting Horizons* 189–205; SA Zeff, 'How the US Accounting Profession got Where It Is Today: Part II' (2003) 17 *Accounting Horizons* 267–86.

[80] This type of two-tiered regulatory structure, where the government oversees a private regulatory body, is known as meta-regulation. C Coglianese and E Mendelson, 'Meta-Regulation and Self-Regulation' in R Baldwin, M Cave and M Lodge (eds), *The Oxford Handbook of Regulation* (Oxford University Press 2010) 147–51.

they can also apply various penalties. There is a caveat though: these regulators can only enforce rules in respect of their members because their authority arises out of the membership of the regulatee in the regulatory scheme.

The last set of enforcement mechanisms is more direct. The investor that is harmed due to a breach of a rule in the regime may start legal proceedings to obtain redress as long as there are mechanisms available. These proceedings can either be judicial, in a court of law, or be initiated through other means, such as arbitration; this depends on the contractual or corporate scheme governing the relationship.

ii. Standards for Private Enforcement: the Interplay Between Public Law and Private Law

The common conceptual distinction between public law and private law is that the first has the goal of pursuing collective goals, while the second serves as a regulatory background for private transactions to take place.[81] Even though conceptually this is a clear-cut distinction, in practice the relationship between these two legal domains is much more intertwined.

The reality is that not only can private law be shaped by public law, but that public law may also need to rely on private law to achieve its goals.[82] This is especially relevant in the field of securities regulation, where many of the regulatory standards enshrined in what would be considered within the domain of public law (eg standards used for supervision duties) create expectations for the parties engaging in private transactions, and in many instances actually serve as the basis for private law redress.

Private standards can be the basis for the creation of public standards, which in turn can be used to create duties within private law. An interesting example of this public/private relationship in the field of investments is the duty to one's client when providing investment advice. The duty started as a purely private law standard in the *Bond* case in Germany, being transposed to the public law realm with its inclusion in MiFID,[83] an instrument used for supervision standards.[84] The journey back to the private law realm is evident when the national instruments transposing MiFID are used as a basis for liability in a private relationship,[85] as is allowed in many jurisdictions, either directly or indirectly.[86]

Within the EU context, this relationship needs special attention since differences in the interaction between public law and private law may create wholly

[81] A Robertson, 'Introduction: Goals, Rights and Obligations' in A Robertson and TH Wu (eds), *The Goals of Private Law* (Hart Publishing 2009) 5–6.

[82] See generally M Moran, 'The Mutually Constitutive Nature of Public and Private Law' in A Robertson and TH Wu (eds), *The Goals of Private Law* (Hart Publishing 2009).

[83] Dir 2004/39/EC on markets in financial instruments [2004] OJ L145/1 (MiFID), art 19(4).

[84] O Cherednychenko, 'European Securities Regulation, Private Law and the Investment Firm-Client Relationship' [2009] *European Review of Private Law* 925, 931–37.

[85] ibid 937–46.

[86] ibid 946–51.

different private law regimes, despite the harmonised supervisory approach; this might create difficulties for the single market due to the divergent private law standards being applied in different Member States.

Therefore, both legal categories (public and private law) may find a way to be used as a basis for recovery through private enforcement.

B. The Importance of Private Enforcement in Securities Regulation

The mere presence of substantive rules is not sufficient for them to accrue any value, since a proper system of enforcement is necessary for well-designed black-letter law to be deployed.[87] The architecture of the enforcement mechanisms of a given regime is a policy choice that must be made. To this extent, both the public and private enforcement of securities regulation play an important role in the securities regulation system.[88]

Public enforcers are government agencies that are established with clear objectives to promote market efficiency and investor protection and are given the power to warn, fine or even suspend market actors from engaging in their professional roles as they relate to securities transactions. In some specific systems they are given the power to sue in court, shifting the decision-making process of the enforcement mechanisms to an impartial judge. Private enforcers are the persons that have been defrauded or otherwise have a claim against an issuer or a financial intermediary in respect of a harm inflicted upon them while transacting securities, and who can decide, given the incentives for the dispute resolution system, to sue.

The basic differences between public and private enforcement can be summarised along the following lines:[89] while public enforcers obtain a salary to perform their duties,[90] private enforcers are remunerated either for the specific task at hand

---

[87] For an overview on the impact of enforcement in securities regulation see L Hail and C Leuz, 'International Differences in the Cost of Equity Capital: Do Legal Institutions and Securities Regulation Matter?' (2006) 44 *Journal of Accounting Research* 485; JC Coffee, 'Law and the Market: the Impact of Enforcement' (2007) 156 *University of Pennsylvania Law Review* 229 (Professor Coffee hypothesises that the difference in enforcement may explain the difference in share value increase when cross-listed firms in the US and the UK are compared).

[88] Compare R LaPorta, F Lopez-de-Silanes and A Shleifer, 'What Works in Securities Law?' (2006) 61 *The Journal of Finance* 1 (arguing that 'securities laws matter because they facilitate private contracting rather than provide for public regulatory enforcement') and HE Jackson and MJ Roe, *Public and Private Enforcement of Securities Laws: Resource-Based Evidence* (Harvard Law School 2009) (demonstrating that there is a strong association between outcomes in securities regulation and public enforcement, when it is measured by resources).

[89] This section has benefited from the literature review carried out in M Lemos and M Minzner, 'For-Profit Public Enforcement' (2014) 127 *Harvard Law Review* 853, 858–63.

[90] WB Rubenstein, 'On What a "Private Attorney General" Is—and Why It Matters' (2004) 57 *Vanderbilt Law Review* 2129, 2139 ('public attorneys work for the public and are paid a salary to do so. The amount of time they invest in an issue, the amount of sanction they recover, or the amount of harm they deter, has no bearing on their fee. Their priorities, the uses of their billable hours, are generally determined by politics, not money').

or through the spoils of their efforts.[91] Another consideration relates to the goals of enforcement: public seeks deterrence, while private aims at compensation.[92] This is a simplified portrayal of the matter as there are, for example, public enforcers that receive remuneration for their efforts[93] and private enforcers that work for the public good, not expecting an economic advantage from their work;[94] notwithstanding, this distinction is the basic starting point from which the 'pure' public and private types of enforcement differ.

As the state is the source of authority for legal rules, enforcement is in its own interest since non-compliance would be considered a failure of the legal system and consequently of the state itself. This is especially important in areas where the legal rules purport to regulate behaviour in the public interest; these are often the types of rules that need justification, as explained in Chapter 2. Public enforcement, however, is not without its shortcomings. At the outset, the creation and maintenance of an enforcement apparatus requires the expenditure of a substantial amount of resources, which could be used in more productive governmental activities. Then there are the problems to which the public enforcement apparatus is subject, creating the possibility of inadequate enforcement: on one hand, bribes,[95] political influence,[96] capture,[97] the individual interest of the enforcer in

---

[91] On this second case, they can either have their interests aligned to the person who will be compensated, or they can be looking for their own interest by acting as bounty hunters with no compensatory interest where this is allowed. See MH Redish, 'Class Actions and the Democratic Difficulty: Rethinking the Intersection of Private Litigation and Public Goals' [2003] *University of Chicago Legal Forum* 71, 90–91.

[92] Rubenstein (n 90) 2140–42.

[93] Professors Lemos and Minzer explain that until the 20th century the remuneration of public officials through what they obtained through their efforts was common in the US, such as with tax collectors that were allowed to retain some of the taxes they collected. Even though this incentive set-up was mostly abandoned by the turn of the 20th century, it has been returning since public enforcement started to be used to compensate victims. Lemos and Minzner (n 89) 861–63.

[94] In Professor's Coffee terminology, these are the ideological private attorneys general, who are financed by foundations or membership donations, being controlled by the social and political groups that they serve. JC Coffee, 'Rescuing the Private Attorney General: Why the Model of the Lawyer as a Bounty Hunter is not Working' (1983) 42 *Maryland Law Review* 215, 235.

[95] There are three important aspects to the mechanics of a bribe: (1) honesty: a person who is subject to a fine is willing to pay the enforcer a sum up to the value of that fine to forego enforcement. The enforcer, acting in his self-interest, may accept the bribe if the perceived profit from it is higher than the perceived cost of the action; (2) structure of incentives: enforcers gain in enforcing law and violators gain in violating the law, but the variation in the gain of violators is higher than the gain of enforcers, consequently giving such violators more resources than enforcers, giving them more power to bribe; (3) temporal pattern of violations: repetitive violation is more likely to create situations where the enforcer can be bribed. See GS Becker and GJ Stigler, 'Law Enforcement, Malfeasance, and Compensation of Enforcers' (1974) 3 *Journal of Legal Studies* 1, 3–5.

[96] Lemos and Minzner (n 89) 859 ('Politicians may undermine enforcement efforts by replacing key personnel or cutting budgets, and limited resources may prevent public enforcers from uncovering and pursuing violations').

[97] For a general overview of the literature, see ED Bó, 'Regulatory Capture: a Review' (2006) 22 *Oxford Review of Economic Policy* 203; RE Barkow, 'Insulating Agencies: Avoiding Capture through Institutional Design' (2010) 89 *Texas Law Review* 15.

moving to the private sector,[98] shirking[99] and on the other, overreaction due to scandals.[100]

Private enforcement is mainly a self-interested activity;[101] as long as the expected benefits outweigh the costs of litigation, private parties will have an incentive to engage in enforcement. The risk with private enforcement is over-enforcement, which is created when the rules allow a plaintiff to recoup more from the procedure than the harm actually suffered;[102] this is a problem that is created through institutionally designed incentives and which can be controlled in the same way.

The other problem with private enforcement, if it were to be used exclusively, is that enforcement will only be executed where expected benefits outweigh litigation costs. From a social point of view, it is not always true that a lawsuit that costs more than the amount at stake is undesirable, as it may create deterrence effects that are more beneficial than the amount that will be spent on it.[103]

Therefore, from this initial discussion, it can be implied that private enforcement is more adequate when there are incentives for plaintiffs to pursue it. If this is the case, in situations where a private party is harmed and the conduct does not constitute something that should be considered a crime,[104] the best approach to enforcement would be to leave it to private parties. This is justified because the state would not have to invest in an enforcement structure for these cases, saving resources for other activities and avoiding the problems that are susceptible in public enforcement operations. In addition, private enforcers also are free from the bureaucratic structure of government, being able to move more quickly than the public counterpart.[105]

Public enforcement, on the other hand, is justified in two situations: when, even though there is a social benefit in enforcing a particular rule due to its deterrence effects, the cost of the lawsuit for the private party is higher than its expected benefit, and where the prohibited conduct is victimless, as there will be no private party interested in enforcing the rules.[106] This is a general approach that can be applicable

---

[98] This is known as the revolving door phenomenon, where the individual is interested in being part of the public enforcement agency only to gain expertise to move to the private industry later on. See Revolving Door Working Group, 'A Matter of Trust: how the revolving door undermines public confidence in government—and what to do about it' (2005), pogoarchives.org/m/gc/a-matter-of-trust-20051001.pdf.

[99] On the question of individual incentives for public employees, see Lemos and Minzner (n 89) 886–95.

[100] See AC Pritchard, 'The SEC at 70: Time for Retirement?' (2005) 80 *Notre Dame Law Review* 1073, 1078–83.

[101] S Shavell, 'The Fundamental Divergence Between the Private and the Social Motive to Use the Legal System' (1997) 26 *Journal of Legal Studies* 575, 579 ('private parties are not usually concerned, or are not exclusively concerned, with the social purposes of litigation, whatever may constitute these purposes; private parties are primarily concerned with their selfish benefits from litigation').

[102] WM Landes and RA Posner, 'The Private Enforcement of Law' (1975) 4 *Journal of Legal Studies* 1, 15.

[103] Shavell (n 101) 584–85.

[104] Which varies depending on the cultural values of the specific jurisdiction.

[105] See Coffee (n 94) 226.

[106] See Becker and Stigler (n 95) 4–5.

in any area when the deterrence function of litigation is at stake—to minimise costs, it is interesting to design the system in such a way that public enforcement will be used as little as possible, allowing private parties to seize the enforcement function when they have the incentives to do so, leaving public enforcement for cases when such incentives are absent.

The purpose of securities law is twofold: namely, efficient markets and investor protection,[107] where the latter is also important for economic efficiency.[108] Deterrence, therefore, is not the only objective as a system needs to be in place for investors to be protected so that they can be compensated in case they are harmed by behaviour that violates securities laws.

Therefore, as securities laws have a dual purpose of deterrence and compensation, the claim that private enforcement should be the first step in designing an enforcement regime becomes even stronger; an exclusive public enforcement system for compensation would be at high risk of capture by the industry, especially in financial markets where there is often a lot of money at stake. For proper investor protection and the creation of market confidence, the best approach is to allow a regime for private enforcers, where enforcers are more likely to have their interest aligned with those of investors. With the compensation regime set, deterrence objectives should then be engaged and other enforcement mechanisms created to calibrate the system, as a non-calibrated enforcement system may lead to either under-deterrence, which may breed abuse and trigger many of the social costs of inefficient markets discussed above, or it may cause over-deterrence, creating other kinds of costs that are unnecessary, consequently undermining economic efficiency.[109]

The point I make for private enforcement and investor protection is an important one for this book. Its central aspect is to create dispute resolution systems where private enforcement can be effectively deployed transnationally, enhancing the scope of protection of securities laws—be they national or foreign—to investors who wish to participate in foreign markets, or in transactions with foreign securities aspects.

---

[107] 'The mission of the US Securities and Exchange Commission is to protect investors, maintain fair, orderly, and efficient markets, and facilitate capital formation'. See SEC, 'The Investor's Advocate', www.sec.gov/about/whatwedo.shtml. See also CVM, 'The Commission', www.cvm.gov.br/ingl/indexing.asp ('The Law that instituted the CVM established that it should observe the following objectives: to assure the proper functioning of the exchange and over-the-counter markets; to protect all securities holders against fraudulent issues and illegal actions').

[108] For an overview on the discussion of investor protection and economic efficiency, see A Georgosouli, 'The Debate over the Economic Rationale for Investor Protection Regulation: a Critical Appraisal' (2007) 15 *Journal of Financial Regulation and Compliance* 236.

[109] For a general overview on the potential problems of multiple enforcers, see AM Rose, 'The Multienforcer Approach to Securities Fraud Deterrence: a Critical Analysis' (2010) 158 *University of Pennsylvania Law Review* 2173.

4

The Liability Regime for Securities Disputes

Legal disputes arise out of the breach of a right. Recovery is only possible if a party that owes a legal obligation to another fails to comply with it. Rules on liability establish the standards that should be followed and are an essential part of any legal framework that purports to regulate conduct, guarantee rights and fix market failures. It is composed of both the basis used by plaintiffs to present their argument to a court and the defences available to avoid the payment of damages.

Securities transactions are executed in a fairly similar fashion across different jurisdictions; yet, depending on the legal relationship that is at stake, the standards of conduct may differ, as might the liability regime available. Much of the design of a liability system for transactions with securities depends on the characteristics chosen to define the concept, yet there is no universal definition of what a security is, despite its conceptual similarity in every jurisdiction. The exact legal contours of the definition are, of course, set out within each different legal system. The American definition is quite broad, ranging from the more commonly known legal category of a company's share to the more complicated investment contract, encompassing all sorts of derivatives in between.[1] Securities law is applicable if there is a transaction involving a security where there are no exemptions either to the security being transacted or to the transaction itself.

The backbone of securities law and the liability regimes involved at every step of securities transactions are based on regulating information asymmetry and diminishing the costs thereof, from the issuance of shares to the certification of financial statements by auditors.

---

[1] The exact language is: 'the term "security" means any note, stock, treasury stock, security future, bond, debenture, evidence of indebtedness, certificate of interest or participation in any profit-sharing agreement, collateral-trust certificate, preorganization certificate or subscription, transferable share, investment contract, voting-trust certificate, certificate of deposit for a security, fractional undivided interest in oil, gas, or other mineral rights, any put, call, straddle, option, or privilege on any security, certificate of deposit, or group or index of securities (including any interest therein or based on the value thereof), or any put, call, straddle, option, or privilege entered into on a national securities exchange relating to foreign currency, or, in general, any interest or instrument commonly known as a 'security', or any certificate of interest or participation in, temporary or interim certificate for, receipt for, guarantee of, or warrant or right to subscribe to or purchase, any of the foregoing' (Securities Act of 1933 s 2(a)(1)). Security-based swap agreements do not fall within the definition of a 'security' (Securities Act of 1933, s 2A).

The objective of this chapter is to identify and classify the types of disputes arising out of securities transactions and to demonstrate, through a brief analysis, that the standards of conduct in different jurisdictions may differ depending on the type of dispute that is at stake and on the relevant liability regime. Moreover, the identification of the different types of disputes is relevant because the available dispute resolution mechanisms are closely related to the specific category of dispute.

This chapter explains the securities commercialisation process and its relationship to disputes and identifies the legal framework for securities liability on disclosure, the legal framework for financial intermediaries in securities transactions and the legal framework for informational gatekeepers, and analyses the specific aspects of each type of dispute.

I. Transacting Securities and Disputes

To understand securities disputes, it is important to first understand the securities issuance process and the role that each actor plays in it. The basis for securities liability is the placement of securities in the market and the ongoing regulatory disclosure duties after securities are placed and remain in commerce, and the commercialisation efforts by intermediaries.

A. Issuing Securities

Securities are issued and placed in the 'primary market' and traded in the 'secondary market'. There are many reasons for issuing securities but the main one is to raise capital to finance a business. There is a great deal of effort involved in marketing securities, finding buyers and pricing them before the initial offering. This is a role that is assigned to an underwriter, that is, a financial services provider that helps the issuer with the placement of securities in the market. There are two ways in which the underwriter performs this function: the firm commitment and the best efforts methods. In the first case the underwriter assumes the risk of the issuance by committing to buy a percentage of the shares issued at an agreed price, while in the second the risk does not shift and the underwriter maintains the right to return any unsold shares.

Before the securities are placed on the market it is common for the legal rules of the country in which the securities will be issued to require audited financial statements from the issuer.[2] These statements are signed by the relevant issuer's officers and then certified by auditors, who are accountants belonging to a regulatory body that authorises them to perform audits.[3]

---

[2] eg Spanish Law 22/2015 (Financial Audit Law Recast (Spain)), first additional disposition.
[3] eg Sarbanes-Oxley Act of 2002, s 102.

Another requirement is the filing of a registration statement and the distribution of prospectuses before the securities are placed on the market. These documents have to contain all the relevant information about the issuance and the company to allow investors to make informed decisions. The responsibility for the information's veracity falls on both the issuer and the underwriter. Credit rating agencies also play a role by evaluating the risk of a given security.

Finally, after the legal requirements have been complied with, the underwriter can place the securities on the market, which can be done either through qualified investors or via the general public.[4] There are direct selling efforts made by banks and securities brokers; they can also incur liability depending on the information they provide to their customers.

After the securities are placed, they can be traded openly through exchanges or on the over-the-counter markets. When the securities are traded on public markets, ongoing disclosures about the securities and the financial health of the company that has issued them are often required; this is a duty that falls on the issuer. At the same time, auditing firms certify financial statements and credit rating agencies (CRAs) continue to evaluate the riskiness of certain securities and/or the companies issuing them.

The commercialisation of securities is made through financial intermediaries, banks, brokers and dealers, who engage in contractual relationships with investors to sell the securities and to provide financial services in relation to them.

B. Types of Disputes

From this account of how securities are issued and traded it is possible to identify three main categories of disputes arising out of securities transactions, which are dependent on the relationship that the investor has with the party from whom recovery is sought.

Some legal relationships are clear; the investor who buys securities through a financial intermediary has a contract with him, creating a direct relationship between the parties. Other relationships are not so clear; this includes the investor who relied on a CRA's rating to buy securities.

In any event, disputes arising out of securities transactions can be grouped into three categories: issuer–investor, financial intermediary–investor and informational intermediary–investor. While each type of dispute is not exclusive for each particular basis of liability—for example, financial intermediaries may fall within both disclosure liability as well as contractual liability—this categorisation of disputes is helpful in order to analyse the dispute resolution systems available to each of them, as the duties in different regulatory systems are usually divided in this manner.

---

[4] The legal requirements vary depending on which process is chosen.

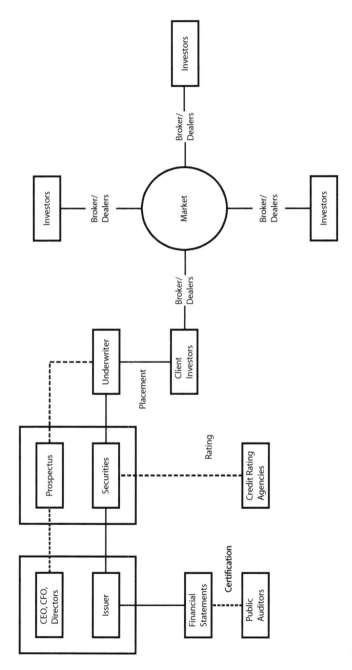

Figure 1: Issuance process

C. Transacting Transnationally

To establish the transnational character of securities transactions it is necessary to start with the understanding that markets are, at least legally, tied to certain national regulatory schemes. There is no such thing as a global market in the legal world; what exist are local markets regulated by specific jurisdictions.

A Brazilian company that wishes to raise money in the United States has to register its securities with the SEC and place them through financial intermediaries that are registered to do business there. Selling efforts made to the US market through a Brazilian financial intermediary without registration would be illegal under US law; the same is true the other way around.[5]

There are two consequences of this: first, legal access to a market requires registration and compliance with local market rules regarding both securities and financial intermediaries. Secondly, disputes with financial intermediaries, when the relationship has been started at the initiative of the financial intermediary, will most likely be national since the financial intermediary will usually be required to have a local presence.[6]

Even though the relationship between financial intermediaries and investors will be mainly national, a legal transnational transaction with a financial intermediary is also possible when the investor is the one going after a foreign financial intermediary to obtain access to different markets.[7]

The securities, on the other hand, while they have to be registered nationally, do not have to be from a company incorporated nationally. National depositary shares, such as American Depositary Shares (ADSs), are a common occurrence, as are cross-listed companies. The transnational aspect and the problems arising from it become evident; while the company issuing securities is regulated in a given jurisdiction, its assets can mostly be found in another one. As such, it may be difficult for the investor to resolve a dispute effectively with a company if an event creating liability occurs due to the lack of effective transnational dispute resolution mechanisms.

In these cases, CRAs and auditor liability may also present the same type of problem, for example where an American investor relies on a rating issued by a Brazilian CRA of a Brazilian company that has its shares traded on a US stock exchange. Absent an effective dispute resolution system, the CRA becomes immune to foreign investors.[8] Therefore, despite the national character of securities regulation,

---

[5] Transactions regarding the general public. See Securities Act of 1933, s 5; Securities Exchange Act of 1934, s 15(a)(1); Investment Advisers Act 1940, s 203(a); Brazilian Law 6.385/1976, art 16.

[6] This affirmation does not apply to the EU area due to the passport scheme that exists there.

[7] For example, Charles Schwab has a service for international investors to open a brokerage account in the US and invest directly in the US Markets. See Charles Schwab, 'Open an Account', international. schwab.com/public/international/nn/open_an_account?country=BR.

[8] They might be immune as a matter of law and have no, or at least, a very low level of liability in certain jurisdictions. For a comparative perspective of CRA liability in different jurisdictions, see A Scarso, 'The Liability of Credit Rating Agencies in a Comparative Perspective' (2013) 4 *Journal of European Tort Law* 163.

these examples show that there are situations in which transnational disputes over securities transactions may occur.

The European landscape regarding transnational securities transactions is slightly different from the one presented above. The European Union has a passport mechanism,[9] regarding both prospectuses and financial intermediaries, which makes transnational securities transactions easier. Regarding the prospectus, its approval is required by only one of the Member States, being automatically valid within all other Member States. It is only required that the competent authority of the host Member State is notified.[10] Financial intermediaries, when authorised in their home Member State, can provided services, as long as they fall within the scope of the services that they have been authorised to provide in their home state, within other Member States either directly, by using tied agents or by establishing a branch.[11]

This mechanism is based on the more general goal of the European Union, that is the construction of an internal market,[12] which, for the purposes of this discussion, is strongly tied to the right of establishment,[13] the freedom to provide services[14] and the free movement of capital.[15] Such passport regime increases the likelihood of transnational securities transactions as it relieves the burden of registration in every single jurisdiction, whether for the securities being issued or for the financial intermediary, decreasing the costs of foreign market operation and capital raising.

II. Legal Framework for Securities Liability—Issuers

As the basis of securities regulation is information asymmetry, the main duty that persons involved with the issuance and distribution of securities have is the duty of information disclosure. Relevant information about the company has to be disclosed at the issuance stage of the process as well as periodically thereafter. The breach of these duties creates a right for the person who has been harmed by false

---

[9] The passport mechanism is based on the mutual recognition principle established in the *Cassis de Dijon* judgment (Case 120/78 *Rewe-Zentral AG v Bundesmonopolverwaltung für Branntwein (Cassis de Dijon)* [1979] ECR 649), which comprises the mechanism of the single passport and home state supervision. See H Ásgeirsson, 'Integration of European Securities Markets' [2004] *Monetary Bulletin—The Central Bank of Iceland* 50, 51.

[10] Dir 2003/71/EC on the prospectus to be published when securities are offered to the public or admitted to trading [2003] OJ L345/64 (Prospectus Dir), art 17.

[11] Dir 2004/39/EC on markets in financial instruments [2004] OJ L145/1 (MiFID), arts 31–32; Dir 2014/65/EU on markets in financial instruments [2014] OJ L173/349 (MiFID II), arts 34–35.

[12] Consolidated Version of the Treaty on European Union [2012] OJ C326/15 (TEU), art 3(3) and Consolidated Version of the Treaty on the Functioning of the European Union [2012] OJ C326/47 (TFEU), art 26.

[13] TFEU, art 49.

[14] TFEU, art 56.

[15] TFEU, art 63(1).

or misleading information or by an omission made by those obliged to provide such information.

The breadth of this private right of action and the extent to which it can be effective for investors to recover is dependent not only on the substantive rules of conduct, but also on the procedural requirements that have to be met for a claim to prevail. While the purpose of this section is mainly to identify the standards of conduct of the jurisdictions under study, some of the procedural developments, especially in the US system for securities disputes, must be considered because they have evolved together with the substantive reforms on the securities regulation system and are an essential part of the liability regime.

A. The United States

Securities regulation at the federal level in the United States appeared in a moment where there was great concern and frustration with the economic depression, just after the 1929 crash.[16] The Securities Act of 1933 was designed to avoid the *caveat emptor* logic for selling securities by imposing extensive duties of truthfulness on issuers and on persons related to the issuance of securities, while the Securities and Exchange Act of 1934 focused on the regulation of speculative trading.[17]

Contrary to the civil law countries under analysis, the liability regime for securities transactions in the United States is heavily informed by the provisions of its securities laws.[18] Most of the securities claims arise under the concept of misrepresentation and securities fraud, mainly under Rule 10b-5.[19] In 2013, 84 per cent of class action lawsuits in securities litigation presented a Rule 10b-5 claim.[20]

Two other important causes of action for private securities litigation in the United States, but not nearly as relevant as the Rule 10b-5 claims, are Section 11 and Section 12 of the Securities Act of 1933. Section 11 claims were present in 9 per cent of the filings in 2013, while the 12(2) variety of Section 12 was present in only 7 per cent.[21]

i. The Securities Act of 1933

A security, unless exempted under Section 3(a) of the Securities Act of 1933, must be registered with the SEC. A transaction of, or an attempt to transact, an

---

[16] J Burk, 'The Origins of Federal Securities Regulation: A Case Study in the Social Control of Finance' (1985) 63 *Social Forces* 1010, 1012.

[17] ibid 1012–13.

[18] Even though securities regulation standards also play a role in liability in civil law countries, the backbone of private enforcement relies more on general contractual and tort standards.

[19] 17 CFR § 240.10b-5 (2013).

[20] Cornerstone Research, 'Securities Class Action Filings—2013 in Review' (2013) http://securities.stanford.edu/research-reports/1996–2013/Cornerstone-Research-Securities-Class-Action-Filings-2013-YIR.pdf.

[21] ibid.

unregistered security is expressly prohibited by Section 5 of the Securities Act of 1933, unless the transaction itself is also exempted by section 4 of the Act.[22]

The Securities Act of 1933 provides grounds for recovery under its Sections 11 and 12. According to this piece of legislation, the information that is required in a registration statement is extensive, including a business description, an outline of property owned, a description of the material legal proceedings that the company is facing, financial information, and management structure, among other information.[23] If, by its effective date,[24] any information in the registration statement is untrue regarding a material fact or if it is misleading by omission, the buyer of the security has a private right to sue under Section 11 of the Securities Act of 1933.[25] In general, proving reliance on the statement is not necessary, the plaintiff being required only to prove the existence of the falsity or of the omission made.[26] One caveat is that if the pleading is 'sound in fraud', it has to satisfy the heightened pleading standard of Section 9(b) of the Federal Rules of Civil Procedure, requiring the party to plead with particularity the circumstances consisting of fraud or mistake.[27] This is a cause of action linked with the issuance of securities, and it creates a limited class of possible plaintiffs; only those who made the purchase of a primary offering are allowed to sue under Section 11(a).[28]

The statute is generous in lining up defendants: the issuer, everyone who signed the registration statement, directors at the time of the filing, persons responsible for certifying statements in the filing and the underwriters can all be sued.[29] With the exception of outside directors, who are proportionally liable for their statements,[30] all defendants are jointly and severally liable.[31]

---

[22] See also Rule 144, 17 CFR § 230.144 (2013), Rule 144A, 17 CFR § 230.144a (2013), Reg D (Rules Governing the Limited Offer and Sale of Securities Without Registration Under the Securities Act of 1933), 17 CFR §§ 230.501–230.506 (2013) and Reg S (Rules Governing Offers and Sales Made Outside the United States Without Registration Under the Securities Act of 1933), 17 CFR §§ 230.901–230.905 (2013).

[23] See Reg S-K, 17 CFR § 229 (2013).

[24] The effective date of a registration statement is deemed to be 20 days after it is filed and has to be calculated according to 17 CFR § 230.459 (2013).

[25] For the materiality requirement to be fulfilled, it is necessary that 'there must be a substantial likelihood that the disclosure of the omitted fact would have been viewed by the reasonable investor as having significantly altered the "total mix" of information made available'. *Basic Inc v Levinson*, 485 US 224, 231–232 (1988) (quoting *TSC Indus, Inc v Northway, Inc*, 426 US 438, 449 (1976)).

[26] Reliance is presumed under this section if the purchase is made before the first 12-month earnings report covering a period of 12 months after the registration's effective date (Securities Act of 1933, s 11(a)). See also *Herman & MacLean v Huddleston*, 459 US 375, 382 (1983) ('if a plaintiff purchased a security issued pursuant to a registration statement, he need only show a material misstatement or omission to establish his *prima facie* case').

[27] See also TR David, JP Corley and AA Delawalla, 'Heightened Pleading Requirements, Due Diligence, Reliance, Loss Causation, and Truth-on-the-Market—Available Defenses to Claims under Sections 11 and 12 of the Securities Act of 1933' (2009) 11 *Transactions Tennessee Journal of Business Law* 53, 61–63.

[28] See *APA Excelsior III LP v Premiere Technologies Inc*, 476 F 3d 1261, 1276 (11th Cir 2007).

[29] Securities Act of 1933, s 11(a)(1)–(a)(5).

[30] Securities Act of 1933, s 11(f)(2); see also Securities Exchange Act of 1934, s 21D(f).

[31] Securities Act of 1933, s 11(f)(1).

While the statute allows for various different defendants, it also provides them with various defences: knowledge of the untrue or misleading statement by the plaintiff,[32] resignation from office and information to the SEC by non-issuers that they were not responsible for the registration statement before its effective date,[33] lack of knowledge regarding the part of the registration statement for which the person is liable coupled with steps towards resignation and giving public notice that the statement became effective without his knowledge,[34] and reasonable belief.[35]

Besides these statutory defences, there are also other important defences created in the judicial context. Among them are the impossibility of reliance and the lack of loss causation. Reliance on the registration statement, for the purposes of a plaintiff's claim in a class action, is presumed. If, from the facts, it is clear that plaintiffs could not have relied on the statements because they had committed themselves to the transaction before the filing of the registration statement, liability does not arise.[36] The other defence comes from the logical link between the misleading or false statement and the harm suffered. If the defendants prove that there was no loss causation, liability does not attach.[37]

Damages under this cause of action can be the price paid for the security minus its value at the time of the suit; the price for which the securities were sold before the suit; or the price for which it should have been disposed after the suit but before judgment, but only if such damages are less than the difference in the price paid for the securities (in which case it shall not be in excess of the price offered to the public) and their price at the time of the suit.[38]

In sum, Section 11 of the Securities Act is a straightforward provision: if there is a registration statement with false or misleading information when shares are sold to the public and there is a subsequent price drop, any buyer of securities to whom the statement refers may recover the price difference only by proving that the statements were false or that there was a misleading omission contained within it.

Section 12(a) of the Securities Act of 1933 provides grounds for recovery in two different situations. The first is for any offering or selling of securities that is made without a registered statement[39] while the second is for the offering or selling of securities by means of prospectus or oral communications that contain an untrue statement of material fact or are otherwise misleading.[40]

---

[32] Securities Act of 1933, s 11(a).
[33] Securities Act of 1933, s 11(b)(1).
[34] Securities Act of 1933, s 11(b)(2).
[35] Securities Act of 1933, s 11(b)(3).
[36] See *APA Excelsior III LP* (n 28) 1277 ('In sum, we hold that the Section 11 presumption of reliance does not apply in the limited and narrow situation where sophisticated investors participating in an arms-length corporate merger make a legally binding investment commitment months before the filing of a defective registration statement'). For an extensive review on the recent judicial developments on section 11, see M Steinberg and B Kirby, 'The Assault on Section 11 of the Securities Act: a Study in Judicial Activism' (2010) 63 *Rutgers Law Review* 1.
[37] See *In re Merck & Co, Inc Securities Litigation*, 432 F 3d 261, 274 (3rd Cir 2005).
[38] Securities Act of 1933, s 11(e).
[39] Securities Act of 1933, s 12(a)(1).
[40] Securities Act of 1933, s 12(a)(2).

In respect of the identification of the defendants that the plaintiff can bring to court, the language in Section 12(a) of the Securities Act of 1933 is more restrictive than Section 11: these two subsections state open with 'offers or sells' and further down also make clear that the defendant 'shall be liable ... to the person purchasing such security from him'.[41] The language of the statute defines 'sale' or 'sell' to include 'every contract of sale or disposition of a security or interest in a security, for value' and 'offer' as 'every attempt or offer to dispose of, or solicitation of an offer to buy'.[42] A strict reading of the statute would lead to the conclusion that only direct sellers would be liable for a violation of Section 12, but the Supreme Court has already decided that those who engage in solicitation may also be sued under this section, as long as a sale has taken place.[43] For Section 12(a)(2), the SEC has enacted a rule providing that only issuers can be deemed sellers.[44]

Some of the defences are also similar. Knowledge by the plaintiff of the untrue statement or omission or the existence of a reasonable belief that the information was true and not misleading, if proved by the defendants, will exempt them from liability.[45]

The remedy in this section is either rescission of the transaction where the plaintiff still has the securities, with payment of interest minus any dividends received, or, where the securities have been sold, damages.[46] Similarly, as per Section 11 in respect of the cause of action regarding untrue and misleading statements, if the defendant proves that the losses were not due to the statements, damages are not recoverable.[47]

ii. Claims under the Securities and Exchange Act of 1934

The backbone of securities fraud liability in the United States is Rule 10b-5, promulgated under Section 10 of the Securities and Exchange Act of 1934. Section 10(b) of the Securities and Exchange Act of 1934 provides that

> It shall be unlawful for any person, directly or indirectly, by the use of any means or instrumentality of interstate commerce or of the mails, or of any facility of any national securities exchange ... to use or employ, in connection with the purchase or sale of any security registered on a national securities exchange or any security not so registered, or any securities based swap agreement, any manipulative or deceptive device or contrivance in contravention of such rules and regulations as the Commission may prescribe.[48]

---

[41] Securities Act of 1933, s 12(a). See also *Pinter v Dahl*, 486 US 622, 641–647 (1988).

[42] Securities Act of 1933, s 2(a)(3).

[43] *Pinter* (n 41) 643 ('the inclusion of the phrase "solicitation of an offer to buy" within the definition of "offer" brings an individual who engages in solicitation, an activity not inherently confined to the actual owner, within the scope of §12'); ibid 644 ('The purchase requirement clearly confines §12 liability to those situations in which a sale has taken place ... The requirement, however, does not exclude solicitation from the category of activities that may render a person liable').

[44] See 17 CFR § 230.159A (2013).

[45] Securities Act of 1933, s 12(a)(2).

[46] Securities Act of 1933, s 12(a)(2).

[47] Securities Act of 1933, s 12(b).

[48] Securities Exchange Act of 1934, s 10. See also *Blue Chip Stamps v Manor Drug Stores*, 421 US 723 (1975) and *Birnbaum v Newport Steel Corp*, 193 F 2d 461 (2nd Cir 1952).

Under this section, the SEC prescribed Rule 10b-5, which establishes the prerequisites of forbidden behaviour regarding securities transactions subject to US law. The rule prohibits the employment of devices, schemes or artifices to defraud, the making of untrue statements or omissions of material facts that are misleading and engagement in business that would operate as fraud, if such conduct is made in connection with the purchase or sale of securities. Even though the rule is also known as the securities fraud rule, it covers both fraudulent and non-fraudulent behaviour.[49]

The framework of Rule 10b-5 for private actions is not only based on statutory grounds. Most of its contours were judicially established, as expressed by Chief Justice Rehnquist's famous statement that Rule 10b-5 is 'a judicial oak which has grown from little more than a legislative acorn'.[50] The private right of action itself is nowhere to be found in the legislative text, being an 'implied' right that emerged from judicial decisions.[51]

The recognition of the rights under Rule 10b-5 and its scope has gone through an initial growth followed by a subsequent narrowing, both through the development of jurisprudence[52] and the requirements of the Private Securities Litigation Reform Act (PSLRA).[53]

The PSLRA was enacted at the end of 1995 due to concerns about meritless and abusive suits.[54] It was a statute intended to lower capital costs without destroying the incentives for meritorious lawsuits.[55] The relevant changes were the safe-harbour provision for forward-looking statements, the heightened pleading standards and the change from joint and several to proportionate liability for some actors.

The safe-harbour provision diminished the range of application of Rule 10b-5. Its objective was to 'encourage issuers to disseminate relevant information to the market without fear of open-ended liability'[56] regarding forward-looking statements that are identified as such or are immaterial.[57] Before, forward-looking statements would fall within the same category of other general statements, and the PSLRA made it harder

---

[49] Fraud is 'a knowing misrepresentation of the truth or concealment of a material fact to induce another to act to his or her detriment'. BA Garner, *Black's Law Dictionary* (9th edn, West 2009). For an overview of the concept of fraud in securities regulation, see S Buell, 'What is Securities Fraud?' (2011) 61 *Duke Law Journal* 511.

[50] *Blue Chip Stamps* (n 48) 737.

[51] The first court to recognize this right of action was the US District Court for the Eastern District of Pennsylvania in 1946. See *Kardon v National Gypsum Co*, 69 F Supp 512 (DC Pa 1946). The US Supreme Court only dealt with the issue in 1971, in *Superintendent of Insurance of State of New York v Bankers Life and Casualty Co*, 404 US 6 (1971).

[52] As an example see *Central Bank of Denver, NA v First Interstate Bank of Denver, NA*, 511 US 164 (1994) (finding that there are no private right of action against aiders and abettors of violators of Rule 10b-5).

[53] Private Securities Litigation Reform Act of 1995 (PSLRA), Pub L 104–67, 109 Stat 737 (1995).

[54] HR Rep No 104–369, at 31 (1995) (Conf Rep).

[55] See S Rep No 104–98, at 4 (1995).

[56] HR Rep No 104–369, at 32 (1995) (Conf Rep).

[57] Securities Act of 1933, s 27A(c); Securities Exchange Act of 1934, s 21E(c).

for a plaintiff to prevail on a suit based on misleading forward-looking statements.[58]

Regarding the heightened pleading standard, the PSLRA instituted a change, imposing a requirement that, in lawsuits made under the Securities and Exchange Act of 1934, alleging an untrue statement of material fact or the omission of information that would make a statement misleading, the plaintiff must specify each alleged statement and the reason why they are deemed to be misleading.[59] In respect of each of these statements or omissions attributed to the defendant, the plaintiff must also state 'with particularity facts giving rise to a strong inference[60] that the defendant acted with the required state of mind', what is known as the scienter standard.[61] It also became necessary to establish proof of loss causation.[62]

Therefore, to prevail on a Rule 10b-5 lawsuit, it is necessary for plaintiff to prove '(1) a material misrepresentation or omission by the defendant; (2) scienter; (3) a connection between the misrepresentation or omission and the purchase or sale of a security; (4) reliance; (5) economic loss and (6) loss causation'.[63] If these elements are not present, the defendant prevails on a motion to dismiss.[64]

Finally, the last modification by the PSLRA was the change from joint and several liability to proportionate liability.[65] Joint and several liability is only available to the extent that the defendants knowingly committed the securities violation.[66]

There were many empirical studies after the PSLRA was enacted testing its consequences in the securities class action environment. The statute had the effect of reducing both nuisance and non-nuisance litigation.[67] The PSLRA had two important strands of impact related to litigation: first, smaller companies or those with a lower market turnover became less likely to be defendants in respect of a securities class action; secondly, companies engaging in fraud where there was no hard evidence before the suit also became less likely to be sued. The greatest impact was on suits between US$2 million and US$4 million.[68] Even though there was a

[58] For an analysis of problems that may arise when forward-looking statements are mixed with general statements about the business, see WG Couture, 'Mixed Statements: the Safe Harbor's Rocky Shore' (2011) 39 *Securities Regulation Law Journal* 257.

[59] Securities Exchange Act of 1934, s 21D(b)(1).

[60] The strong inference requirement was addressed by the US Supreme Court in *Tellabs Inc v Makor Issues & Rights Ltd,* 551 US 308, 324 (2007) ('a complaint will survive, we hold, only if a reasonable person would deem the inference of scienter cogent and at least as compelling as any opposing inference one could draw from the facts alleged').

[61] Securities Exchange Act of 1934, s 21D(b)(2)(A). For CRAs or controlling persons the required state of mind is a different one, Securities Exchange Act of 1934, s 21D (b)(2)(B).

[62] Securities Exchange Act of 1934, s 21D(b)(4).

[63] See *Dura Pharmaceuticals, Inc v Broudo,* 544 US 336, 341–342 (2005).

[64] Securities Exchange Act of 1934, s 21D(b)(3)(A). These are requirements for pleading and not for the plaintiff to obtain final judgment. If the plaintiff prevails on a motion to dismiss, it is still necessary to go to the end of the trial. Most lawsuits settle after this point.

[65] Securities Exchange Act of 1934, s 21D(f)(2)(B).

[66] Securities Exchange Act of 1934, s 21D(f)(2)(A).

[67] Nuisance litigation is the type of lawsuit where plaintiffs sue, even without a proper case, to try to reach a settlement due to the costs of the lawsuit to defendants.

[68] SJ Choi, 'Do the Merits Matter Less After the Private Securities Litigation Reform Act? ' (2006) 23 *The Journal of Law, Economics, & Organization* 598, 623.

reduction in nuisance suits, there is scepticism that this reform was beneficial to the general welfare of investors.[69]

Another important aspect in the liability design under Rule 10b-5 is the question of who can be a defendant in the lawsuit. The starting point is that the illegal conduct must occur in connection with the sale or purchase of securities.[70] Buyers, sellers, brokers and the issuer may be defendants, but only those responsible for the statement may be put in this position. Aiders and abettors contributing to a statement, but who do not 'make' it, cannot be sued for a violation of Rule 10b-5.[71]

On the question of damages, they are generally limited to the difference between the transaction price of the security and its mean trading price during the 90-day period starting on the day that the correct information was disseminated to the market.[72]

In order to complete the overview of the liability system in securities litigation in the United States, one more topic must be addressed: the fraud-on-market doctrine.

An important aspect of the liability regime in the United States for Rule 10b-5 violations is procedural. Since the class action mechanism is constantly used in securities litigation, the class certification and pleading requirements play a major role in the development of the litigation. Most of the lawsuits settle after the motion to dismiss stage, and the number of cases that reach a verdict is minimal.[73]

The *Basic Inc v Levinson*[74] decision brought a major change in the traditional reliance requirements for securities litigation in the United States.[75] Classically, to succeed in a claim for securities fraud, the plaintiff had to prove not only that had he known the truth, he would have acted differently, but also that the untruthful statement had a direct or proximate relation to the loss.[76] This is the transactional causation, a 'but for' argument that absent the untruthfulness the plaintiff would have acted in another way, and the loss causation, a connection between the statement and the loss caused.[77]

The fraud-on-the-market theory[78] was developed to deal with the plaintiff's reliance requirement in class actions. Requiring that every single member of a class

---

[69] Through a quick mathematical exercise, Professor Choi estimates that the benefit from eliminating nuisance suits during the period of the study would be around US$16.2 million, while the lost deterrence arising out of the legislative reform was US$93.9 million. ibid.

[70] 17 CFR 240.10b-5.

[71] See *Central Bank of Denver, NA* (n 52).

[72] Securities Exchange Act of 1934, s 21D(e)(1).

[73] In the dataset of the Cornerstone Research for the period of 1996 to 2011, only 8% of the securities class actions reached a ruling on summary judgment, while the rest were either dismissed or reached a settlement beforehand. Cornerstone Research, *Securities Class Action Filings—2011 in Review* (2011) 18.

[74] *Basic Inc* (n 25).

[75] For a discussion of the subject, see MB Fox, 'Demystifying Causation in Fraud-on-the-Market Actions' (2005) 60 *The Business Lawyer* 507.

[76] *Huddleston v Herman & Maclean*, 640 F 2d 534, 549 (5th Cir 1981).

[77] Fox (n 75) 508–11.

[78] For a historical perspective of the doctrine and a discussion about its functioning, see DC Langevoort, 'Basic at Twenty: Rethinking Fraud on the Market' [2009] *Wisconsin Law Review* 151.

prove that they relied on the allegedly false misstatement to certify the class would curb the possibility of the procedure since individual questions would overwhelm common ones.[79]

The presumption adopted was that shares traded on well-developed markets incorporate all available information into their securities prices, including any misrepresentations.[80] Therefore, by engaging in securities transactions in the marketplace, there is a presumption that the buyer (or seller) has relied on the integrity of the price to do so, and to this extent also on any material misrepresentations made since they are incorporated into that market price.[81]

By transforming the question of reliance into a common problem, the fraud-on-the-market theory allows for the use of the class mechanism for securities litigation. Under the theory there is no requirement that the purchaser had actually relied on, or even read, the misstatement under scrutiny. The important aspect is the presumption of reliance on market prices and the transfer of the misleading information to them.

Since the fraud-on-the-market theory consists of a presumption, defendants do have the possibility to rebut it. As long as it is demonstrated that the misstatement did not travel through the mechanisms of price incorporation, liability can be avoided.[82]

The doctrine has been the object of much criticism. Commentators have pointed out that it may cause overcompensation, and to the extent that it is usually the issuer that pays for the outcome of these suits, it may even reduce the general welfare of investors, increasing social costs.[83] Despite the criticisms, the doctrine is still in use.[84]

B. European Union

The liability regime in securities regulation in the European context has a two-tiered framework: the first level is the legal instruments of the European Union, the Treaties, directives and regulations, while the second is the internal legislation of the country. The securities markets are heavily regulated by European directives, which oblige Member States to implement legislation in compliance therewith, even though the liability provisions are left for national legislation.

---

[79] *Basic Inc* (n 25).
[80] ibid 246.
[81] ibid.
[82] ibid 248 ('Any showing that severs the link between the alleged misrepresentation and either the price received (or paid) by the plaintiff, or his decision to trade at a fair market price, will be sufficient to rebut the presumption of reliance').
[83] PG Mahoney, 'Precaution Costs and the Law of Fraud in Impersonal Markets' (1992) 78 *Virginia Law Review* 623.
[84] See *Halliburton v Erica P John Fund*, 573 US ___ (2014).

i. *The European Perspective*

Disclosure in capital markets is regulated at the European level mainly through three different directives and their amending and implementing legislative provisions: the Prospectus Directive,[85] the Transparency Directive[86] and the Market Abuse Directive.[87]

[85] See also Commission Reg (EC) 809/2004 implementing Dir 2003/71/EC of the European Parliament and of the Council as regards information contained in prospectuses as well as the format, incorporation by reference and publication of such prospectuses and dissemination of advertisements [2004] OJ L149/1, Commission Reg (EC) 211/2007 amending Reg (EC) No 809/2004 implementing Dir 2003/71/EC of the European Parliament and of the Council as regards financial information in prospectuses where the issuer has a complex financial history or has made a significant financial commitment [2007] OJ L61/24, Commission Reg (EC) 1569/2007 establishing a mechanism for the determination of equivalence of accounting standards applied by third country issuers of securities pursuant to Dirs 2003/71/EC and 2004/109/EC [2007] OJ L340/66, Dir 2010/73/EU amending Dirs 2003/71/EC on the prospectus to be published when securities are offered to the public or admitted to trading and 2004/109/EC on the harmonisation of transparency requirements in relation to information about issuers whose securities are admitted to trading on a regulated market [2010] OJ L327/1, Commission Delegated Reg (EU) 486/2012 amending Reg (EC) No 809/2004 as regards the format and the content of the prospectus, the base prospectus, the summary and the final terms and as regards the disclosure requirements [2012] OJ L150/1, Commission Delegated Reg (EU) 862/2012 amending Reg (EC) No 809/2004 as regards information on the consent to use of the prospectus, information on underlying indexes and the requirement for a report prepared by independent accountants or auditors [2012] OJ L256/4, Commission Delegated Reg (EU) 759/2013 amending Reg (EC) No 809/2004 as regards the disclosure requirements for convertible and exchangeable debt securities [2013] OJ L213/1, Delegated Reg (EU) 382/2014 supplementing Dir 2003/71/EC of the European Parliament and of the Council as regards regulatory technical standards for publication of supplements to the prospectus [2014] OJ L111/36.

[86] Dir 2004/109/EC on the harmonisation of transparency requirements in relation to information about issuers whose securities are admitted to trading on a regulated market [2004] OJ L390/38 (Transparency Dir), Commission Dir 2007/14/EC laying down detailed rules for the implementation of certain provisions of Dir 2004/109/EC on the harmonisation of transparency requirements in relation to information about issuers whose securities are admitted to trading on a regulated market [2007] OJ L69/27, Commission Reg (EC) 1569/2007 establishing a mechanism for the determination of equivalence of accounting standards applied by third country issuers of securities pursuant to Dirs 2003/71/EC and 2004/109/EC [2007] OJ L340/66, Commission Decision 2008/961/EC on the use by third countries' issuers of securities of certain third country's national accounting standards and International Financial Reporting Standards to prepare their consolidated financial statements [2007] OJ L340/112, Dir 2013/50/EU amending Dir 2004/109/EC of the European Parliament and of the Council on the harmonisation of transparency requirements in relation to information about issuers whose securities are admitted to trading on a regulated market, Dir 2003/71/EC and Commission Dir 2007/14/EC laying down detailed rules for the implementation of certain provisions of Dir 2004/109/EC [2013] OJ L294/13.

[87] Dir 2003/6/EC on insider dealing and market manipulation [2003] OJ L96/16 (Market Abuse Dir), Commission Reg (EC) 2273/2003 implementing Dir 2003/6/EC of the European Parliament and of the Council as regards exemptions for buy-back programmes and stabilisation of financial instruments [2003] OJ L336/33, Commission Dir 2003/124/EC implementing Dir 2003/6/EC of the European Parliament and of the Council as regards the definition and public disclosure of inside information and the definition of market manipulation [2003] OJ L339/70, Commission Dir 2003/125/EC implementing Dir 2003/6/EC of the European Parliament and of the Council as regards the fair presentation of investment recommendations and the disclosure of conflicts of interest [2003] OJ L339/73, Commission Dir 2004/72/EC implementing Dir 2003/6/EC of the European Parliament and of the Council as regards accepted market practices, the definition of inside information in relation to derivatives on commodities, the drawing up of lists of insiders, the notification of managers' transactions and the notification of suspicious transactions [2004] OJ L162/70.

The European framework for securities regulation is structured around two main axes, market efficiency and the creation of a pan-European market for securities.[88] Therefore, the set of problems arising at the European level that are addressed through regulation go beyond those discussed above, arising within the national spheres.

As is the case with the other two systems of civil liability discussed herein, the provisions of these directives are designed to impose extensive disclosure duties on issuers, underwriters and other participants of capital markets. As a matter of EU law, these directives do not have horizontal direct effect[89] since they constitute obligations imposed on the Members States to implement measures internally.[90] The details of civil liability for disclosure are thus left to the Member States.[91] The Prospectus Directive, for example, provides only that responsibility for the information should attach at least to the issuer (or its administrative, management or supervisory bodies), the offeror, the person asking for the admission to trading in a regulated market or the guarantor, as the case may be.[92] The way in which liability should be deemed to arise and the relevant remedies are not provided for, yet Member States have to adapt their systems so they are in compliance with the general framework of the directives.[93]

ii. Implementation in Domestic Systems: the Case of Spain

Spanish Law 24/1988 was created in 1988 to give coherence to the reforms that had been made in the Spanish securities market regulations in the years before and to modernise the Spanish markets due to the possibility of a European capital market being established by 1992.[94] The law created the Comisión Nacional del Mercado de Valores (CNMV),[95] the agency responsible for regulating and supervising

[88] See also Dir 2009/65/EC on the coordination of laws, regulations and administrative provisions relating to undertakings for collective investment in transferable securities [2009] OJ L302/32 (UCITS Dir), the European legislative instrument on the coordination of laws, regulations and administrative provisions relating to undertakings for collective investment in transferable securities.

[89] They have vertical direct effect if the Member State does not implement the directives in the allotted time. See Case C-41/74 *Van Duyn v Home Office* [1974] ECR 1337 and Case C-148/78 *Pubblico Ministerio v Ratti* [1979] ECR 1629.

[90] See D Chalmers, G Davies and G Monti, *European Union Law* (2nd edn, Cambridge University Press 2010) 286–93. The exception to this rule is that directives may be directly effective against the Member States if the Member State has not transposed a given directive into internal legislation by the end of the transposition period. See also *Minister of the Interior v Cohn-Bendit* [1980] 1 CMLR 543.

[91] N Moloney, *EC Securities Regulation* (2nd edn, Oxford University Press 2008) 164–65; IHY Chiu, *Regulatory Convergence in EU Securities Regulation* (Kluwer Law International 2008) 160–62. See also Case C-174/12 *Hirmann v Immofinanz AG* (19 December 2013).

[92] Prospectus Dir, art 6.

[93] See N Moloney, *How to Protect Investors: Lessons from the EC and the UK* (Cambridge University Press 2010) 444–47.

[94] See Spanish Law 24/1988, Introduction.

[95] Spanish Law 24/1988, art 13.

financial markets in Spain,[96] and set out the framework for the duties of market participants at many different levels.

A prospectus is required for securities that are to be admitted to trading in a secondary official market[97] or for an initial public offering,[98] which also brings disclosure requirements. Under Spanish law a prospectus must provide sufficient information for investors to evaluate the financial situation of the issuer and their future possibilities; it must be drafted in an easily readable and comprehensible manner.[99] The responsibility for the prospectus' information lies with the issuer, the offeror, the entity asking for the admission to trade in a regulated market and all of their managers.[100]

After the securities are issued and are trading in a regulated market, issuers have a duty to disclose their annual financial statements,[101] which have to be audited.[102] Every three months, issuers must also make a statement which includes information about significant operations in the time period and their impact on the financial situation of the company.[103] The responsibility for the annual financial statements falls to at least the issuer and its officers, under conditions that the CNMV may establish.[104] This responsibility encompasses all the damage that the owners of such securities may suffer if the information provided does not faithfully reflect the situation of the issuer.[105]

A similar duty of information is also imposed on financial intermediaries. They are obliged to give clear and non-misleading information to their clients, with extra obligations when these institutions provide advisory services for their clients.[106]

Like the US and Brazilian systems, the Spanish system also has disclosure requirements for relevant information[107] and explicitly puts forward a 'disclose or abstain' policy for privileged information.[108] Relevant information is deemed to be any information that may affect a reasonable investor in transacting with securities, influencing their price in the secondary market.[109] Issuers have to make this kind of information public,[110] unless, under their own responsibility, they believe it may prejudice their legitimate interests.[111]

---

[96] The CNMV can impose normative instruments that are known as *Circulares*, as long as there is previous authorisation either by a *Real Decreto* or an *Orden del Ministerio de Economía y Hacienda*. Spanish Law 24/1988, art 15.

[97] Spanish Law 24/1988, art 26.

[98] Spanish Law 24/1988, art 30 *bis*.2.

[99] Spanish Law 24/1988, art 27.1.

[100] Spanish Law 24/1988, art 28.1.

[101] In case of debt securities, the statements must be issued every semester. Spanish Law 24/1988, art 35.2.

[102] Spanish Law 24/1988, art 35.1.

[103] Spanish Law 24/1988, art 35.3.

[104] Spanish Law 24/1988, art 35 *ter*.1.

[105] Spanish Law 24/1988, art 35 *ter*.2.

[106] Spanish Law 24/1988, art 79 *bis*.

[107] Spanish Law 24/1988, art 81.

[108] Spanish Law 24/1988, art 82.

[109] Spanish Law 24/1988, art 82.1.

[110] Spanish Law 24/1988, art 82.2.

[111] Spanish Law 24/1988, art 82.4.

Even though there is a clear liability system against issuers, there is very little litigation on the subject. Most of the litigation regarding financial markets is of the financial intermediary–investor type.

iii. Other Liability Regimes

Liability systems for issuers in other EU Member States vary to the extent that there are different legal regimes. They can be based on the country's tort liability, on its contractual liability, or specifically on the liability arising out of the relevant prospectus and transparency regulations available. Three examples, regarding prospectus liability, are sufficient to illustrate the difference: namely, France, Germany and the United Kingdom.

In France, liability is based either on the general tort regime or on the contractual liability regime.[112] In any event, for liability to attach it must be proven that there exists loss or damage, fault on the part of the persons who signed the prospectus and a causal link with the harm suffered.[113]

In Germany the liability regime is a specific one, implemented in the German Securities Prospectus Act, but complemented by the application of German tort law.[114] The purchaser has to prove that the prospectus is incorrect or incomplete, that the securities were purchased after the prospectus was published, and that the purchase was made within six months after the first trading of the securities or the public offering.[115] Pre-contractual liability only arises where the transaction is a direct one between the purchaser and the issuer.[116]

Finally, in the United Kingdom, prospectus liability can be based on section 90 of the Financial Services and Markets Act 2000, common law negligence or common law deceit.[117] Under section 90, untrue or misleading statements, or omissions that were required to be included, constitute sufficient grounds for liability, with the available defence being reasonable belief or reliance on an expert.[118]

The standards for liability of these countries, and overall in Europe, are similar[119] but notwithstanding this similarity the actual operation of liability may differ, sometimes because there are additional aspects that must be proved[120] or because the standard of proof is diverse.[121] The recoverable damages can also be different.[122] Therefore, the liability regime will depend on the applicable legal regime, which can differ substantially notwithstanding EU harmonisation efforts, having

---

[112] ESMA, *Report: Comparison of Liability Regimes in Member States in Relation to the Prospectus Directive* (2013) Annex III, 77.
[113] ibid Annex III, 79.
[114] ibid Annex III, 87.
[115] ibid Annex III, 89.
[116] ibid Annex III, 88.
[117] ibid Annex III, 313.
[118] ibid Annex III, 313–15.
[119] ibid para 41.
[120] ibid para 44.
[121] ibid para 42.
[122] ibid paras 48–50.

the potential to create legal uncertainty for issuers and consequently undermine the free-movement-of-capital principle. The positive aspect of the EU framework is that despite these differences in liability regimes, the operation of the directives and regulations function as a convergence tool, continuously approximating them.

C. Brazil

Securities regulation in Brazil is also extensive. Similarly, Brazil has an agency in charge of regulating the securities market. The agency is known as Comissão de Valores Mobiliários (CVM), created by Brazilian Law 6.385/1976. The CVM has the power to define what can be considered fraudulent and non-equitable practices in the initial offering or intermediation of securities.[123]

Through different legal instruments the CVM has imposed many duties to issuers and market participants both in the initial offering of securities as well as duties regarding the trading of securities in the secondary market. Like the SEC, the CVM not only sets the rules of the game, but also has a strong enforcement presence in securities regulation, having the power to bring administrative proceedings for irregularities.

In a way that differs from the United States though, the regime for securities liability in private litigation is not based predominantly on particular provisions of securities law, but relies heavily on the general provisions on civil liability in the Brazilian Civil Code.[124] It is interesting to note that the litigation of these cases in Brazil is well below the US level.

With its authority derived from Brazilian legislation, the CVM has issued many different legal rules organising the securities market in Brazil and imposing duties to market participants regarding their behaviour. Disclosure obligations are widespread and specific obligations are dependent on what transactions are made and the identification of the person committing the act.

Different regulations are applicable, imposing different disclosure duties, depending on whether what is relevant is an issuance of securities or secondary market trading. There are basically two different Instructions[125] that impose disclosure duties to market players.[126] They are Instruction CVM 400, regulating the issuance of securities to the public, and Instruction CVM 358, regulating the disclosure of material information and insider trading.

The first duty is the preparation of the prospectus for the issuance of securities, the responsibility for which falls to both the offeror and the lead underwriter.[127]

---

[123] Brazilian Law 6.385/1976, art 18, II, b).

[124] Brazilian Law 10.406/2002.

[125] An Instruction is one of the legal mechanisms through which the CVM regulates the market.

[126] There are also other Instructions with more specific disclosure duties, but their analysis is beyond the scope of this chapter.

[127] Instruction CVM 400, art 38.

The information in the prospectus should neither omit relevant facts nor have information that may mislead investors.[128]

While responsibility for the prospectus falls to both the offeror and the lead underwriter, the duty of care is distinct: the offeror is responsible for the 'truthfulness, consistency, quality and sufficiency of the information',[129] while the lead underwriter is under a duty to exercise due care to guarantee the accuracy of the information.[130]

The second duty is one of disclosure of material facts. The list of facts considered to be material is extensive and comprises occurrences that are likely to influence securities prices, the investor's decision to buy or sell them or the investor's decision to exercise any rights arising out of the above-mentioned security.[131]

Within the corporate structure, the person responsible for disclosing material facts is the Director of Investor Relationship, but where disclosure is not made, if other actors (such as controlling shareholders, directors, board of directors members, fiscal counsel or any other technical or consulting body within the corporation that is created by the corporate charter) have any knowledge about it, they also become responsible if they do not communicate the material fact promptly to the CVM.[132] The disclosure may be exempted after a request to the CVM if there is a belief that it may harm a legitimate interest of the company.[133] Even though the legislation is not explicit about the liability of the issuer, it can be implied from the goals of the legal framework; such liability has already been affirmed by the São Paulo Justice Tribunal.[134]

Compared to the US system, the standards of conduct under the Brazilian system are similar: the issuer and underwriter have a duty to disclose information in an initial offering while the issuer and its officers have an ongoing duty to disclose relevant facts to the market.

Following this brief overview of the legal duties of market participants, it is possible to move on to the analysis of liability, which arises out of the provisions of the Brazilian Civil Code. The relevant provision provides the following: 'anyone that, by an illicit act ..., causes harm to another, is obliged to repair the harm'.[135] Illicit acts are those that violate rights and cause harm to others, whenever they are made by a voluntary action or omission, negligence or imprudence.[136] Therefore,

---

[128] Instruction CVM 400, art 39.
[129] Instruction CVM 400, art 56 (trans by the author).
[130] Instruction CVM 400, art 56 § 1.
[131] Instruction CVM 358, art 2°.
[132] Instruction CVM 358, art 3° §§ 1–2.
[133] Instruction CVM 358, arts 6°, 7°.
[134] See *Asa Administradora de Bens v ABN Amro Bank* (TJSP, 5th Private Law Chamber, Civil Appeal n 9247433-87.2005.8.26.0000) (2011).
[135] Brazilian Civil Code, art 927 (trans by the author).
[136] Brazilian Civil Code, art 186. The specific language is: 'anyone that, by voluntary action or omission, negligence or imprudence, violates a right and causes harm to other, even if exclusively moral, commits and illicit act' (trans by the author).

from the language of the statute, not only the duty and its breach are necessary for liability to arise, but harm must also be suffered.

The harm caused will constitute the measure of damages to be paid in this kind of lawsuit, but the problem is that the jurisprudence has not yet developed a method on how to measure harm arising from securities litigation. After a survey of the São Paulo and Rio de Janeiro Tribunals' jurisprudence repositories, the only reference to damages in this type of case was found in the *Asa Adminstradora de Bens* case.[137] The case was about the non-disclosure of a contract where ABN Amro SA would buy shares of Banco Real SA and assume its control. After the contract was signed, but before the shares were effectively traded and the control of Banco Real SA had changed, ABN Amro made tender offers and bought shares of these companies in the market. The court determined that the defendant should 'indemnify the harm suffered by plaintiffs arising out of the sale of these shares, harm which corresponds to the difference between the value effectively owed and the one paid'.[138] Then the court enrolled a specialist to calculate the amount of harm done.[139]

In this particular case, not only was harm not proven, but moreover there were no reasonable grounds to believe that the plaintiffs were harmed. It is dangerous to imply harm from the mere lack of information disclosure, since it is not always clear, depending on the information that was not disclosed, if the security price would go up or down in the event the particular information had indeed been released to the public.[140] Harm therefore should not be assumed abstractly, implied from the mere breach of duty to inform by the issuer, but must be proved, even if a lax standard of proof is used.

This was the concern of James Siano, the dissenting Justice.[141] In fact, after the announcement of the material fact underpinning this dispute, the share price of the securities that were sold by plaintiffs actually fell,[142] a situation that would leave the plaintiffs with fewer assets in the event they had not sold their securities. This constitutes strong evidence that if there was a mispricing due to the non-disclosure of material information to the market, it was one that worked in the plaintiffs' favour. This suggests the plaintiffs were not harmed and no liability should have arisen out of this breach of disclosure duties by Banco Real SA,[143] at least concerning the specific plaintiffs in this case.[144]

---

[137] *Asa Administradora* (n 134).

[138] ibid 32 (trans by the author).

[139] ibid.

[140] Of course there are some cases where actual harm can be implied, for example when an oil company hides the fact that one of its main oil platforms has exploded.

[141] See Dissenting Opinion in *Asa Administradora* (n 134).

[142] According to estimates of the defendants, the share price fell by 30% to 35%, but this assertion was not specifically contested by plaintiffs in the lawsuit.

[143] Banco Real SA, and not ABN Amro SA, was the party that had the duty to disclose relevant information to the market.

[144] If it were the plaintiffs that bought the shares, harm would be more evident.

D. Disclosure Liability Standards: Similar But Not Equal

The private liability standards among the jurisdictions studied are fairly similar. Issuers of securities have to be truthful and disclose material information to their investors; many surrounding service providers are under a duty of due diligence to assert that the information provided is correct.

The objective behind these regulatory regimes is to diminish informational asymmetry by promoting a market where there is disclosure of truthful information. Some differences can be identified in respect of the scope of liability, if joint and several or if proportional to the act performed; the calculation of damages, which may be done through different methods, depending on the standard that is breached; and finally the available defences.

Moreover, another important difference is the legal background structuring the private right of action in securities litigation: in the United States this has been created and extracted from the legal statutes on securities regulation and by judicial decisions; in Spain it is based on securities laws;[145] while in Brazil it is a corollary of the general liability framework available within its legal system.

Finally, even though the standards of conduct may be generally similar, the operation of liability can vary substantially, even in places where the standard of conduct is harmonised, such as in the European Union,[146] creating the necessity for efficient private international law rules so as to avoid legal uncertainty.[147]

III. Legal Framework for Securities Liability—Financial Intermediaries

Financial intermediaries are those that operate between markets and investors. They can trade on their own account, buying and selling securities for themselves, or they can act as pure intermediaries, executing trades for investors. In any event, together with the execution of these transactions, they may also provide other types of financial services, such as advising their clients as to the kinds of investments in which they should invest or by managing their portfolios.

As a general matter, when financial intermediaries are transacting in securities, they are subject to the disclosure regime, being prohibited from engaging in these transactions through the use of false or misleading information, as well as to specific regimes regulating their conduct in providing financial services.

In the United States, the securities regulation liability regime for financial intermediaries is also anchored to Rule 10b-5, having another layer of protection—either

---

[145] Spanish Law 24/1988, art 28.
[146] See ESMA (n 112).
[147] See Ch 10.

through the Investment Advisers Act of 1940 or the rules of FINRA, the self-regulatory organisation in charge of regulating the securities industry[148]—coupled with the common contractual liability regime.

The difference between the legal sources that are applicable to financial intermediaries depends on whether they are classified as broker-dealers or as investment advisers. In theory, while broker-dealers have to comply only with the suitability standard in advising clients about products,[149] investment advisers owe clients a complete fiduciary duty, including the duties of loyalty and care.[150] In practice, this distinction may be blurred when brokers hold discretionary accounts of their clients[151] or act as their client's agent, in which case fiduciary duties would also be owed, even though the extent of the duty or the determination of when it should be applied is not quite clear in the American legal system.[152] The institutional background for dispute resolution is also distinct since not only are broker-dealers subject to the regulatory overview of FINRA, but disputes arising with investors are also resolved through arbitration by a panel organised according to FINRA's arbitration system.[153]

In any event, the distinction between the fiduciary duty owed by investment advisers and the suitability standard with which broker-dealers must comply when selling securities to clients has to be made clear. The suitability standard requires that the broker-dealer or an associated person 'have a reasonable basis to believe that a recommended transaction or investment strategy involving a security or securities is suitable for the customer, based on the information obtained through the reasonable diligence … to ascertain the customer's investment profile',[154] while the fiduciary duty provides, in addition to the suitability requirement, that the adviser acts in the best interest of the client and prohibits, absent disclosure, conflicts of interest between the fiduciary and the principal or between principals of the same fiduciary.[155]

The situation in the United States at the moment is complicated in respect of the standard of conduct applicable to financial intermediaries. Broker-dealers at times do provide investment advice while being held to a lower standard than investment advisers. There have been some proposals for reform,[156] especially after the

---

[148] The provisions regulating SROs in the US are found in s 19 of the Securities and Exchange Act of 1934. On the formation of FINRA, see SEC Release No 34-56145 (26 July 2007).

[149] SEC, 'Study on Investment Advisers and Broker Dealers' (2011), www.sec.gov/news/studies/2011/913studyfinal.pdf, 59–66.

[150] ibid 21–22.

[151] A discretionary account exists when a client opens an account with a broker or an investment adviser and they can trade on that account without the client's consent. See also ibid 54–55.

[152] AB Laby, 'Selling Advice and Creating Expectations: Why Brokers Should Be Fiduciaries' (2012) 87 *Washington Law Review* 707, 724–25.

[153] On the institutional design of the FINRA arbitration system and its flaws, see Ch 7.

[154] FINRA Rules, s 2111.

[155] The fiduciary duty under the Investment Advisers Act of 1940 requires utmost good faith, full and fair disclosure of all material facts and reasonable care to avoid misleading clients. See *SEC v Capital Gains Research Bureau, Inc*, 375 US 180 (1963); See also Laby (n 152) 725.

[156] See Laby (n 152); SEC (n 149); G Ravdin, 'One Step Forward, Two Steps Back: Arguing for a Transatlantic Investor Protection Regime' (2012) 50 *Columbia Journal of Transnational Law* 490.

enactment of the Dodd-Frank Act and the study by the SEC on the subject, but it still is not clear if this will continue to constitute the liability regime for financial intermediaries in securities transactions.[157]

In a manner different from the United States, which defines the intermediary liability according to the intermediary classification within the regulatory system and the activity performed,[158] in the European Union the standard of conduct is defined according to the category of client with whom the financial intermediary is transacting and the type of service offered.[159] There are three main categories of duties owed by financial intermediaries, which arise depending on whether the party with whom they are transacting is a retail client, professional client or eligible counterparty.[160]

Fundamentally, investment services intermediaries must 'act honestly, fairly and professionally in accordance with the best interests of [their] clients',[161] while they are also obliged to execute orders on the terms most favourable to the client[162] and to implement measures to 'provide for the prompt, fair and expeditious execution' of orders.[163] Depending on whether the financial intermediary is providing investment advice, other types of investment services or execution-only services, a duty of suitability or appropriateness may also exist.

The suitability requirement is applicable when investment advice is provided and necessitates that the investment firm obtains the 'necessary information regarding the client's or potential client's knowledge and experience in the investment field …, his financial situation and his investment objectives' so that the firm can assess and recommend financial instruments that are suitable to the client.[164] The appropriateness standard is applicable when investment services other than investment advice are provided, and requires that the investment firm ask the 'client to provide information regarding his knowledge and experience in the investment field relevant to the specific type of product offered or demanded', so the

---

[157] President Trump recently signed an executive order requesting a review of the 'fiduciary rule', indicating that some changes might occur. M Konczal, 'Trump Picks Wall Street Over Main Street', *New York Times* (New York, 4 February 2017).

[158] At least theoretically, since broker-dealers are not supposed to give investment advice that is not 'solely incidental', although they often end up doing so. See Investment Advisers Act of 1940, s 202 (a) (11)(C).

[159] Moloney (n 91) 396–97. The regulatory framework is set by the MiFID and its implementing regulation: Commission Dir 2006/73/EC implementing Dir 2004/39/EC of the European Parliament and of the Council as regards organisational requirements and operating conditions for investment firms and defined terms for the purposes of that Dir [2006] OJ L241/26; Commission Reg (EC) 1287/2006, implementing Dir 2004/39/EC of the European Parliament and of the Council as regards record-keeping obligations for investment firms, transaction reporting, market transparency, admission of financial instruments to trading, and defined terms for the purposes of that Dir [2006] OJ L241/1. Starting from January 2018, the current regulatory framework will be replaced by MiFID II and Reg 600/2014 on markets in financial instruments [2014] OJ L173/84 MiFIR.

[160] See MiFID, arts 19(10) and 24(2); MiFID II, recitals 10, 11, 104, art 30 and Annex II.

[161] MiFID, art 19(1); MiFID II, art 24(1).

[162] MiFID, art 21(1); MiFID II, art 27(1).

[163] MiFID, art 22(1); MiFID II, art 29(1).

[164] MiFID, art 19(2); MiFID II, art 24(3).

investment firm can assess whether the product is appropriate for the client.[165] Not only is the scope of the appropriateness standard requirement lower, necessitating only the provision of information regarding the investor's knowledge about the product, but moreover, it is not conditional on the provision of services; if the intermediary finds that the product is not appropriate or if the client fails to inform the intermediary about his knowledge and experience, the intermediary may still proceed and provide the service as long as a warning is provided.[166]

Remaining within the 'type of service' categorisation, the execution-only service does not impose any kind of information duty on intermediaries; however, certain requirements must be fulfilled for this category to be applicable: the instruments covered must be shares traded in a regulated market, money market instruments, bonds or other forms of securitised debt (excluding those embedding a derivative); the service must be provided at the initiative of the client; the client must be informed that the suitability requirement is not applicable; and the conflict of interest duties must be complied with.[167]

Moving up the ladder of investor sophistication, the requirements when transacting with professional investors are different. In this case, in respect of the suitability and appropriateness requirements, the financial intermediary is entitled to assume that professional investors have the necessary experience and knowledge in respect of the products for which they are classified as professional investors and that as such, the client is financially able to bear the risks of such investment;[168] this reduces considerably the duties of the financial intermediary.

Finally, the last category of clients is that of the eligible counterparty; this category imposes the fewest requirements on investment intermediaries. When dealing with this category of client, the duties of suitability, appropriateness, most favourable terms execution and measures for prompt, fair and expeditious execution are not required.[169]

While these categories set out the framework for the standard of conduct of investment intermediaries, they are not excessively rigid; generally, the client has the option to ask for a higher or lower level of protection, though there might be some limitations. For example, eligible counterparties may request, either generally or on a trade-by-trade basis, to have the financial intermediary subjected to the general standard of conduct regime;[170] professional clients may also opt to be treated as retail clients, and retail clients who comply with some requirements may request to be treated as professional clients.[171]

---

[165] MiFID, art 19(5); MiFID II, art 25(3). If the financial intermediary fails to obtain the information about the client it may not recommend investment services or financial instruments to the client. Commission Dir 2006/73/EC, art 35(5).
[166] ibid.
[167] MiFID, art 19(6); MiFID II, art 25(4).
[168] Commission Dir 2006/73/EC, arts 35(2) and 36.
[169] MiFID, art 24(1); MiFID II, art 30(1).
[170] MiFID, art 24(2); MiFID II, art 30(2).
[171] MiFID, Annex II; MiFID II, Annex II.

A brief comparison of the US and EU systems on financial intermediary standards of conduct and liability shows that the EU system, while being quite complex, is more straightforward and less confusing than the American system; the latter seems to suffer from a pathological regulatory overburden created by the imposition of two different systems of regulation that apply to theoretically different institutions but that in practice provide virtually the same services, the difference being only the (self-)determination of classification. As the focus in the EU system is on the service provided rather than on how the institution is classified, absent the requirements for a lesser standard of conduct, the higher standard will be applicable, guaranteeing greater legal certainty in respect of the market regulation operation and the standards of conduct that should be followed; this consequently establishes a more homogeneous level of protection for investors and creates less confusion for financial intermediaries.

In the European context it is important to draw attention to the fact that even though the standards of conduct that are expected from the financial intermediaries are the same, as they have been harmonised by European legislation, the specific imposition of liability regarding non-compliance with these norms is left to Member States since no provision is made in MiFID I or II; this creates a different regime for the private enforcement of these rules depending on which specific Member State law will be applicable.[172] There is an ongoing discussion regarding the extent to which the MiFID standards displace private law in EU Member States, as the directive was created as supervision legislation.[173] The trend seems to indicate that MiFID can also be a basis for private law litigation, complementing national private law standards, even though it still is not clear whether this is a mandatory outcome as a matter of EU law, leaving Member States with a considerable margin of discretion regarding their private liability regime.[174]

Finally, in Brazil, the manner in which the regulatory structure is set up is similar to the one in the United States, since it is divided according to the category in which the person is registered in the regulatory system. There are two categories: autonomous investment agents, who perform client prospection activities, among other things, and provide information about the investment products and services being offered,[175] and investment managers, who can manage their clients' portfolios.[176] Autonomous investment agents have to act diligently and with good faith, acting with the care expected from a professional in his position towards his

---

[172] See Case C-604/11 *Genil 48 SL v Bankinter* (30 May 2013), para 59.3 ('it is for the internal legal order of each Member State to determine the contractual consequences where an investment firm offering an investment service fails to comply with [the suitability and appropriateness standards], subject to observance of the principles of equivalence and effectiveness').

[173] O Cherednychenko, 'European Securities Regulation, Private Law and the Investment Firm-Client Relationship' [2009] *European Review of Private Law* 925, 927–31.

[174] For a discussion on the issue, see D Busch, 'Why MiFID Matters to Private Law – The Example of MiFID's Impact on an Asset Manager's Civil Liability' (2012) 7 *Capital Markets Law Journal* 386; S Grundmann, 'The Bankinter Case on MIFID Regulation and Contract Law' (2013) 9 *European Review of Contract Law* 267.

[175] Instruction CVM 497, art 1, I and III.

[176] Instruction CVM 306, art 2.

clients and the institutions of the securities markets.[177] Investment managers must use the care and diligence that an active and honest man uses for his own business, acting with loyalty in relation to their clients' interests.[178] A person may not be both an autonomous investment agent and an investment consultant at the same time; he must choose one of the activities.[179]

This section has demonstrated that the standards of care that are owed in financial intermediary–investor disputes are different depending on the jurisdiction at hand. Moreover, even in the European Union with its harmonised regime, the actual enforcement of the rules by private parties can vary since the liability regime is left to Member States.

IV. Legal Framework for Securities Liability— Informational Intermediaries

The third type of disputes that investors may have in securities transactions are those related to the information providers with whom they do not have a direct relationship, such as CRAs and auditing firms. These are market players that provide information to the market and currently are an essential service provider in many securities regulation frameworks, with a legal mandate that changes their status from being mere information providers to market gatekeepers, to the extent that their use is mandatory for certain types of transactions.[180]

The role of these players in the market is a simple one—to provide information to investors so they can make better investment decisions, be it through the provision of an analysis of a given financial product, a service provided by the CRAs, or the lending of their reputation to financial statements and guaranteeing that they are correct, as in the case of the service provided by financial auditors. The legal status of the opinions and statements of these players is relevant to investors; depending on how they are treated and the relevant standard of liability in case the opinion or information is wrong, investors may be able to successfully sue.

In the beginning, CRAs and auditors developed their services to provide investors with information, either directly to the client, as in the case of the initial practice of CRAs of selling subscriptions to their newsletters, or through the provision of audits hired by audited companies and given to investors. The market developed because there was value to be provided by these market actors, which could only

---

[177] Instruction CVM 497, art 10.
[178] Instruction CVM 306, art 14, II.
[179] Instruction CVM 497, art 13, para 1.
[180] For a development on the regulatory role of CRAs and the obligation of certain institutions to purchase only rated investments, see fn 161 of N Ellis, L Fairchild and F D'Souza, 'Is Imposing Liability on Credit Ratings Agencies a Good Idea?: Credit Rating Agency Reform in the Aftermath of the Global Financial Crisis' (2011–2012) 17 *Stanford Journal of Law, Business and Finance* 175, 213.

be sustained if the information they provided was more or less accurate, as inaccuracy of ratings or audits would put these information providers out of business.

Later, these players were given a special legal status, as was the case for the Nationally Recognized Statistical Rating Organization (NRSRO) status for the CRAs, or the SEC registered status for auditors, as it became a government policy that information provided to investors was presumably relevant. The only reason for the existence of this obligation was a belief that certified financial statements would reduce the probability of false or misleading information. Under both schemes, informational accuracy is an objective to be achieved, and the system of incentives to which these information providers are subject must be calibrated to allow them to provide investors with accurate information.

There are two ways to align interests: compensation and liability. In an economic environment an action will be performed according to the gains that the actor might obtain from the action. This section discusses the transformation of the compensation structure of these industries and the importance of a liability regime for informational intermediaries.

A. Compensation

In 1909 the activity of rating securities started with John Moody rating US railroad bonds that had already been in existence since 1850.[181] The emergence of credit rating agencies was a convergence of the activities of credit reporting agencies, the specialised financial press and investment bankers, with each having their own particular role in providing financial information.[182] Compensation in the industry was straightforward: those who wanted to obtain financial information prepared by the rating agencies would subscribe to their services, which would be made available through periodic publications.[183] The rating agencies then had an incentive to provide the most accurate information as they could by undertaking analysis in a manner that could reflect reality and provide useful information to their clients, since they would be hired on the basis of their reputational capital.[184]

The change in the industry's compensation scheme occurred in 1970 when issuers started paying rating agencies to rate bonds, an activity which today constitutes the main source of income for rating agencies.[185] This modification of the CRA

---

[181] R Sylla, 'A Historical Primer on the Business of Credit Rating Agencies' (prepared for the conference 'The Role of Credit Reporting Systems in the International Economy', 2001) 6–7. For a general overview on the development of credit ratings, see F Partnoy, 'The Siskel and Ebert of Financial Markets?: Two Thumbs Down for the Credit Rating Agencies' (1999) 77 *Washington University Law Quarterly* 619.

[182] Credit Reporting Agencies provided information about the creditworthiness of businesses, the specialised financial press provided information about specific industry sectors and investment bankers provided internal information from a business, usually by being part of the company's board. Sylla (n 181) 7–10.

[183] Partnoy (n 181) 640.

[184] See ibid 627–55.

[185] Sylla (n 181) 24.

business model was a direct effect of securities regulation within the CRA activities domain after CRAs were elevated to the status of NRSROs and were given the power to grant 'regulatory licenses'.[186] One of the most important regulatory changes that had an effect on this business model was the requirement that certain investors could only invest in 'safe' assets, which would be classified as such according to a rating from one of the CRAs. Issuers would then start to pay CRAs to rate their products, as they would want to be able to access this restricted investor market. The change in the compensation structure also reflected a change in the client being served and the product being provided. The initial client was the user of financial information and the product was high-quality information; after this shift, the client became the issuer and the product became the highest rate possible within the models used by the rating agency. Regulation transformed the CRA market completely as all issuers became legally obliged to have a high rating to be able to tap a given market, incentivising the practice of gaming the CRA models and, in the worst cases, even corrupting CRAs outright so that every product received a rating that would comply with the minimum requirements. Therefore, regulation in this case created incentives for ratings to be inflated.

This brief discussion shows that in the first business model scheme the CRA interests are aligned with those of the information users, who are in fact also their clients; in the second case, where there is a regulatory licence that the CRAs can use to extract rent from issuers, the interests of CRAs are not aligned with those of the information users, leading to a deterioration in ratings quality.

The auditing industry also experienced a similar development; emerging as information intermediaries in colonial times,[187] the industry was later granted regulatory licences and made legally essential to securities transactions.[188] Like the credit ratings market, the market for audited financial statements, based on the reputation of auditors, became a market for certified financial transactions.

In a manner that differs from the CRAs, the conflict of interest in the auditing industry did not arise exclusively from the regulatory licence granted by the government. In the US history of auditing, UK investors initially used auditors to certify that economic activities taking place overseas were being performed properly.[189] As the economy grew and capital markets developed, auditors were increasingly hired by securities issuers to increase the reliability of their financial statements.[190] At this point, the conflict of interest between the auditor and the information user was already more acute than before since the party remunerating

---

[186] Partnoy (n 181) 623. See also CA Hill, 'Regulating the Rating Agencies' (2004) 82 *Washington University Law Quarterly* 43, 43.

[187] See DL Flesher, GJ Previts and WD Samson, 'Auditing in the United States: a Historical Perspective' (2005) 41 *Abacus* 21.

[188] For example, in the US public companies need to have their accounts audited by independent auditors (eg Securities and Exchange Act of 1934, s 13(a)(2)).

[189] Flesher et al (n 187) 24–26.

[190] See PM Healy and KG Palepu, 'Information Asymmetry, Corporate Disclosure, and the Capital Markets: A Review of the Empirical Disclosure Literature' (2001) 21 *Journal of Accounting and Economics* 405, 415.

the auditor was no longer the party using its information. Nonetheless, the business continued to be based on reputation, since any credibility that an auditing firm could attribute to a financial statement from an unknown or unreliable company was the credibility of the auditing firm itself, giving it an incentive to perform a thorough audit service.

In a similar fashion to the experiences of the CRA industry, regulation in the auditing industry operated to guarantee a perpetual market to those that were already in it: a requirement that financial statements had to be audited was created[191] and it became increasingly difficult for an accounting firm to be considered a public accounting firm able to perform audits. Since the number of audits became more or less guaranteed and since competition is not likely to arise, regulation removes an important incentive for auditors to maintain their reputation.

As the objective of information intermediaries is to provide reliable information, the regulatory changes that were made to the industries in the sector were, to a certain extent, prejudicial to this objective. As compensation might not be the main driver of information accuracy in respect of the services provided by information intermediaries, liability standards and the risk of being held responsible for an information inaccuracy have become an important aspect of guaranteeing that the information reaching investors is accurate.

B. The Liability Regime

The problem in the case of informational intermediaries is that liability is more complicated to establish than in the case of issuers and financial intermediaries, as there is no direct legal relationship between the investor and the informational intermediary; in a general liability system, the applicable standard would fall within the tort category. In the United States the situation was even worse for the investor who had relied on a credit rating; CRAs were considered to have the same level of protection for their ratings as journalists had for their news, and could only be held liable for their ratings if plaintiffs could show 'actual malice' by the CRA,[192] even in cases where the issuer was suing the rating agency in respect of ratings for which it had contracted for.[193] By 2003 this requirement was softened and some American courts started excluding CRAs from the legal protection that was afforded to news companies in cases in which issuers constituted their clients or they were involved in the transaction being rated.[194]

---

[191] eg, Securities and Exchange Act of 1934, s 13(a)(2).
[192] See *Dun & Bradstreet, Inc v Greenmoss Builders*, 472 US 749 (1985); *NY Times v Sullivan*, 376 US 245 (1964).
[193] *In re Enron Corp, Sec, Derivative & ERISA Litigation*, 511 F Supp 2d 742 (SD Tex 2005).
[194] T Nagy, 'Credit Rating Agencies and the First Amendment: Applying Constitutional Journalistic Protections to Subprime Mortgage Litigation' (2009) 94 *Minnesota Law Review* 140, 151–54.

The level of protection that the CRAs had was lowered even more following the Dodd-Frank Act, which required, for purposes of pleading, that the sufficient state of mind for CRA liability is one of knowingly or recklessly failing

> (i) to conduct a reasonable investigation of the rated security with respect to the factual elements relied upon by its own methodology for evaluating credit risk; or (ii) to obtain reasonable verification of such factual elements … from other sources that the credit rating agency considered to be competent …[195]

In addition, the act also repealed the protection that CRAs had against expert liability in registration statements.[196] This led CRAs to refuse to accept the inclusion of their ratings in registration statements, which froze the markets for asset-backed securities.[197] Not long after the US House Financial Services Committee approved the removal of the expert liability for CRAs.[198]

In other parts of the world the status of CRA liability and their standard of care in respect of their activities varies. Contractual claims are almost impossible to advance as there are no specific laws other than general contract law governing these transactions; in this case, exclusion of liability is a common clause.[199] Moreover, in tort, it is not an easy task to attach liability to CRAs as proving causation may be a complicated task.[200]

In the EU context, a recent regulation enacted in 2013 imposed civil liability on credit rating agencies.[201] The system is two tiered: at the European level, liability can be established when the CRA has infringed any of the rules of Annex III of Regulation (EC) 1060/2009,[202] either intentionally or with gross negligence, causing damage to the investor, who has to establish reliance.[203] To define what these terms mean, national legislation, determined according to the rules of private international law, will be applicable.[204] This is a minimum harmonisation measure, as the regulation allows for further civil liability if national law provides for it.[205]

Finally, another important development worth mentioning in respect of CRA liability arose in Australia. In *Bathurst Regional Council v Local Government Financial Services Pty Ltd*,[206] Standard & Poor's was found liable for one of its

---

[195] Dodd-Frank Act, s 933(b).

[196] The repeal was of Rule 436(g) of the Securities Act of 1933.

[197] B Haar, 'Civil Liability of Credit Rating Agencies—Regulatory All-or-Nothing Approaches between Immunity and Over-Deterrence' 2013-02 University of Olso Faculty of Law Legal Studies Research Paper Series 1, 8.

[198] ibid 8–9.

[199] Except in France, in which the Finance and Banking Regulation Law forbids this kind of clause. See ibid 3.

[200] ibid 5–6.

[201] Reg (EU) 462/2013 amending Reg (EC) 1060/2009 on credit rating agencies [2013] OJ L146/1, including art 35a.

[202] Reg (EC) 1060/2009 on credit rating agencies [2009] OJ L302/1.

[203] ibid, art 35a(1).

[204] ibid, art 35a(4).

[205] ibid, art 35a(5).

[206] *Bathurst Regional Council v Local Government Financial Services Pty Ltd* (No 5) [2012] FCA 1200.

ratings based on misrepresentation and negligence claims. An interesting aspect of the decision was that, despite all the language on the documentation disclaiming liability, the CRA was held liable due to the function it performed in the market. As its role is to provide information to investors,[207] it was decided that it owed a duty of care to potential investors.[208] This approach to CRA liability, if adopted elsewhere, will have an important impact on the industry, realigning CRA interests to those of the external users of information.

On the auditors' side, liability follows either the securities liability regime standards, with slight modifications in the specific case of auditors, or tort law in civil law countries—sometimes with certain limitations, as in Spain—but nonetheless following the logic of general tort law.[209]

In the United States the standard required to hold an auditor liable for misstatements is even higher in securities transactions than that imposed on other players. In addition to other pleading requirements, to properly plead scienter[210] in an auditor liability case, the plaintiff

> must allege sufficient facts to show that the accounting practices were so deficient that the audit amounted to no audit at all, or an egregious refusal to see the obvious, or to investigate the doubtful, or that the accounting judgments which were made were such that no reasonable accountant would have made the same decisions if confronted with the same facts.[211]

The standard for pleading a strong inference of scienter could be met when allegations of red flags coupled with Generally Accepted Accounting Principles (GAAP) or Generally Accepted Auditing Standards (GAAS) violations are made,[212] as long as they can show that the auditor's practice amounts, at best, to a pretend audit.[213] Auditor protection from liability seems to be a trend in common law jurisdictions; in the United Kingdom it is also complicated to hold an auditor liable; '[absent] special circumstances, an auditor of a public company owes no duty of care to an outside investor or an existing shareholder who buys stocks in reliance on a statutory audit'.[214]

---

[207] In a passage, the judge explains that '[t]he issuer of the product is willing to pay for the rating not because it may be used by participants and others interested in financial markets for a whole range of purposes but because the rating will be highly material to the decision of potential investors to invest or not. S&P knew this was why it was being paid which is why it authorised ABN Amro to disseminate the rating in its ratings letters', ibid, 1038–39.

[208] ibid 1157–60.

[209] Another example is Belgium, where liability is not limited. See ID Poorter, 'Auditor's Liability towards Third Parties within the EU: A Comparative Study between the United Kingdom, the Netherlands, Germany and Belgium' (2008) 3 *Journal of International Commercial Law and Technology* 68, 73 ('By virtue of article 140 of the Belgian Company Code and the common liability principles, a Belgian auditor is liable towards each interested party').

[210] As seen before, scienter is the state of mind of the defendant.

[211] *In re Scottish Re Group Securities Litigation*, 524 F Supp 2d 370, 385 (SDNY 2007) (quoting *In re Refco, Inc Sec Litig*, 503 F Supp 2d, 611, 657 (SDNY 2007) (internal quotation marks omitted)).

[212] See *In re AOL Time Warner, Inc Sec and ERISA Litigation*, 381 F Supp 2d 192, 240 (SDNY 2004) (citing *In re Complete Mgmt Inc Sec Litig*, 153 F Supp 2d 314, 334 (SDNY 2001)).

[213] *Rothman v Gregor*, 220 F 3d 81, 98 (2nd Cir 2000) (citing *McLean v Alexander*, 599 F 2d 1190, 1198 (3rd Cir 1979)).

[214] Poorter (n 209) 70. The case in which the comment was made is *Caparo Industries v Dickman* [1990] 1 All ER 568. See also *Al Saudi Banque v Clarke Pixley* [1990] Ch 313; *James McNaughton Papers v Hicks Anderson Court* [1991] 1 All ER 134.

At the EU level there has been an ongoing discussion about auditor liability, but so far no concrete actions have been taken; rather, the focus on solutions falls at the Member State level.[215] In Spain, for example, the law regulating auditors changed in 2015 (Spanish Law 22/2015). The new law provides that liability will be imposed for harm caused by auditing firms due to the breach of their obligations as imposed by the Civil Code.[216] This law regulates the extent of the liability, rendering it proportional to the direct harm that the accounting firm could have caused to the audited entity or to a third party (eg investors) and excluding the harm caused by the audited company.[217] Finally, the auditors signing the auditing statements are put on the same level as the auditing firms, thus being liable to the same extent.[218]

The Brazilian system can be characterised as even more 'general'; the law regulating the liability of independent auditors only provides that auditing firms will be liable, by wilful or negligent conduct, for the harm they cause in exercising their auditing duties.[219] This law does nothing more than to borrow from the general tort regime existing under Brazilian law.

Even though CRAs and auditors perform similar functions in the market, the liability regimes to which they are subject are different: moreover, the differences between regimes within these two industries are also dependent on the laws of the specific country.

The focus of this section has not been the discussion of which liability regime for third parties is better,[220] but rather to establish that there are many industry-specific and country-specific differences.

V. Concluding Remarks

The objective of this chapter was to identify the types of dispute that may arise out of securities transactions, the standards of conduct in different countries to which the relevant persons involved are subject and the important aspects of the liability regime in each legal system.

---

[215] For an overview of the discussion, see Commission, 'Commission Recommendation Concerning the Limitation of the Civil Liability of Statutory Auditors and Audit Firms—Impact Assessment' C (2008) 2274 final.

[216] Art 26.1.

[217] Art 26.2.

[218] Art 26.3. For a discussion of the auditor's liability system in Spain, see C Humphrey, MAG Benau and ER Barbadillo, 'El Debate de la Responsabilidad Civil de la Auditoría en España: la Construcción del Discurso sobre la Limitación de Responsabilidades por las Corporaciones Profesionales' (2003) XXXII *Revista Española de Financiación y Contabilidad* 1091.

[219] Brazilian Law 6.385/1976, art 26, para 2.

[220] For discussion of CRAs, see Nagy (n 194) and Haar (n 197); for discussion on auditors' liability, see EL Talley, 'Cataclysmic Liability Risk among Big Four Auditors' (2006) 106 *Columbia Law Review* 1641 and HT Al-Shawaf, 'Bargaining for Salvation: How Alternative Auditor Liability Regimes Can Save the Capital Markets' [2012] *University of Illinois Law Review* 502.

The types of dispute differ depending on the legal relationship that the investor has with the defendant. The issuer–investor dispute arises mainly out of securities law, being based on the information disclosure duties that issuers owe to investors. The financial intermediary–investor dispute arises out of the contractual relationship between the financial intermediary who is buying or selling a security to the investor, advising him or managing his assets, where either suitability or fiduciary duties may play a role in the litigation. Finally, the last category of disputes is those involving informational intermediaries, such as CRAs and auditors, who do not have a contractual relationship with the investor and are subject to duties arising mainly out of a general tort framework, if at all, notwithstanding the increase in the discussion regarding the need to impose liability on these actors.

The relevance of these dispute categories for dispute resolution methods is related to the type of legal connections that the players have with each other. Investors and issuers, at some point in their relationship, had a connection through the securities that had been purchased or sold: there was a direct legal link between the two. The same is true with the investor and the financial intermediary, who are bound by a contract. In the latter case, unless the investor is subscribing for credit ratings or hiring the auditor himself, there is no direct legal connection between the parties, leaving liability to be established through general tort law or regulatory law.

Different regulatory regimes with different liability frameworks have important consequences for cross-border transactions: in this situation, legal certainty can only be achieved if a strong private international law mechanism is in place. This is true also in the European Union; even though their standards of conduct are highly harmonised for the different areas of securities regulation, the regulation of the liability aspects are left to the Member States, creating different frameworks for private enforcement that are dependent on the law applicable to the transaction.

The next chapters will explore the dispute resolution design for each type of dispute, the shortcomings that these systems have in a transnational environment and the possible solutions that can be designed for a more efficient dispute resolution system.

5

Building a Transnational Securities Dispute Resolution System

As securities markets become transnational, it is important that legal structures for dispute resolution of securities transactions are also created to deal with securities transactions involving transnational elements. This in turn will ease the enforcement of securities regulation principles and guarantee that market participants can effectively rely on a legal solution for their disputes. Access to justice, therefore, is an important background for the development of strong transnational securities markets.

The objective of this book is to provide solutions to improve the legal infrastructure for transnational securities transactions. In this chapter I briefly explain the problems with the current framework for each type of securities dispute, caused by the different securities regulation systems that exist today and the inadequacy of private international law to bring legal certainty for securities transactions, and propose solutions to each of them.

For mass disputes, namely those of an investor–issuer and investor–informational intermediary type, I propose an arbitration model to allow for aggregate litigation and to ease the structuring of the dispute resolution system, while at the same time diminishing most of the transaction problems that arise out of cross-border litigation. For the investor–financial intermediary disputes, I propose a network model based on the European Fin-Net system, rescaled to the global environment, providing adequate information to foreign investors, therefore increasing access to justice.

The rationale underpinning the choices made herein will be duly analysed in the subsequent chapters. Chapter 6 analyses the institutional aspects of dispute resolution, Chapter 7 surveys alternative models of dispute resolution systems, Chapter 8 discusses aggregate litigation design, Chapter 9 surveys aggregate litigation models and, finally, Chapter 10 analyses the transnational aspects of dispute resolution.

I. Problems with Transnational Dispute Resolution of Securities Transactions

Securities are regulated because they tap into the savings pool of the general population, creating the need to avoid inequitable practices. Transnationally, there are two questions that are important—first, is there a legal infrastructure available to resolve the dispute and protect investors, and second, is it accessible?

Any country that has a legal system will most likely have a dispute resolution system that will be able to deal locally with securities transactions; the range of different dispute resolution systems is broad and depends on policy choices made in each particular jurisdiction.[1]

In any developed legal system there will be a forum for securities disputes, but what is not given is if the country will have links with other legal systems to enforce a decision that is rendered by one of its courts. From the investor perspective, the transnational problems arise when (a) the investor purchases securities of a foreign company or securities listed in a foreign country, (b) the intermediary is based in a foreign country, and finally (c) the investor relies on a rating or an audit of a foreign informational intermediary.

Private international law is the area that deals with these problems, but there is no simple solution to them as various different approaches exist depending on where the dispute will be resolved and where the judgment will be enforced. The question here is one of jurisdiction over the defendant and enforceability of the decision in the location where the defendant has his assets.

Matters of jurisdiction, as well as of the enforceability of foreign decisions, are country specific and will vary depending on the public policy choices of a given country. For the transnational system to work, the forum of the investor will have to be able to exercise jurisdiction over a foreign defendant on terms that are acceptable to the foreign forum, otherwise enforceability will be at risk.[2] Alternatively, the foreign system needs to provide paths so that outside investors can obtain redress; this then becomes a problem of access. In other words, either there are bridges available to connect the different legal systems, allowing for a decision in one system to be enforced in another, or the investor has available access to the foreign system.

Access, nationally or transnationally, is a basic problem of dispute resolution; if the investor is harmed, the costs and incentives should be adequate to allow the investor to pursue his claim. There are two paths that can be used to solve the problem as will be explained in the next chapters: low access costs to the dispute

---

[1] For example, the FINRA arbitration forum, which was developed through self-regulation mechanisms and industry practice, and the alternative dispute resolution mechanisms in Europe, encouraged by Dir 2004/39/EC on markets in financial instruments [2004] OJ L145/1, art 53.

[2] Richard Fentiman frames this problem as 'Enforcement Risk', explaining that its absence is what allows for the dispute to proceed. R Fentiman, *International Commercial Litigation* (Oxford University Press 2010) 691.

resolution system or aggregate litigation mechanisms. Each of these paths has its advantages and disadvantages.

While with a low-cost system any person can decide whether to pursue their claim, the incentives might not be high enough for them to start the lawsuit, either due to the small advantages that may accrue from it or due to the complexity of the claim.[3] On the other hand, with aggregate litigation a lawyer, an investor with a more substantial stake in the dispute or a third-party may take the lead in the lawsuit but a single set of facts common to all investors pursuing the claim is necessary for the aggregate litigation system to work. Also, a system that binds those who are absent from the lawsuit is not common and can be complicated to implement in countries that are not familiar with it. Therefore, the solutions for access to justice regarding transnational securities transactions need to be tailored to the specific types of dispute, as there is no one-size-fits-all solution.

II. Dispute Resolution Systems in Transnational Securities Transactions—Institutional Considerations

In Chapter 4, three types of disputes in securities transactions were identified: investor–issuer, investor–financial intermediary and lastly, investor–informational intermediary. The different institutional frameworks for dispute resolution proposed herein were considered according to the particular characteristics of these different disputes.

A. Investor–Issuer

The common investor–issuer dispute involves multiple investors harmed due to an omission or false statement made in connection with the purchase of securities. The factual pattern for the persons harmed in these types of case is similar as it arises out of the same information that has been given to the market.

Even though a dispute resolution mechanism that functions on an individual basis can be used for this type of dispute, aggregate litigation could enhance the incentives for litigation as the amount at stake in the dispute would be increased, creating the possibility for third parties to assume coordination costs.[4] Aggregate

---

[3] This is an economic question—the more complex the claim is, the more expensive it will be to litigate, even if a low-cost dispute resolution system is available. For a brief overview on how to calculate the value of a claim, see R Cooter and T Ulen, *Law and Economics* (6th edn, Addison Wesley 2016) 388–91.

[4] JC Coffee, 'Understanding the Plaintiff's Attorney: the Implications of Economic Theory for Private Enforcement of Law Through Class and Derivative Actions' (1986) 86 *Columbia Law Review* 669, 679.

litigation would also lower the aggregate social costs for solving a single dispute with many claimants as fewer judicial procedures would be necessary to resolve all of the disputes arising out of the same factual pattern.[5] For the type of dispute at stake, the use of an arbitration framework may be adequate to avoid the prohibitions on aggregate litigation and guarantee enforceability at the transnational level.

i. Setting the Incentives

For aggregate litigation to work, a party has to be able to increase the stakes of the litigation by aggregating claims of other parties and to benefit from it, enhancing the personal profit that can be achieved by doing so.[6] Any aggregation mechanism that does not take this economic logic into account is prone to failure since there would be no benefit for a person to pursue this line of action otherwise.

It does not matter who that person will be; a claimant, a lawyer or a third-party funder can function as the litigation manager, assuming the risks of failure and some of the profits of litigation.[7] This principle works both in simple aggregate litigation and class action-style mechanisms; the important aspect is that there should be additional advantages for the party who will be managing the claimant side of litigation so there is an economic reason to sue, while at the same time, aligning their incentives with claimants.[8]

In the absence of opt-out mechanisms, and given the fact that lawyers are suitable candidates for this leading position in aggregate litigation, rules on maintenance, champerty and solicitation, which can be identified across different jurisdictions, have to be softened for aggregate litigation to become a suitable mechanism for the resolution of mass disputes.[9] At the same time, in order to

---

[5] A Layton, 'Collective Redress: Policy Objectives and Practical Problems' in D Fairgrieve and E Lein (eds), *Extraterritoriality and Collective Redress* (Oxford University Press 2012) 93.

[6] This is important to solve the free-rider and other collective action problems, especially when the harm is too small for a single person to pursue it. JR Macey and GP Miller, 'The Plaintiffs' Attorney's Role in Class Action and Derivative Litigation: Economic Analysis and Recommendations for Reform' (1991) 58 *University of Chicago Law Review* 1, 8–9; see generally M Olson, *The Logic of Collective Action: Public Goods and the Theory of Groups* (Harvard University Press 1971).

[7] For a discussion of the lawyer as the litigation manager, see Macey and Miller (n 6). For a discussion on third-party financiers as litigation managers, see EC Burch, 'Litigating Together: Social, Moral, and Legal Obligations' (2011) 91 *Boston University Law Review* 87 and J Molot, 'Litigation Finance: a Market Solution to a Procedural Problem' (2010–2011) 99 *Georgetown Law Journal* 65.

[8] In these situations, the other side of the coin is that defendants may reach out to the plaintiff's lawyers to settle at a price that is below the 'fair value' of the claim. The solution would be to set limits on the fee that the lawyer can obtain, linking it to a maximum percentage of the outcome for claimants. See DR Hensler and TD Rowe, 'Beyond "It Just Ain't Worth It": Alternative Strategies for Damages Class Action Reform' (2001) 64 *Law and Contemporary Problems* 137, 138.

[9] Due to the needs of economies of scale for litigation to be economically feasible, lawyers would have to be able to market and line up a multitude of claimants with small claims. For a discussion on maintenance and champerty, see A Sebok, 'The Inauthentic Claim' (2011) 64 *Vanderbilt Law Review* 61. For other problems that professional ethics rules may bring, see C Silver, 'Ethics and Innovation' (2011) 79 *George Washington Law Review* 754.

avoid abuses, mechanisms should also be developed to make lawyers accountable so that frivolous lawsuits can be avoided.[10]

ii. Overcoming the Prohibition of Opt-Out Aggregate Litigation

Opt-out aggregate litigation, with preclusion operating to all of those that would have a claim arising out of the same factual pattern, is a device that exists only in certain jurisdictions. Its advantage is that it creates a single lawsuit that definitely resolves all the claims arising out of the same facts, putting an end to the dispute and avoiding the need for multiple defences, thus diminishing litigation costs. In addition, by allowing the aggregation of all possible claims, it increases the incentive for the matter to be litigated when contingent fee schemes are allowed. At the same time, due to its size, it may also become a bet-the-company type of dispute, since a decision against the defendant may destroy the company financially as well as its reputation; some argue that it is a form of legalised blackmail.[11] In any event, if a liability rule can create too much harm for a defendant, the substantive rule is the one that should be reformulated, not those shaping access to justice.

As the opt-out system can be an interesting alternative to resolve disputes regarding issuer–investor claims, the prohibitions on it have to be overcome; this can be done through the use of arbitration.[12] Operationally, this can be done by including an arbitration clause in the corporate charter of the issuer, obliging all investors to resolve any disputes with the company through arbitration.[13] This excludes the judicial forum as an alternative for dispute resolution, but it also provides for alternative procedural rules that can be more flexible than those in national civil procedural codes, such as rules regarding notice and service of process.[14]

The main problem for the enforceability of the decision—apart from public policy considerations regarding securities disputes—would be due process concerns regarding notice to each and every possible claimant.[15] With this problem in mind, it is possible to devise a scheme which provides that when litigation ensues, the issuer becomes obliged to notify every investor in the lawsuit, allowing them to join or be represented by the lead claimant and thus making them aware that a dispute resolution procedure is being initiated and that they will be bound by it,

---

[10] For example, in cases in which lawyers take the lead in the litigation, a fee-shifting provision making the lawyer liable for any loss could be an option. For a discussion in the class action context, see Hensler and Rowe (n 8) 152–59.

[11] Analysing the claim that class actions are legalised blackmail, see C Silver, ' "We're Scared to Death": Class Certification and Blackmail' (2003) 78 *New York University Law Review* 1357.

[12] Despite the problems that class arbitration may encounter outside the US, a legal structure can be imagined where an 'opt-out' procedure based on arbitration is developed. For a discussion on these problems in Europe, see P Billiet (ed), *Class Arbitration in the European Union* (Maklu 2013).

[13] See generally C Ravanides, 'Arbitration Clauses in Public Company Charters: an Expansion of the ADR Elysian Fields or a Descent into Hades? ' (2007) 18 *The American Review of International Arbitration* 371.

[14] See G Born, *International Commercial Arbitration* (Kluwer Law International 2009) 1742–44.

[15] Under the New York Convention, one of the grounds for non-enforcement of an arbitral award is lack of notice of the proceedings (art V(1)(b)). This also is a basis under national legislation (see Uncitral Model Law on International Commercial Arbitration (2006), art 36(1)(a)(ii)).

guaranteeing due process standards and a fair trial. With the information technology available today, this should not be much of a problem, as notice could easily be given by email.

iii. Transnational Aspects

In addition to allowing easier means of notification, arbitration also facilitates the resolution of problems arising out of the transnational character of the transaction. As soon as the arbitration becomes international, the framework of the NY Convention[16] can be used for the enforcement of foreign arbitral awards.

As long as the arbitral tribunal's jurisdiction can be established by the existence of a proper arbitration clause within the corporate charter, it is unlikely that there will be issues on the recognition and enforcement of a foreign arbitral award. To avoid the need for recognising and enforcing the award, the system could even be set up in such a way that the arbitration would have its seat where the decision has to be enforced. This would work as long as the legal system in which the seat were located had a pro-arbitration regime operating at least to the same extent as the rules of the NY Convention.

The only problem that may exist concerns the public order character of securities rules. If national legal systems provide that securities regulation is a public policy matter arising out of their own securities regulation regime, they may deny recognition and enforcement of arbitral decisions.

iv. System Design and Rule of Law

Due to the public policy character of securities regulation and the necessity for information in order for investors to assess their risks in these transactions, including legal risks, it is very important that the system operates within the parameters of the rule-of-law principle.

Independence and accountability of the decision maker and reasoned decisions that are made public are paramount to the success and efficacy of the system in providing a serious alternative to courts that could be used for transnational transactions. The absence of reasoned decisions, or their confidentiality, can harm the legal certainty of the system as it would be impossible to know where the law stands at any given moment. This is the case in Brazil today, which has an arbitration system designed for companies listed at the higher corporate governance levels. This creates a paradox since those companies, which should exercise best practices of corporate governance and provision of information to the market, hide behind the veil of arbitration in the event of disputes with shareholders. A solution to this would be to oblige arbitration systems that deal with disputes between investors and public companies to publish their decisions; this could be

---

[16] Convention on the Recognition and Enforcement of Foreign Arbitral Awards (entered into force 07 June 1959) 330 UNTS 38 (NY Convention).

done through industry self-regulation or legislation. Arbitral decisions would then have, at least, a de facto precedential value for future disputes.

v. Implementation Aspects

An important question concerns how such a system could become reality. Companies may prefer litigation regimes that make it harder for investors to obtain redress, so the chances of being sued and having a harmful financial setback from litigation is diminished. As it is the company that would have to decide to include an arbitration clause in its corporate charter, it seems unlikely that this would be done without any other incentive.

A path for an arbitration system for issuer–investor disputes might engage the use of different corporate governance levels when the company is listed, to encourage its use. In Brazil, for example, the companies listed at higher corporate governance levels are obliged to have an arbitration clause in their corporate charter.[17]

With the globalisation of capital markets this would provide an interesting way to use the existing legal infrastructure already available throughout the world to promote a level playing field for the investors of a given company, regardless of where they are from. It would then be easier for the company to tap foreign markets, as the rights attached to the shares, including procedural ones, would be uniform across countries, thus avoiding some of the problems that arose in foreign cubed securities class actions in the United States, where foreign plaintiffs were not able to pursue litigation in US courts due to their foreign status.[18]

For the company, this would imply a higher level of transparency since actual rights from share ownership would vary less and possibly attract a higher valuation due to it.[19] It would be important for securities exchanges to create differentiated corporate governance levels with arbitration and opt-out dispute resolution mechanisms and to market them as such to make investors aware of the characteristics of these systems.

B. Investor–Financial Intermediary

An ideal dispute resolution system would give investors easy access to justice, allowing them to pursue their claims from any country in which they are situated, against any financial intermediary with whom they have transacted; this would be done under rules that they can comprehend and can manage without causing themselves serious harm for minor mistakes.

---

[17] Novo Mercado, Nível 2, Bovespa Mais and Bovespa Mais Nível 2. See BM&FBOVESPA, 'O que são Segmentos de Listagem', www.bmfbovespa.com.br/pt_br/listagem/acoes/segmentos-de-listagem/sobre-segmentos-de-listagem/.

[18] See *Morrison v National Australia Bank*, 561 US 247 (2010).

[19] For a discussion of the effects of transparency when coupled with good governance, see L Gu and D Hackbarth, 'Governance and Equity Prices: Does Transparency Matter?' [2013] *Review of Finance* 1.

Regarding access, contrary to the investor–issuer dispute, the investor–financial intermediary dispute is one in which the fact pattern is highly individual. The determination of what the financial intermediary did or said to the investor is what will be of most significance in this type of dispute, forbidding the use of aggregate litigation as a mechanism to resolve it.[20]

The problem of access can therefore only be solved by using alternative procedural mechanisms or alternative dispute resolution systems, such as the small claims court in Brazil or the Financial Ombudsman Service (FOS) in the United Kingdom. By having low or non-existent access costs and allowing a party to proceed without a lawyer, these systems enable any person to engage in a dispute if he deems the financial loss to be sufficiently relevant to be worthwhile. The forum could even be an online platform, where the investors would fill out a form with their claims and arguments, making access to the system extremely easy.[21]

The question that then arises concerns how these mechanisms would be structured when transnational transactions are involved as in most countries there is already some type of alternative dispute resolution system that addresses these issues.

i. Transnational Aspects

The transnational aspect in financial intermediary–investor disputes becomes complicated because most countries have strong regulations to protect investors and to regulate investment services. Securities regulation and civil liability arising out of non-compliance are specific to the legal system and can have important differences.

There are two situations in which a transnational dispute may arise between an investor and a financial intermediary: first, when the investor wants to invest in a foreign country and seeks a financial intermediary of that country which can provide services to allow him to invest there, and secondly, when the financial intermediary reaches out to an investor in a foreign country.

In the first case the investor will hardly be able to bring the financial intermediary to his own forum. If the financial intermediary has no contacts with the country of the investor there will be no basis for the investor's forum to exercise jurisdiction over the defendant, and even if it does, the decision would still have to be recognised in the financial intermediary's forum. The option then is for the

---

[20] For example, in Europe there are plenty of cases involving the demise of Lehman Brothers against financial intermediaries that were selling products based on Lehman Brothers' credit risk. To illustrate some of these disputes in the UK, see the decisions of the FOS DRN 1570597, DRN 191087 and DRN 3824818 (denying the investor's claim), and DRN 3727359 and DRN 2604832 (upholding the complaint); in Spain, see Tribunal Supremo, Sentencia 244/2013 (RJ 2013/3387) and AP Madrid (Sección 20a), Sentencia 427/2013 (AC 2014/156).

[21] Such as has been proposed in the consumer context in Europe through the ODR Regulation, where the online 'platform should take the form of an interactive website offering a single point of entry to consumers and traders seeking to resolve disputes out-of-court', 'allow[ing] consumers and traders to submit complaints by filling in an electronic complaint form' (Reg (EU) 524/2013 on online dispute resolution for consumer disputes [2013] OJ L165/1, recital 18).

investor to sue in the financial intermediary's forum, which may be complicated due to costs and lack of information regarding the legal system, as well as possible language barriers.

In the second case, when the financial intermediary is the one reaching out to the investor, the regulatory regime of the investor's forum comes into play, as do the dispute resolution mechanisms that exist there. In any event, in the event the financial intermediary lost the case and decided not to pay, the investor would still have to recognise the judgment in the location where the financial intermediary had assets. As a result of the differences in securities regulation regimes and liability standards, it is important for an investor to have easy access to a dispute resolution system that is binding and allows for the enforcement of a decision against the financial intermediary. An overarching dispute resolution system at the international level that could resolve this type of dispute is unlikely; its implementation would be extremely difficult due to the costs involved and the idiosyncrasies of each legal system.

In the absence of a treaty on securities regulation rules that could in fact harmonise the regulation of investment services and create an international court to resolve disputes arising from them, the best approach to dispute resolution would be to engage the local dispute resolution bodies to create a mechanism that would facilitate foreign investor access. Some ways in which this could be done are through information disclosure and the use of easy procedures for dispute settlement, for example by using the internet for the submission of claims and maybe even as a means to conduct hearings. This would be advantageous both to the investor, who would have a forum that would be able to deal properly with the issue, and for the market that offers these services to foreign investors, which would be seen as an attractive venue for investment.

The language barrier may be an issue and realistically no single system will be able to deal with all the languages of different investors. While this could be a problem, an investor would probably not invest in a place where the language is completely unknown to him. A solution that could diminish the problem would be for the dispute resolution system to offer the possibility of conducting the procedure in English, which is a language widely known in the financial industry. Another possibility is to offer cheap translation services for those who need it.

Therefore, the idea is, following the model of the European approach, to develop a network of dispute resolution systems in charge of forwarding investors to the appropriate dispute resolution bodies. It is true that this solution is based on the premise that the alternative dispute resolution bodies will be adequate and able to provide easy access to investors; this might not always be the case.

ii. Implementation Aspects

For this system to be effective, two conditions need to be satisfied. The first is to guarantee that the dispute resolution systems that will be part of the network have the ability to definitively resolve the disputes between investor and financial intermediaries, in addition to giving adequate protection regarding the industries within which they are supposed to operate.[22]

Its legal aspect depends on the binding nature of the decision being issued by the system; otherwise, the system is nothing more than a conciliation forum. It does not matter whether the body is based on direct or consent jurisdiction. Systems based on consent jurisdiction, where the granting of decision-making power is based on the consent of the parties, are preferable because they can rely on the arbitration framework and take advantage of the NY Convention regime. A locally based arbitration system that is mandatory for industry members and may allow foreign investors to opt in after a dispute has arisen would be an interesting option as it would resolve many transnational questions, provide an alternative forum for the investor and at the same time protect due process; the forum would be accessible only by the investor's acceptance after the dispute was ripe, weakening any investor's argument of lack of due process in his own forum at a later proceeding if there is no success in arbitration.[23] Moreover, the preconditions for the operation of the rule-of-law principle are also important; the scheme should guarantee independent decision makers and publish reasoned decisions, bringing legal certainty to its users.

As soon as legally binding dispute resolution systems are in place, the second step is for the network to develop. This has to be done through discussions and agreements between the different systems. The development is a political one that will need the input of industry members, from both the investor and financial intermediary sides.[24]

C. Investor–Informational Intermediary

The usual case in which an informational intermediary harms an investor occurs where the information provided is based on false or misleading representations, for example when a CRA rates a bond as triple-A, even though the company is on the verge of bankruptcy, and relying on the information provided by the CRA, the investor buys the security.

The relationship between investor and informational intermediary is, most of the time, non-existent as the rating is created to inform the general market and

---

[22] In the Fin-Net context, there have been some problems with national ADR schemes that were not comprehensive enough to provide investors with alternative forums, undermining access to justice and consequently, investor protection. See N Moloney, *How to Protect Investors: Lessons from the EC and the UK* (Cambridge University Press 2010) 455–58.

[23] This design, conceptually, would not be pure arbitration as it would require the use of both direct and consent jurisdictional bases. A pure arbitration system could also be imagined but this would require the will of the industry to accept such a mechanism, which is unlikely.

[24] For a 2009 discussion on the development of Fin-Net, see DG Internal Market and Services, 'Evaluation of FIN-NET' (Final Report, June 2009); European Commission, 'Summary of the Responses to the Public Consultation on Alternative Dispute Resolution in the Area of Financial Services' (September 2009).

not a specific investor. There is no contract or corporate link between the parties. The same is true for information prepared by auditors as the investor who relies on it has no direct legal relationship with them, unless the auditor has been hired by the investor to do due diligence on the company, which is not usually the case in public market transactions.

This creates an extremely hard-to-solve scenario for a comprehensive and investor-friendly dispute resolution mechanism. As there is no direct contact between the informational intermediary and the investor, the only forum available would be the courts of the place in which the informational intermediary is located. The courts of the place in which the investor is located would be an option where it is allowed by the forum state, but enforcement would be extremely hard due to requirements of proper notice and the acceptance of the exercise of exorbitant jurisdiction by foreign courts in these cases.

As to the extent of the harm caused, this situation is similar to the one where the investor purchases securities based on information provided by the issuer. False or misleading information provided by informational intermediaries can be harmful to many people, having far-reaching effects to all of those who have transacted based on such information. Aggregate litigation could therefore be an option to resolve the dispute.

Another problem concerns the scope of different laws applicable to the transaction at stake as different countries have different approaches to the liability of informational intermediaries. For example, while the United States is lenient in its approach, Australia has a tighter grip on the standard of care that informational intermediaries owe to the market. From the investor's perspective, the applicability of Australian law would be more interesting when there is an Australian aspect involved in the transaction, but the only certainty of its applicability would be when the CRA is also Australian.[25]

One way to facilitate the venue and access issues would be to have credit rating or auditing contracts, when requested by the company issuing the securities, imposing an obligation on the informational intermediaries to accept arbitration within the same parameters as the system proposed for investor–issuer disputes; this would allow for aggregate litigation, which would connect the CRAs to the dispute resolution scheme put in place by the investor.

To resolve the applicable law question, a provision could be added to the contract between informational intermediaries and issuers, identifying the law applicable to any disputes arising out of their relationship and their relationship with third parties. In addition, a clause should also be included in the corporate charter of the company issuing securities, identifying a law that would also apply to that relationship and creating an indirect legal link between investor and informational intermediary.

Informational intermediaries would most likely oppose this proposition as it would increase the risk of their business. Therefore, for such a system to be

[25] See Ch 4.

implemented, pressure would have to come from the companies using their services, which in turn would imply powerful investors pressuring the companies to do so. An alternative way to introduce such rules would be through the imposition of regulation by regulatory agencies; this would be more complicated to implement at the transnational level due to the local reach of regulatory systems.

III. Two Systems for Transnational Dispute Resolution of Securities Transactions

The objective of this book is to provide solutions to improve the legal infrastructure for transnational securities transactions. The ideal solution would be an overarching system, an international court, composed only of specialist judges and providing easy access for any investor that had been harmed. This court would have compulsory jurisdiction, where any securities disputes with a transnational character would be resolved. Of course, this solution is not feasible due to the costs and political constraints of creating such a system, in addition to the regulatory diversity that is present in securities regulation today. Nonetheless, dispute resolution systems for transnational securities transactions could be socially beneficial as they would strengthen cross-border confidence in different markets, increasing the incentives to invest in a foreign jurisdiction.

Starting from the current landscape, there are paths that can be used to build a better transnational legal infrastructure. Private international law problems are tied to questions of jurisdiction, applicable law and enforcement; they can become quite complex depending on the situation at hand, especially when the public policy aspects of the jurisdiction in which a decision has to be enforced come into play.

Moreover, private international law problems can be more or less prevalent depending on the dispute at stake; cross-listed companies will be subject to at least two regulatory systems, and may have investors from even more jurisdictions. Another regulatory system would also apply if there were any selling efforts that could have been seen as directed towards another jurisdiction, thus engaging an extra set of liability rules to be managed. On the other hand, financial intermediaries will only be subject to foreign law where they are the ones pursuing the investor outside the jurisdiction in which they are licensed to work, otherwise they will be regulated safely within the confines of their own jurisdiction, even if the investor is a foreigner.

In the previous section, I outlined the main aspects of how different dispute resolution systems could be improved depending on the type of dispute at stake, discussing the parties' incentives for litigation, the transnational aspects at stake and the incentives for implementation. In this section I outline how these systems can be legally operationalised. As discussed throughout this work, within the broad topic of 'transnational dispute resolution of securities transactions' there are three different types of disputes, each with different problems that require different solutions, for which I propose aggregate litigation through arbitration for the mass type of disputes and a network of alternative dispute resolution (ADR) providers for disputes with financial intermediaries.

A. Aggregate Litigation Through Arbitration

The mass type of dispute, involving many investors from different jurisdictions who have been harmed as a result of information provided by relevant market actors, needs a better solution for access and for the centralisation of the dispute resolution process to avoid litigation in too many different jurisdictions and the costs that come with multiple proceedings. The proposal is the use of arbitration with an aggregate dispute resolution mechanism; this solves most of the problems discussed as it centralises the dispute in a single forum and to a certain extent also avoids some of the private international law issues such as enforcement and applicable law. This can work for both the investor–issuer and the investor–informational intermediary types of dispute. The main aspects of the legal operationalisation of the system are related to the seat of arbitration, the existence of adequate arbitration clauses and the importance of the arbitral institution.

i. Seat of Arbitration and Arbitrability

The arbitral seat is the 'home' of the arbitration and has important consequences for the legal framework under which the arbitration will fall.[26] These consequences include the national law applicable to the arbitral procedure, the law applicable to the relationship with national courts and their power to annul the award, the law applicable to the validity of the agreement, and the definition of the place where the award is 'made', among other issues.[27]

The objective of the system is twofold: to increase access to investors, including foreign ones, and to provide an efficient mechanism that guarantees that the issuer will not have to engage in many different dispute resolution procedures for a dispute involving a single set of facts. The choice of the seat is closely related to the second issue.

Efficiency, for these purposes, can be translated in a legal framework that allows for innovation in arbitration since the proposal will include an opt-out aggregate litigation mechanism that is functionally similar to the American class action, while at the same time guaranteeing, to the greatest extent possible, that the award

---

[26] Born (n 14) 1679.
[27] ibid 2053.

will be enforceable in other jurisdictions. Liberal national legislation and a status as part of the NY Convention and other international arbitration regimes are important aspects that have to be taken into consideration when making the choice. These are prerequisites for this proposal to work.

Another important aspect is that the arbitral seat must be closely connected with the place in which the issuer has assets, where the issuer is incorporated or where the issuer is listed. The best scenario would be if all three places were the same, anchoring the issuer to a single national jurisdiction.

From the issuer's perspective this is important because if the assets are located in a jurisdiction that considers securities matters non-arbitrable, investors may side-step the arbitration agreement contained in the charter and sue directly in the courts of such a place, defeating the purpose of the arrangement. The same is true regarding the place in which the company is incorporated and where it is listed. If it is incorporated in one jurisdiction, listed in another and has most of its assets in a third, the issuer must verify whether all three jurisdictions would accept the use of arbitration for securities disputes, which would increase legal risk and due diligence costs for the company.

The limitations are clear: the issuer and its relevant connections must be in a jurisdiction with a pro-arbitration mentality so a comprehensive dispute resolution system based on arbitration can be deployed for securities disputes.

ii. Arbitration Clauses

The second important aspect of the operation of a global dispute resolution system for securities transactions based on arbitration is well-drafted arbitral clauses within the relevant documents. The foundational arbitration clause regulating the dispute resolution procedure between investors and issuer is to be found in the corporate charter of the issuer. Additional clauses could also be included in the services contract between issuer and informational intermediary include the latter in the dispute resolution process in the event it can also be held liable under substantive law for its acts. Finally, if the issuer uses depositary receipts mechanisms to reach other markets, an arbitration clause should also be included in the depositary agreement. I provide clauses that could be used to construct such a system below.

Corporate Charter Clause

The corporate charter clause has to address the main aspects of the dispute resolution mechanism, including who will be bound by the clause, the subject matter of the dispute, the applicable law governing the subject matter and procedure of the arbitration, the arbitral institution that will manage it and its rules, and the language and the seat of arbitration. In addition, specific due process guarantees should also be articulated in the clause. The proposal here is a combination of personal notice through email and the publication of the beginning of the arbitration procedure in major newspapers.

Dispute Resolution and Applicable Law

a. The Corporation, its shareholders, former shareholders, directors, executives, former directors, former executives and any other party engaging in contractual relations with the Corporation with a clause in their contract referring to this arbitration clause agree to finally solve all disputes, claims, controversies and disagreements, relating or arising out of the Corporate Law or Securities Law provisions governing this Corporation, or relating to or arising out of the transaction of its securities, by arbitration.

    i. The laws of [Jurisdiction] shall be applicable to the substantive matters of any disputes, claims, controversies or disagreements related to this clause, as well as to the submission to arbitration and the arbitral proceedings.

    ii. The arbitration shall be administered by [Arbitral Institution], the Rules of which [Specify the Rules] are deemed to be incorporated by reference into this clause.

    iii. The language to be used in the arbitral proceedings shall be [Specify the language].

    iv. The place of arbitration shall be [City/Country].

b. To guarantee due process, notification shall be provided to every party included in the arbitration procedure by any means that can effectively inform them, including but not limited to emails, which shall be regarded as the main method of communication.

    i. Each shareholder, beneficiary or of record, shall inform the issuer an email address to which notice under this arbitration procedure shall be given.

    ii. In aggregate proceedings, notice by email together with the publication of notice on three different occasions within two weeks in a major newspaper of the country in which the arbitration will take place shall be considered sufficient to include any interested party in the arbitration procedure.

Informational Intermediary Services Contract Clause

To bind the informational intermediary to the aggregate arbitration procedure an arbitration clause in the contract between the issuer and the informational intermediary is necessary. It is important to note that CRAs issuing ratings that are not requested by the issuer will not be included in the arbitration procedure as there will be no basis capable of bringing them to arbitration.

Dispute Resolution

Any dispute arising out of or in connection with this contract, including third parties relying on the information provided by the Informational Intermediary, shall be referred to and finally resolved by arbitration in accordance with the Dispute Resolution and Applicable Law clause provided in the Corporate Charter of the Issuer.

Depositary Agreement Clause

In cases in which the issuer enters foreign markets through the use of depositary receipts an arbitration clause should also be included in the deposit agreement. One interesting example is the Baidu and Bank of New York agreement, which provides for arbitration 'in the event the Depositary is advised that a judgment of a court in the United States may not be recognized'.[28] In this proposed dispute resolution system, a more straightforward arbitration clause referring to the corporate charter of the issuer is preferred.

Dispute Resolution

> Any dispute arising out of or in connection with this Deposit Agreement shall be referred to and finally resolved by arbitration in accordance with the Dispute Resolution and Applicable Law clause provided in the Corporate Charter of the Issuer.

iii. Importance of the Arbitral Institution

Arbitral institutions do not decide the cases themselves but serve as case managers, guaranteeing the integrity of the arbitral procedure. In the particular discussion on aggregate litigation, the arbitral institution will also need to have rules that are adequate for the arbitration procedure and expertise on dealing with such matters as they may become complicated.

Important issues that need to be outlined in advance with clear rules are the minimum threshold of claimants that could start the aggregate arbitration procedure, the mechanism to select the lead claimant, the notice procedure and the mechanism for choosing arbitrators. Furthermore, another interesting aspect, related to the incentives of the parties that could be included in the rules, is a fee-shifting provision, to avoid unmeritorious claims and to compensate the defendant, at least to a certain extent, if an unmeritorious claim is nevertheless arbitrated.

Below I provide language for institutional rules to deal with these four issues.

Aggregate Arbitration Procedure

a. Minimum Threshold. Any person having at least a 10% stake in the dispute (Initial Claimant) may initiate an aggregate arbitration procedure by giving notice to the Arbitral Institution and to the person or company against whom a claim is being made (Respondent) of the request for aggregate arbitration.
    i.   Respondent will have 10 days to respond to the request for aggregate arbitration.
    ii. The Arbitral Institution, after analysing the request and the response to the request for aggregate arbitration, will decide, based on a prima facie analysis of the claim, if the procedure is adequate for the dispute and initiate proceedings to constitute the Arbitral Tribunal.

---

[28] Deposit Agreement between Baidu.com, Inc, The Bank of New York and Owners and Beneficial Owners of American Depositary Receipts (2005) www.sec.gov/Archives/edgar/data/1329099/000119312505140785/dex43.htm, 28.

b. Notice and Opt-out. If the Arbitral Institution decides that the aggregate arbitration procedure is adequate, the Initial Claimant will give notice to any other persons who may be part of the dispute (Other Claimants).

    i. Where Respondent has information regarding the identity of any of the Other Claimants, Respondent shall be obliged to provide such information to the Initial Claimant.

    ii. Notice shall be given by email or by any other written means, such as mail. Only those duly notified will be bound by the arbitration procedure.

    iii. Any Other Claimant who does not wish to participate in the aggregate proceeding may opt out of it by informing the Arbitral Institution in writing, having 60 days from the decision establishing the Lead Claimant to do so.

c. Lead Claimant. Any claimant or group of claimants may apply to be Lead Claimant in the arbitration procedure. The Lead Claimant will represent all claimants that did not opt out in the arbitration procedure, exercising all actions necessary to protect and defend their interests, such as, but not limited to, hiring lawyers, deciding on the legal strategy to be taken and negotiating settlements.

    i. The selection of Lead Claimant shall be made by the Arbitral Institution according to the highest amount the applicant or group of applicants has at stake in the dispute.

    ii. In case the selected Lead Claimant is different from the Initial Claimant, the Lead Claimant shall reimburse any reasonable costs incurred by the Initial Claimant in starting the arbitration procedure, such as, but not limited to, giving notice to Other Claimants.

d. Arbitration Costs and Attorney's Fees. The party that loses the arbitration shall pay the other party's costs and attorney's fees.

    i. Each party shall deposit in an escrow account the amount established in Annex I for Arbitration Costs and Attorney's Fees at the beginning of the Arbitration Procedure.

    ii. The Initial Claimant shall be responsible for the initial deposit, and shall be reimbursed in case a different claimant is appointed as Lead Claimant.

    iii. Only the Lead Claimant shall be responsible for Arbitration Costs and Attorney's Fees, but in case the claims are upheld the Lead Claimant will also be the only one to be reimbursed for such costs and fees.

iv. *Possible Problems Remaining*

The proposed scheme solves the access problem for small investors, while at the same time discouraging unmeritorious suits, thus protecting issuers from nuisance litigation. Even though this scheme can provide an interesting option in respect of the current landscape, there are still some problems that may arise in the transnational realm due to the public policy aspect of securities laws.

Assuming that the system is duly established in a jurisdiction that accepts the arbitrability of securities disputes, the problem of foreign investors suing overseas will still be present, as long as those investors are under a jurisdiction that does not accept the arbitrability of securities disputes. This is not a problem as long as the issuer has no assets or can otherwise be forced to comply with that jurisdiction's decision.

Another question that comes to mind concerns the case that arises if this problem emerges in the context of the European Union. How can a duly performed arbitration, that is recognised by the state where the issuer is situated stand in face of a contrary decision of another Member State's court in a procedure for enforcement in the issuer's state? Recital 12 of Brussels I Recast[29] excludes decisions on the validity of arbitration agreements from its recognition and enforcement rules. However, where such a decision is made and there is also a decision on the substance of the matter, this decision on the substance should not be precluded from recognition, but the courts of the Member States may decide on the recognition and enforcement of the award itself, as the NY Convention has precedence over Brussels I Recast. The problem remaining is if the award is made in the issuer's jurisdiction, therefore falling outside the scope of the NY Convention. The solution here would be to consider such award as a 'judgment given between the same parties in the Member state addressed', applying art 45(1)(c) by analogy,[30] or as a last resort determine that such a Member State judgment would be contrary to public policy and refuse recognition based on art 45(1)(a).

In any event, the aggregate arbitration mechanism proposed here can at least solve the access problem faced by foreign investors who do not have the money or energy to engage in this type of litigation, as it allows other parties with a bigger risk appetite to do so for all those who potentially have a valid claim, and present a strong argument to uphold the arbitration agreement and the arbitral award.

B. A Network of ADR Systems

The investor–financial intermediary type of dispute requires a different solution due to the personal character of the relationship. A mass procedure would not be adequate and the question of access still remains open. The investor should have an easy path to resolve the dispute: a dispute resolution body that would hear his complaint, notify the financial intermediary and give a binding decision.

As most countries already have ADR systems for these disputes, and they usually do not involve complex private international law questions, the best approach would be to engage the national dispute resolution bodies in a network so they can cooperate with one another and point the investor to the appropriate body that could deal with the dispute. The premise here is that these bodies need to offer easy access to the investor, solving the disputes fairly and according to rule-of-law

---

[29] Regulation (EU) 1215/2012 on jurisdiction and the recognition and enforcement of judgments in civil and commercial matters [2012] OJ L351/1 (Brussels I Recast).

[30] See JV Hein, 'The Protection of Arbitration Agreements within the EU after West Tankers, Gazprom and the Brussels I Recast' (*Conflictoflaws.net*, 17 July 2015) http://conflictoflaws.net/2015/the-protection-of-arbitration-agreements-within-the-eu-after-west-tankers-gazprom-and-the-brussels-i-recast/.

standards. The Fin-Net system in Europe could be used as a model to create a global network that could deal with these cases.

To operationalise such a system there is not much that can be done legally, absent a full treaty creating a worldwide arbitral institution or court to deal with such cases, which would obviously be complicated to enact. Agreements between dispute resolution bodies would rather provide the best approach to coordinating and creating mechanisms for disputes involving foreign investors.

One shortcoming of this system would arise in those cases in which the financial intermediary approaches the foreign investor in his jurisdiction, while not having a presence there. This can be a problem when the investor's law is more beneficial than the financial intermediary's as the ADR body would not be familiar with it and might not be willing to apply such rules. The option left would be either for the investor to sue in his court and try to enforce the judgment in the financial intermediary's forum, or for the investor to accept the less favourable approach in exchange for a possible forum to resolve the dispute.

An argument could also be made for arbitration in these situations but due to the consensual character of the procedure and the limits imposed by investor and consumer protections laws, this solution could be difficult to implement. In addition, financial intermediaries searching for retail foreign investors without establishing a presence in the country are likely to be acting illegally and not in good faith; their acceptance of the inclusion of an arbitration clause with a fair mechanism of dispute resolution is unlikely, leaving the investor with his own court, when that is possible, or the ADR of the place in which the financial intermediary is established.

A network of ADR providers could at least facilitate access, providing a higher level of protection for retail investors and consequently increasing confidence in foreign investments made with foreign financial intermediaries.

IV. Concluding Remarks

So far I have tried to show that private enforcement is an important mechanism for the application of securities laws and the construction of confidence on capital markets, which can be considered a prerequisite for its full development.

Despite the globalisation of capital flows, the strength of the legal infrastructure for the protection of small and medium investors who may participate, willingly or not in transactions with transnational elements is low due to the strong national character of legal systems and securities regulations; this raises a variety of problems related to access to justice and legal uncertainty generated by public policy conflicts and the operation of private international law.

The objective of this book is not to respond to the question of whether or not it is a good idea to involve small and medium investors in transnational securities transactions; however, to the extent that various investors have come to find themselves involved in such investments and the global securities market has also started to develop in this direction, it becomes important to provide alternatives that could solve, or at least diminish, the legal problems surrounding transnational dispute resolution, increasing access to justice and reducing legal uncertainty. This is especially true in places where the transnational aspect of securities transactions is becoming more and more prevalent due to the quest for market integration, such as in the European Union.

The legal infrastructure for resolving transnational disputes therefore comes to form a crucial background to enable a higher degree of market integration since more people would be able to rely on it and develop confidence in the system. Arbitration and institutional cooperation can go a long way to achieve these objectives for the development of truly global capital markets.

The next chapters frame the categories of analysis and develop the themes that are necessary to understand the proposals that were made in this chapter.

6

Institutional Aspects of Dispute Resolution

The objective of this chapter is to set parameters to analyse the institutional framework of dispute resolution systems and to understand the policy choices that can be made in respect of its design. For the purposes of this analysis, there are two categories of institutional aspects that have to be considered: the legal aspects and the economic aspects of a dispute resolution system. The legal aspects define the political and legal structures within which the dispute resolution system is embedded, while the economic aspects define the means through which the system will finance itself, engaging at the same time with the question of incentives to litigate. This second economic aspect is especially relevant as it relates directly to the efficiency of the system and the procedural level of protection that is given to litigants.

These institutional aspects are essential for the construction of a dispute resolution system as they give shape to the structure of the system and are their minimum necessary components. Therefore, this chapter is divided into two parts: the legal aspects of the institutional framework and the economic aspects of the institutional framework.

I. Legal Aspects of the Institutional Framework

In respect of the legal aspects, it is important to anchor the discussion to the premise that any dispute resolution system is tied to the legal framework of the state. This is a necessary condition of its existence because, without the power of the state, the dispute resolution system would be ineffective absent the will of the losing party to comply with the decision. The legitimacy of the system and the legal framework underpinning its operation therefore becomes essential to justify its binding effects.

In addition, to provide a just method for dispute resolution, the decision makers have to be independent, while at the same time the logic in which their decisions are reached has to be made known, allowing society to develop legitimate expectations on the rules of the legal system.[1]

---

[1] The concept of 'just' used here is a formalistic one—a just decision is one that is or could be reasonably expected in a given legal system.

These institutional legal aspects are necessary for a system based on the rule of law, which has important consequences in respect of the mechanisms underpinning the economic organisation of society, as explained in Chapters 2 and 3.

A. The Legal Basis of the Dispute Resolution System

Since the legal power of a dispute resolution system has to be linked to the legal system in which the decision arising out of it has to be enforced, the legal basis for the system becomes an important aspect of its design. The legal basis for the authority of a dispute resolution system can either have a direct link to the state's power or it can be indirect, having an additional requirement for legality to operate. At the same time, the dichotomy of the direct jurisdictional basis/consent jurisdictional basis defines the transnational legal infrastructure that is available for the cross-border operation of dispute resolution systems. This section explains each of them.

i. Direct Jurisdictional Basis

The main dispute resolution system with a direct jurisdictional basis is the judiciary. As a part of the state structure and normally created and designed by a constitution, the judiciary is in charge of solving disputes. It is the institution that applies and maintains the law.

Its main characteristic is that it is a direct part of the state structure; judges are authorised to decide matters that are brought to them independently of the will of the parties of the dispute. It does not matter that one of the parties does not wish to be bound by the decision; as long as the requirements to make the party part of the legal procedure are satisfied, the judge may decide the dispute and the decision will be legally enforceable.

Even though the court structure is the main body with a direct legal jurisdictional basis, it may not be the only one. Alternative dispute resolution arrangements can also be created on the basis of direct jurisdictional powers. Within this idea, the important characteristic of direct jurisdiction is the possibility of binding decisions without some prior authorisation of the party being bound.

Systems built on a direct jurisdictional basis are either constitutionally designed or created by legislation, always having support from the state that is attributing jurisdiction to it. This implies that in order to be created or modified, these systems require political energy.

Another problem is the effects that decisions based on direct legal jurisdiction have on foreign jurisdictions. Today there is no wide-ranging mechanism for the recognition of foreign judgments, creating piecemeal solutions, or none at all, for cross-border dispute resolution.[2]

---

[2] Attempts were made to create an international convention on jurisdiction and judgments, but the efforts were unsuccessful. See R Michaels, 'Two Paradigms of Jurisdiction' (2006) 27 *Michigan Journal of International Law* 1003, 1009–10.

ii. Consent Jurisdictional Basis: Arbitration

Systems with a consent jurisdictional basis require not only the authorisation of the legal system, but also the consent of the parties in submitting their dispute to it. This is the premise of arbitration, which is the use of a private third party to decide a dispute between two litigants, binding them as to the outcome.[3] Arbitration is a creature of consent. Parties are bound by it if they have agreed to the dispute resolution mechanism that settles their dispute. In addition, only those matters that are authorised, or not prohibited by law, can be arbitrated; as such, not all disputes can be decided via arbitration.

The practice of employing third parties to resolve disputes through the application of rules pervades ancient history. From the Middle East to Rome, there are many accounts of parties designing their dispute resolution methods and using third parties to give binding decisions.[4] It is true that the institutional setting of arbitration as we know it today was only possible after the development of the modern nation states, creating the interplay between public and private that permeates this dispute resolution process.[5] Even though there is an extensive body of literature that sees arbitration as a kind of *lex mercatoria*, the efficacy of an arbitral award depends on the legal framework in which it will be enforced; therefore, the decision to use arbitration should be made considering both the national legal infrastructure and the international legal infrastructure.[6]

Arbitration therefore has two levels of legitimacy: the first is the legal authorisation allowing parties to empower a third party to decide their dispute with finality, while the second is the agreement between the parties to empower the third party. This section briefly surveys some of the legal framework enabling arbitration at the national and the transnational levels.

The National Legal Framework for Arbitration

Even though arbitration could theoretically be envisioned based only on the legal principle of *pacta sunt servanda*, it is usually regulated by legislative provisions.

---

[3] O Ashenfelter and R Iyengar (eds), *Economics of Commercial Arbitration and Dispute Resolution* (Edward Elgar 2009) ix.

[4] See G Born, *International Commercial Arbitration* (Kluwer Law International 2009) 21–27. Such practice was also common during the Middle Ages, where it had a relevant role in guilds and trading places. See J Baker, 'From Lovedays to ADR: Arbitration and Dispute Resolution in England 1066–1800' [2006] *Transnational Dispute Management* 1.

[5] Arbitration during the 18th and 19th centuries faced strong hostility from some states; in France this started to change only after its ratification of the Geneva Protocol of 1923, which made agreements to arbitrate enforceable, while in the US, this hostility was only overcome with the enactment of the FAA and similar state rules. See Born (n 4) 37–49.

[6] '[I]nternational commercial arbitration, no less than arbitration within nation-states, while conducted in the sphere of private law, is a public legal creation whose operation and effectiveness is inextricably linked to prescribed actions by national courts' (WM Reisman and B Richardson, 'Tribunals and Courts: An Interpretation of the Architecture of International Commercial Arbitration' in AJ Berg (ed), *Arbitration—The Next Fifty Years* (Kluwer Law International 2012) 17).

The United States, for example, has a strong tradition of arbitration. The Federal Arbitration Act (FAA) was enacted in 1925,[7] covering both domestic and international arbitration.[8] It was the result of a movement from the business community in the years before its enactment, which pressed for legislation due to the concern over the costs and delays of litigation and the problems with the enforceability of arbitration agreements.[9] As it is today, the FAA is a strong statute and pre-empts most state arbitration laws in the United States if they try to diminish or limit the contractual agreement of the parties to arbitrate,[10] creating a generous environment for arbitration. Also, the case law developed in the United States broadened the possibilities of situations in which disputes could be submitted to arbitration, encompassing a wide array of cases.[11]

Arbitration in Spain also has deep historical roots, to the extent that it was considered a fundamental right in the Cadiz Constitution, in 1812.[12] The institution has undergone various changes since then,[13] reaching its current institutional design with Law 60/2003. Inspired by the UNCITRAL Model Law,[14] the Spanish arbitration law is a modern law, encompassing all the necessary requirements for a strong environment for arbitration.

Brazil, on the other hand, has a much younger arbitration culture. Having taken the same position as most Latin American countries and having embraced the 'Calvo Doctrine' in the past,[15] Brazil was strongly opposed to the use of arbitration to resolve international disputes.[16] This approach started to change in the 1980s with the opening of the Brazilian economy to foreign investment; the development of this area only reached maturity in 2002, with the ratification of the NY Convention.[17]

Meanwhile, the journey to an efficient arbitral framework in Brazil was a turbulent one. The Brazilian arbitration law was enacted in September 1996,[18] but soon

---

[7] Federal Arbitration Act, ch 213, § 1, 43 Stat 883 (1925).

[8] IS Szalai, 'The Federal Arbitration Act and the Jurisdiction of the Federal Courts' (2007) 12 *Harvard Negotiation Law Review* 319, 325.

[9] ibid 354–55.

[10] See CR Drahozal, 'Federal Arbitration Act Preemption' (2004) 79 *Indiana Law Journal* 393, 407–20.

[11] C Ravanides, 'Arbitration Clauses in Public Company Charters: an Expansion of the ADR Elysian Fields or a Descent into Hades?' (2007) 18 *The American Review of International Arbitration* 371, 373–74.

[12] See JFM Merchán, 'La Constitución de 1812 y el Arbitraje' (2012) 14 *Revista del Club Español del Arbitraje* 33.

[13] The modifications came with the Civil Procedure Law of 1855, the Jurisdiction Unification Decree of 1855, the Civil Procedure Law of 1881, the Arbitration Law of 1953, the Arbitration Law of 1988, and finally Spanish Law 60/2003; ibid 34–35.

[14] Spanish Law 60/2003, exposition of motives.

[15] The Calvo Doctrine, named after Carlos Calvo, was a foreign policy principle that foreign investors had to use local courts to resolve their disputes.

[16] R Brazil-David, 'An Examination of the Law and Practice of International Commercial Arbitration in Brazil' (2011) 27 *Arbitration International* 57, 57.

[17] ibid 58. Convention on the Recognition and Enforcement of Foreign Arbitral Awards (entered into force 07 June 1959) 330 UNTS 38 (NY Convention).

[18] Brazilian Law 9.307/1996.

enough its constitutionality was being challenged as violating article 5, XXXV of the Brazilian Constitution, which provides that 'the law will not exclude from the appreciation of the Judicial Power a harm or threat to a right'.[19] This challenge was only resolved in 2001, and until then arbitration clauses were seen as mere promises to arbitrate, without any legal certainty as to their efficacy. The only way to resolve the dispute by arbitration was through an agreement to arbitrate after the dispute had arisen.[20] With the decision in 2001, the constitutionality of the arbitration law was confirmed by the Supremo Tribunal Federal (STF),[21] bringing to an end the legal insecurity that was present in the use of arbitration clauses in the Brazilian legal system.

The International Framework for Arbitration

The first international legal instrument that initiated the development of international arbitration was the Geneva Protocol on Arbitral Clauses of 1923. Ratified by various countries, it was the first truly wide-ranging instrument backing arbitration.[22] This Protocol made agreements to arbitrate in connection with contracts valid, even though each country could limit the application of the Protocol to commercial contracts.[23] Its practical advantage was that the courts of the signatories, when facing a valid arbitration clause, had to refer the parties to arbitration.[24]

As the beginning of the modern framework for international arbitration, this instrument had some important limitations. The Protocol was only applicable when the agreement to arbitrate was made between parties of different jurisdictions,[25] and through this instrument contracting parties had the duty to execute arbitral awards if they were made within their own territory.[26] Even with the

---

[19] Translation by the author.

[20] Brazil-David (n 16) 58.

[21] *MBV Commercial and Export Management Establishment v Resil Industria e Comercio Ltda* (STF, SE 5206 AgR) (2004).

[22] The treaty was ratified by Albania, Austria, Belgium, Brazil, the UK and some of its colonies, New Zealand, India, Czechoslovakia, Denmark, Estonia, Finland, France, Germany, Greece, Iraq, Italy, Japan, Luxembourg, Monaco, Netherlands, Norway, Poland, Portugal, Romania, Spain, Sweden, Switzerland and Thailand.

[23] 'Each of the Contracting States recognises the validity of an agreement whether relating to existing or future differences between parties subject respectively to the jurisdiction of different Contracting States by which the parties to a contract agree to submit to arbitration all or any differences that may arise in connection with such contract relating to commercial matters or to any other matter capable of settlement by arbitration ... Each Contracting State reserves the right to limit the obligation mentioned above to contracts which are considered as commercial under its national law' (Protocol on Arbitration Clauses (entered into force 28 July 1924) 27 LNTS 158 (Geneva Protocol on Arbitration Clauses), art 1).

[24] See Geneva Protocol on Arbitration Clauses, art 4.

[25] See Geneva Protocol on Arbitration Clauses, art 1.

[26] '[E]ach Contracting State undertakes to ensure the execution by its authorities and in accordance with the provisions of its national laws of arbitral awards made in its own territory under the preceding articles' (Geneva Protocol on Arbitration Clauses, art 3).

presence of such limitations the Protocol was indeed useful to many parties who wished to compel arbitration.[27]

Soon came the second important international instrument for international arbitration, the Geneva Convention for the Execution of Foreign Arbitral Awards of 1927. The Geneva Convention extended the territorial enforceability of arbitration made pursuant to a valid agreement under the Geneva Protocol, increasing the efficiency of the international arbitral system.[28] Another positive aspect of the Convention was the limitation of the substantive review of the merits of awards.[29]

Even though there were improvements in the system, it still was fairly burdensome. The party enforcing the award had to prove that the award was valid, the subject matter was capable of settlement by arbitration under the law of the country it would be relied upon, that the award was made by an arbitral tribunal composed according to the will of the parties, that it was a final award and that its recognition was not contrary to the public policy of the country in which it was to be relied upon.[30] Such requirements created a double-exequatur situation; the enforcing party first had to confirm the award in the country in which it was made to then pursue enforcement in another country.[31] These two instruments provided a comprehensive framework for international arbitration in the first half of the twentieth century, preparing the field for the developments that were about to come.

Due to concerns from the business community regarding the instruments in place backing international arbitration, the International Chamber of Commerce (ICC) issued a preliminary Draft Convention with the objective of substituting the Geneva instruments of the 1920s.[32] The main idea behind the project was the creation of truly international awards, in other words awards that are independent from the national rules of procedure where the arbitration took place.[33]

This idea of international arbitration completely detached from states was not well considered. The ICC Draft Convention was presented to the UN Economic and Social Council (ECOSOC), which, in 1955, came up with a new Draft Convention[34] that was closer to the already-established international arbitration

[27] See A Nussbaum, 'Treaties on Commercial Arbitration: a Test of International Private-Law Legislation' (1942) 56 *Harvard Law Review* 219, 231–32.

[28] 'In the territories of any High Contracting Party to which the present Convention applies, an arbitral award made in pursuance of an agreement whether relating to existing or future differences … covered by the Protocol on Arbitration Clauses … shall be recognised as binding and shall be enforced in accordance with the rules of the procedure of the territory where the award is relied upon' (Convention for the Execution of Foreign Arbitral Awards (signed 26 September 1927) 92 LNTS 302 (Geneva Convention for the Execution of Foreign Arbitral Awards), art 1).

[29] Born (n 4) 61.

[30] Geneva Convention for the Execution of Foreign Arbitral Awards, art 1.

[31] Born (n 4) 62.

[32] ICC, 'Enforcement of International Arbitral Awards: Report and Preliminary Draft Convention' (ICC Brochure No 174, Paris, 1953) text available at www.newyorkconvention.org/11165/web/files/document/1/5/15940.pdf.

[33] ibid 7.

[34] See ECOSOC 'Report of the Committee on the Enforcement of International Arbitral Awards', UN Doc E/2704 (28 March 1955).

system.[35] This new draft received comments from various governments and non-governmental organisations,[36] leading to a 'Conference on International Commercial Arbitration' that was held at the UN in New York from 20 May to 10 June 1958.[37] This conference ended with the signature of the NY Convention.

Today, the NY Convention is in force in 157 countries.[38] Already considered for some time as the 'cornerstone of current international commercial arbitration',[39] it provides a global framework for the recognition and enforcement of arbitral awards and arbitration agreements. The scope of its application comprises arbitral awards made in the territory of a state other than the one in which the recognition or enforcement is sought or awards not considered domestic in the state in which it is to be recognised or enforced.[40] By analogy, the same rationale is applicable to arbitration agreements[41] when the seat is outside the forum state.[42] If the seat is in the same state, the applicability of Article II will be subject to domestic law.[43]

The Convention provides specific rules for the recognition and enforcement of arbitral awards and agreements. Under the Convention, an arbitration agreement has to be in writing in respect of a defined legal relationship of which the subject matter can be settled by arbitration.[44] For the recognition and enforcement of the arbitral award, the plaintiff only has to provide the original award and the arbitration agreement or certified copies of these documents, translated into the language of the court in which recognition or enforcement is sought, if necessary.[45] These conditions are the only two necessary for the recognition and enforcement of an arbitral award; national implementing legislation requiring more from plaintiffs is contrary to the NY Convention.[46]

Compared to the Geneva Convention, the NY Convention presents an important evolution in this aspect since it is no longer necessary for the plaintiff to prove either that the award is final in the country where it was made or that the arbitral tribunal was constituted in the manner agreed upon by the parties,[47] removing the necessity of the double-exequatur.[48]

---

[35] AJ Berg, *The New York Arbitration Convention of 1958* (Kluwer Law and Taxation 1981) 7.

[36] See ECOSOC 'Recognition and Enforcement of Foreign Arbitral Awards: Report by the Secretary-General' UN Doc E/2822 (31 January 1956).

[37] Berg (n 35) 8. See also UN Doc E/CONF 26/SR 1–UN Doc E/CONF 26/SR 25.

[38] See UNCITRAL, 'Status of the Convention on the Recognition and Enforcement of Foreign Arbitral Awards', www.uncitral.org/uncitral/en/uncitral_texts/arbitration/NYConvention_status.html.

[39] Berg (n 35) 1.

[40] NY Convention, art 1(1).

[41] Recognition and enforcement of arbitration agreements is governed by art II of the NY Convention.

[42] See D Schramm, E Geisinger and P Pinsolle, 'Article II' in N Port, D Otto, P Nacimiento and H Kronke (eds), *Recognition and Enforcement of Foreign Arbitral Awards: a Global Commentary on the New York Convention* (Wolters Kluwer Law and Business 2010) 41.

[43] ibid 42.

[44] Art II(1)(2).

[45] Art III(1)(2).

[46] Berg (n 35) 248.

[47] Geneva Convention for the Execution of Foreign Arbitral Awards, art 1(c)(d).

[48] Even though the plaintiff does not have to prove these two aspects, they are still the basis for a court to refuse enforcement of an arbitral award. NY Convention, art V(d)(e).

The burden is now on the defendants, who, to avoid the enforcement of arbitral awards, have to prove one of the grounds available in article V, subject to the discretion of the enforcing courts.[49] Even though the approach to judicial discretion may vary depending where enforcement is sought, in practice the results are similar, independently of the approach taken by the court.[50]

The improvements of the global international arbitration framework introduced by the NY Convention and the number of countries that have ratified it render it an important component regarding the discussion of transnational dispute resolution.

iii. Considerations of the Legal Basis of a Dispute Resolution System

There are two important aspects that are relevant regarding the legal basis used to design a dispute resolution system for transnational securities transactions.

The first is the level of entrenchment of the dispute resolution system within the institutional framework of governments. Nationally or internationally, systems that have a direct legal basis are harder to create, and when they are created, they are not so easily dismantled. They are often part of a greater state or inter-state design, such as the judiciary or the WTO.

On the other hand, systems based on indirect legal jurisdictional basis do not need the same political capital to be built. Anyone could start an arbitral institution from their home, as it does not usually require previous approval from authorities. The success of the system would require convincing those persons who are party to disputes to use it; this however, is more of a marketing question.

The second aspect is the enforcement of the decisions across borders. The direct legal jurisdiction systems often depend on treaties made on a piecemeal basis or on considerations of 'comity' in order to operate across borders, presenting serious legal barriers and legal uncertainty. The indirect legal jurisdiction systems are more effective due to the NY Convention, which allows for the worldwide enforcement of any decision made through them. This second aspect will be discussed in more depth in Chapter 10.

B. The Decision Maker's Independence and Accountability

In the context of legal decision making, independence is the absence of external factors influencing the decision-making process, whether from other political branches of the state or from private interests. Independence therefore is an

---

[49] Art V reads: 'Recognition and enforcement of the award *may* be refused, at the request of the party against whom it is invoked, only if that party furnishes to the competent authority where the recognition and enforcement is sought, proof that: ...' (emphasis added).

[50] P Nacimiento, 'Article V(1)(a)' in N Port, D Otto, P Nacimiento and H Kronke (eds), *Recognition and Enforcement of Foreign Arbitral Awards: a Global Commentary on the New York Convention* (Wolters Kluwer Law and Business 2010) 207–09.

essential characteristic of the rule of law, since for it to exist, those who are in charge of applying the law have to take their decisions on the basis only of the legal rules and principles of a given legal system.

External influence in the decision-making process in dispute resolution systems is a dangerous path as it jeopardises the rule-of-law ideal by bringing alien concepts into it; if allowed, law becomes pure politics, thus changing all the beneficial aspects that a legal system may have in solving disputes in a just and fair system.[51] In the modern state context, judicial independence is so important that it is considered to be a fundamental human right.[52] To avoid unwarranted influences[53] and guarantee independence, formal institutional safeguards have to be put in place.[54] The adjudicator, as a neutral third party, can only dispense justice and fairness according to the law if there is independence,[55] and this is valid both for judges as public officers as well as arbitrators acting through the power delegated by the parties to the dispute.

The flipside of independence is accountability. Too much independence is also problematic, since, if left unchecked, judges may become the tyrants themselves, foregoing the application of the law for their own private interests.[56] This is a matter of fine-tuning the institutional design of a political system as judges are the gears in the wider machinery of the state. To the same extent that judges should not be allowed to decide based on bribes, nor should they be allowed to forego what has been politically established as 'law', apart from constitutional violations, within a democratic legal system.[57] To address this problem, accountability mechanisms have to be created to provide some sort of control over decision makers, who will have different characteristics depending on whether the decision-maker is a public official (direct legal jurisdiction) or an arbitrator (consent-based jurisdiction).

---

[51] See JA Ferejohn and LD Kramer, 'Independent Judges, Dependent Judiciary: Institutionalizing Judicial Restraint' (2002) 77 *New York University Law Review* 962, 967 ('A legislature required to generalize when crafting its rules will, we fear, be all too quick to abandon or distort those rules in particular cases involving favoured or disfavoured parties, thus subverting the law's generality for improper reasons').

[52] Universal Declaration of Human Rights, art 10.

[53] The influences to be concerned with are the illegal ones—those arising out of private bribes or political pressure, disfiguring the legal process and adding elements for the judge to consider that should be absent for a decision based solely on legal arguments.

[54] G Vanberg, 'Establishing and Maintaining Judicial Independence' in K Whittington, D Kelemen and G Caldeira (eds), *The Oxford Handbook of Law and Politics* (Oxford University Press 2008) 100.

[55] C Larkins, 'Judicial Independence and Democratization: a Theoretical and Conceptual Analaysis' (1996) 44 *The American Journal of Comparative Law* 605, 608.

[56] See Ferejohn and Kramer (n 51) 972–73 ('Making judges independent of politicians and other lawmakers may free them from certain pressures to ignore the law ..., but it also frees them from any pressure to follow it, and it allows them to make law in ways that could be problematic').

[57] The power aspect is not the only relevant problem with judges who are too independent, as the legal uncertainty arising out of such a legal system design also has considerable economic impact due to the uncertainty that this brings into the legal system.

i. Public Officials

The judge is the person holding a public office within the political structure of a state. If the state is a democratic one abiding by the rule of law standard, the judge's independence has two essential aspects.[58]

The first aspect is that of the judge as a public officer within a state branch vis-à-vis the other state branches and his role in guaranteeing compliance with the rules of the political system. In this respect, the judge must be insulated from political pressures from other sectors of the state[59] as he is acting as a guarantor that the state will not be able to execute its will outside of what is authorised by law.[60]

Some of the mechanisms to guarantee a judge's independence are a strong selection process, tenure of the job, irreducibility of salaries,[61] prohibition of transfers, judicial immunity and a country's budget percentage guaranteed to the judicial branch.[62] These mechanisms soften any concerns that a judge might have regarding the continuity of his standard of living and the proper work of the judicial institutions since there is guaranteed income both at a personal and institutional level. By ensuring these mechanisms are in place, the judges are free to decide as they please, without being afraid of retaliation from other political bodies.

As the fairness of decisions depends on judges deciding based on the law, their independence has to be balanced with other mechanisms that ensure that judges will not stray too far from the possibilities of decision within the legal system and applicable norms of which they are part. The structure of the judiciary itself already presents some accountability mechanisms that counterbalance the judge's independence, such as the right to an appeal. Alongside it, another incentive for judges to remain within some widely acceptable boundaries of the law is to have the rate of reversal of their decisions as one of the yardsticks for promotion within the judicial career. An instrument of a more political character that is also used to control the exercise of the judiciary's power is the possibility of impeachment or the discharge of duties for judges; this is a serious mechanism usually reserved to the most egregious offences, such as outright corruption.[63]

The second aspect is judicial independence from external influences of the parties to the dispute. The practice of selling decisions or of deciding on the basis

---

[58] Borrowing from the definition of C Larkins, '[j]udicial independence refers to the existence of judges who are not manipulated for political gain, who are impartial toward the parties of a dispute, and who form a judicial branch which has the power as an institution to regulate the legality of government behaviour, enact "neutral" justice, and determine significant constitutional and legal values' (Larkins (n 55) 611).

[59] ibid 609.

[60] Constitutional courts are an important aspect of limiting a state's power and guaranteeing that some rights will be left unaltered by the state.

[61] The salary standard should be linked to its purchasing power since inflation can deeply erode what the judges can effectively obtain from it. See K Rosenn, 'The Protection of Judicial Independence in Latin America' (1987) 19 *The University of Miami Inter-American Law Review* 1, 29–30.

[62] ibid 15–23.

[63] See F Thompson and DH Pollitt, 'Impeachment of Federal Judges: an Historical Overview' (1970–1971) 49 *North Carolina Law Review* 87; Brazilian Supplementary Law 35/1979, art 26.

of friendship or family ties (with a party to the dispute) undermines the fairness and justice of the legal system, disrupting the rule of law. There are a few measures available to discourage this type of behaviour. The first is to give judges sufficient income for the position they occupy in society. Guaranteeing a good income diminishes the incentives underpinning the judge's acceptance of a bribe to decide in favour of a given party. The second measure is to provide the parties with a procedural mechanism to exclude a judge from a dispute due to the ties he might have with a party.[64] Finally, criminalising corruption is also another means by which the institutional design might be structured to avoid judge partiality and guarantee independence.[65]

ii. Private Decision Makers

In the same manner that judges need to be independent and impartial to provide litigants with fair and just decisions, so do arbitrators. In fact, from the perspective of a single dispute, the independence of the arbitrator has to be even higher than that of the judge because in a state-based judicial system appellate review is normally available, which is uncommon in arbitration.[66] Since arbitration is a matter of choice on the part of those who submit their disputes to it, the parties will necessarily only agree to do so if they believe that there is a certain level of honesty in the process.[67]

Even though for the litigants in a specific case importance of independence in arbitration may be even higher than in a judicial proceeding, the mechanisms guaranteeing independence from undue influence are not the same as in state structures. This difference between state mechanisms of independence and arbitration mechanisms is due to the different structural relationships that arbitrators and judges have with the parties.

The difference is found in the identification of the judge or the arbitrator to decide the dispute. In a lawsuit, the dispute will be randomly assigned to a judge competent to hear the matter.[68] In other words, even though there might be a pool of judges that can decide the dispute, or only one judge that can decide the dispute depending on the size of the jurisdiction in which the dispute will be heard, the judge is not explicitly chosen by the parties. On the other hand, arbitrators are normally chosen by parties; they either act together, or each party will nominate an arbitrator, and the arbitrators nominate a third.

---

[64] Ideally this would be done by a second-level review mechanism and not by the judge presiding over the case.

[65] For a general overview on judicial corruption, see Transparency International, *Global Corruption Report 2007* (Cambridge University Press 2007).

[66] Born (n 4) 1463–64.

[67] 'The perceived legitimacy of the international arbitration process cannot be greater than the degree of confidence that litigants have in the ethical standards of the arbitrator.' J Paulsson, 'Ethics, Elitism, Eligibility' (1997) 14 *Journal of International Arbitration* 13.

[68] eg, Brazilian Civil Procedure Code, art 285.

The second difference reflects remuneration. Judges are public employees and are therefore paid by the government through revenue that is secured from the general population by taxation and sometimes from fees that the litigants pay to the judicial system.[69] Arbitrators are usually exclusively remunerated by the parties to the dispute, who have to proportionally fund the costs of the dispute resolution process.

Even though judges and arbitrators resolve disputes for a living, it is a business only for arbitrators, since they depend on 'clients' to select them to decide their cases and to generate revenue. This characteristic unpacks a wide array of considerations that are relevant to their independence. At the same time, while it is important to prevent arbitrators from being too close to one of the parties to the dispute, it is also important not to decrease too extensively the requirements authorising a claim of partiality, since this could lead to problems in finding arbitrators for some disputes, especially in cases where, due to their geographical traits or subject matter, there are not that many arbitrators available. This could be a problem in a field as specialised as securities transactions.

There is no single standard for assessing an arbitrator's independence worldwide, but the one that is commonly used is 'justifiable doubts'.[70] The concept is used to assess the risk of partiality since it is not necessary that a party demonstrates an actual lack of independence or impartiality, but only that there is a justifiable doubt in the mind of a reasonable third party.[71] The standard is also coupled with the use of possible conflict disclosure requirements by arbitrators, which, if not made, may generate sufficient grounds for disqualification, even if the possible conflict that should have been disclosed is not by itself sufficient for a partiality claim.[72] With an obligation of disclosure, the parties have a higher awareness of the possible conflicts that the arbitrator may have in deciding their dispute, impeaching the arbitrator if necessary.

These mechanisms are important to guarantee the integrity and legitimacy of the arbitration process, helping to lift it to the same level as the public justice system.

C. The Reasoning and Publicity of Decisions

The reasoning behind legal decisions is an important aspect of any legal system. Law is dynamic, always evolving through new legislation and legal decisions. There are two special aspects of reasoned decisions that are important for a modern legal

---

[69] Only a few countries have a system where what is paid by the litigants is supposed to cover the costs of the justice system. See C Hodges, S Vogenauer and M Tulibacka (eds), *The Costs and Funding of Civil Litigation: a Comparative Perspective* (Hart Publishing 2010) 13–15.

[70] See UNCITRAL Model Law on International Commercial Arbitration (2006), art 12; IBA Guidelines on Conflicts of Interest (2004), Part I(2).

[71] See Born (n 4) 1475–79.

[72] ibid 1524.

system: first, they constrain the judges in reaching a decision since they are obliged to use reason and the decision has to logically follow from the premises that were accepted in a judgment. If the premises themselves are being disputed, practical reason has to be used through the frame of reference of the law in general or of particular branches of law.[73] Secondly, they give the legal system new material to operate, clarifying situations that were previously unclear and serving as the basis for the discussion and decision of similar cases.

In respect of the first aspect, legal reasoning in a legal system functions as a guidepost for judges as it limits the range of decisions that can be taken. The lack of a reasoning obligation would allow them to reach any decision without having to provide justification. By imposing a duty to reason, judges have to do so through legal arguments, which can be made only according to the logic of the legal system itself. Reasoning therefore has to be developed based on legal norms, with the effect of constraining the possible arguments that can be made, and consequently the possible outcomes of a legal decision.[74] This aspect of reasoning in law leads towards the ideal of certainty that is necessary for the rule of law to operate.

In respect of the second aspect, which follows directly from the first, legal decisions are utterances of what the law is at a given moment, and as such they also function normatively in regulating the conduct of the population subject to it. The reasoning behind a decision, whether the precedent doctrine operates within the legal system or not, is informative of the state of the law and is used as a yardstick for legal/illegal behaviour. Lawyers will advise their clients about the legality of a given path of behaviour based both on statute and on the decisions of the relevant courts in the jurisdictions in which the client operates; where a dispute arises out of a similar fact pattern as had been decided before, the previous judgment will be used as an argument as to the current state of the law, even if it is not strictly binding under the rules of that particular legal system.[75]

As established in the previous paragraphs, the existence of reasoned decisions is an important aspect of the operation of a legal system which purports to regulate effectively the conduct of those subject to it. Even though reasoned decisions are

---

[73] N MacCormick, *Rhetoric and The Rule of Law: A Theory of Legal Reasoning* (Oxford University Press 2005) 254–55.

[74] '[T]he legal answer "always has to be capable of being framed in terms of law, through interpretation of statutes or of precedents, or of legal principles developed through reflection on law as practically coherent normative order". In this vein, a primary requirement of legal reasoning is to show that the ruling "does not contradict validly established rules of law". A second requirement is to show that the decision is supported by established legal principles' (F Carbonell, 'Reasoning by Consequences: Applying Different Argumentation Structures to the Analysis of Consequentialist Reasoning in Judicial Decisions' in C Dahlman and E Feteris (eds), *Legal Argumentation Theory: Cross-Disciplinary Perspectives*, vol 102 (Springer 2013) 6).

[75] As in Brazil, which does not have a doctrine of *stare decisis*, even though many commentators argue that judicial decisions have legal value for future cases. See F Didier, *Curso de Direito Processual Civil*, vol 2 (5th edn, Juspodivm 2010) 386–87. With the recently published Brazilian Civil Procedure Code, there are mechanisms by which legal decisions may become binding. See F Didier, PS Braga and RA Oliveira, *Curso de Direito Processual Civil—Teoria da Prova, Direito Probatório, Decisão, Precedente, Coisa Julgada e Tutela Provisória*, vol 2 (11th edn, Juspodivm 2016) 468–469.

important, something more is needed for them to comply with their function of being the substrate of legal arguments and future legal decisions. Any person who wants to access a judicial decision should be able to do so without incurring any major costs (and preferably, be able to do so for free), therefore creating an environment of transparency in the operation of the legal system.

Transparency in legal decision-making bodies brings important advantages to their operation and the efficiency of the legal system as a whole. An interesting study about transparency in the civil justice system in the United States was published in 2012, underlining its importance and the benefits accruing from it.[76] Essentially, the study concluded that transparency would improve the functioning of the market in claim settlements, decrease fraud, increase confidence and decrease transaction costs.[77] The conclusions are intuitive; if information is concentrated in a single database that is easily accessible, the general costs that the system creates will be lower since duplicative efforts to produce the same information will be avoided.[78] To a certain extent, the argument is the same as with disclosure duties for securities regulation.

Also, at a more fundamental level, justice should be accessible to everyone; differentiating access to crucial information about the law through the financial capabilities of the parties—by allowing access only through paid means, for example—would create an unnecessary and unjust bias towards the party with greater financial means.[79]

Whether it is a matter of the efficiency or of the fairness of the system, reasoned decisions and easy access to them should be pursued as objectives in any proposal for a dispute resolution system.

II. Economic Aspects of the Institutional Framework

There are two sides to consider regarding the economic aspects of a dispute resolution system: the costs of maintaining a dispute resolution system and the costs of accessing a dispute resolution system.

---

[76] JW Doherty, RT Reville and L Zakaras (eds), *Confidentiality, Transparency, and the US Civil Justice System* (Oxford University Press 2012).

[77] ibid xxv.

[78] Think, for example, of the case of a legal system that implemented a central database accessible through the Internet. Before the implementation each party would have to ask for the production of a copy of the judgment on paper, which would have to be mailed to the parties. After the implementation of the system the parties will only print the judgment if they feel the need to read it on paper, as it could be accessible through the Internet at any time.

[79] See LM LoPucki, 'The Future of Court System Transparency' in JW Doherty, RT Reville and L Zakaras (eds), *Confidentiality, Transparency, and the US Civil Justice System* (Oxford University Press 2012) 170–71. It is true that in any event the party with less money will be disadvantaged, but the difference is that at least theoretically, the lawyer of this party will have the same possibility of preparing a strong case as the lawyer of the richer party. In the event money is charged to access court decisions, access to law itself is impaired.

A. Costs of Maintaining a Dispute Resolution System

Dispute resolution systems need to be funded. They will require a physical location and employees to carry out the activities they perform. The total costs will depend on the size of the institution and the array of services offered; for example, those institutions that only coordinate dispute resolution but do not maintain the decision makers on their payroll will have lower fixed costs when compared to court systems, which will necessarily need judges and support staff that will be paid on a regular basis, regardless of the number of cases filed.

Such considerations are important because the success of a dispute resolution system will depend on its costs and how the costs will be borne. A completely private design will create a dispute resolution body that is a business, which will lead to incentives for pleasing the users of the system. On the other hand, a system that is public will have a higher degree of independence but will also require financial commitment from states to be able to properly perform its activities.

The choice then is how to allocate the costs between the users of the system and the political community supporting it. In most cases where the jurisdictional legal basis is direct, the system will be funded both by the political community through taxation and the requirement that the users pay a fee to access the system. On the other hand, when the legal basis for jurisdiction is indirect, the model of the dispute resolution system will be more of a business, receiving money from the users of the system and sometimes from the business community that has an interest in supporting it.

B. Costs of Engaging in a Dispute Resolution Procedure

Every decision to engage in a legal dispute has to take into account the costs that the dispute will entail compared to the likelihood of the claim's success. The best-case scenario for someone considering engaging in litigation is a high-value claim with a high likelihood of success. Each legal system differs substantially regarding the costs of litigation, which can amount to millions of dollars for each party.[80] Even though securities disputes costs may amount to millions, individual investors rarely have a high amount at stake in their dispute; therefore, they may be precluded from obtaining redress exclusively because of costs.

Here there is an inherent tension between costs and access to justice. The higher the costs, the harder it is to obtain access, which then requires alternative methods of access and legal support for those parties that do not have it. Costs can be divided into costs of access and costs of evidence and representation.

---

[80] For a comparative view on the costs of civil litigation, see Hodges et al (n 69).

Table 6.1: Access cost of dispute resolution systems

	US[1]	Brazil[2]	Spain[3]	FINRA[4]	ICC[5]
Filing fees	US$400	US$1,000	US$695.15	US$1,425	US$5,365
Arbitrator's Fees[6]	–	–	–	US$450	US$10,060
Total	US$350	US$1,000	US$695.15	US$1,875	US$15,424

Notes

[1] US District Court—Southern District of NY, 'District Court Fee Schedule and Related Information', www.nysd.uscourts.gov/fees.

[2] São Paulo Tribunal, 'Taxa Judiciária', www.tjsp.jus.br/Egov/IndicesTaxasJudiciarias/ DespesasProcessuais/TaxaJudiciaria.aspx.

[3] J Albert, *Study on the Transparency of Costs of Civil Judicial Proceedings in the European Union— Final Report—Annex 48—Spain* (European Commission 2007) 22.

[4] FINRA Customer Code, ss 12900 and 12902.

[5] ICC, 'ICC Cost Calculator', www.iccwbo.org/Products-and-Services/Arbitration-and-ADR/ Arbitration/Cost-and-payment/Cost-calculator/.

[6] The arbitrator's fees are based on the median value of those displayed in the documents regulating each system.

i. Costs of Access

Every court system or arbitral institution requires the payment of a fee for access to the dispute resolution system. The fee can be applied either at the beginning of the litigation or at various steps along the way.[81] In any event, the minimum cost that should be considered for matters of dispute resolution should be the amount dispensed from the beginning of the lawsuit until the first instance decision, which is the first stage at which the dispute has been effectively resolved by a third party to the dispute.[82] Within this idea of cost of access, the remuneration of arbitrators has also to be taken into account since in many systems it has to be paid up front. These costs can vary immensely.

To illustrate the difference Table 6.1 shows a comparison for a dispute valued at US$100,000 among different dispute resolution systems.

In this comparison, it becomes clear that stepping through the door of arbitration can be more expensive than proceeding to litigation. Even at FINRA, the securities arbitration institution in the United States that is prepared to handle customer (investor) arbitrations, the cost of simply engaging in arbitration amounts to almost 2 per cent of the total value of the dispute, whereas in the courts this would not exceed 1 per cent. At the ICC, one of the most prestigious arbitration institutions in the world, the cost of engaging in a U$100,000 dispute is simply prohibitive, amounting to more than 15 per cent of the claim just for the filing of the dispute and remuneration of the arbitrator.

[81] ibid 14.

[82] The dispute could be resolved by settlement after the beginning of a lawsuit, but this would not entail the full use of the dispute resolution system.

ii. Costs of Evidence and Representation

Evidence production and review are other important aspects of the cost structure of dispute resolution in securities disputes. Here the main culprits are common law-style discovery and expert witnesses.

Discovery is a civil-procedure institution that is not well known to civil law lawyers. It allows one party to demand the production of information by the other party on an extensive basis, encompassing more or less anything that is relevant to the claim or defence;[83] this imposes extreme burdens both on the party who has to organise the documents and also on the party requesting the documents who will be required to review them.

To the extent that any given type of dispute has a wide factual background that can be accessed through discovery, institutional designs that allow for this procedural possibility will be much costlier for litigants than the systems that have these methods capped. Document collection, review and production are tasks that are often done by the parties' lawyers, combining this type of costs with the costs of representation to some degree.

Lawyers' fees depend largely on the jurisdiction and the profile of the law firm providing the service. Smaller law firms may charge by the lawsuit being pursued, while larger law firms usually charge an hourly rate for the service provided, which averages, at least in the United States, at US$250 an hour per lawyer.[84]

At these rates, any type of dispute that would require even a not-so-extensive discovery process would, as a matter of fact, make it impossible for the average investor to pursue a lawsuit, unless the investor was joined by similarly situated investors to proceed with a mass claims proceeding. When low values are at stake, the dispute resolution system design has to allow for low costs of evidence and representation, otherwise low-value claims will be precluded from legal protection.

III. Implications of the Institutional Framework for a Dispute Resolution System

Legal systems exist to manage expectations and to coordinate social interactions. In economic transactions they are important because they allow the parties to plan for the future, relying on the legal system to guarantee that promises will be kept and assets will be protected. With regard to this aspect, private enforcement is highly important to its efficiency, as explained in Chapter 3.

The reliability of the legal system is dependent on the operation of the rule-of-law principle through institutions designed to operate as objectively as possible.

---

[83] See Federal Rules of Civil Procedure, s 26(b).
[84] NM Pace and L Zakaras, *Where the Money Goes: Understanding Litigation Expenditures for Producing Electronic Discovery* (Rand Institute for Civil Justice 2012).

Since the dispute resolution forum is where the law will be applied in the specific case, it has to be designed so as to avoid subjective considerations as much as possible.

The first part of this chapter showed that two of the most essential component parts for this to be accomplished are the balance between the independence and accountability of the decision makers and the transparency of their decisions. These considerations, while not definitely tied to the type of jurisdiction-granting mechanism, are to some extent defined by it.

By having a well-designed balance between the independence and the accountability of the decision maker the dispute resolution system guarantees that it will operate according to the rule of law, bringing to it all the positive aspects related to economic efficiency.

Regarding transparency, it is not so important if a single dispute is considered; an arbitration, the main focus of which is simply to definitively resolve a dispute, will most likely be tailored to the needs of the parties engaging in it. For example, confidentiality may be important because the parties do not want other parties to know about their dealings. The problem is that a dispute resolution system, with a specific focus on solving single disputes, may create problems for the legal system as a whole. Decisions that are not made public impair the development of law as other players will not be able to be guided by these decisions and develop expectations around them; this brings back one of the most important issues that law has been created to resolve, namely certainty in social relations. Therefore, if a dispute resolution system purports to be comprehensive in a given field of disputes, be it vested with direct or indirect jurisdiction, it has to be designed in a manner whereby decision makers have strong incentives to consider only legal arguments and where the transparency of decisions is allowed so the legal system can evolve.

The second dimension of this chapter is related to the economic considerations of a dispute resolution system. On the one hand, the system has to be funded; the two pure models are state-funded systems and business-funded systems. In practice, this has some relationship to the type of jurisdiction-granting mechanism upon which the dispute resolution system is based; systems with direct jurisdiction are usually financed by taxation, either of the population in general or of specific users of the system, while systems based on consent jurisdiction mechanisms are funded by the users of the system or by businesses that feel it is appropriate to have a parallel dispute resolution system in place.

Finally, the second economic aspect, the costs of engaging in litigation, is essential to the analysis undertaken in the next chapters as it is linked to the incentives for the exercise of private enforcement. For claims to be litigated, they have to bring an expected benefit to the claimant. If the value of the claim is lower than the cost of engaging in litigation, the claim will not be litigated. Even if the system allows claims to be litigated for free, as in some small claims systems, the claim value might be so low that it is not worthwhile for the claimant to pursue it. Aggregate litigation mechanisms then become interesting options, allowing for the collection of claims to increase the possible economic output of the dispute, creating an opportunity for other parties to get involved and providing a wider avenue for access to justice.[85]

The rule of law and access to justice, therefore, are paramount to the efficiency of private enforcement of securities laws, both in respect of the compensation and the deterrence aspects of securities regulation. The next chapter surveys different dispute resolution systems that could be used as models to create a system working within the principles of the rule of law and providing wider access for securities disputes, enabling self-reliance on the private enforcement of securities laws. Thereafter, Chapter 8 analyses the incentives for private enforcement in aggregate litigation and the possible pitfalls that this type of procedural mechanism may create.

---

[85] See C Hodges, *The Reform of Class and Representative Actions in European Legal Systems* (Hart Publishing 2008) 187–91; S Issacharoff, 'Governance and Legitimacy in the Law of Class Actions' [1999] *Supreme Court Review* 337.

7

Alternative Models of Dispute Resolution Systems

The previous chapter established core institutional aspects of a dispute resolution system and provided some insight on how such a system could comply with the rule-of-law principle and be an adequate mechanism for private enforcement. This chapter will use this previous discussion as a basis to analyse some of the important dispute resolution systems that could be used to resolve financial transactions. Its objective is to outline how different dispute resolution mechanisms that could be potentially used for securities disputes are structured in practice. Due to the transnational character of the problem proposed by this book, this chapter is divided into national models and transnational models.

I. National Models

National models of dispute resolution systems are those based within the bounds of a state. Even though they can deal with disputes that are transnational, their institutional structure is nation based.

A. Small Claims Court Model

Small claims courts are dispute resolution systems within the state structure that are an alternative to the normal procedure of the court system. They are designed to provide easy access to the justice system by allowing a person to sue without a lawyer and by having low access costs. The decision maker is either a judge or a person overseen by a judge; the authority of the decision is the same as the one given through normal proceedings. Funding for the small claims courts comes from the state. Small claims courts have a limited jurisdictional scope based on the claim value, while at the same time they may restrict those who have standing to sue.[1] The small claims courts model is completely public.

---

[1] For example, in the New York Small Claims Court System, businesses are not allowed to sue. See JS Kaye and J Lippman, 'A Guide to Small Claims in the NYS City, Town and Village Courts'

The Brazilian system is an interesting one. Small claims courts in Brazil have existed since 1984.[2] Their introduction into the Brazilian legal system had the initial goal of opening access to justice to a part of the population that otherwise could not use the judiciary to seek legal relief.[3] Subsequently, the justification for the system has also been broadened to encompass the overburdened courts that existed (and continue to exist) in Brazil.[4]

Bureaucracy was previously a much uglier monster than it is today in Brazil. In 1979 the Brazilian government started the National Programme of Debureaucratization to diminish the bureaucratic requirements that were widespread in the Brazilian government.[5] In the same period, the Rio Grande do Sul judiciary was testing a simpler method of dispute resolution that would avoid the high costs and the delay that were common in Brazilian courts.[6] This setting, and the inspiration that the Secretary from the Debureaucratization Ministry gained from the small claims court in New York,[7] formed the background against which the Brazilian small claims courts were created.

In 1995 the legal and institutional structures of the small claims courts were broadened, both regarding the amount of the disputes that were accepted within their jurisdiction as well as the legal problems at stake. Brazilian Law 9.099/95, currently in force, was the legal instrument that provided for these changes.

The procedure in the small claims courts is simpler than in normal courts. For disputes up to 20 minimum salaries a lawyer is not necessary to assist in the lawsuit.[8] The procedure is basically divided into two hearings: during the first, a conciliator will try to lead the parties to an agreement;[9] if an agreement is not reached, a second hearing will be organised so evidence can be presented and the judge can be instructed.[10] Appeals are possible and are made to a court of three career judges.[11]

There are three main figures in the dispute resolution method of the small claims courts in Brazil: the career judge, the lay judge and the conciliator. The career judge is the only one who is a proper judge, approved by public examination and invested with judicial powers. Any actions that are taken by the lay judge or the conciliator are under the supervision of the career judge. The difference is a

---

(New York State Unified Court System Rev 8/05) www.nycourts.gov/courts/8jd/pdfs/NYS_Small-ClaimsGuideSept05.pdf.

[2] Brazilian Law 7.244/1984.

[3] ACM Chasin, *Uma Simples Formalidade: estudo sobre a experiência dos Juizados Especiais Cíveis em São Paulo* (LLM, USP 2007).

[4] ibid.

[5] ibid 42–43.

[6] See ibid 51–54.

[7] ibid 50.

[8] Brazilian Law 9.099/95, art 9. Small claims courts can entertain disputes up to 40 minimum salaries (Brazilian Law 9.099/95, art 3, I). A 'minimum salary' is the minimum amount an employer must pay someone for a month's work. At the time of writing, a minimum salary is R$ 937,00.

[9] Brazilian Law 9.099/95, art 22.

[10] Brazilian Law 9.099/95, arts 27–29.

[11] Brazilian Law 9.099/95, art 41 §1.

functional one; the lay judge will preside over the instruction and judgment hearings and proffer decisions subject to the career judge's approval,[12] while the conciliator can only preside over conciliation hearings.[13]

This structure allows for a smaller cost in dispensing justice and resolving disputes. For example, while a judge earns around R$20,000,[14] a lay judge can be remunerated up to R$3,000 a month,[15] depending on the amount of work that has been done. The difference is substantial.

Criticisms have been advanced that the quality of justice would be different, depending on the proceeding chosen; those who could afford a full proceeding would have more 'justice' than those subject to the small claims system.[16] Even though there is some truth to such an argument, since those who are paid more tend to be better trained than those who are paid less and more evidence results in more facts being provided to the decision maker, this is also highly dependent on the institutional structure of the small claims courts.[17]

A compromise must also be reached between costs, quality of justice and access to justice. A slightly poorer justice is better than no justice at all, a situation which might arise because the costs are too high for disputes to be entertained or because the proceedings for the 'better-quality' justice become too long due to the demand on the court system, such that it becomes virtually impossible for a judicial decision to be of any use.

B. The Financial Ombudsman Service Model

The financial ombudsman service model is a different scheme in comparison to the small claims court model. Its funding is more specific, the decision makers are not judges and the binding effects of the decision are different from those of a judicial decision.

One of the most successful financial ombudsman services is the UK FOS. It is a public body that was created by the UK Parliament in 2000[18] and is run by a 'company limited by guarantee and not having a share capital',[19] the Financial

---

[12] Brazilian Law 9.099/95, art 40.

[13] Brazilian Law 9.099/95, art 22.

[14] For example, in Mato Grosso do Sul a judge at the beginning of his career receives R$23.512,65. See TJMS, 'Estrutura Remuneratória—Cargos Efetivos', www.tjms.jus.br/transparencia/resolucao102/anexo3a-2016-01.php.

[15] In the State of Mato Grosso do Sul, this would mean deciding around 42 cases, the lay judge receiving R$ 71.00 for each case. Resolution TJMS 564 (2010), art 2.

[16] Chasin (n 3) 54–58.

[17] Chasin has shown in her work that despite being under the same 'small claims court' legislation and within the same city, there were significant differences in the operation of the 'small claims court' system in the two courts that she studied. See ibid 87–163.

[18] Financial Services and Markets Act 2000, pt XVI, sch 17.

[19] Articles of Association of Financial Ombudsman Service Limited, www.financial-ombudsman.org.uk/faq/pdf/articles_of_association.pdf.

Ombudsman Service Limited, the 'scheme operator' under the Financial Services and Markets Act 2000.[20]

The idea behind the scheme was to resolve 'quickly and with minimum formality by an independent person'[21] disputes regarding services provided within the financial services industry in the United Kingdom; it appears that this service has been successful: the 2012/2013 annual review showed that there were 2,161,439 calls to their helpline and 508,881 new cases. Their track record was also good; 81 per cent of all cases were resolved in less than 12 months in 2012/2013[22] and 90 per cent in 2014/2015.[23] During the 2015/2016 period, there were fewer enquiries (1,631,955).[24]

These are substantial numbers, which show that the service has attracted a considerable number of users. As substantial as the number of cases with which the FOS is dealing is, the budget for its operation, which was £191.1 million for 2012/2013[25] and £257.9 million for 2015/2016,[26] is also substantial. Its financing structure is interesting. It depends on a levy imposed on financial firms as a cost of doing business and, mainly, on the income that is also received from these firms according to the cases that are brought against them.[27] Even though the levy is a form of taxation and the burden of sustaining the system falls on financial firms, it is a fair structure as it provides access to justice to financial customers and to some extent the financing also comes from the consumers themselves, since they will be paying for the services they obtain from financial firms, who have to take into account their costs of doing business when deciding how much they will charge.

The scheme derives its authority from the Financial Services and Markets Act 2000,[28] the Consumer Credit Act 2006[29] and from regulations enacted by the Financial Conduct Authority (FCA),[30] the UK body in charge of regulating

---

[20] Financial Markets Act 2000, s 225.

[21] Financial Services and Markets Act 2000, s 225(1).

[22] See FOS, 'Annual Review 2012/2013', www.financial-ombudsman.org.uk/publications/ar13/dealt.html.

[23] FOS, 'Our Plans and Budget for 2016/2017—Consultation', www.financial-ombudsman.org.uk/publications/PB-2016-17-consultation.pdf.

[24] FOS, 'Annual Review 2015/2016', www.financial-ombudsman.org.uk/publications/annual-review-2016/ar16.pdf.

[25] There was an expected deficit of £6.4 million but this was due to a surge in PPI cases and the necessity to hire and train new staff (FOS, 'Annual Review 2012/2013' (n 22)).

[26] FOS, 'Annual Review 2015/2016' (n 24).

[27] The levy ranges from £100 to £300,000, depending on the size of the firm, and it covered 9.3% of the budget in 2012/2013 (FOS, 'Our Plans and Budget for 2012/2013—Finalised and Approved', www.financial-ombudsman.org.uk/news/updates/planandbudget-2012-13-approved.html). Case fees are currently £550 per case, but are charged only on the cases after the 25th case that is brought against the company. There used to be a surcharge of £350 for cases involving payment protection insurance, which is not being charged anymore (see FOS, 'Our Plans and Budget for 2013/2014—Finalised and Approved', www.financial-ombudsman.org.uk/news/updates/plan_and_budget_13-14.html; FOS, 'Our Plans for the Year Ahead—March 2016', www.financial-ombudsman.org.uk/publications/our-plans-2016-17.pdf).

[28] Pt XVI and sch 17.

[29] Section 59.

[30] FCA Handbook.

financial services firms and financial markets in the United Kingdom.[31] More limited in scope than those in courts, the disputes entertained within this system are only those related to regulated activities from investment firms in the United Kingdom or collective portfolio management services provided by a European Economic Area (EEA) Undertakings for the Collective Investment of Transferable Securities (UCITS) management company or by an EEA Alternative Investment Fund Manager (AIFM);[32] the jurisdiction is also only available to consumers or otherwise low-asset-value institutions,[33] with maximum awards of £150,000.[34]

The dispute resolution system is mainly informal and is operated first through a conciliation/mediation procedure that is performed by the 'adjudicators', who try to resolve the matter and issue an opinion on how the case should be resolved. This opinion is not binding and if the parties do not reach an agreement they can make a request that the case be decided by the ombudsman. After the ombudsman decision is issued, the consumer can either accept it or not. If the decision is accepted, it is binding on both parties, otherwise it is not binding and the consumer can still seek redress through the court system.[35]

The FOS is under the supervision of a Board, with its members being appointed by the FCA.[36] Board members are appointed to serve in the public interest, and not as the representatives of any sector of the financial services industry.[37] The Board is then in charge of appointing and maintaining a panel of ombudsmen.[38]

Finally, regarding the decision made, the FOS is becoming more transparent. It has already started publishing the decisions taken, as required by the amendments to the Financial Services and Markets Act 2000 introduced by the Financial Services Act 2012. The publicity of the decisions is a positive change since it makes the system more transparent and gives businesses more resources to understand better what is expected of them, improving legal certainty.

For the purposes of this work, this is a very interesting scheme. It finances roughly 80 per cent of its operation through case-related revenue, it is consumer friendly, it resolves disputes within a relatively short period of time and it renders binding decisions. Such characteristics could be interesting for a transnational system for securities disputes, especially when having in mind the small and medium investor.

---

[31] See FCA, 'About the FCA', www.fca.org.uk/about/the-fca.

[32] FCA Handbook, DISP 2.3.1 and 2.6.1.

[33] FCA Handbook, DISP 2.7.6.

[34] FCA Handbook, DISP 3.7.4.

[35] See FOS, 'The Ombudsman and Larger Businesses', www.financial-ombudsman.org.uk/publications/pdf/guide_complaints_handlers.pdf, 7–9; FCA Handbook DISP, 3.6.6(4); 4(A).

[36] The chairman also needs the approval of HM Treasury. Financial Services and Markets Act 2000, sch 17, 3(2).

[37] FOS, 'Information for Businesses Covered by the Ombudsman Service', www.financial-ombudsman.org.uk/faq/businesses/answers/rules_a8.html.

[38] See Articles of Association of Financial Ombudsman Service Limited, s 15.

C. Self-Regulation Model

Another option is to have the dispute resolution system embedded in the market control mechanisms that are overseen by the organised securities markets, under a self-regulation model.

In Brazil, this is the option that has been chosen for disputes up to R$70,000[39] that involve financial intermediaries and investors when the dispute concerns the intermediation of securities transactions or custody services.[40] The mechanism is run by BMF&Bovespa through its regulatory body, the BM&FBovespa Supervisão de Mercados (BSM), which has rules and regulations that govern the procedure for the dispute resolution mechanism.[41]

Decisions are made either by the Director of Self-Regulation, the President of the Supervision Council or the Supervision Council,[42] who are appointed by the General Assembly of the BSM.[43] The arrangement does not guarantee much independence since the decision makers are under the complete control of BM&FBovespa, the Brazilian securities market. Even though decisions are made by persons who are members of this private body, due to the public aspect of a securities market, the decision can be appealed to the CVM, the Brazilian public agency in charge of regulating the securities market,[44] which then renders an administrative decision.[45] Since administrative decisions in Brazil do not preclude the use of the judiciary, both parties can still start a lawsuit over the same subject matter of the dispute if they are not satisfied with the decision proffered.

Regarding the reasoning of decisions and transparency, the mechanism can be used as a good example because both the BSM and the CVM decisions are published on their websites and legal reasoning is provided, allowing a body of precedent to develop.

Access is not as easy as it is for other mechanisms; it is highly bureaucratised, requiring the recognition of the claimant's signature by a public notary. The good part about it is that it is free and a form and manual are provided to make it easier for a complaint to be made.

---

[39] Instruction CVM 461, art 80 para 1.
[40] Instruction CVM 461, art 77.
[41] See BM&FBOVESPA Regulamento do Mecanismo de Ressarcimento de Prejuízos—MRP, www.bsm-autorregulacao.com.br/assets/file/Novo-RegulamentoMRP.pdf (Bovespa Regulation of the Loss Recovery Mechanism).
[42] Bovespa Regulation of the Loss Recovery Mechanism, art 15 and art 19, I and II.
[43] Estatuto Social da BM&FBOVESPA Supervisão de Mercados—BSM (2014), www.bsm-autorregulacao.com.br/assets/file/codigo-conduta/BSM-Estatuto-Social.pdf, art 16, I and II. This means that legally BSM is totally controlled by the BM&FBovespa, since BSM associated parties are BM&FBovespa and Banco BM&F de Serviços de Liquidação e Custódia SA, which is controlled by BM&FBovespa (see Banco BM&FBOVESPA, 'Quem Somos', www.bmfbovespa.com.br/bancobmf-bovespa/institucional.asp).
[44] Instruction CVM 461, art 82, para 1, and Regulation of the Loss Recovery Mechanism, art 19, III.
[45] Bovespa Regulation of the Loss Recovery Mechanism, art. 22.

D. Arbitration

Continuing from the most to the least public dispute resolution scheme, arbitration may be divided into schemes that have some degree of public influence, the state-supervised model, and the more general arbitration schemes that operate only through the enabling legislation of a state.

i. State-supervised Model

Arbitration is supposedly a purely private mechanism of dispute resolution. Even though this is how arbitration initially developed, there are schemes that are based on an arbitration framework but in which there is a strong public presence, to the extent that it is stripped of its 'voluntary' character and becomes the only de facto method for solving disputes.

This is the case for the Financial Industry Regulatory Authority (FINRA), the dispute resolution scheme in the United States for disputes between consumers and financial intermediaries. '[FINRA] is the largest independent regulator of securities firms doing business with the public in the United States.'[46] FINRA arose out of 'the consolidation of NASD and the member regulation, enforcement and arbitration operations of the New York Stock Exchange'.[47] It is an industry self-regulatory organisation, falling under the supervision of the SEC.

The power exercised by FINRA derives from its registration with the SEC under Section 15A of the Securities and Exchange Act 1934. Since any broker-dealer must be registered with a Section 15A-registered securities association, FINRA being the only one at the moment, it exercises a public power since registration and compliance with its rules is mandatory for brokers-dealers to be legally able to exercise their activity.[48]

FINRA maintains a dispute resolution scheme based on arbitration, which is imposed on its members either by a contractual commitment with investors or by FINRA Rule 12200.[49] The option for the investor is only theoretical as most financial intermediaries include an arbitration clause in their contract, imposing the use of the FINRA forum for dispute resolution.[50] On the other hand, and characterising the public aspect of the FINRA scheme, the broker-dealers cannot escape this dispute resolution method since they must be registered with FINRA to exercise their functions.

---

[46] FINRA, 'About Finra', www.finra.org/AboutFINRA/.
[47] FINRA, 'NASD and NYSE Member Regulation Combine to Form the Financial Industry Regulatory Authority—FINRA' (July 2007) www.finra.org/newsroom/2007/nasd-and-nyse-member-regulation-combine-form-financial-industry-regulatory-authority.
[48] Securities and Exchange Act 1934, s 15(b)(1).
[49] 'Parties must arbitrate a dispute under the Code if: Arbitration under the Code is either: (1) Required by a written agreement, or (2) Requested by the customer'.
[50] See NASAA, 'Mandatory Binding Arbitration: Is it Fair and Voluntary?' (15 September 2009) www.nasaa.org/807/mandatory-binding-arbitration-is-it-fair-and-voluntary/.

Arbitrators for a particular dispute are selected from a list that is randomly generated from FINRA's roster. Parties then will be able to strike arbitrators from the list and rank their choices. Since 31 January 2011, on a three-arbitrator panel, customers have had the choice of requesting the appointment of a panel composed by public arbitrators only; previously, one arbitrator connected to the securities industry was always present.[51]

FINRA arbitrators do need to have some qualifications, such as five years of professional experience and two years of college-level credits, in addition to completing a training programme.[52] These do not seem to be particularly stringent requirements and anyone who fulfils them is able to become a FINRA arbitrator. Therefore, there are no strong checks regarding arbitrator independence; moreover, reputation does not seem to be a proper mechanism to guarantee it in this context.[53]

Another negative point of the FINRA arbitration process is that decisions are usually not reasoned. As mentioned above, the lack of reasoning is a problem for the operation of the rule of law, especially in an institutional setting where almost all similar disputes are resolved through this forum.

Fees are paid along the way, depending on the acts required. For example, a party has to pay a fee to file a claim, but if the other party wants to counterclaim, they also have to pay a fee. If a hearing is requested, additional fees are due.

A positive aspect of this approach, however, is that most decisions against financial intermediaries are complied with voluntarily. As FINRA has regulatory power over its members, it can suspend or revoke their licences if they do not comply with the arbitrators' decision within 30 days and is therefore an extremely efficient dispute resolution mechanism.[54]

The interesting characteristic of this scheme is that it is privately managed under the supervision of a public authority, which will be in charge of guaranteeing that the scheme remains truthful to its goals. There are a few shortcomings, namely the lack of proper mechanisms to guarantee arbitrator independence and the lack of reasoned decisions, which are important aspects of a legal system operating under the rule of law.

---

[51] See FINRA, 'Optional All Public Panel Rules', www.finra.org/ArbitrationAndMediation/ Arbitration/Rules/NoticestoArbitratorsParties/NoticestoParties/P123997.

[52] See FINRA, 'FINRA's Arbitrators', www.finra.org/ArbitrationAndMediation/Arbitrators/ BecomeanArbitrator/FINRAArbitrators/index.htm.

[53] In a manner that differs from commercial arbitration, which involves high-stakes disputes and has a small community of arbitrators that are chosen based on their reputation due to the repeat-player nature of the law firms involved in them, securities arbitration involves smaller claims that are brought mainly by consumers who are not likely to be coming back and learning about the institutional characteristics of the forum and the specific arbitrators.

[54] See JI Gross, 'The End of Mandatory Securities Arbitration?' (2010) 30 *Pace Law Review* 1174, 1189; FINRA Rules 12904.

ii. Private Arbitration Model

The private arbitration model[55] is the general arbitration model. Even though this sub-section falls within the 'national' division of this section, the private arbitration model functions both for national as well as transnational disputes; the decision to place it here was because their institutional structure is tied to a state, which is to say that it differs from the international arbitration model discussed in the next section, which is tied to more than one state.[56] It is characterised by complete freedom of the parties to engage in arbitration, whether through a contractual clause agreed upon before the dispute arises or by an agreement to arbitrate afterwards.

The only role of the state in a private arbitration model is to guarantee that agreements to arbitrate will be legally binding—which means that once someone agrees to arbitrate, the dispute has to be submitted to arbitration and the decision of the arbitrator will be executable through the courts of law of that state. The whole scheme is characterised by the exclusive presence of parties acting in their private capacity.

An arbitral institution usually manages a private arbitration procedure. This institution is in charge of guaranteeing that the procedure develops seamlessly and that the decisions made by the arbitrators will be legally enforceable. Remuneration of the arbitral institution and of the arbitrators is paid by the parties to the dispute; the manner in which remuneration accrues varies depending on the arbitral institution.

The guarantee of arbitrator independence is based mostly on reputational aspects. There are a few mechanisms within the legal framework for arbitration that can cure a lack of independence but these are ex post mechanisms of control, such as non-enforcement based on the arbitrator's partiality.

The specific dispute resolution schemes are tied to the arbitral institutions that manage the arbitration. Arbitration is usually used in the following manner: parties choose an arbitral institution to manage the dispute and then the selection of the arbitrators and the constitution of the arbitral panel will be carried out according to the rules of that arbitral institution.[57]

There are various famous arbitral institutions, such as the International Court of Arbitration of the International Chamber of Commerce, the American Arbitration Association and the London Court of International Arbitration. Two that are worth a closer look are the Câmara de Arbitragem do Mercado (CAM) and PRIME Finance, since they purport to deal with disputes tied to financial transactions.

---

[55] In arbitration scholarship, this is the commercial arbitration model, as investment arbitration always involves the state as one of the parties to the dispute and is based on treaties.

[56] An arbitral institution has to be constituted according to the laws of a state unless created by an international treaty.

[57] For example, the ICC Rules of Arbitration, iccwbo.org/dispute-resolution-services/arbitration/rules-of-arbitration/.

CAM is an arbitral institution based in Brazil. It was created by BOVESPA (now BM&FBovespa), the Brazilian stock exchange, in 2001. CAM was designed to manage arbitral procedures based on conflicts originating from companies listed on BM&FBovespa.[58] The use of CAM to arbitrate corporate disputes is mandatory for those companies that are listed on the higher corporate governance levels of BM&FBovespa: Novo Mercado, Nível 2 and BOVESPA Mais.[59]

The arbitrator roster is a limited one, with 62 people.[60] Independence therefore is based on reputation, as there are no other mechanisms of control besides the request to change arbitrators in the event a suspicion of impartiality arises.[61]

It is interesting that CAM uses the word transparency as something important for listed companies since the arbitral procedure that they offer is confidential,[62] giving no publicity for the decisions and actually diminishing transparency when compared to the Brazilian judicial procedure.[63] It is true that there is no obligation for listed companies to resolve their disputes through CAM arbitration, but those who wish to comply with higher corporate governance standards tend to be the bigger companies, a situation that necessarily leads to more complex disputes. Therefore, the decisions of these disputes will most likely not be made public, making it hard to understand the reasons through which the decisions are reached and how they would be applicable in different cases.

The second arbitral institution mentioned is PRIME Finance. Its model is the more general arbitral institution, without any formal links to government or government-authorised organisations.[64] According to its website, PRIME Finance was created after discussions with various market participants and government officials in which the need for an arbitral institution focusing on complex financial transactions was recognised.[65]

PRIME Finance had its opening conference on 16 January 2012 but so far its operation seems to be highly secretive as there are no reports on the amount or type of disputes that have been handled by this arbitral institution. As this is a more general arbitral institution, it is not something that should be criticised. On the other hand, such an institutional design would not be adequate as the main method of dispute resolution in a particular field of law.

---

[58] This information is on their website. See BM&FBOVESPA, 'Câmara de Arbitragem do Mercado', www.camaradomercado.com.br/.

[59] See BM&FBOVESPA, 'O que são Segmentos de Listagem', http://www.bmfbovespa.com.br/pt_br/listagem/acoes/segmentos-de-listagem/sobre-segmentos-de-listagem/.

[60] Other arbitrators can be chosen but have to be confirmed by the President and one of the Vice-Presidents of CAM. Regulamento da Câmara de Arbitragem de Mercado, www.bmfbovespa.com.br/pt_br/servicos/camara-de-arbitragem-do-mercado-cam/regulamentacao/ (Câmara de Arbitragem do Mercado Regulation), s 3.7.

[61] See Câmara de Arbitragem do Mercado Regulation, ss 3.11–3.14.

[62] Câmara de Arbitragem do Mercado Regulation, s 9.1.

[63] The publicity of judicial acts is constitutionally guaranteed in Brazil. See Brazilian Federal Constitution, art 5, LX.

[64] Such as stock exchanges with self-regulatory powers.

[65] PRIME Finance, 'About Us', primefinancedisputes.org/about-us/.

II. International Models

International dispute resolution mechanisms are those established with the authority of more than one state. As with national dispute resolution models, there is a wide array of different settings for international dispute resolution models.

A. International Courts

The defining characteristic of an international court or tribunal is the presence of sitting judges who are remunerated by the institution as their decision makers. There are no other defining characteristics in the taxonomy of international organisations that can be used to make this distinction, as the other characteristic that is also used to define what is commonly understood as a court in the national sphere, compulsory jurisdiction, is not always present in the international sphere.

International courts are established by treaties. Their initial authority derives from the authority attributed to them by the states entering the treaty to establish the international tribunal. While they may broaden their power by their own operation,[66] it is necessary for this to be accepted by the relevant countries involved in order for the tribunal to continue exercising authority.

The typical example of an international court with non-compulsory jurisdiction is the International Court of Justice (ICJ).[67] The Court is composed of 15 independent judges.[68] In a given dispute, if a country does not have a judge of its nationality as part of the Court, it may appoint an ad hoc judge.[69] The use of ad hoc judges is seen as problematic because it goes against the ideal of judicial independence, even though their use is justified as serving the 'function of maintaining the confidence of the parties in the judicial process before the ICJ'.[70] The ICJ has jurisdiction over any cases between states that refer their dispute to it, and in 'matters specially provided for in the Charter of the United Nations or in treaties or conventions in force'.[71]

The International Tribunal for the Law of the Sea also has a similar institutional design. Jurisdiction is only exercisable if accepted by state parties, judges

---

[66] For example, the European Court of Justice. See K Alter, 'The European Court's Political Power Across Time and Space' (2009) Northwestern Law & Econ Research Paper No 09-03.

[67] Its jurisdiction becomes compulsory only when a country makes a declaration under the Statute of the International Court of Justice, www.icj-cij.org/documents/?p1=4&p2=2, art 36(2) (ICJ Statute), and only when the other country submitting the dispute for consideration has also made the same declaration.

[68] They are elected by the General Assembly and Security Council of the UN for a renewable nine-year term. ICJ Statute, arts 3(1), 4(1), 13(1).

[69] See R Mackenzie, C Romano and Y Shany, *The Manual on International Courts and Tribunals* (Oxford University Press 2010) 6–8.

[70] ibid 8.

[71] ICJ Statute, art 36(1).

are elected and ad hoc judges can be appointed when there are no judges of the nationality of one of the states in the dispute.[72]

At the other end of the spectrum, having compulsory jurisdiction over disputes, is the World Trade Organization (WTO) Dispute Settlement Body (DSB),[73] established in accordance with the Dispute Settlement Understanding. The DSB has the authority to establish panels and adopt reports.[74] The dispute resolution procedure is embedded in a complex institutional setting and encompasses various steps before a final resolution is made. The first formal step is consultation, where the parties try to resolve their disagreements without engaging in litigation.[75] If consultation does not work, the second step is the establishment of a panel to decide the dispute. The panel procedure is more similar to arbitration since panellists are selected ad hoc, not being part of any permanent body within the WTO.[76] The panel decision may either be adopted by the DSB or appealed.[77]

If the panel report is appealed, then it goes to a Standing Appellate Body for review. This is where the dispute resolution system of the WTO becomes more aligned to the idea of a 'court' than an 'arbitral tribunal'. Appellate Body members are appointed for a four-year term with the possibility of one reappointment.[78]

Panels and Appellate Body reports have to be adopted by the DSB unless there is a consensus on not adopting them.[79] When a WTO member is applying measures that are inconsistent with a covered agreement, the panel or Appellate Body recommends that the member bring the measure into conformity with the agreement.[80]

These decisions are binding and if the member does not comply with them, the complainant may either request compensation from the breaching party or resort to countermeasures after authorisation by the DSB.[81]

Even though the international court model may be adequate to resolve diverse types of disputes, it might not constitute the best forum for transnational securities transactions. There are two problems that are quite clear from this model: the necessity of establishing the body through a treaty, which requires spending a lot of political energy, especially with the broad scope of signatories required for a truly transnational dispute resolution system; and the high maintenance costs of maintaining sitting judges and the structure of the body.

---

[72] Mackenzie et al (n 69) 40–44.
[73] Agreement Establishing the World Trade Organization, Annex 2 (15 April 1994) (Dispute Settlement Understanding), art 23.
[74] Dispute Settlement Understanding, art 2.1.
[75] Dispute Settlement Understanding, art 4.
[76] There is an indicative list of panellists that is maintained by the WTO but they are not formally tied to it. For the procedure for selecting panellists, see Dispute Settlement Understanding, art 8.
[77] Dispute Settlement Understanding, art 16.4.
[78] Dispute Settlement Understanding, art 17.2.
[79] Dispute Settlement Understanding, art 16.4 and 17.14.
[80] Dispute Settlement Understanding art 19.
[81] Dispute Settlement Understanding, art 22.

B. International Arbitral Institutions

The difference between international arbitral institutions and national arbitral institutions is that the former are constituted on the basis of international treaties, while the latter are constituted on the basis of articles of incorporation, in accordance with national law.

International arbitral institutions perform the function of administering arbitrations. They do not decide cases, but provide rules, facilities and personnel to ensure that the arbitration process follows smoothly.

The two most recognised international arbitral institutions are the Permanent Court of Arbitration (PCA), in The Hague, and the International Centre for Settlement of Investment Disputes (ICSID), in Washington.

The PCA is the older of the two, established in 1899 by The Hague Conference through the adoption of the Convention for the Pacific Settlement of International Disputes.[82] The ICSID was established in 1966 and the cases that it administers are more limited in scope than those administered by the PCA, being restricted to investment disputes.[83]

C. The European Cross-Border Mechanism for Financial Disputes: a Network of Dispute Resolution Bodies

The mechanism developed in Europe for cross-border consumer financial disputes involving the financial intermediary–investor type of dispute is Fin-Net, a financial dispute resolution network. It is not a dispute resolution body but only a network in which its members, national dispute resolution schemes such as the UK FOS, agree to cooperate with each other regarding financial disputes. For example, if an Italian has a problem with a UK financial company, the Italian may bring his problems to the Italian dispute resolution body for financial disputes, which will then guide the Italian consumer to contact the UK scheme that can help him with his dispute, or it will forward the dispute directly to that scheme.[84]

Clearly, Fin-Net is a cooperation forum as it only organises and orients national dispute resolution schemes in the European Economic Area countries on how to deal with complaints that are cross-border or outside their jurisdictional scope.[85]

---

[82] Mackenzie et al (n 69) 102.

[83] Convention on the Settlement of Investment Disputes between States and Nationals of other States (10 April 2006), art 25.1.

[84] See Memorandum of Understanding on a Cross-Border Out-of-Court Complaints Network for Financial Services, https://ec.europa.eu/info/sites/info/files/memorandum-of-understanding_en.pdf, 3–4.

[85] I use 'jurisdictional' here in the sense of what disputes these schemes can entertain.

Fin-Net was created in 2001 by the European Commission. It has a very modest budget.[86] The number of complaints coming through the system has risen, from 1,041 in 2007 to 1,854 in 2011.[87] This remains a small number of cases when compared to more local dispute resolution schemes,[88] which indicates that consumer cross-border financial transactions are not that common when compared to similar national transactions.

The Fin-Net was created to bring information to consumers on out-of-court redress mechanisms, to ensure information exchange between different ADR schemes, to improve the provision of dispute resolution services and to ensure that there is a common set of principles governing the different ADR schemes.[89] Basically, the broad objectives of the scheme are to 'assist consumers in the resolution of cross-border disputes' and to 'raise consumer confidence in buying financial services cross-border'.[90]

The positive aspect of Fin-Net is that it provides information and mechanisms, through local ADR schemes, to consumers on how to obtain redress on cross-border financial transactions and it does this at a low cost. By improving the prospect of information access and redress, this scheme is helpful in increasing confidence in the market for cross-border financial transactions.

The negative aspect of the scheme is that it does not go far enough. Despite improving information and redress mechanism access, these ADR mechanisms vary depending on the jurisdiction at stake. They have a widely different range, from non-binding to binding and from private based to public based.[91] Someone who would like to engage in a cross-border financial transaction would have to perform a detailed study of the redress mechanisms that are available in the countries in which the investor would like to invest, defeating, at least to some extent, the purpose of the Fin-Net network itself. If someone has the need to look for information beforehand to be protected, a network that provides information would then become less useful, as the investor who has done his homework would already have it.

Even though Fin-Net represents a step forward in increasing confidence in markets through the provision of more information about the functioning of dispute resolution in financial transactions within the European context, the construction of a single market would profit from a European-wide dispute resolution system, or at least systems connected by the network that are similar in how they operate.

---

[86] The budget in 2008 was €65,326 (DG Internal Market and Services, 'Evaluation of FIN-NET—Final Report' (June 2009) 50).

[87] European Commission, 'FIN-NET Activity Report 2011' (June 2012).

[88] For example, the UK FOS dealt with 508,881 formal disputes in the 2012/2013 year (see FOS, 'Annual Review 2012/2013' (n 22)).

[89] DG Internal Market and Services, 'Evaluation of FIN-NET—Final Report' (June 2009) 8.

[90] ibid 9.

[91] ibid 19.

III. Implications

A. General Implications

A serious dispute resolution system for securities transactions has to provide a high degree of certainty on its outcomes based on clear rules that are known by the parties before they engage in a transaction. In a perfect world, dispute resolution systems would operate only for enforcement of decisions, as everyone would know beforehand what the decision would be. Certainty requires institutional structures to isolate the decision maker from unwarranted external influence, be it from the political process or from parties to the dispute; yet at the same time, checks and balances are necessary to avoid the decision maker going rogue, becoming the tyrant himself.

A consequence of the need for certainty in the legal system and the dispute resolution process is the need for reasoned decisions. Legal rules may need to be interpreted due to the impossibility of having ex ante a complete set of rules that would apply seamlessly to every single situation, creating the need that for every dispute, which by definition involves uncertainty, a decision is made to clarify the status of the law. The development and functioning of the dispute resolution system based on legal mechanisms therefore also depends on reasoned decisions.

Finally, the cost of the system should be as low as possible while providing the necessary certainty for the dispute resolution process. High costs of access limit the availability of the system to those who have fewer resources, excluding them from the possibility to use formal redress mechanisms. This consequently removes confidence in the market as investors may feel helpless when facing unjust situations without having a forum for the discussion of their dispute. As lack of confidence in a market may create the lemons problem, it is better if a properly structured system is in place. There is a prior question that arises concerning the desirability of having low-asset investors in financial markets; this is not a question that this work is trying to answer. Nevertheless, to the extent that low-asset investors are included in the securities market, proper means of redress have also to be made available.

Some of the alternative systems discussed in this chapter have these characteristics. The UK FOS, for example, is free for the complainant, provides fast decisions and provides reasons for the decisions, even though the decisions are not legally justified.[92] The drawback of the system is that, with a simpler design than a full court procedure, it deals only with limited types of cases, namely those involving investors and financial intermediaries, up to the limit of £150,000.

For a dispute resolution system to be an efficient tool for transnational securities transactions, all of the characteristics discussed above and in the previous chapter

---

[92] There has been a trend towards more justification in the UK FOS decisions, but the downside is that too much formalisation may increase the amount of time necessary for a decision to be made.

have to be included in its design, so the objectives of access to justice and legal certainty can be achieved.

B. EU Implications

In respect of the cross-border provision of financial services, the European Union already has in place a solution for the transnational problem, which is the coordination of different out-of-court dispute resolution systems for financial consumer transactions. Even though this might be a very simple mechanism, it seems to be adequate for current EU needs, at least in the investor–financial intermediary type of dispute. The problems of certainty and access to the dispute resolution system would therefore have to be discussed on a case-by-case basis, depending on the EU Member State being analysed. The difference between the out-of-court settlement procedures could create distortion in competition, as the level of justice provided would differ. For example, in Italy the out-of-court dispute resolution system is not binding, while in the United Kingdom it is, as long as the consumer accepts the decision. Therefore, some kind of harmonisation and similarity in access to justice and in the consequences of the dispute resolution process are objectives that should be pursued to normalise legal redress and to guarantee a level playing field for different investors within Europe. This rationale could also be extended beyond Europe, in a global Fin-Net system, as proposed in Chapter 5.

Outside the financial consumer context, the dispute resolution method in Europe is also local, but based on national courts. The interaction among EU members' courts is done through the European international private law mechanisms, a regime that can create some legal certainty problems in transnational securities transactions, as will be explained in Chapter 10.

8

Aggregate Litigation Design

Civil procedure is a defining aspect of litigation in general. The mechanisms available to the parties and the rules of procedure are always taken into account when deciding whether to engage in litigation.

Aggregate litigation mechanisms can play an important part in the determination of what cases go forward and who is able to obtain redress for an act that caused harm to a party. The bundling of economic incentives from different parties and the enrolment of a third party in the economic benefits that may accrue from the lawsuit can unlock justice for people that would otherwise not be able to achieve it.[1] Aggregate litigation can be a particularly good solution in securities disputes, especially those involving disputes between issuer and investor and information intermediary and investor, due to the widespread effects that false or misleading information may have on the market, linking all claims by the same facts.

Procedural aspects are as important as substantive ones in the operation of the legal system; 'the mechanisms of law—what courts are to deal with which causes and subject to what conditions—cannot be dissociated from the ends that law subserves'.[2] Aggregate litigation mechanisms can be an interesting option for access to justice and the enforcement of substantive law, but their design may encounter constitutional limits based on juridical values such as fairness and due process, which vary depending on the specific legal system under consideration.

The broad questions that aggregate litigation design has to resolve are twofold: how to create proper incentives for claims to be brought forward without overburdening possible defendants due to too many unsubstantiated claims[3] and how to achieve finality on a particular dispute. Even though the focus of this book is on securities disputes, the discussion on aggregate litigation has a more general tone.

The objective of this chapter is to establish a framework to analyse aggregate litigation and understand how it can be applied to securities disputes. The chapter

---

[1] See H Erichson, 'Beyond the Class Action: Lawyer Loyalty and Client Autonomy in Non-class Collective Representation' [2003] *University of Chicago Legal Forum* 519, 576 ('By combining the stakes of many plaintiffs, collective representation provides group lawyers sufficient incentive to invest heavily in the litigation. It allows lawyers to take advantage of economies of scale, reducing the per-plaintiff cost of litigating').

[2] SB Burbank, 'The Class Action Fairness Act of 2005 in Historical Context: a Preliminary View' (2008) 156 *University of Pennsylvania Law Review* 1439, 1439.

[3] A Layton, 'Collective Redress: Policy Objectives and Practical Problems' in D Fairgrieve and E Lein (eds), *Extraterritoriality and Collective Redress* (Oxford University Press 2012) 94.

is divided into two parts: aggregate litigation design and the role of aggregate litigation in securities disputes.

I. Aggregate Litigation Design: a Framework for Analysis

Aggregate litigation mechanisms can be designed to achieve diverse goals, such as access to justice, enhancing the economy and regulation through litigation, among other means.[4] The two basic goals that aggregate litigation can accomplish are deterrence and compensation,[5] in addition to saving public resources due to widespread litigation. The discussion of this book focuses more on aggregate litigation as a means of compensation and access to justice than on deterrence; this second goal is a matter more closely related to the prevention of abuses and law enforcement—the broader regulatory design of securities regulation—than to dispute resolution and redress. Even though aggregate litigation has been around in the United States for some time, it has recently become an important topic in the European context.[6]

Conceptually, aggregate litigation is a mechanism where a decision issued by a court binds many persons. It becomes especially relevant when private claims are of so little value that no single litigant would engage in litigation to have his rights protected because it would be more expensive in respect of time and/ or money than to do nothing, as a result of the small value of the claim relative to litigation costs.[7] By allowing claims to be put together and litigated as a group, the total value of the pie increases. As long as the total value that can be recuperated is higher than the costs of bringing the suit, there are sufficient incentives for the claim to be litigated; the bigger the group of claims, the bigger the incentive. Even claims that could be litigated individually could also be grouped, as there would be more resources available for the lawsuit and the transaction costs would be proportionally smaller than if litigation was pursued on an individual basis.

---

[4] C Hodges, *The Reform of Class and Representative Actions in European Legal Systems* (Hart Publishing 2008) 187–222.

[5] C Hodges, 'Objectives, Mechanisms and Policy Choices in Collective Enforcement and Redress' in J Steele and WH Boom (eds), *Mass Justice: Challenges of Representation and Distribution* (Edward Elgar 2011) 102; G Miller, 'Compensation and Deterrence in Consumer Class Actions in the US and Europe' in F Cafaggi and HW Micklitz (eds), *New Frontiers of Consumer Protection: the Interplay Between Private and Public Enforcement* (Intersentia 2009) 264–66.

[6] See European Commission, 'Towards a European Horizontal Framework Collective Redress' (Communication) COM (2013) 401 final.

[7] This is the concept of a negative claim. See R Cooter and T Ulen, *Law and Economics* (6th edn, Addison Wesley 2016) 388–91.

So far, there are two main actors that can be identified in the plaintiff's side: the owners of the claims that will be grouped and the agent that will coordinate the litigation efforts on the part of the plaintiffs.

This second player on the plaintiff's side of the aggregate litigation game, the one who may benefit from the lawsuit in addition to the claim owners, constitutes a necessary piece of the puzzle as claimants themselves would otherwise have no interest in pursuing litigation due to its cost.[8] This player might have a private role, seeking profit from the activity, or a public one, seeking to correct a wrongful act or be in charge of enforcing the law. Its role can be either to coordinate the lawsuit and seek the most appropriate redress for the case or to provide funding when necessary, sometimes both.

On the private side, this can either be a lawyer, who will receive money from the service performed for the group, or a third-party funder, who will provide money for the costs of the lawsuit. The incentives can be either the return on the investment from the lawsuit, or the sense of duty performed if the party is an association that has as its mission the defence of a particular group.[9]

Depending on the identification of the manager/financier of the litigation and the different interest positions of group members, different conflicts of interest may arise. The first aspect of an aggregate litigation design revolves around the incentives of the parties to bring the claim forward, the costs of the lawsuit and the conflicts between those different players. Within this context, there are additional concerns that come into play as the financial aspect is not the only one that influences the possibilities of aggregate litigation. Ethical rules of the legal profession can also limit the schemes that can be designed for aggregate litigation and for financing incentives.

The second consideration, closely tied to the first, concerns whether the mechanism of aggregation will be an opt-in mechanism or an opt-out one. An opt-in mechanism requires each claimant to express their desire to participate in the lawsuit and to be bound by it, while the opt-out procedure binds absent claimants without their consent. This characteristic of the opt-out procedure also has implications for conflict-of-interest analysis, but this option is not available to every single legal system due to constitutional limitations.[10]

Due to this, aggregate litigation differs widely in practice, especially when contrasting the American class action system with civil law systems; notwithstanding, the underlying problems that these systems are designed to solve are similar. This section analyses the conflicts in the relationships among the different parties

---

[8] This is part of the collective action problem, where even though it is beneficial for the members of a group to act in conjunction to achieve their own common goal, they fail to do so. See generally M Olson, *The Logic of Collective Action: Public Goods and the Theory of Groups* (Harvard University Press 1971).

[9] The availability of these mechanisms is highly jurisdiction specific due to differences in procedural law and ethical standards for lawyers.

[10] Opt-out procedures are allowed in some common law jurisdictions such as the US, Canada and Australia. See R Mulheron, *The Class Action in Common Legal Systems* (Hart Publishing 2004) 5–15.

involved in aggregate litigation, ethical limitations on aggregate litigation and the limitations on choosing the opt-in or opt-out character of the mechanism. This section does not attempt to exhaustively cover the subject, but only to give a broad overview of the main issues that are present in aggregate litigation design and its possible limitations.

A. Conflicts in Aggregate Litigation

The purpose of an aggregate litigation system is to allow for litigation that otherwise would not exist due to cost/benefit constraints, or at least improve the economies of scale of it. Due to the inherent tensions of agency–principal relationships, exacerbated by the multiple claimants setting, aggregate litigation presents a wide array of conflict-of-interest problems.[11]

These conflicts can be divided into three groups: conflicts between the lawyer and plaintiffs, conflicts within the group and conflicts involving third-party financiers.

i. Conflicts Between Plaintiffs and Lawyer

The role of lawyers in legal disputes is to advise what the best course of action for a particular problem is and to represent the client in litigation if necessary. To perform this role, lawyers expect to be compensated; there is a wide array of different schemes that can be designed for this purpose. The commonly used schemes are the contingency fee, the hourly rate and the fixed sum.

In the contingency fee[12] arrangement, the lawyer is paid a part of plaintiff's recovery, becoming directly interested in a high outcome for the client. Even though their interests seem to be aligned, the alignment is not a complete one when a settlement possibility is introduced into the equation. If lawyers have the power to settle, they may be tempted to settle early to avoid costs of litigating, even though litigation might be more economically efficient to the client.[13]

---

[11] See J Steele and WH Boon, 'Mass Justice and Its Challenges' in J Steele and WH Boon (eds), *Mass Justice: Challenges of Representation and Distribution* (Edward Elgar 2011); on conflicts regarding the class action, see G Miller, 'Conflicts of Interest in Class Action Litigation: an Inquiry into the Appropriate Standard' [2003] *University of Chicago Legal Forum* 581, 581–90; more generally on the conflict of interest problems, see J Armour, H Hansmann and R Kraakman, 'Agency Problems and Legal Strategies' in R Kraakman, J Armour and L Enriques (eds), *The Anatomy of Corporate Law: a Comparative and Functional Approach* (2nd edn, Oxford University Press 2009); on the conflict-of-interest problems when there is legal representation by a public officer, see M Lemos, 'Aggregate Litigation Goes Public: Representative Suits by State Attorneys General' (2012) 126 *Harvard Law Review* 486.

[12] For some examples of where the contingency fee arrangement is allowed, see HM Kritzer, *Risks, Reputations, and Rewards: Contingency Fee Legal Practice in the United States* (Stanford Law and Politics 2004) 258–59.

[13] See G Miller, 'Some Agency Problems in Settlements' (1987) 16 *Journal of Legal Studies* 189, 198–202. The author in this article explains that any system besides the contingency fee system, where the plaintiff has control over settlement, tends to be non-optimal.

In the hourly fee arrangement the lawyer will sell his time and work by the hour, receiving a fee according to the amount of time that was dedicated to the case. This scheme does not combine with lawyer control for settlement, as the lawyers will have the incentive to go to trial to spend as many hours as possible working on the case.[14]

Finally, in the fixed sum agreement, the lawyer will receive what has been agreed in the contract with the client, regardless of the outcome of the case; the lawyer has the incentive to work as little as possible for the benefit of the client, settling at the first possible opportunity.

As long as the plaintiff has an important stake in the litigation and the information asymmetry between lawyer and plaintiff is low, the selection of the compensation scheme will not be a very important problem as both parties will be able to strike a deal that is in their best interest. Conflict-of-interest problems start to become serious when the monitoring power of plaintiff(s) over lawyer diminishes.

This is the case in situations where aggregate litigation is most adequate, as plaintiffs tend to be less well informed[15] and have a weakened lawyer–client relationship due to the number of similar cases that lawyers are handling and the small interest of each client compared to the overall amount at stake.[16] To a certain extent, market incentives take care of this problem. As these tend to be claims that would not be pursued by each claimant alone, it is unlikely that they would be willing to pay up front for litigation or commit to pay an hourly fee to the lawyer by whom they are being represented, leaving the contingency fee as the lawyer compensation scheme of choice, which aligns the interest of lawyers with those of claimants, even though not perfectly.[17] The decision of the lawyer in taking a case in these circumstances will depend on the profit that he will make; this is a function of the number of claims he can aggregate and the percentage he would be able to take home, which depends on the availability of an opt-out mechanism and on ethical obligations, regarding both solicitation and the manner in which the lawyer can charge the clients.

ii. Conflicts Between Group Members

Different group members may have different interests, economic or personal, even if the claims are based on the same factual circumstances giving rise to liability.

---

[14] ibid 203–04.

[15] The information asymmetry comes from the fact that lawyers will understand better the chances of success of the lawsuit, whether due to their legal experience or due to their knowledge of the facts surrounding the case.

[16] See EC Burch, 'Litigating Together: Social, Moral, and Legal Obligations' (2011) 91 *Boston University Law Review* 87, 97 ('Moreover, although aggregating clients makes litigation economically viable and more efficient, it makes effective client monitoring nearly impossible').

[17] The litigation becomes a joint venture where the lawyer assumes the costs and shares the benefits of the outcome, becoming the agent and the creditor of the clients at the same time, which creates an incentive to pay attention to stronger cases and settle quickly weaker cases. See ibid 97–98.

An example of diverse economic interests in securities litigation can be seen in a case where false or misleading statements were used to inflate the securities price and in which, at later moments, there are various securities price drops after several curative disclosures made during an extended period of time. In this situation, there will be a difference of interest between those who bought the security after one of these disclosures and those who sold it.[18] While buyers will want to maximise price inflation in the litigation so that they will receive more due to the stock price decrease, sellers will want to minimise it since this will also maximise their recovery.[19]

Interests may also differ depending on the cohesion and goals of the individuals that may be part of the group, which leads to different perspectives and expectations about the autonomy of the lawsuit and its outcome, having consequences in respect of how the solutions for aggregate litigation should be designed regarding procedural fairness. Between the two extremes of individual litigation and class litigation (opt-out procedure), the concepts of individual-within-the-collective and group-oriented individuals can be used as a basis for the discussion.[20] While in the first claimants are strongly tied due to overlapping egocentric interests and/or joint intent,[21] in the second they are mainly self-interested but might have advantages in terms of acting collectively.[22]

In this second case, plaintiffs may have different approaches in respect of how they would prefer to pursue the case and as to their different risk tolerances; this would lead to different strategies for each plaintiff. The problem is that to profit from the lawsuit collectivisation, some of the plaintiffs would have to give away their autonomy and their preferences to be able to participate in the process.[23] When designing aggregate litigation procedures, these differences have to be taken into consideration, allowing different groups to exercise their different preferences.

iii. Third-Party Financiers

One recent development in the legal market that has been getting increasing academic attention is the use of third-party financiers to finance litigation. Third-party financing has the advantage of dismantling the double role that lawyers play—as both financier and agent—in many procedures of aggregate litigation, while it also engages a more sophisticated party and someone with more at stake in the litigation to monitor the lawyers;[24] moreover, it broadens the opportunities

---

[18] This example is based on *Seagate Technology II Securities Litigation*, 843 F Supp 1341 (ND Cal 1994).

[19] See Miller (n 11) 594.

[20] EC Burch, 'Procedural Justice in Nonclass Aggregation' (2009) 44 *Wake Forest Law Review* 1, 11–24.

[21] ibid 16.

[22] ibid 20.

[23] ibid 22.

[24] EC Burch, 'Financiers as Monitors in Aggregate Litigation' (2012) 87 *New York University Law Review* 1273, 1277.

for costly litigation to proceed when lawyers are not comfortable enough to risk their assets in a specific case.

The downside of a third-party financier is that another party is added to the already complex conflict-of-interest matrix that is present in litigation. One of the practices of consumer litigation lenders is to lend money on a non-recourse basis, having only the outcome of the litigation as the source of future repayment.[25] In one case a third-party financier provided U$200,000 to a plaintiff expecting to receive U$600,000 plus a percentage of the recovery; this led the plaintiff to reject a U$1 million offer to settle.[26] The lawyers were not pleased, as they were going to be paid on a contingency fee basis, and sued the financing company.[27]

Moreover, in these schemes, even though the lawyer loses some of the conflicts that were present before as a result of the contingency fee system, these conflicts are simply transported to the financier, who will have similar incentives as the lawyer to suggest a quick settlement. The lawyer would then have a divided loyalty to the client, whom he is supposed to represent, and the financier, who is a repeat player and might bring more business to the lawyer.

In any event, the use of external litigation finance may be beneficial. For example, Professor Molot suggests that allowing third-party finance empowers plaintiffs by providing alternatives to settlement with the defendant, creating a market for claims that would increase the efficiency of settlements by allowing transactions that would reflect to a greater extent the merits of the case than simply the bargaining power of the parties.[28]

iv. Conflicts in an Opt-out Procedure

The most famous system of an opt-out procedure is the American class action. In an opt-out procedure the concerns about conflicts of interest are even more acute than in opt-in aggregate litigation since the decision of the court binds absent parties, some of whom would not even know they are involved in litigation or that they could be bound by it. The legitimacy of the decision becomes the central problem in these mechanisms.

The legitimacy of a judicial decision is usually guaranteed because the parties to a dispute have the right and opportunity to participate in the judicial process, presenting its case and defending it in front of an impartial judge, who will issue a reasoned decision. The guarantee of someone's 'day in court'[29] is one of the tenets of the principle of the due process of law, legitimating the final decision reached

---

[25] Other practices can be commercial lending, also recovering the investment from the outcome of the lawsuit, or lending money to law firms involved in litigation at high interest rates. See ibid 1301–04.

[26] See *Weaver, Bennett & Bland, PA v Speedy Bucks, Inc,* 162 F Supp 2d 448 (WDNC 2001).

[27] ibid.

[28] See J Molot, 'Litigation Finance: a Market Solution to a Procedural Problem' (2010–2011) 99 *Georgetown Law Journal* 65.

[29] In the US, the Supreme Court was explicit about the right to a 'day in court' in *Martin v Wilks,* 490 US 755, 762 (1989).

by the court.[30] Parties consent to being represented by a lawyer of their choice and to engaging in litigation.

The central added value of the opt-out procedure mechanism is exactly the absence of this guarantee, binding persons that were not part of the judicial proceeding. This increases the economic benefits of aggregation since all of those who have a similar case will be bound by the decision.[31]

The same conflicts of interest that are present in normal aggregate litigation are also present in opt-out procedures, such as collusion between class counsel and defendants, leading to unfair settlement agreements.[32] The important background question to the opt-out procedure, which has a link with the operation of preclusion principles, is how a judicial decision can legitimately bind someone who has not participated in the proceedings.

Operationally, the answer lies in the use of alternative legitimating mechanisms, which, in the classic class action/corporate governance literature, are typified as voice, exit and loyalty.[33] At its core, this is a governance design problem,[34] which involves the main players of the civil justice system and their incentives to act.[35] In the United States, contrary to other common principal–agent situations that are extensively regulated by legal standards and have legitimacy mechanisms to control the agent's behaviour, such as in corporate law and bankruptcy law, in the opt-out procedure context they are either lacking or are inadequate to address the conflict issues that arise.[36]

From a normative perspective, the bases for legitimising a decision for a person that has not had their 'day in court' are consent, majoritarian control, prior

---

[30] The right to be heard guaranteeing the legitimacy of a judicial decision may even have constitutional status in some countries. The Brazilian Constitution, for example, provides that 'the law won't exclude from judiciary appreciation a harm or threat to a right' (art 5 XXV) and 'no one will be deprived of liberty or property without due process' (art 5 LIV) (trans by the author). See also *Phillips Petroleum Co v Shutts*, 472 US 797 (1985).

[31] See *Mace v Van Ru Credit Corp*, 109 F3d 338, 344 (7th Cir 1997) ('The policy at the very core of the class action mechanism is to overcome the problem that small recoveries do not provide the incentives for any individual to bring a solo action prosecuting his or her rights. A class action solves this problem by aggregating the relatively paltry potential recoveries into something worth someone's (usually an attorney's) labor').

[32] See DR Hensler and TD Rowe, 'Beyond "It Just Ain't Worth It": Alternative Strategies for Damages Class Action Reform' (2001) 64 *Law and Contemporary Problems* 137, 138 ('some defendants who face stronger claims may seek out plaintiffs' attorneys who are willing to settle such claims at less than their true value in exchange for fees that arguably are more generous than they deserve, given what they have obtained for their class clients').

[33] See JC Coffee, 'Class Action Accountability: Reconciling Exit, Voice and Loyalty in Representative Litigation' (2000) 100 *Columbia Law Review* 370; AO Hirschman, *Exit, Voice, and Loyalty: Responses to Decline in Firms* (Harvard University Press 1970).

[34] See S Issacharoff, 'Governance and Legitimacy in the Law of Class Actions' [1999] *Supreme Court Review* 337.

[35] DR Hensler, *Class Action Dilemmas: Pursuing Public Goals for Private Gains* (RAND Institute for Civil Justice, 1999) 8–23.

[36] See Coffee (n 33) 376 (criticising the governance mechanisms to reduce agency costs identified by Jensen and Meckling as inadequate in the class action context); see also MC Jensen and WH Meckling, 'Theory of the Firm: Managerial Behavior, Agency Costs and Ownership Structure' (1976) 3 *Journal of Financial Economics* 305.

association/community of interests and homogeneous preferences.[37] The strength of these bases varies and is dependent on the circumstances. The strongest is consent; someone who consented to participate in a proceeding knowing beforehand that the results of it will have concrete effects will be more likely to accept the decision as legitimate.[38] The prior association/community of interests basis may be more appropriate as a normative argument to bind a community that share the same interests, inherent in the status of the group.[39] The majoritarian control basis is either linked to consent, through a contractual framework where a representative entity is created, or other policy goals, when the entity created for representation has a basis in statutory provisions, such as a consumer association. Finally, homogeneous preferences can be justifiable to bind absent members to the extent that their claims and preferences are in fact 'homogeneous', demonstrating that the different class members have aligned interests.

The consent basis, usually the strongest one to legitimise a judicial decision, has a lesser role in the case of the opt-out procedure; at the same time, other bases are used to make the decision more legitimate.

The logic of the benefits of aggregate litigation applies even more to the case of the opt-out procedure; as class members do not have an actual interest in pursuing the lawsuit on an individual basis due to its value or its cost, someone has to take the lead. This is a job usually done by class counsel, who acts as the propelling engine for litigation by seeking situations in which class actions could be brought and by financing them.[40] Litigation is highly expensive in the United States, and by assuming the costs, lawyers invest a significant stake in the class action,[41] frequently having a much greater interest in the outcome of the dispute than class members themselves.[42] As class members have a small stake in the dispute their incentive to monitor lawyers is also small; this often means that lawyers end up being free to act as they please.[43]

---

[37] Coffee (n 33) 380–85.

[38] The problem with consent in opt-out procedures boils down to what constitutes consent—the opt-out procedure assumes consent was given if the person has not opted-out, therefore other guarantees are built in to legitimise the decision, such as the requirement of adequate representation. ibid 381.

[39] For example, a decision binding asbestos victims only based on prior association/community of interests criteria would hardly be seen as legitimate if every single person did not consent to it or had the opportunity to participate in the proceedings, since the consequences of asbestos exposure vary greatly from victim to victim.

[40] One author explained that class actions are 'characterized by a rent-seeking entrepreneur pursuing her own interests with little oversight by her principals.' WB Rubenstein, 'On What a "Private Attorney General" Is—And Why It Matters' (2004) 57 *Vanderbilt Law Review* 2129, 2162–63.

[41] Class action lawyers have been seen as self-interested entrepreneurs for quite a long time. See JC Coffee, 'The Regulation of Entrepeneurial Litigation: Balancing Fairness and Efficiency in the Large Class Action' (1987) 54 *University of Chicago Law Review* 877.

[42] Of course, this is not always the case; many class actions involve highly emotionally charged situations—such as in asbestos litigation—in which the class representatives would clearly have an interest in the outcome of the dispute that surpasses mere economic recovery. These cases, though, tend to involver higher stakes for class members than other simpler consumer cases.

[43] See JR Macey and G Miller, 'The Plaintiffs' Attorney's Role in Class Action and Derivative Litigation: Economic Analysis and Recommendations for Reform' (1991) 58 *University of Chicago Law*

The incentives, therefore, are a clear departure from the classic representative role of the lawyer. Class counsel will perform in court with his own interests in mind rather than those of the class; therefore plaintiffs become a mere conduit for the lawyer to play his role. In many types of case this is not a serious problem since class members either accept their condition of claimants, with the possibility of receiving a small sum at the end of the litigation, or they exercise their right to opt out and receive nothing. The stakes are so low that it is not economically profitable for a claimant to pursue the claim on his own.[44] Even if lawyers are thinking about themselves and profiting more than they should be entitled to, claimants are still better off in this situation than otherwise. Legitimacy here is based both on consent and homogenous preferences[45] even though the consent basis is extremely weak.[46]

Some conflicts are specific to the opt-out procedure; these includes the 'reverse auction' practice, where there are many class actions on the same subject matter and the defendant's counsel seeks the best settlement deal by 'shopping' options among different classes' counsel.[47]

Another problem arises when members of the class, individually considered, have a stronger economic interest than the rest of the members and would prefer to pursue litigation themselves.[48] In such situations the class action mechanism shifts from being the plaintiff's sword and may become the defendant's shield.[49] As they have higher stakes, particular class members may disagree with class counsel on the direction of the lawsuit; however, depending on how far the procedure has already been developed, they may not be able to opt out. Since disagreements may occur when the procedure is more advanced and plaintiffs may not opt out anymore, class members may be precluded from litigating their rights to the fullest extent.[50] In this situation, the normative legitimacy grounds are weak; they are based solely on consent inferred from a failure to opt out at an ex ante moment when it was not clear that class counsel would not represent adequately the interests of the particular class member.

Review 1, 3 ('[P]laintiff's class and derivative attorneys function essentially as entrepreneurs who bear a substantial amount of the litigation risk and exercise nearly plenary control over all important decisions in the lawsuit').

[44] See M Gilles and GB Friedman, 'Exploding the Class Action Agency Costs Myth: the Social Utility of Entrepreneurial Lawyers' (2006–2007) 155 *University of Pennsylvania Law Review* 103, 132–36.

[45] By having a preference in receiving something rather than nothing.

[46] Consent here is based on the decision not to opt out of the class action. Of course, this presumption of consent is problematic because the parties may not have had a real chance to know the possible claims to which they might be entitled. Such justification only has some appeal in situations where claimants would not otherwise have had an interest in pursuing the claim themselves.

[47] Gilles and Friedman (n 44) 161–62.

[48] JC Coffee, 'Class Wars: the Dillemma of the Mass Tort Class Action' (1995) 95 *Columbia Law Review* 1351, 1351–52.

[49] ibid 1350.

[50] See Coffee (n 33) 419–25.

Therefore, some conflicts of interest can be present specifically in relation to the opt-out mechanism of aggregate litigation. These conflicts have to be considered so they can be addressed in any new design of an opt-out system.

B. Ethical Limitations

Aggregate litigation can be an interesting alternative for litigating securities claims and for providing access to justice to investors; however, the ways in which claims can be financed and aggregated can be drastically limited by the ethical obligations of the legal profession in different countries. Rules on champerty and maintenance,[51] client solicitation, attorney–client relationships and attorney–third-party relationships can all be impediments to the formation of a group for litigation purposes.

Champerty and maintenance rules limit how lawyers and third-parties can participate in the funding of a lawsuit and how they can influence its direction.[52] If lawyers and third parties are limited to too great an extent, no one will be willing to assume any of the risks of litigation, either because it is outright prohibited or because the control over litigation becomes too narrow and the investment becomes too risky.

Rules on client solicitation preclude lawyers, or even third parties, from searching for and engaging clients to initiate the lawsuit. This is true in Brazil, where it is forbidden for a lawyer to 'recruit or capture cases, with or without the help of a third-party'.[53] Any active attempt to amass a critical number of similar cases for litigation will be seen as an ethical violation, rendering it almost impossible for a private lawyer to pursue litigation where the value of each individual claim is low.

Other types of prohibition might also limit the compensation design that could further plaintiffs' interests in aggregate litigation; these include the prohibition on lawyers providing cash to clients for their claims and the prohibition against lawyers sharing fees with non-lawyers.[54]

I do not imply here that all of these limitations are bad, as some have their foundations in convincing policy rationales;[55] however, their existence limits mechanisms that could be used by lawyers and other third parties to stimulate

---

[51] Maintenance is the 'assistance in prosecuting or defending a lawsuit given to a litigant by someone who has no bona fide interest in the case [or] meddling in someone else's litigation' and champerty is '[a]n agreement between an officious intermeddler in a lawsuit and a litigant by which the intermeddler helps pursue the litigant's claim as consideration for receiving part of any judgment proceeds'. A Sebok, 'The Inauthentic Claim' (2011) 64 *Vanderbilt Law Review* 61, 72–73 (Citing *Black's Law Dictionary*, 9th edn, 2009).

[52] ibid 109.

[53] Brazilian Law 8.906/1994, art 34, IV (trans by the author).

[54] Molot (n 28) 109–11.

[55] For example, the prohibition on sharing fees with non-lawyers allows lawyers to remain independent of outside influence; ibid 110.

the aggregation of claims in cases that otherwise would not be litigated, opening access to justice and generating an efficient mechanism for compensation.

C. Preclusion Principles and Limits on Choosing an Opt-in or Opt-out Mechanism

Aggregate litigation can be based either on an opt-in system, where claimants express their consent to be bound by the decision by initiating the lawsuit, or an opt-out procedure, where the decision involving a class binds all members of the class even though specific consent was not given.

While an opt-in procedure guarantees each person the right over his or her claim and to be bound by the decision only if consent is expressly given to participate in the litigation, the opt-out procedure disposes of mass questions collectively and more efficiently, as it definitely resolves the dispute and binds all those that might have been involved in it, even if consent is not given.

The possibility of using one of the systems is closely tied to the operation of preclusion; each legal system has its own preferences as to what normative basis should be accepted. Common law systems are more lenient in what to accept, while civil law systems tend to be more conservative, limiting the scope of preclusion in aggregate litigation to very specific circumstances. The choice of one system or another is not only a matter of policy design. Underlying the discussion there are constitutional limits that vary widely depending on the jurisdiction; these are imposed through the operation of preclusion.

i. The Operation of Preclusion – General Aspects

Preclusion is the backbone of any legal procedure, including those of collective redress. The concept of preclusion is essential to the construction of a dispute resolution method capable of putting an end to disputes. It prevents the re-litigation of claims and issues already decided by a court, bringing stability to the relationship between the parties to a dispute. Preclusion guarantees that the parties will be able to rely on a judicial decision. A party that prevails in a claim will not have to worry about being brought to court in respect of the same disagreements over which a decision has already been rendered, providing social pacification. To understand the operation of a collective redress system and the choice between an opt-in and an opt-out procedure, a general understanding of the rules of preclusion and its limits are necessary.

The scope of preclusion varies depending on the jurisdiction, usually being more expansive in common law countries and more restricted in civil law ones, even though there have been some recent expansionist changes in the latter.[56] The

---

[56] See L Silberman, 'Preclusion Doctrine' in OG Chase and H Hershkoff (eds), *Civil Litigation in Comparative Context* (Thomson West 2007) 458; 461.

basic questions addressed by the doctrine concern who is bound by the decision and what legal questions and factual issues are encompassed by it.

There is a tension between preclusion and fairness of legal proceedings;[57] every legal system has to strike a balance between the two, especially because the second is a tenet of the rule-of-law principle.[58] This balance is usually struck through the requirements for the operation of claim preclusion, which are mutuality, identical causes of action and the existence of a judgment on the merits of the dispute.[59]

Mutuality

Fairness through the operation of preclusion is anchored in the idea that everyone should have their day in court;[60] this is one of the most basic requirements for preclusion to operate. To be bound by a judgment, a party has to be part of the litigation process; this is true both in common and in civil law systems.

In the United States, the Supreme Court explained that 'in Anglo American jurisprudence ... one is not bound by a judgment *in personam* in a litigation in which he is not designated as a party or to which he has not been made a party by service of process'.[61]

In the EU context, the right to a fair trial is enshrined both in the Charter of Fundamental Rights of the European Union,[62] which since the Treaty of Lisbon[63] has had the same value as the EU Treaties,[64] and in the European Convention on Human Rights. The Convention establishes that 'everyone is entitled to a fair and public hearing within a reasonable time by an independent and impartial tribunal established by law';[65] this comprises the right of access to a court, even though this right can be limited.[66] This is important because all the countries that are members of the Council of Europe are also party to the Convention, and soon the European Union itself will accede to it,[67] submitting to the jurisdiction of the European Court of Human Rights. Therefore, the idea of a fair trial, as developed both under

---

[57] ED Cavanagh, 'Issue Preclusion in Complex Litigation' (2009–2010) 29 *The Review of Litigation* 859, 870–71.

[58] Maintaining the rule of law is essential to fair dispute resolution, but from the state's perspective it is even more so, since the rule of law is one of the bases of the legitimacy of the state's authority. See Ch 2.

[59] Cavanagh (n 57) 862.

[60] *Richards v Jefferson County*, 517 US 793, 803 (1996).

[61] ibid 798, citing *Hansberry v Lee*, 311 US 32, 40 (1940).

[62] Charter of Fundamental Rights of the European Union [2012] OJ C326/391, art 47.

[63] Treaty of Lisbon [2007] OJ C307/01.

[64] Consolidated Version of the Treaty on European Union [2012] OJ C326/15 (TEU), art 6(1).

[65] Convention for the Protection of Human Rights and Fundamental Freedoms (European Convention on Human Rights, as amended), Art 6(1).

[66] This is not an absolute right; the European Court of Human Rights will evaluate whether the limitations pursue a legitimate aim, whether there is a reasonable relationship of proportionality between the means employed and the aim sought to be achieved, and whether they restrict or reduce the access of the individual in a way that the very essence of his right is impaired. See *Ashingdane v the United Kingdom* (1985) Series A no 93, para 57; *Tinnelly & Sons Ltd and Others and McElduff and Others v the United Kingdom* ECHR 1998-IV, para 72.

[67] TEU, art 6(2), mandates the EU to accede to the European Convention on Human Rights.

the Charter and the Convention, becomes an important concept regarding the extent to which the mutuality principle may be weakened in the design of aggregate litigation procedures.

The Brazilian Civil Procedure Code clearly states that a judicial decision on the merits creates *res judicata* for the parties in respect of whom it is issued, not benefiting or harming third parties.[68] The same is true in the Spanish Act of Civil Procedure.[69]

By requiring that in order to be bound by a judgment the parties are present at a legal proceeding, the law guarantees that both parties will be heard and will be able to present their case, engaging in a fair dispute in front of a judge. As will be demonstrated, there are many instances in which this requirement has been relativised, especially in the United States.

Identity of Causes of Action

Generally, a cause of action can be understood as comprising the facts that are legally relevant and the legal reasons that give rise to a claim, both in common and civil law; however, both the theory and operation of causes of action, regarding the preclusive effects of a decision, are highly dependent on the individual legal system.

In the US system, the concept of the cause of action has suffered a transformation, shifting from one based on theories of recovery to one based on transactions. Initially, a cause of action would have been substantiated on the legal theory that was used for recovery and as such it would have been possible to raise multiple lawsuits in respect of the same factual situation, based, for example, on torts for the first lawsuit and breach of contract in the second.[70] Later, the cause-of-action concept became more practical, not only admitting, but requiring, that different theories of recovery be used in a single lawsuit when these theories are based on the same 'transaction' or factual proof at trial;[71] parties would thus be precluded from using a new theory based on the same factual circumstances for another lawsuit.[72] Therefore, the element 'identity of causes of action', for claim preclusion purposes, is nowadays based on the factual circumstances for the theories of recovery; if the circumstances are the same, there is identity of the causes of action for claim preclusion purposes.[73]

---

[68] Brazilian Law 13.105/2015 (Brazilian Civil Procedure Code), arts 502, 506.

[69] Spanish Law 1/2000 (Spanish Act of Civil Procedure), art 222.3 ('La cosa juzgada afectará a las partes del proceso en que se dicte').

[70] Cavanagh (n 57) 866–67.

[71] ibid.

[72] See § 24.1, Restatement (Second) of Judgments ('When a valid and final judgment rendered in an action extinguishes the plaintiff's claim pursuant to the rules of merger and bar, the claim extinguished includes all rights of the plaintiff to remedies against the defendant with respect to all or any part of the transaction, or series of connected transactions, out of which the action arose').

[73] Cavanagh (n 57) 867; Restatement (Second) of Judgments § 24 (1982); See also *O'Brien v City of Syracuse*, 429 NE 2d 1158, 1159 (NY 1981) ('once a claim is brought to a final conclusion, all other claims arising out of the same transaction or series of transactions are barred, even if based on different theories or if seeking a different remedy'); *Farmers High Line Canal v City of Golden*, 975 P 2d 189, 203 (1999) ('Furthermore, "[t]he best and most accurate test as to whether a former judgment is a bar

The Brazilian system has gone through a recent change; even though the cause of action is considered to be the facts and legal arguments giving rise to the claim of the lawsuit,[74] article 508 of the Brazilian Civil Procedure Code states that 'when a decision on the merits becomes final, all the allegations and defences that a party could have used to grant or deny the claim are considered presented and repealed'.[75] The exact limits of this article are still being debated, especially regarding its effects on claimants.[76] The majority of Brazilian authors understand that the preclusive effect does not encompass all causes of action that could have been used for a given claim, but only the ones that were effectively raised in the lawsuit.[77] Therefore, a change either in the facts or legal reasons would create a new cause of action, avoiding preclusion.[78]

The Spanish system, on the other hand, uses the concept of the actual and virtual object of the civil procedure, enshrined in article 400.1 of the Spanish Act of Civil Procedure, which states that 'when what is claimed in a lawsuit can be based in different facts or different legal theories or titles, all of them will be deemed pleaded at the time of the request, without their use being admissible in a later lawsuit'.[79]

Therefore, the definition of the cause of action and what causes of action a decision encompasses for preclusion purposes vary; this also has consequences for collective redress mechanisms. A more encompassing theory guarantees greater efficiency and protection to the defendant, while a less encompassing theory allows the claimant to sue over and over again for the same claim, on the basis of facts and legal reasons that could have been used in the first procedure.

Judgment on the Merits

A judgment on the merits of the dispute is nothing more than a decision over the substantive portion of the claim made by the plaintiff. Generally, decisions that are not on the merits of the dispute, such as those related to lack of jurisdiction, do not have preclusion effects.[80] There are exceptions, such as the issue preclusion in the United States and the decisions on prejudicial issues in Brazil.[81]

---

in subsequent proceedings ... is whether the same evidence would sustain both, and if it would the two actions are the same, and this is true, although the two actions are different in form." *Pomponio v Larsen*, 80 Colo 318, 321 (1926)').

[74] Brazilian Civil Procedure Code, art 319, III.

[75] Brazilian Civil Procedure Code, art 508 (trans by the author) ('[t]ransitada em julgado a decisão de mérito, considerar-se-ão deduzidas e repelidas todas as alegações e as defesas que a parte poderia opor tanto ao acolhimento quanto à rejeição do pedido').

[76] DAA Neves, *Manual de Direito Processual Civil* (8th edn, Juspodivm 2016) 810–811.

[77] F Didier, PS Braga and RA Oliveira, *Curso de Direito Processual Civil—Teoria da Prova, Direito Probatório, Decisão, Precedente, Coisa Julgada e Tutela Provisória*, vol 2 (11th edn, Juspodivm 2016) 563.

[78] Neves (n 76) 810.

[79] See AO Santos and IDP Gimenez, *Derecho Procesal Civil: El Proceso de Declaracion* (3rd edn, Editorial Universitaria Ramon Areces 2004) 71–75.

[80] See Cavanagh (n 57) 867; Brazilian Civil Procedure Code, art 486; Spanish Act of Civil Procedure, art 222.2.

[81] Brazilian Civil Procedure Code, art 503 §1°.

ii. Types and Scope of Preclusion

The scope of preclusion delineates the matters that a judgment will cover and prohibits re-litigation. It is the last calibration element between the efficiency and fairness of the legal system as it defines the aspects of the dispute that will be definitively resolved. Here the difference between the common law and the civil law is considerable.

In the United States preclusion can be separated in two groups, claim preclusion and issue preclusion.

The notion of claim preclusion can be dissected into the common law doctrines of bar and merger. When a plaintiff is successful in a lawsuit, the claim merges into the judgment and the plaintiff is then not allowed to pursue another lawsuit with the same claim.[82] On the other hand, if the plaintiff loses the litigation, his claim is extinguished and the judgment acts as a 'bar' to him.[83] In practice this means that when litigation comes to an end the plaintiff is not allowed to start another lawsuit based on the same claim, whether the previous lawsuit was successful or not. The doctrine operates throughout the court systems of the United States, in the sense that a claim unsuccessfully pursued in a federal court may not be re-litigated in a state court. This is an important characteristic of the doctrine since the American legal system has a wide variety of court structures existing throughout the country, each of which might differ from the other due to the political design of the American state.[84]

Issue preclusion, on the other hand, is narrower than claim preclusion and prohibits only the re-litigation of 'an issue of fact or law necessary to [a court's] judgment'.[85] The issue will be barred from being discussed in another lawsuit based on different causes of action between the same parties.

In the European context, where there are many different legal systems operating and interacting with one another under EU law, *res judicata* has also been recognised as an important principle.[86] Courts do not have to review a final decision adopted in breach of EU law unless, under their own national law, they have the

---

[82] See *Kasper Wire Works, Inc v Leco Eng'g & Mach, Inc*, 575 F 2d 530, 535–36 (5th Cir 1978) ('When the plaintiff obtains a judgment in his favor, his claim "merges" in the judgment; he may seek no further relief on that claim in a separate action').

[83] ibid ('Conversely, when a judgment is rendered for a defendant, the plaintiff's claim is extinguished; the judgment then acts as a "bar"').

[84] See *Baker v General Motors Corp*, 522 US 222, 233 (1998) ('A final judgment in one State, if rendered by a court with adjudicatory authority over the subject matter and persons governed by the judgment, qualifies for recognition throughout the land. For claim and issue preclusion (*res judicata*) purposes, in other words, the judgment of the rendering State gains nationwide force').

[85] See *Kremer v Chem Constr Corp*, 456 US 461, 466 fn6 (1982).

[86] Case C-234/04 *Rosmarie Kapferer v Schlank & Schick GmbH* [2006] ECR I-2585, para 20 ('attention should be drawn to the importance, both for the Community legal order and national legal systems, of the principle of res judicata. In order to ensure both stability of the law and legal relations and the sound administration of justice, it is important that judicial decisions which have become definitive after all rights of appeal have been exhausted or after expiry of the time limits provided for in that connection can no longer be called into question ((Case C-224/01 *Köbler v Republik Österreich* [2003] ECR I-10239, para 38)').

power to do so.[87] Generally, under the Brussels/Lugano regime, the extension of the claim preclusion effect will be according to the rules of the country where the judgment was made, but this depends on the approach taken by each Member State.[88]

In the civil law countries under study, preclusion effects are deployed through their own doctrine of *res judicata*, which can be explained through two different aspects: the formal *res judicata*, having its effects within the legal procedure, and the material *res judicata*, which extends the effects of the decision beyond the boundaries of the procedure.

The formal *res judicata* operates through the immutability of the decision within the process due to the impossibility of appeal, either because the law does not allow for such an appeal or because the party that had the right to appeal did not launch it in due time or decided not to appeal.[89] It is related not to the effects of the decision, but to the decision itself as an act of the procedure.[90]

The material *res judicata*, on the other hand, 'is the immutability of the substantial effects of a decision on the merits'.[91] As a technical legal matter, the majority of Brazilian doctrine adopts the concept of material *res judicata* as relating to the quality of the judicial decision that makes its effects immutable.[92] *Res judicata* therefore operates by precluding those affected by it from discussing the matter again following the conclusion of the process (formal *res judicata*) and protecting the effects of the decision from any further modifications (material *res judicata*).

As to the object of the lawsuit, *res judicata* operates differently in the Brazilian and the Spanish systems. In Brazil, *res judicata* is more limited and operates only in respect of the dispositive part of the judgment;[93] it does not encompass its *ratio decidendi* concerning the necessary questions underpinning the outcome of the judgment,[94] unless expressly decided by the judge and when the matter being decided is essential to the claim of the party.[95] The Spanish system, on the other

---

[87] See *Kapferer* (n 86) para 24; in the arbitration context, see Case C-126/97 *Eco Swiss China Time Ltd v Benetton International NV* [1999] ECR I-3055, para 48.

[88] See J Velden and J Stefanelli, *The Effect in the European Community of Judgments in Civil and Commercial Matters: Recognition, Res Judicata and Abuse of Process* (British Institute of International and Comparative Law 2008) 51–62.

[89] See H Theodoro, *Curso de Direito Processual Civil—Teoria Geral do Direito Processual Civil e Processo de Conhecimento*, vol 1 (Forense 2012) 558; Juan Montero Aroca, Juan Luis Gómez Colomer and Silvia Barona Vilar, *Derecho Jurisdiccional II—Proceso Civil* (Tirant Lo Blanch 2004) 468.

[90] CR Dinamarco, 'Relativizar a Coisa Julgada Material' (2001) 55/56 *Revista da Procuradoria Geral do Estado de São Paulo* 31, 36.

[91] ibid 35.

[92] See ibid 32; N Calixto and VA Marins, 'Eficácia da Sentença e Coisa Julgada Perante Terceiros' (1989) 25 *Revista da Faculdade de Direito da UFPR* 93, 94 ('Sendo um elemento imunizador dos efeitos que a sentença projecta para fora do processo e sobre a vida exterior dos litigantes, [a utilidade da coisa julgada] consiste em assegurar estabilidade a esses efeitos, impedindo que voltem a ser questionados depois de definitivamente estabelecidos por sentença não não [*sic*] mais sujeita a recurso').

[93] See Brazilian Civil Procedure Code, art 489 III; art 504, I.

[94] The exception to this would be if a contrary decision would put the dispositive part of the first decision in danger. See Neves (n 76) 802–03.

[95] Brazilian Civil Procedure Code, art 503, § 1.

hand, operates differently as it extends the *res judicata* effects to the reasoning that underpins the outcome of the decision; it is thus closer to the US system of preclusion.[96]

In respect of these characteristics of the operation of preclusion, the mutuality requirement is the most important with regard to the limits on the use of the opt-out procedure.

iii. Preclusion and Non-Mutual Parties: Possibility of the Opt-out Procedure

The starting point for the subjective limits of preclusion is the mutuality requirement, which is cornerstone of this institution. The mutuality requirement is justifiable because, as a matter of due process and fairness, parties that did not have an opportunity to present their case or to defend themselves should not be bound by a decision. As is common with rules, for this particular one there also are exceptions, which vary widely depending on the relevant jurisdiction.

United States

In the United States, exceptions to the mutuality requirement vary depending on the type of preclusion being discussed. There are six exceptions[97] that can be reduced into three groups: the agreement of a non-party to be bound by a judgment to which it is not a party, a legal relationship between the party that was party to the previous judgment and the non-party suffering its preclusion effects, and finally, statutory schemes giving preclusive effects in respect of non-parties to a judgment, as long as there are no due process violations.

In respect of issue preclusion, the discussion is slightly different. Even though parties who are not party to a judgment cannot be bound by it, the US system allows strangers to a judgment to use the decision reached in it.[98]

Issue preclusion can be used both defensively and offensively. A defensive use of preclusion occurs when a party uses a previous decision to prevent a plaintiff who was present in a previous lawsuit from pursuing his claim. The recognition

---

[96] See SC López, 'La Cobertura Actual de La Cosa Juzgada' (2009) 20 *Revista Jurídica de la Universidad Autónoma de Madrid* 67; Santos and Gimenez (n 79) 554–57.

[97] (1) 'A person who agrees to be bound by the determination of issues in an action between other is bound in accordance with the terms of his agreement' (Restatement 2nd of Judgments, § 40); (2) pre-existing substantive legal relationships between the non-mutual party to be bound and the party to the judgment, such as in the assignor–assignee relationship (see *Taylor v Sturgell*, 553 US 880, 881 (2008)); (3) adequate representation may be sufficient to bind a non-party in certain limited circumstances, such as the class action (see *Martin* (n 29) 762); (4) assuming control over litigation in which the judgment was rendered is also a way of being bound by the decision (see *Montana v United States*, 440 US 147 (1979)); (5) a lawsuit through proxy is also preclusive—in other words, a person who brings a lawsuit as an agent or representative of a party bound by a previous decision also suffers its preclusive effects (see *Taylor* (above) 881); and (6) when a statutory scheme that does not violate due process is sufficient to 'foreclose successive litigation by non-litigants (see *Martin* (n 29) 762). This categorisation can be found in *Taylor* (above).

[98] Cavanagh (n 57) 869.

of its use in federal courts was made in the *Blonder-Tongue Laboratories, Inc v University of Illinois Foundation* case,[99] where the Supreme Court overruled the holding of *Triplett v Lowell*[100] 'that a determination of patent invalidity is not *res judicata* against the patentee in subsequent litigation',[101] allowing the defendant to use a prior determination in a judgment where only the plaintiff was a party, against the plaintiff himself. The rationale for the decision was that '[i]n any lawsuit where a defendant, because of the mutuality principle, is forced to present a complete defence on the merits to a claim which the plaintiff has fully litigated and lost in a prior action, there is an arguable misallocation of resources'.[102] Therefore, the question of allowing estoppel against a plaintiff would rest on the determination of whether the plaintiff had 'a full and fair opportunity to litigate' the issue.[103]

The offensive use of preclusion for non-mutual parties is also possible, but it has more complications than its defensive counterpart. *Parklane Hosiery Co v Shore*[104] was a stockholder's class action in which the claim was made that the corporation and its officers had issued false and misleading statements in violation of the Federal Securities Act. While the class action was ongoing the SEC brought suit against the same defendants regarding the same issue of facts, and after a non-jury trial, the case was decided in favour of the SEC. The plaintiffs in the stockholder's action moved for summary judgment, arguing collateral estoppel on the issues that had already been decided in the SEC suit; this argument was denied by the District Court, a decision which was reversed by the Court of Appeals, and the latter judgment affirmed by the Supreme Court.[105] The general rule established in the case was that

> in cases where a plaintiff could easily have joined in the earlier action or where, either for the reasons discussed above or for other reasons, the application of offensive estoppel would be unfair to a defendant, a trial judge should not allow the use of offensive collateral estoppel.[106]

The textbook example of unfairness in collateral estoppel is the case where the defendant is sued for a small amount of money and does not have an incentive to defend himself vigorously and as such loses the case; thereafter, other plaintiffs linked to the same set of facts try to sue the defendant for millions of dollars and use collateral estoppel in respect of the decision in the first case.[107]

---

[99] *Blonder-Tongue Laboratories, Inc v University of Illinois Foundation*, 402 US 313 (1971).
[100] *Triplett v Lowell*, 297 US 638 (1936).
[101] *Blonder-Tongue Laboratories, Inc* (n 99).
[102] ibid 329.
[103] ibid.
[104] *Parklane Hosiery Co v Shore* 439 US 322 (1979).
[105] See ibid.
[106] ibid 331.
[107] eg *Berner v British Commonwealth Pac Airlines*, 346 F 2d 532 (2nd Cir 1965).

General Exceptions in Civil Law: Brazil and Spain

The Brazilian Civil Procedure Code clearly states that a judicial decision on the merits creates *res judicata* for the parties in respect of whom it is issued, not harming third parties.[108] The same is true for the Spanish Act of Civil Procedure.[109] Mutuality is so important that it is a constitutional guarantee.[110]

In Brazil the new Civil Procedure Code has no exceptions. In the old one, the exceptions were very specific and were related to cases where the third-party *res judicata* effect was necessary or followed from the decision itself; this was the case, for example, in matters concerning the mental state of the person. Even though there was a third-party effect, there were guarantees in place for protection. The binding effect of the decision would only operate if all those who might have an interest in the lawsuit were served with process.[111]

In Spain *res judicata* also affects successors in title and heirs, as well as those who are entitled to the right that constitutes the basis legitimating one of the parties to the lawsuit.[112] The third-party effect in the Spanish system, concerning successors and heirs, only operates if the acquisition title was formed after the lawsuit regarding the object of dispute was initiated,[113] simply protecting the party in a lawsuit from an unfair disposition of the defendant's assets. The second case regarding the application of *res judicata* to third parties arises where the condition of the person constitutes the legal question of the subject of the procedure. The operation of *res judicata* and the *erga omnes* effect of the decision is a necessary precondition for the effectiveness of the decision. For example, a person who is judged incompetent for civil acts and the consequent change in legal status derived from the decision has to be opposable to everyone, and not only in respect of the parties to the lawsuit. The *erga omnes* effect occurs only after the registration of the change of status in the civil registry, giving constructive legal notice about the status of the person to everyone.[114]

Mutuality, therefore, is a strong principle in civil law systems, to the extent that the development of a full-blown opt-out aggregate litigation procedure might be highly unlikely in such systems; nevertheless, alternatives have been created in respect of mass procedures, in particular in the consumer context.

---

[108] Brazilian Civil Procedure Code, art 508.

[109] Art 222.3 ('La cosa juzgada afectará a las partes del proceso en que se dicte').

[110] Art. 5, LV of the Brazilian Constitution guarantees litigants the right to answer (contraditório) and the right to a full defence. An article that provides a similar guarantee in the Spanish Constitution is article 24.1 ('Todas las personas tienen derecho a obtener la tutela efectiva de los jueces y tribunales en el ejercicio de sus derechos e intereses legítimos, sin que, en ningún caso, pueda producirse indefensión').

[111] Brazilian Law 5.869/1973 (Old Brazilian Civil Procedure Code), art 472.

[112] Spanish Act of Civil Procedure, art 222.3. This provision points to art 11 of the same legal text, which establishes the use of some forms of class actions for consumer disputes within the Spanish legal system.

[113] Aroca et al (n 89) 479.

[114] Spanish Act of Civil Procedure, art 222.3.

The Operation of Preclusion in Representative Actions: How the Mutuality Requirement is Circumvented in Brazil and Spain

A special topic in both Brazil and Spain is preclusion in collective litigation. As mutuality has a constitutional status, the design of collective means of redress and their effects on third parties is more limited than in the United States.

Despite this seemingly insurmountable obstacle, the Brazilian and Spanish legal systems have designed and deployed collective means of redress for some specific situations, with the most important having been developed in the consumer context; for these purposes, a workaround had to be made with regard to the operation of *res judicata*, which can be explained through the categories of collective rights created, those which have been legitimated to pursue collective actions and the mitigated effects of *res judicata*.

In Brazil there are basically three categories of collective rights: diffuse rights, collective rights and individual homogeneous rights.[115] Diffuse rights are transindividual and indivisible rights belonging to a group of unidentified people; collective rights are also trans-individual and indivisible, but the group to which they belong can be identified; finally, individual homogeneous rights belong to individuals and are divisible, albeit having a common origin.[116]

The persons authorised to launch a collective action are highly limited, even in cases of individual homogeneous rights; most of the legal entities authorised to bring such an action are public.[117] In fact, the only private entity category that could pursue a lawsuit for collective redress is associations that have been constituted for at least one year and that include within their objectives the defence of a specific public interest;[118] this would also give a public spin to its operation.

These entities are authorised to go before a court and engage in a lawsuit against a company that has violated the rights of a multitude of people, without the need for their participation in the lawsuit. As a logical matter, within the Brazilian legal system, while the *res judicata* cannot bind those who were not a party in the lawsuit, at least to the extent that it might be prejudicial to them, it will operate against the defendant. Due to this particularity there are a few different ways in which the *res judicata* will operate; this will depend on the class of rights being discussed.

Due to the nature of the diffuse types of rights, which are trans-individual, indivisible and belonging to an unidentified group of people, the *res judicata* will be *erga omnes*, unless the claim for relief is denied due to lack of evidence;[119] this is

---

[115] For an overview of the topic, see E Talamini, 'A dimensão coletiva dos direitos individuais homogêneos: ações coletivas e os mecanismos previstos no Código de Processo Civil de 2015' in H Zaneti (ed), *Coleção Repercussões do Novo CPC—Processo Coletivo*, vol 8 (Juspodivm 2016) 109–132; F Didier and H Zaneti, *Curso de Direito Processual Civil—Processo Coletivo*, vol 4 (Juspodivm 2011) 75–98.

[116] Brazilian Consumer Defence Code, art 81.

[117] Prosecutor's office, political entities (Union, States and Municipalities) and entities from the public administration. See Brazilian Law 7.347/1985, art 5°, I, II, III and IV; Brazilian Consumer Defence Code, art 82, I, II and III.

[118] Brazilian Law 7.347/1985, art 5, V; Brazilian Consumer Defence Code, art 82, IV.

[119] Brazilian Consumer Defence Code, art 103, I; Law 7.347/1985, art 16.

known as *res judicata secundum eventum probationis*.[120] In the first case, both those legitimised to pursue the lawsuit and the defendant will not be able to discuss the same matter again, while in the second, any legitimised party will be able to start another lawsuit as long as new evidence is presented. In respect of the collective type, the effect is *ultra partes*, encompassing the members of the group that has been harmed.[121] To clarify, it is important to underline that the rights in question for these kinds of actions are those with a trans-individual character, and not the individual rights of the persons who were harmed due to the transgression of a trans-individual right. For example, in air pollution cases, the group of persons living close to a factory have a right to clean air, but the harm that they may suffer due to air pollution is an individual right, which is not encompassed by the concept of collective rights *lato sensu*.[122] Therefore, a decision against the individuals in these collective lawsuits does not preclude them from proceeding with their own claims arising out of the same factual circumstances.[123]

In respect of the individual homogeneous rights collective lawsuit, the *res judicata* is *secundum eventum litis*, in other words its effect depends on its outcome. If the claim for relief is accepted, the effect of the *res judicata* is *erga omnes*, and thereafter any of the individuals may execute the decision individually. On the other hand, if the claims are dismissed, even with prejudice, the individuals who have not assisted in the lawsuit may file another lawsuit for damages on an individual basis.[124] One detail to be considered is that if the lawsuit is dismissed with prejudice, the *res judicata* operates in respect of those who are legitimised to propose a collective lawsuit on the matter, therefore precluding them from starting a new collective lawsuit on the basis of the same questions.[125] This system protects the individuals from being bound by a decision against them when they were not able to participate and defend their rights, while at the same time being an effective mechanism to resolve mass disputes in the event that the decision is favourable to the plaintiffs.

Therefore, in Brazil, even though preclusion has a strong connection to the concept of mutuality, there are some exceptions that allow for third-party effects in respect of those who have not participated in the proceedings; this never operates to their detriment.

In Spain the practical effect of representative litigation can be broader than in Brazil. A group that consists of more than half of the harmed, in cases where identity can easily be ascertained, are allowed to choose a person to represent them in the lawsuit.[126] Consumer associations are also legitimised to represent

---

[120] Talamini (n 115) 114.
[121] Brazilian Consumer Defence Code, art 103, II.
[122] Diffuse and collective rights.
[123] The law is clear on this point—see Brazilian Consumer Defence Code, art 103 §1.
[124] Brazilian Consumer Defence Code, art 103 §2.
[125] International Law Association, 'Interim Report: "Res Judicata" and Arbitration' (Berlin Conference 2004) www.ila-hq.org/download.cfm/docid/446043C4-9770-434D-AD7DD42F7E8E81C6, 19.
[126] Spanish Act of Civil Procedure, arts 6.7, 7.7 and 11.2.

consumers.[127] The decision in these cases has to provide an identification of those who will benefit from the lawsuit; when the individualised determination is not possible, the characteristics and requirements to demand payment have to be made clear[128] so the individual consumers can execute the decision afterwards.[129] Also, if the decision declares a certain type of behaviour illegal, it must also declare whether there will be effects on those who have not been a party to the lawsuit.[130] Since these representative actions may have an effect on those who have not been party to the lawsuit, the Spanish system demands that notice is given either to every individual consumer when they are easily identifiable[131] or through communication channels that cover the territory where those who have been harmed may be found.[132]

iv. Preclusion in Arbitration: What Law Will Govern Its Operation?

The analysis of preclusion in arbitration should begin first at the national level. In most jurisdictions, the arbitral award will have the same preclusive effects as a judgment of a national court.[133] Within the national context, preclusion in arbitration is no more problematic than preclusion of legal decisions; as long as the award comprises the necessary requirements, it will have the effects of a judicial decision in the national jurisdiction.

The complexity of the question increases when the object of analysis is transposed to the transnational realm, as the clarity of what kind of preclusion will be applicable fades. When the dispute is transnational and arbitral awards become international, the legal infrastructure regulating them reflects such change through the applicability of the international treaties on the matter. Article III of the NY Convention[134] provides that '[e]ach Contracting State shall recognize arbitral awards as binding', implicitly imposing some kind of preclusion effects on the award, even though it does not provide any clear rule on how preclusion should operate. This 'binding' quality of an arbitral award attributed by Article III of the New York Convention is a 'constitutional statement of principle'[135] that 'impl[ies] at least equally broad principles of preclusion as those applicable to national courts judgments'.[136] Since the preclusion rules vary from jurisdiction to jurisdiction, the

---

[127] Spanish Act of Civil Procedure, art 11.
[128] Spanish Act of Civil Procedure, art 221.1.1.
[129] Spanish Act of Civil Procedure, art 519.
[130] Spanish Act of Civil Procedure, art 221.1.2.
[131] Spanish Act of Civil Procedure, art 15.2.
[132] Spanish Act of Civil Procedure, art 15.1.
[133] For an analysis of the difference between judicially confirmed and unconfirmed awards in the US, see G Born, *International Commercial Arbitration* (Kluwer Law International 2009) 2895–904; Brazilian Arbitration Law, art 31; Spanish Arbitration Act, art 43.
[134] Convention on the Recognition and Enforcement of Foreign Arbitral Awards (entered into force 07 June 1959) 330 UNTS 38 (NY Convention).
[135] Born (n 133) 2892.
[136] ibid 2893.

problem that is to be solved concerns the preclusion rule that will be applicable in a given case.

At least four possibilities are available: (a) the law of the jurisdiction where the new lawsuit is brought; (b) the law of the arbitral seat; (c) the law applicable to the arbitration agreement or to the merits of the dispute; and finally (d) international preclusion rules.[137]

Each of these possibilities has its own rationale for its applicability. The idea that *res judicata* is a procedural aspect could justify the applicability of the law in the jurisdiction where the second lawsuit is brought.[138] On the other hand, this same aspect could also be used to sustain the position that the applicable law for preclusion should be the law of the place where the award was rendered.[139] Since arbitration agreements are creatures of consent, the substantive applicable law approach to define the *res judicata* effects of an arbitral award is also justifiable.[140] Finally, the international preclusion rules approach is defended by Gary Born;[141] with the idea that preclusion effects are, in a substantial manner, private rights derived from the arbitration agreement between the parties, he argues that international preclusion principles derived from the NY Convention and from the international arbitral process should be applicable, instead of a national preclusion rule.[142]

There is no single correct solution to this question; pragmatically, both the law of the arbitral seat and the law of the enforcing forum are highly important when discussing the preclusive effects of an arbitral award. In any event, at a minimum, arbitral awards will have preclusive effects that encompass, at least, the dispositive part of the decision, generating what is known in the US system as claim preclusion. These international arbitral awards do have to be confirmed in order to have preclusion effects,[143] but once they have been confirmed, they have the same preclusive force as national court decisions.[144] In the United States, the reach of the preclusion effects of an arbitral award is broader since issue preclusion also operates,[145] even though its third-party effects are more limited than in US court decisions.[146]

---

[137] See ibid 2909–13.
[138] International Law Association (n 125) 14.
[139] A Sheppard, 'Res Judicata and Estoppel' in B Cremades and J Lew (eds), *Parallel State and Arbitral Procedures in International Arbitration* (ICC 2005) 229. Sheppard is in favour of using this approach for international arbitration (ibid 231).
[140] Sheppard has acknowledged that this has already happened in an ICC Award; ibid 230.
[141] Born (n 133) 2911–13.
[142] ibid 2912.
[143] Unconfirmed awards in the US do not have the full faith and credit of a judicial judgment as a statutory matter, but nonetheless they do have comparable preclusive effects developed under the jurisprudence of US courts. See ibid 2896–98.
[144] In the US, see *Lewis v Circuit City Stores, Inc*, 500 F 3d 1140, 1147 (10th Cir 2007).
[145] For exceptions on the application of preclusion, see Born (n 133) 2900.
[146] ibid 2901.

As the type of preclusion and its extension are important to legal certainty, the question becomes an important one that has to be considered when designing an aggregate mechanism for dispute resolution based on arbitration.

D. Final Considerations on Aggregate Litigation Design

Aggregate litigation functions as a mechanism both to enable compensation and to guarantee the application of the law.[147] The design of an aggregate litigation system has to consider the conflicts of interest that arise out of the different classes of claimants in the same legal procedure, the conflicts with legal counsel and the conflicts with third-party financiers, if they will be a part of the system.

In addition, the design must engage the limitations of the legal system in which the aggregate mechanism has to be applicable. Constraints of both ethical and procedural nature, which sometimes are tied to constitutional principles, may limit the range of options that are available. Procedural constraints on preclusion become an especially important topic when the dispute is transposed to the trans-national realm.[148]

II. Aggregate Dispute Resolution and Securities Disputes

Throughout this chapter it has been established that one of the purposes of aggregate litigation is to provide economies of scale to facilitate litigation that otherwise would not be initiated due to the costs or low value of the claims at stake, in addition to facilitating the management of claims by courts and ensuring the application of the law. Aggregate litigation, therefore, is a manner of pursuing redress in respect of claims that otherwise would not be litigated, thus providing access to justice.

Aggregate dispute resolution design has to consider the incentives of the parties who will be part of the process; at the same time, it is important that in such design, consideration is given to the ethical and procedural limits relevant in specific jurisdictions. As a result of the different approaches of different legal systems, a one-size-fits-all solution may not be achievable. In any event, it is important to understand those situations in which aggregate litigation can be used with securities disputes. As shown in Chapter 4, in the securities context there are three main

---

[147] See Layton (n 3) 93–96.
[148] The transnational problems will be addressed more extensively in Ch 10.

different types of dispute: investor–issuer, investor–financial intermediary and investor–informational intermediary.

Each of these disputes has their intrinsic characteristics, and some can benefit much more from an aggregate litigation approach than others. Aggregate litigation is only adequate where there are similar issues between the members of the group; otherwise, managing such a procedure would become impossible. In the securities context, disputes that have this characteristic are those that involve one act which has consequences for a multitude of persons, such as a false or misleading statement made by an issuer or the issuing of a credit rating made with minimum regard for the fundamentals of the investment. In these cases, disputes concerning both the falsity of the statement and the lack of fundamentals of a rating would greatly benefit by being resolved in an aggregate manner, since the question would be applicable to all those that were harmed by the statement or the rating.[149] This is most likely to occur in relation to investor–issuer and investor–informational intermediary disputes.

The other type of dispute—investor–financial intermediary—is unlikely to benefit from an aggregate procedure. The transaction between an investor and a financial intermediary is highly personal; the duties of the financial intermediary, such as the duty to assess the suitability of the investment, is so linked to the personal characteristics of the investor that it would be highly unlikely that an aggregate procedure would provide any benefit, even if the same practice creating harm has been employed with different clients.

Another consideration is that aggregate litigation procedures are national, tied to specific jurisdictions and thus lacking a very strong transnational appeal. Class or aggregate arbitration could be a possible solution to transnationalise aggregate dispute resolution solutions.

In respect of the disputes discussed previously, the likelihood of creating a class arbitration system is higher from the first to the last type of dispute due to their intrinsic characteristics. The first relationship arises out of the purchase or sale of a security, the most common types of which are shares of a company. Even though the harm has to arise out of a purchase or sale of securities, the link tying the buyer or holder to the company issuing the fraudulent statement is based on the shareholder–company legal relationship. To this extent, an arbitration agreement with a class arbitration provision could be inserted into the corporate charters of companies, which would bind all those who have a claim arising out of the shareholder relationship, even if it is based on the violation of securities law. In addition, the class aspect is stronger than in the other two types of dispute because there is an aspect to the shareholder–company relationship that is absent in those disputes,

---

[149] Causation and individual damages may have to be litigated individually; nonetheless, the question of whether the information was false or the rating had no fundamentals to back it up still is a common issue for the class.

namely the fact that every single shareholder has something in common with the others—the company. If they are similarly situated, they could be considered as a class or as members of a group.[150]

The second set of disputes is the one in which investors sue the intermediaries buying or selling securities from them. The basis for arbitration would be the contractual agreement between investor and intermediary, and here the consumerist aspect of the relationship is much more relevant than in the previous case, which may prevent the use of arbitration in some countries.[151] Even if arbitration is allowed, the use of class arbitration still encounters other barriers. While the use of contracts of adhesion might be common, creating a single legal matrix for disputes with different customers, the relationships are mainly bilateral, and as mentioned above, the class aspect that is present in shareholder–company relationships is missing in this type of dispute. It is also highly unlikely that intermediaries would include a class arbitration clause in their contracts and set up a mass arbitration system so their customers could pursue their claims collectively, since a piecemeal approach to litigation would most likely reduce their costs in dispute settlement due to the transaction costs faced by single plaintiffs bringing arbitration claims against them.

Finally, the last type of dispute would involve investors against informational intermediaries, when the latter have provided false or misleading information to the market. Even though a system of aggregate litigation would be beneficial in this case, the possibility of class arbitration is even lower than in the other two types of disputes. There would be no legal basis to confer jurisdiction to an arbitral tribunal since there are no direct legal relationships between investors and the possible defendants; all of the links would have to go through the company. One way to allow for arbitration in these cases would be through the contractual arrangement between the company and the rating agencies and auditors, or through statutory provisions that could require that these kinds of disputes have to be arbitrated. In any event, strong public support for the arbitration system would be necessary for this to work.

A first look at this question would then lead to a conclusion that class arbitration in the securities area outside the United States would only be viable in cases of securities fraud where the company charter provides for class arbitration. Of course, the use of this mechanism is dependent on the inclusion of clear arbitration agreements in company charters allowing for class arbitration and structuring a system that would not deny due process to the plaintiffs, since the question of notice might be an issue that should be considered to guarantee the effectiveness

---

[150] Depending on when the securities were bought, different shareholders might have different interests according to the misleading statements that were made and the answers that the market gave to such misstatements; in any event they have a link, namely being shareholders of an enterprise, one which is not present in the other types of dispute.

[151] For example, mandatory arbitration is forbidden in consumer relationships in Brazil. Consumer Defence Code, art. 51 VII.

of the arbitral award. Therefore, outside jurisdictions that admit US-style class actions and class arbitration, the major possibility for the use of this mechanism would be one arising within the context of issuer–investor disputes, assuming that this would be an acceptable arrangement regarding public policy considerations of the jurisdiction in which the award would have to be enforced.

Having established in this chapter that there are some types of securities disputes that may benefit from an aggregate dispute resolution approach, in the next chapter I will give some examples of aggregate litigation mechanisms that currently exist, and then present more coherently in Chapter 10 the transnational questions which will subsequently be combined with those presented herein, in order to justify the model proposed in Chapter 5 for transnational dispute resolution for securities transactions.

9

Aggregate Litigation Models

The objective of this chapter is to illustrate some of the different aggregate litigation models that are available today. Broadly there are three different models of aggregate litigation: the first is the joinder of the parties in a single lawsuit, where individuals participate and have standing in the legal procedure; the second is the use of test cases, where even though each individual claimant still has standing and participates in the procedure, some cases are used to determine general common issues for those involved in litigation; finally, the last mechanism is where a representative has the legal standing for a group of people, who will be bound by the decision even though they have not participated in the procedure. This chapter provides a brief overview of the American class action, representative actions in Brazil and Spain, the Dutch Act on Collective Settlement of Mass Damages, the English Group Litigation Order, the German Capital Market Model Claims Act, and a discussion of aggregate litigation in the European Union and class arbitration.

I. The American Class Action

Conceptually, the American class action is a mechanism where one or a few persons represent a whole group with similar characteristics in a lawsuit; all of those sharing these characteristics are bound by the decision, even if they are not active participants in the proceedings.

A. A Brief History of the Class Action

Historical records show that while the class action has roots dating back as far as the twelfth century,[1] it became a more commonly used mechanism only later in the seventeenth century. At this point in time, group litigation, both in England and the United States, was used mostly to regulate relationships within social groups.[2]

---

[1] The earliest case found by Professor Yeazell is *Martin, Rector of Barkway v Parishioners of Nuthamstead*, from 1199. See SC Yeazell, 'The Past and Future of Defendant and Settlement Classes in Collective Litigation' (1997) 39 *Arizona Law Review* 687, 688.

[2] The social structure at that time was different from that which exists today, and so was the role performed by the judiciary. Aggregate litigation was the means through which a given social group would

Contrary to the modern American class action, aggregate litigation in the seventeenth century required the consent of all members of the class, a requirement that was easily achievable due to the social structures in place at the time.[3] The decisions proferred had less of an all-or-nothing character and more of a regulatory one, where the judicial system would perform a legislative function with the judgment serving as the basis for a change in the substantive law governing the relationship between the parties.[4]

In 1842, in the United States, Equity Rule 48 started governing group litigation in federal courts, even though it still was a mechanism that did not bind absent parties.[5] Despite this rule, 11 years later, in *Smith v Swormstedt*,[6] the US Supreme Court stated:

> [W]here the parties interested are numerous, and the suit is for an object common to them all, some of the body may maintain a bill on behalf of themselves and of the others; and a bill may also be maintained against a portion of a numerous body of defendants, representing a common interest.[7]

The Supreme Court, with the language used in this decision, effectively established the possibility of binding effects of class actions on absent class members, which in fact created a contradiction with Equity Rule 48[8] and generated important practical effects. From the date of this judgment until the revision of the Equity Rules, there were not only federal decisions binding absent class members based on *Smith v Swormstedt*, but also decisions based on Equity Rule 48 preserving the

claim or resist claims from its direct administrative unit. Aggregate litigation therefore was a matter of status and not of economic efficiency: not only did every single member of the group have identical rights to one another, since the relationship they had with their superiors was the same, but they were also organised as a political group, with institutions in place and communication channels with the manorial proprietor or the parishioner against whom they usually had to litigate. See SC Yeazell, 'Group Litigation and Social Context: Toward a History of the Class Action' (1977) 77 *Columbia Law Review* 866, 867, 877; GC Hazard, JL Gedid and S Sowle, 'An Historical Analysis of the Binding Effect of Class Suits' (1998) 146 *University of Pennsylvania Law Review* 1849, 1865.

[3] Groups were small and cohesive. See Yeazell (n 2) 878.

[4] ibid 882, 884. One of the first reported cases where the contours of aggregate litigation started moving towards the class action as seen today was *Brown v Vermuden* (22 Eng Rep 796 (Ch 1676)), a case from 1676, where a miner who had not been a part of previous proceedings was contesting the effects that they could have with regard to him. The court rejected the miner's claim based on the argument that, in the event that the court would not bind similarly situated parties, it would be impossible for suits of such a nature finally to come to an end.

[5] See FED R EQ 48 (1842) (repealed 1912), quoted in 42 US (1 How) lvi (1843) in DL Bassett, 'Constructing Class Action Reality' [2006] *Brigham Young University Law Review* 1415, 1433 ('Where the parties on either side are very numerous, and cannot, without manifest inconvenience and oppressive delays in the suit, be all brought before it, the court in its discretion may dispense with making all of them parties, and may proceed in the suit, having sufficient parties before it to represent all the adverse interests of the plaintiffs and defendants in the suit properly before it. But in such cases the decree shall be without prejudice to the rights and claims of all the absent parties').

[6] *Smith v Swormstedt*, 57 US 288 (1853).

[7] ibid 301.

[8] Hazard et al (n 2) 1901–02.

right of absent class members to sue, thus creating legal uncertainty.[9] In 1912 the equity rules were revised, Equity Rule 48 was repealed and the procedure to deal with aggregate litigation was incorporated into Equity Rule 38.[10] This rule did not explicitly state that class actions could be binding on absent class members but in 1921 this became clear under the new framework shaped by the Supreme Court decision of *Supreme Tribe of Ben-Hur v Cauble*.[11]

The next development of the American class action came with the Federal Rules of Civil Procedure. In 1934 the US Congress passed the Rules Enabling Act[12] giving the Supreme Court the 'power to prescribe general rules of practice and procedure and rules of evidence for cases in the United States district courts', which was duly exercised in 1938 with the promulgation of the Federal Rules of Civil Procedure. Rule 23 provided for class actions, allowing for 'persons constituting a class … so numerous as to make it impracticable to bring them all before the court'[13] to sue or be sued on behalf of all, as long as the character of the right was joint or common, the adjudication of claims forming the object of the action could affect a specific property involved in the action or there was a common question of law or facts and a common relief was sought.[14]

Even though the 1938 Rule 23 was prima facie clear, it raised many different problems, including, among others, the proper labelling of a class action, the effects arising from it,[15] the extent of the judgments in class actions and the lack of binding effect of a 'spurious' class action on non-party class members.[16] In 1966, with the revision of the Federal Rules of Civil Procedure, Rule 23 was significantly altered,[17] bringing it to its current design.

---

[9] See ibid 1902–09.

[10] Which provided that '[w]hen the question is one of common or general interest to many persons constituting a class so numerous as to make it impracticable to bring them all before the court, one or more may sue or defend for the whole', containing therefore both the 'aggregate' and 'representative' characteristics of the modern class action. JG Harkins, 'Federal Rule 23—The Early Years' (1997) 39 *Arizona Law Review* 705, 705 citing JL Hopkins, *The New Federal Equity Rules* (1930) 231. On the aggregate and representative characteristics of the class action, see Bassett (n 5) 1418–31.

[11] *Supreme Tribe of Ben-Hur v Cauble*, 255 US 356, 367 (1921) ('if the federal courts are to have the jurisdiction in class suits to which they are obviously entitled, the decree when rendered must bind all of the class properly represented').

[12] Current version at 28 USC § 2072 (2014).

[13] The text of the 1938 Rule 23 is available at 39 Federal Rules Decisions 69.

[14] These are the 'true', 'hybrid' and 'spurious' characters of the class action under the former Rule 23. See Bassett (n 5) 1434–36.

[15] T Ford, 'The History and Development of Old Rule 23 and the Development of Amended Rule 23' (1966) 32 *Antitrust Law Journal* 254, 257.

[16] For other issues that the former Rule 23 created, see the Advisory Committee's Notes on 39 Federal Rules Decisions 69.

[17] 39 Federal Rules Decisions 69.

B. Types of Class Action and Their Prerequisites

Under the current Rule 23 of the Federal Rules of Civil Procedure, the basic prerequisites of a class action are numerosity,[18] commonality,[19] typicality[20] and adequate representation.[21]

The first requirement, numerosity, is concerned more with the impracticability of joinder of all members of the class than with the actual quantity of members; it is not a highly contested issue.[22]

The commonality and typicality requirements are the parameters in place for the efficiency of the class action and the protection of interests of class members. As stated in *General Telephone Co v Falcon*,[23] they

> serve as guideposts for determining whether under the particular circumstances maintenance of a class action is economical and whether the named plaintiff's claim and the class claims are so interrelated that the interests of the class members will be fairly and adequately protected in their absence.

While commonality concerns the relationship of the class members to one another, typicality is a matter of the relationship of the class representative with the absent members of the class.[24]

Adequate representation was a prerequisite even before the current Rule 23. In *Hansberry v Lee*[25] the petitioners, who were African-American, had bought a piece of real estate property and were sued on the basis of an alleged contractual stipulation between 500 property owners that those owners could not sell the properties to African-American people. To be effective, the agreement had to be signed by 95 per cent of the property owners, which had not in fact happened;[26] this issue of fact had been decided as if the signatures had been made in a previous case to which petitioners had not been a party.[27] The Circuit Court found that the fulfilment of the condition precedent to the agreement was *res judicata*, a decision that the Supreme Court of Illinois affirmed. The question was whether the petitioners were bound by the previous judgment despite the fact that they were neither a part of it nor a successor in interest or in privity with the other parties

---

[18] Federal Rules of Civil Procedure, r 23(a)(1) ('the class is so numerous that joinder of all members is impracticable').

[19] Federal Rules of Civil Procedure, r 23(a)(2) ('there are questions of law or fact common to the class').

[20] Federal Rules of Civil Procedure, r 23(a)(3) ('the claims or defenses of the representative parties are typical of the claims or defenses of the class').

[21] Federal Rules of Civil Procedure, r 23(a)(4) ('the representative parties will fairly and adequately protect the interests of the class').

[22] R Nagareda, *The Law of Class Actions and Other Aggregate Litigation* (Foundation Press 2009) 67.

[23] *General Telephone Co v Falcon*, 457 US 147 (1982).

[24] Nagareda (n 22) 73–74.

[25] *Hansberry v Lee*, 311 US 32 (1940).

[26] As established by the proceedings of the lower courts that led to this decision. See *Lee v Hansberry*, 24 NE 2d 37 (1939).

[27] *Burke v Kleiman*, 277 Ill App 519 (1934).

to the suit. On constitutional grounds, it was a question of due process under the Fourteenth Amendment. Not only was the prior case one exclusively against the defendants, thus not having a class character, but it also was not clear that 'the interest in defeating the contract outweighed their interest in establishing its validity'.[28] The US Supreme Court held that in this situation neither the defendants nor the plaintiffs had assumed the power to represent the petitioner in the previous case, and also that, due to their dual interests, this representation was a responsibility that they could not discharge, reversing the lower court judgment.

If these four prerequisites are satisfied, a class action can be entertained in four different situations: (1) when there is a risk of inconsistent adjudication creating incompatible standards of conduct for the party opposing the class;[29] (2) when adjudications regarding individual class members would be dispositive or affect the interests of other members not party to the adjudication;[30] (3) when 'the party opposing the class has acted or refused to act on grounds that apply generally to the class, so that final injunctive relief or corresponding declaratory relief is appropriate respecting the class as a whole';[31] and finally, (4) when there are questions of law or fact common to class members that predominate over any questions affecting only individual members and the class action is a superior method of adjudication.[32]

The three first types of class action contained in the Federal Rules of Civil Procedure, Rule 23(b)(1) and (2) are mandatory, meaning that the members of the class do not have the right to opt out.[33] The last one, based on the predominance of common questions over individual ones, does provide for the right to opt out, but the class-wide preclusion effect is dependent on discharging the duty of providing the 'best notice that is practicable under the circumstances, including individual notice to all members who can be identified through reasonable effort'.[34]

C. Class Certification

Certification is the procedural step by which the lawsuit is stamped with the class action seal, enabling the use of procedural mechanisms and the incidence of legal effects that are specific to this category. The court has to certify the class '[a]t an early practicable time after a person sues or is sued as a class representative'[35] and at the same time identify the 'claims, issues, or defenses' and appoint class counsel.[36]

---

[28] *Hansberry* (n 25).
[29] Federal Rules of Civil Procedure, r 23(b)(1)(A).
[30] Federal Rules of Civil Procedure, r 23(b)(1)(B).
[31] Federal Rules of Civil Procedure, r 23(b)(2).
[32] Federal Rules of Civil Procedure, r 23(b)(3).
[33] The *res judicata* in these kind of cases is mostly for injunctive and declaratory relief. Monetary relief claims need to have a minimum procedural due process to bind absent members. See *Brown v Ticor Title Insurance Co*, 982 F 2d 386 (9th Cir 1992); *Phillips Petroleum Co v Shutts*, 472 US 797 (1985).
[34] Federal Rules of Civil Procedure, r 23(c)(2)(B).
[35] Federal Rules of Civil Procedure, r 23(c)(1)(A).
[36] Federal Rules of Civil Procedure, r 23(c)(1)(B).

The certification consists of checking whether the lawsuit complies with the requirements of Rule 23(a) and fits within one of the categorisations of Rule 23(b). The inquiry must be comprehensive; trial judges are required to undertake a rigorous analysis and be convinced that the prerequisites of Rule 23(a) have been satisfied.[37] Theoretically, since the *Eisen*[38] decision, substantive merit-related inquiries should not be made at the certification stage, but because of the necessity of a 'rigorous analysis' as to its prerequisites, class certification has a close relationship with the substantive merits of the dispute; depending on the specifics of the case, courts may have to engage in such an inquiry.[39] Courts have to resolve disputes as to whether certification requirements have been met and whether they are based on factual or legal assertions, even though this decision will not be binding on the trier of facts.[40] While this might ease the concern over determinations of substantive issues, in any event the decision must be strictly related to the certification requirements.

Most class actions settle after certification, raising the importance of this stage in the judicial process.[41] In practice, the trial occurs during the pre-trial phase, since the dispute will be resolved promptly afterwards according to the outcome of class certification. Within the reality of such a context, the late Professor Nagareda suggested that it is important for courts to 'say what the law is', especially when the dispute for class certification arises between different accounts of the governing law, an inquiry that is similar to the one that is made within the choice-of-law context in nationwide state law-based class actions.[42] This is a crucial aspect for the development of the law on issues that are more prone to class action disputes.[43]

When a class is certified, all the persons that fall within the category delineated by the court as members of that class will be bound by the decision reached under the preclusion doctrine, meaning that if they do not opt out in the specified time period, none of the persons involved in the class will be able to re-litigate the matters decided therein. The same preclusion effects attach to class settlements, which constitute more than just an agreement of the parties but rather also an exercise of judicial authority.[44]

---

[37] *General Telephone Co* (n 23) 160–161.

[38] *Eisen v Carlisle & Jacquelin*, 417 US 156 (1974).

[39] For example, to assess the predominance requirement on a r 23(b)(3) class action, the judge may have to determine, even if only preliminarily, the questions of law and fact that will be important in the lawsuit, a task which touches on the merits of the dispute. Nonetheless, under *Eisen*, evidence and the likelihood of success should not be considered at this moment. For a discussion on this question, see RG Bone and DS Evans, 'Class Certification and the Substantive Merits' (2001–2002) 51 *Duke Law Journal* 1521; *General Telephone Co* (n 23) 160 ('sometimes it may be necessary for the court to probe behind the pleadings before coming to rest on the certification question').

[40] See *Initial Public Offerings Securities Litigation*, 471 f 3d 24 (2nd Cir 2006) 39–42.

[41] TE Willging, LL Hooper and RJ Niemic, *Empirical Study of Class Actions in Four Federal District Courts: Final Report to the Advisory Committee on Civil Rules* (Federal Judicial Center 1996) 179.

[42] R Nagareda, 'Class Certification in the Age of Aggregate Proof' (2009) 84 *New York University Law Review* 97, 164–73.

[43] See Ch 6 on the importance of reasoned and publicly available judicial decisions.

[44] Federal Rules of Civil Procedure, r 23(e)(2). See also TB Wolff, 'Preclusion in Class Action Litigation' (2005) 105 *Columbia Law Review* 717, 765 ('It is through the issuance of a certification order that a court acquires the power to bind absentees to a settlement agreement—a fact reinforced by Rule

D. Class Action and Securities Litigation

In the United States there have been two important changes to the class action procedure in securities litigation, namely the Private Securities Litigation Reform Act of 1995 (PSLRA) and the Securities Litigation Uniform Standards Act of 1998 (SLUSA).

The PSLRA brought major changes to securities litigation in the United States in order to address the increasingly significant problem of frivolous lawsuits. The Act restructured various procedural mechanisms and created a specific framework for the securities class action. Relevant to this part of this work are the reforms concerning the specific procedures that altered the basic process of a class action.

A problem that was fairly present was the existence of plaintiffs for hire; these were persons paid by law firms to buy securities and be ready to act as a representative plaintiff when necessary. The PSLRA tried to curb the practice by imposing a requirement that plaintiffs should certify that they 'did not purchase the security that is the subject of the complaint at the direction of plaintiff's counsel or in order to participate in any private action arising under [the PSLRA]' and that 'the plaintiff will not accept any payment for serving as a representative party on behalf of a class beyond the plaintiff's pro rata share of any recovery'.[45]

Addressing the same problem, another important procedural mechanism that was changed was the one to appoint the lead plaintiff. The PSLRA created a rebuttable presumption that the most adequate plaintiff, for the purpose of appointing a lead plaintiff, would be the party with 'the largest financial interest in the relief sought by the class';[46] this is a determination that can only be rebutted upon proof that either the chosen plaintiff 'will not fairly and adequately protect the interests of the class'[47] or 'is subject to unique defenses that render such plaintiff incapable of adequately representing the class'.[48] The idea of the rule was to change the power balance between lawyers and plaintiffs, giving control of the litigation to those with more interest in closely monitoring the actions of class counsel and negotiating more fiercely in order to lower their fees.[49] Congress's objective in enacting this provision was to increase the role played by institutional investors in securities class actions.[50]

23(e)'s requirement that a court provide further process to class members and then review and approve any settlement before such an agreement can take effect').

[45] Securities Exchange Act 1934, s 21D(a)(2)(ii) and (vi).

[46] Securities Exchange Act 1934, s 21D(a)(3)(B) (iii)(I)(bb).

[47] Securities Exchange Act 1934, s 21D(a)(3)(B) (iii)(II)(aa).

[48] Securities Exchange Act 1934, s 21D (a)(3)(B) (iii)(II)(bb).

[49] SJ Choi, JE Fisch and AC Pritchard, 'Do Institutions Matter? The Impact of the Lead Plaintiff Provision of the Private Securities Litigation Reform Act' (2005) 83 *Washington University Law Quarterly* 869, 869.

[50] ibid.

The results intended by Congress were partially achieved.[51] Only public institutional investors stepped up as lead plaintiffs, while there was no significant change for private institutional investors.[52] The same is true regarding the amount of recovery, which was higher when public institutional investors were involved.[53] Finally, attorneys' fee awards were not reduced due to the increased participation of institutional investors.[54]

This change therefore altered the framework of class actions in the specific field of securities litigation, providing a more certain basis to the court in deciding who would act as the class representative. Even though the objectives of Congress in enacting the legislation were not completely achieved, the procedure for appointing lead plaintiffs was rationalised, creating, at least theoretically, a sound mechanism to align the incentives of lawyers with those of the class.

The second modification arose from the SLUSA, created to prevent the ongoing flight of securities litigation from federal courts to state courts due to the enactment of the PSLRA. The Act mainly prohibited the use of state law for securities class action litigation in which there were legal arguments that included securities fraud.[55]

Notwithstanding the inconclusive evidence, the argument in favour of the legislation was that plaintiffs were moving their lawsuits to state courts to avoid the higher standards that were created after the PSLRA entered into force.[56]

The statute provided for some exceptions, such that class litigation related to securities could still be pursued at the state level; these exceptions included, for example, the case of the 'Delaware carve-out',[57] where the basis of the claim is the statutory or common law of the state in which the issuer is incorporated and involves equity holders of the issuer, in a situation where the case is related to communications made by the issuer to its equity securities holders or where it

---

[51] For an overview of the effects of the PSLRA, see SJ Choi and RB Thompson, 'Securities Litigation and Its Lawyers: Changes During the First Decade After PSLRA' (2006) 06-26 NYU Law and Economics Research Paper Series 1.

[52] Choi et al (n 49) 870.

[53] ibid.

[54] ibid. It is important to note that there were other studies claiming otherwise, but Professor Choi pointed to methodological problems with them, such as failing to control for the size of the case; ibid 878.

[55] The text of the legislation is:
(f) LIMITATIONS ON REMEDIES.—
(1) CLASS ACTION LIMITATIONS.—No covered class action based upon the statutory or common law of any State or subdivision thereof may be maintained in any State or Federal court by any private party alleging—
(A) a misrepresentation or omission of a material fact in connection with the purchase or sale of a covered security; or
(B) that the defendant used or employed any manipulative or deceptive device or contrivance in connection with the purchase or sale of a covered security.
(2) REMOVAL OF COVERED CLASS ACTIONS.—Any covered class action brought in any State court involving a covered security, as set forth in paragraph (1), shall be removable to the Federal district court for the district in which the action is pending, and shall be subject to paragraph (1).' (15 USC §§ 78bb (f)(1) & (2)).

[56] See JJ Johnson, 'Securities Class Actions in State Court' (2011 Lewis & Clark Law School Legal Research Paper Series No 17) 8–12.

[57] The term was used in ibid 8.

concerns decisions of these holders with respect to their voting rights in tender offers or appraisal rights.[58]

The result is that state law-based claims in class actions are pre-empted,[59] diminishing the scope of remedies that are available to plaintiffs to pursue recovery. This was another step taken by the US Congress, this time through the restriction of avenues available to plaintiffs, to increase the difficulty of obtaining relief in securities fraud cases.

II. Representative Actions: Brazil and Spain

Brazil and Spain also have procedures in place to deal with problems that affect a wide range of plaintiffs, but their characteristics are not quite the same as the American class action model.[60] Standing to sue is limited, preclusion rules are not as broad and, moreover, the background civil procedure system is quite different. These systems seem to be designed in order to protect the interests that are more public, either by their substantive nature[61] or by policy choice.[62]

In Brazil the idea of a legal procedure to address disputes with a collective character is as old as the 1934 Constitution, which introduced the Popular Action mechanism,[63] but its proper regulation came only in 1965, with Brazilian Law 4.717/65. Even though standing was broad,[64] its problem was the limited scope of substantive matters that could be protected, encompassing only public heritage/public property and public morality.[65]

Twenty years later, Brazilian Law 7.347/85 was enacted, introducing the Public Civil Action, a procedure with a broader scope than the former Popular Action; it included the general expression of 'diffuse or collective interests' as a subject matter that could be protected. Nonetheless, what was given with one hand was partially taken away with the other; article 5 of the law limited standing to initiate a Public Civil Action to the Prosecutor's Office, the Union, states, municipalities, state companies and associations that had been constituted for at least one year.[66] Not long afterwards, legislation was passed to protect the collective rights

---

[58] Securities Exchange Act 1934, s 28(f)(3)(i) and (ii).

[59] See also *Dabit v Merrill Lynch*, 547 US 71 (2006).

[60] For a more in-depth overview of class actions in Brazil and Spain, see JJM López, 'Las Acciones de Clase en el Derecho Español' (2001) 3 *InDret* 1; A Gidi, 'Class Actions in Brazil: a Model for Civil Law Countries' (2003) 51 *The American Journal of Comparative Law* 311.

[61] Such as those within the concept of diffuse rights.

[62] As in the case of more common consumer torts, such as false advertisement.

[63] The law regulating the procedure (Brazilian Law 4.717/65) was enacted only in 1965.

[64] Brazilian Law 4.717/65 ('Any citizen may be a legitimate party to propose the annulation or declaration of nullity') (trans by the author).

[65] HDB Pinho, 'A Tutela Coletiva no Brasil e a Sistemática dos Novos Direitos' (2007) 15 *Revista Diálogo Jurídico* 1, 4.

[66] The scope of standing was also expanded later to the Public Defence Office.

of disabled persons,[67] securities investors,[68] children[69] and consumers,[70] and within this legislation, specific changes and special circumstances to launch a Public Civil Action were provided for in each case.[71]

While it had been played around with during the 1980s and 1990s,[72] the concept of aggregate litigation only became entrenched in the Spanish legal system with the new Spanish Civil Procedure Act, enacted in 2000.[73] Only matters related to consumer or user lawsuits, in other words those who are the final purchasers or users of goods and services,[74] can be litigated through a representative mechanism in Spain.

Standing is broader than in Brazil since the group of affected people,[75] in addition to consumer and user associations[76] and entities created for the specific purpose of protecting consumer and users,[77] are allowed to bring a lawsuit. In practice though, this broader standing is of limited significance since the people in the affected group have to be 'determined or easily determinable' and the group has to be constituted by a majority of the affected persons,[78] which is not only a requirement that has to be proven by the group, but also raises questions of who, within the group, would control the direction of the lawsuit.[79]

Therefore, in a manner that differs from the American class action, in which anyone can 'create' a class and sue, the trend of the class action procedure in Brazil and Spain is to enable specific parties in specific circumstances to use the judiciary to correct a wrong inflicted on the collective. The rights protected have either a public character or are rights of weaker groups that the legislator wanted to empower, such as consumers or the disabled.

Another crucial difference that confirms the trend is the preclusion effects arising out of these civil law class actions. In both Brazil and Spain there is a separation between the 'collective right' and the 'individual right', even when the individual right is litigated in a collective fashion. A class action in the United States binds all class members, whether or not they participate in the lawsuit. This is not the case in Brazil or in Spain. In Brazil the effects of the judgment are *secundum eventum probationis* regarding interested persons, in other words the effect depends on

---

[67] Brazilian Law 7.853/89.
[68] Brazilian Law 7.913/89.
[69] Brazilian Law 8.069/90.
[70] Brazilian Law 8.078/90.
[71] eg, the changes on standing for public civil actions in Brazil.
[72] Spanish law had specific legislation giving standing to consumer and user associations to propose class actions in cases of unfair advertisement (Spanish Law 34/1988, art 25.1), antitrust (Spanish Law 3/1991, art 19.2.a) and abusive contract terms (Spanish Law 7/1998, art 16.3).
[73] See López (n 61) 3–4 (according to the author, only in two very specific circumstances were class actions for damages allowed in Spain before the Civil Procedure Act).
[74] ibid 4.
[75] Spanish Act of Civil Procedure, art 6.1.7.
[76] Spanish Act of Civil Procedure, art 11.1.
[77] Spanish Act of Civil Procedure, art 6.1.8.
[78] Spanish Act of Civil Procedure, art. 6.1.7.
[79] López (n 61) 6–7.

the result of the lawsuit.[80] If the plaintiffs are successful the result is binding *erga omnes* in the territory in which the judge (or court) has jurisdiction;[81] if the lawsuit is dismissed for lack of evidence, anyone legitimised for the collective lawsuit can sue again as long as new evidence is available.[82] In the consumer context, even if the lawsuit is dismissed with prejudice, each individual consumer still maintains his right to sue (*res judicata* effects *secundum eventum litis*).[83] The same is true in the Spanish context.[84]

As mentioned above, Brazil has specific Public Civil Action legislation for securities transactions. The procedure to be followed is the same as the one regulated in the Public Civil Action Law,[85] but the scope of standing is limited to the Prosecutor's Office.[86] Only cases of fraud, use of insider information and omission of relevant information when there was a duty to inform, can be raised.[87] Apparently, the mechanism has been used very sparsely in securities cases: a survey of the federal jurisprudence showed only three cases in which the Public Civil Action was used,[88] while a search in the São Paulo state showed only two more relevant cases.[89]

For defendants, the prospect of multiple lawsuits, even after prevailing in a class action, may seem daunting, especially to those not familiar with the operations of civil procedure and the litigation framework in civil law countries. Even though this is not the best solution for the defendant, the differences in these systems alleviate the concerns and the harm that might be caused by this possibility.

---

[80] Pinho (n 66) 16.
[81] Brazilian Law 7.347/1985, art 16. This is becoming a contested matter, as federal judges in the Rio Grande do Sul Judicial Section have been deciding that some Public Civil Actions have a national effect due to the national character of the infringement at hand. See *Instituto Brasileiro de Defesa do Consumidor v Caixa Econômica Federal* (STJ, Special Court, EResp 1134957/SP) (2016); *Defensoria Pública da União v Caixa Econômica Federal* (4th Federal Court of Porto Alegre, Statement of Claim Acceptance in Public Civil Action no 5008379-42.2014.404.7100, 04 February 2014) (deciding on the national effect of the Public Civil Action and citing Federal Judge Andrei Pitten Velloso in *Defensoria Pública da União v União—Fazenda Nacional* (14th Federal Court of Porto Alegre, Relief Anticipation in Public Civil Action no 5019819-69.2013.404.7100, 10 May 2013).
[82] Brazilian Law 7.347/85, art 16.
[83] Brazilian Law 8.078/90, art 103 § 1.
[84] See López (n 61) 13.
[85] Brazilian Law 7.347/85.
[86] Brazilian Law 7.913/89, art 1; *Usiminas v Donaldo Armelin* (TRF3, 6th Chamber, Civil Appeal 1275780) (2008); *Usiminas v Ministério Público Federal* (TRF3, 6th Chamber, Instrumental Appeal 212476) (2004); *Telebrás SA v Ministério Público Federal* (TRF1, 2nd Chamber, Civil Appeal 93.01.04391-2/DF) (1995).
[87] Brazilian Law 7.913/89 art 1; *Ministério Público do Estado de São Paulo v Comind Empreendimentos SA* (STJ, 3rd Chamber, REsp 8878 / SP) (2002) ('There is no basis in Laws n 7.347/85 and 7.913/89 to legitimate the Prosecutor's Office to act as the fiscal of the law in a damages action against financial institutions due to liquidation of debts already paid, when the extrajudicial framework to which they were subject has already come to an end') (trans by the author).
[88] *Usiminas v Donaldo Armelin* (n 87); *Usiminas v Ministério Público Federal* (n 87); *Telebrás SA v Ministério Público Federal* (n 87). There was also a criminal appeal that used the Public Civil Action Law as basis to impose collective moral damages on defendants convicted of insider trading (*Luiz Gonzaga Murat Junior v Justiça Pública* (TRF3, 5th Chamber, Criminal Appeal 45484) (2013)).
[89] *Telesp v Ministério Público* (TJSP, 7th Private Law Chamber, Instrument Appeal 0013965-80.2002.8.26.0000) (2002); *Walter Appel v Ministério Público* (TJSP, 8th Private Law Chamber, Instrument Appeal 9034921-85.2007.8.26.0000) (2007).

In contrast to the American system, litigation in Brazil and Spain is cheaper. A clear reason is lack of discovery,[90] which can consume thousands of man hours, on the part of both defendants and plaintiffs. In civil law procedure the parties need to bring their own evidence to court, without the aid of the adverse party.[91] This difference alone, when compared to the US system, cuts the cost of litigation tremendously. Moreover, the harm of repetitive litigation to a defendant is a minor concern compared to the guarantee of due process of law in deciding on a plaintiff's rights. In other words, in civil law systems the day in court remains an essential foundation of fairness in the judicial system, which, without causing a high degree of harm to defendants, guarantees the possibility of each plaintiff to claim his/her substantive right in court.

The problem is that, for conflict of interest and incentives purposes, the system still does not present the best solutions since it is dependent on either public institutions to pursue litigation[92] or on not-for-profit consumer organisations. Adding this consideration to the ethical restrictions that might be faced by lawyers in respect of solicitation, it becomes almost impossible for this system design to provide incentives that would in fact enable aggregate litigation as an adequate solution for legal questions that involve a wide-ranging group.[93]

III. The Dutch Act on Collective Settlement of Mass Damages

The Dutch Act on Collective Settlement of Mass Damages was designed to solve a specific procedural problem that arose out of a mass dispute in the *DES* case, which had more than 18,000 litigants (and a potential group of up to 440,000).[94]

---

[90] To be fair, there is some possibility of discovery in the Brazilian and Spanish systems, but it is very limited in comparison to the US. In Brazil the Brazilian Civil Procedure Code, art 396, states that the judge may demand that a party shows a document or things in his/her possession. The same is true in Spain, according to article 328.1 of the Civil Procedure Law ('each party may request the others to show documents that are not available and that refers to the object of the procedure or to the efficiency of evidence') (trans by the author). The scope is limited though—in Brazil the evidence has to be described as completely as possible, the reason for which it should be produced, and the circumstances which the party requesting the document uses as basis to affirm that the evidence exists and that it is in the possession of the other party (art 397, I, II and III); while in Spain the consequence is that, in case of failure to show a requested document, the court may give weight to a copy of such document (art 329.1), requiring nonetheless that the party requesting the disclosure of the document must have some evidence of it.

[91] Gidi (n 61) 320.

[92] On the problems of public enforcement in aggregate litigation, see M Lemos and M Minzer, 'For-Profit Public Enforcement' (2014) 127 *Harvard Law Review* 853.

[93] In addition to the system just described, Brazil has recently enacted the new Brazilian Civil Procedure Code (Brazilian Law 13.105/2015), which created two new mechanisms that ease the resolution of mass disputes, the Repetitive Claims Resolution Incident (arts 976–987) and the Repetitive Special and Extraordinary Appeals (arts 1.036–1.041). These systems are modelled on test cases; similar claims are suspended, the disputed issues are defined, and the decision is given by a higher tribunal, obliging judges under them to follow the established decision.

[94] See C Hodges, *The Reform of Class and Representative Actions in European Legal Systems* (Hart Publishing 2008) 70–71.

The Act provides that when there is a settlement between the defendant and an association or foundation representing claimants, the settlement can be sent to the Amsterdam Court of Appeal for approval, binding all those who are potentially claimants unless they opt out of the settlement.[95] As it is an opt-out procedure, notice becomes important; it has to be made directly to all known interested persons as well as through newspapers, both at the moment preceding the declaration that the settlement is binding, and after it.[96]

It is becoming more common for funding to be provided by organisations and special purpose vehicles, which either collect money from individuals or are entitled to contingency fees in a successful settlement.[97] This development is important because Dutch lawyers are not allowed to operate on a contingency fee basis due to ethical restrictions;[98] as such, alternative avenues for dispute resolution funding in mass proceedings are needed.

Other questions on the operation of the Dutch Act on Collective Settlement of Mass Damages in the transnational environment will be dealt with in the next chapter.

IV. The English Group Litigation Order

The English Group Litigation Order (GLO) is a mechanism that provides 'for the case management of claims which give rise to common or related issues of fact or law'.[99] The procedure was primarily developed through judicial discretion, due to the necessity that arose to manage cases with a high number of claimants in the 1980s,[100] and was enshrined in legislation in 2000.[101]

The mechanism allows for claims that present similar issues to be managed together by the same court.[102] A register has to be set up to allow for claimants to join the procedure;[103] a judge is then appointed to manage it and issue the necessary orders for the development of litigation.[104]

The procedure is very flexible; the court can vary the issues that will be decided, pick one or more cases to proceed as test cases, and define the preclusion effects

---

[95] ibid 71.
[96] R Hermans and JBL Tjeenk, 'International Class Action Settlements in the Netherlands since *Converium*' in I Dodds-Smith and A Brown (eds), *The International Comparative Guide to: Class & Group Actions 2013* (5th edn, Global Legal Group Ltd 2012) 7.
[97] I Tzankova, 'Netherlands National Report—part 2' (2008) Global Class Actions Exchange, globalclassactions.stanford.edu/sites/default/files/documents/Netherlands_National_Report_2.pdf, 3.
[98] ibid 4.
[99] English Civil Procedure Rules, r 19.10.
[100] Hodges (n 94) 53.
[101] N Andrews, 'Multi-Party Proceedings in England: Representative and Group Actions' (2001) 11 *Duke Journal of Comparative & International Law* 249, 249.
[102] ibid 259.
[103] English Civil Procedure Rules Practice Direction 19B 6.1.
[104] Hodges (n 94) 53.

for those who might join the register after an issue is decided.[105] As an opt-in procedure, only those who are part of the register will be bound by the decisions rendered by the court.[106]

Even though the flexibility of the court is significant, a practice has emerged whereby test cases are used to decide the issues that are common to the group, allowing for the full litigation of these cases so that a clear picture can arise.[107]

Finally, the loser-pays principle still applies; this might give rise to financial consequences for claimants if no other arrangements between claimants and lawyers or third-party financiers are made.[108]

V. The German Capital Market Model Claims Act

The Capital Market Model Claims Act (KapMuG) was enacted in 2005 due to the need for German courts to deal with a securities case brought by 15,000 investors against Deutsche Telekom.[109] At the time the suits were filed, the German Civil Code did not allow for the coordinated management of all these claims. They had a similar factual background: an alleged false or misleading statement in connection with a public offering of American Depositary Share (ADSs).[110]

The Act is restricted to claims for compensation due to false, omitted or misleading information and to claims regarding the fulfilment of contracts under the Securities Acquisition and Takeover Act.[111]

Similar to the English GLO procedure, the German mechanism requires the creation of a register so claimants are able to apply for the initiation of a model case.[112] If there are 10 cases, a referral is made to a Higher Regional Court so that a model case can be established;[113] the court that will try the matter then has to suspend pending proceedings that are factually or legally related to the model case.[114] The Higher Regional Court will then decide on who will be part of the model case, considering the amount of the claim and whether there is any agreement among the plaintiffs regarding a designated model plaintiff.[115] The decision taken is binding on the inferior courts and binding on all interested parties, regardless of intervention.[116]

---

[105] R Mulheron, *The Class Action in Common Legal Systems* (Hart Publishing 2004) 98–99.
[106] Civil Procedure Rules, r 19.12(1)(a).
[107] Hodges (n 94) 58.
[108] ibid 60.
[109] ibid 77–78.
[110] ibid 78.
[111] Kapitalanlegermusterverfahrensgesetz (KapMuG), s 1(1).
[112] KapMuG, s 2(1).
[113] KapMuG, s (1).
[114] KapMuG, s 7(1).
[115] KapMuG, s 8(2).
[116] KapMuG, s 16(1).

This proceeding was created as a management tool to reduce the common issues that would have to be litigated many times; it is an interim proceeding, and as such, other issues such as causation and individual damages will still have to be litigated in a lower court.[117]

An important problem with the German system is the fee distribution for lawyers. Lawyers of the lead plaintiffs can only recover on the basis of the fees of their own clients, even though the work performed will benefit all of those who might be involved in the litigation;[118] this creates a free-rider problem.

VI. Aggregate Litigation and the European Union

The last sections illustrated some of the developments of aggregate litigation in the Member States of the European Union but, in light of the cross-border character of securities transactions within the EU internal market, it is also important to consider whether, at the moment, the European Union has a plan for the development of aggregate litigation.

The discussion regarding aggregate litigation in the European Union took off in 2007, focusing on the consumer law and the competition law context. In its EU Consumer Policy Strategy 2007–2013, the Commission stated that it would 'consider action on *collective redress* mechanisms for consumers both for infringements of consumer protection rules and for breaches of EU anti-trust rules';[119] it effectively did this. The Commission published a Green Paper on consumer collective redress in 2008[120] and a White Paper on damages for breach of antitrust rules,[121] and launched a public consultation in 2011,[122] which was the basis for the European Parliament to adopt the resolution 'Towards a Coherent European Approach to Collective Redress'.[123]

This debate led the Commission to its current position,[124] which is enshrined in the Commission Recommendation 'on common principles for injunctive and compensatory collective redress mechanisms in the Member States concerning

---

[117] P Rott, 'Evaluation of the Effectiveness and Efficiency of Collective Redress Mechanisms in the European Union—Country Report Germany' (European Commission 2008) http://ec.europa.eu/consumers/archive/redress_cons/de-country-report-final.pdf, 7.

[118] ibid 11.

[119] Commission, 'EU Consumer Policy Strategy 2007–2013' (Communication) COM (2007) 99 final, 11 (emphasis in the orginal).

[120] Commission, 'Consumer Collective Redress' (Green Paper) COM (2008) 794 final.

[121] Commission, 'Damages Actions for Breach of the EC Antitrust Rules' (White Paper) COM (2008) 165 final.

[122] Commission, 'Towards a Coherent European Approach to Collective Redress' (Public Consultation) SEC (2011) 173 final.

[123] European Parliament Resolution 2011/2089/INI.

[124] See Commission, 'Towards a European Horizontal Framework for Collective Redress' (Communication) COM (2013) 401 final.

violations of rights granted under Union Law'.[125] The underlying policy of the Recommendation is primarily access to justice and secondarily harmonisation, even if on very broad terms, of the procedural design for aggregate litigation in Member States.[126]

Despite access to justice being the main underlying policy of the Recommendation, some of the principles established therein do not work towards this goal. These shortcomings are a result of the fear of an approximation to the US system, which is explicit in recital 15,[127] and of the creation of an environment ripe for abusive litigation.[128] The main dimensions of the Recommendation that could have gone further in enhancing access to justice concern standing in representative actions, third-party funding, the preference for the opt-in system and scepticism about contingency fees.

According to the principles established in the Recommendation, representative entities having standing for representative actions 'should have a non-profit making character'.[129] The problem with this approach is one of funding; either the entity will barely have funding, preventing the possibility for representative entities to become involved in complex situations,[130] or the funding will be public, which transforms the representative entity into a de facto public entity, creating unnecessary costs for taxpayers. The imposition of a non-profit character on representative entities undermines their role in mobilising private parties to conduct litigation.

The principles on external funding also complicate matters from an incentives perspective. Third parties providing funding are prohibited from 'seek[ing] to influence procedural decisions of the claimant party, including on settlements'.[131] Such a provision increases the risk for the third-party funder, which consequently either increases the interest/stake that the funder demands or precludes the lawsuit altogether, leaving both funder and claimants worse off.

The opt-in system, in the aggregate litigation context, is also another problem for access to justice.[132] Aggregate litigation mechanisms are better suited for negative claims, and as such it is unlikely that claimants would move to initiate litigation, leaving the responsibility for gathering claimants in the hands of lawyers. As explained before, due to ethical limitations lawyers may not pursue new clients

---

[125] Commission Recommendation 2013/396/EU.

[126] Commission Recommendation 2013/396/EU recital 10.

[127] 'Elements such as punitive damages, intrusive pre-trial discovery procedures and jury awards, most of which are foreign to the legal traditions of most Member States, should be avoided as a general rule'.

[128] Commission Recommendation 2013/396/EU recital 10.

[129] Commission Recommendation 2013/396/EU art 4(a).

[130] See D Fairgrieve and G Howells, 'Collective Redress Procedures: European Debates' in D Fairgrieve and E Lein (eds), *Extraterritoriality and Collective Redress* (Oxford University Press 2012) 2.78.

[131] Commission Recommendation 2013/396/EU art 16(a).

[132] Commission Recommendation 2013/396/EU art 21 provides that 'The claimant party should be formed on the basis of express consent of the natural or legal persons claiming to have been harmed

actively; this situation thus weakens the economies of scale that are at the heart of the benefits arising out of aggregate litigation.

Finally, contingency fees are seen as undesirable and should be avoided if they create 'any incentive to litigation that is unnecessary from the point of view of the interest of any of the parties'.[133] First, it is not clear what an unnecessary incentive would be; however, a contingency fee arrangement is nothing more than a method of funding. Cases in which contingency fees would be used are unlikely to be litigated through a compensation system where the claimant pays up front, especially in the aggregate litigation context where there are many small claims and no claimant with enough economic interest or capability to pursue the lawsuit. What the contingency fee system does is to allow part of the risk, as well as part of the benefits, to shift into the hands of the lawyer.

The nature of all of these prohibitions is to avoid abusive litigation, which is a worthwhile goal since litigation can be a costly endeavour for defendants. The problem is that these measures avoid the problem but to a large extent do so by harming the main access-to-justice goal that aggregate litigation is designed to achieve.[134]

There are other ways to create procedural fairness and avoid abusive litigation— or at least, to avoid the costs incurred by defendants associated with it—when implementing aggregate litigation systems, and the Commission has already picked up some hints for such a solution. The main aspect that would create a just system is the reimbursement of legal costs to the winning party, which is already enshrined in article 13 of the Recommendation. Instead of putting too many regulations around who may be a representative party, limiting the influence of external funders to the litigation and prohibiting contingency fees, the rules should be drafted in a way to give a wide degree of liberty to those taking the risk, but at the same time ensuring that they will be responsible for costs in case claimants lose the litigation. Such an approach is even more relevant in cases where all of the claims are of negative value since no single claimant would rationally take the litigation into his own hands, leaving the role of manager either to the representative entity or to the lawyer representing the claimants, who could fund the litigation themselves or rely on an external third party. In these cases, the representative entity, the lawyer or the external funder should be made responsible for the costs but should also be allowed to recover based on the risk and the possible upside of litigation. The only caveat is that recovery should be limited to a certain amount, the determination of which would depend on what can be deemed fair, to avoid abuse against claimants.

This design is an interesting one because it opens up the possibility for private parties to make use of aggregate litigation mechanisms, not only enhancing access

---

("opt-in" principle). Any exception to this principle, by law or by court order, should be duly justified by reasons of sound administration of justice'.

[133] Commission Recommendation 2013/396/EU 16(a) arts 29, 30.
[134] Fairgrieve and Howells (n 130) 2.79.

to justice, but at the same time limiting the downside faced by defendants, who will be reimbursed for the costs of litigation if they successfully defend the case. Also, since those who will benefit from winning a case will also have to bear the costs of a loss, it is likely that only cases with a considerable amount of merit will be litigated, avoiding the problem of nuisance litigation. If access to justice is the goal to be pursued, this approach is the best way of achieving it without undermining fairness to defendants.

VII. Class Arbitration

Class arbitration is a procedural device similar to the class action, developed to bring a dispute with multiple claimants/respondents to an end. Similarly to the class action, in a class arbitration there will be a decision to certify a class, defining the characteristics that would delineate the group of persons who would be bound by the final decision.[135]

Developed initially in the United States, the class arbitration has been around since at least 1982[136] and it is increasingly becoming an international phenomenon.[137] As a 'born and bred' American device, interesting questions arise in relation to its effective development and efficiency in the transnational forum since many countries may have restrictions against it.

The class arbitration mechanism is an interesting topic of study for this work because it encompasses a mechanism (at least when considered internationally) that could, at least theoretically, be used to efficiently resolve securities disputes in a variety of different legal backgrounds, as proposed in Chapter 5.

A. Historical Development of Class Arbitration

Initially, in the United States, only parties to a contract or a related set of contracts could be parties to a given arbitration, while class arbitrations were impermissible.[138] Soon courts started accepting class arbitration[139] even though the initial prevalent

---

[135] The binding nature of the decision will depend on the due process standards of the arbitral seat or the applicable law and public policy considerations of the enforcing country.

[136] See *Keating v Superior Court*, 645 P 2d 1192 (Cal 1982).

[137] See SI Strong, 'Enforcing Class Arbitration in the International Sphere: Due Process and Public Policy Concerns' (2008) 30 *University of Pennsylvania Journal of International Law* 1, 1; SI Strong, 'From Class to Collective: The De-Americanization of Class Arbitration' (2010) 26 *Arbitration International* 493.

[138] G Born, *International Commercial Arbitration* (Kluwer Law International 2009) 1227. See also *Vernon v Drexel Burnham & Company*, 52 Cal App 3d 706 (Cal 1975).

[139] *Keating* (n 136) 1209–10.

position was that it was only allowed when parties explicitly agreed to it.[140] This changed with a divided Supreme Court decision in *Green Tree v Bazzle*,[141] where the majority opinion concluded that the interpretation of the contract and the kind of procedure allowed by virtue of it was a matter for the arbitrator to decide, and not one for the courts.

One of the reasons why arbitration was used in a widespread manner, especially in consumer and labour contracts, was to avoid class litigation.[142] The use of arbitration was a way identified by businesses to effectively bar class treatment and the possibility of redress for negative claims. This decision effectively opened the doors for class treatment in arbitration proceedings in the United States when arbitration clauses were silent since it gave the power to the arbitrator to decide.[143] The business community reacted promptly, and not only did companies start to insert clauses into their contracts that explicitly barred class arbitration, but arbitral institutions also started to develop specific rules and procedures for these kinds of proceedings.[144]

Two recent decisions confirm the trend of the possibility for class arbitration based on clauses that are silent on the matter. In *JSC Surgutneftegaz v President and Fellows of Harvard College*,[145] Harvard's investment managers complained that the Russian gas company from which they had purchased American Depositary Receipts had depressed its net profits in order to reduce the dividends that the company was required to pay; it then filed a 'demand for class arbitration' with the American Arbitration Association (AAA).[146] The majority of arbitrators decided that class arbitration was allowed, despite the decision in *Stolt-Nielsen SA v Animalfeeds Int'l Corp*,[147] in which Judge Rakoff stated that New York law did not allow for class arbitration when the arbitration clause was silent. Judge Berman confirmed the award, thus allowing Harvard to pursue the claim representing a class on the grounds of *Bazzle*,[148] finding that the arbitrators were competent to decide how to interpret the arbitration clause regarding procedural treatment.

---

[140] See *Champ v Siegel Trading Co*, 55 F 3d 269, para 18 (7th Cir 1995) ('We thus adopt the rationale of several other circuits and hold that section 4 of the FAA forbids federal judges from ordering class arbitration where the parties' arbitration agreement is silent on the matter'); *Dominium Austin Partners, LLC v Emerson*, 248 F 3d 720 (8th Cir 2001) para 23 ('Finally, we note that the goal of the FAA is to enforce the agreement of the parties, not to effect the most expeditious resolution of claims. See *Baesler v Cont'l Grain Co*, 900 F 2d 1193, 1195 (8th Cir 1990). As such, an arbitration agreement should be enforced "in accordance with its terms"').

[141] *Green Tree v Bazzle*, 539 US 444 (2003).

[142] In some countries, consumer and labour regulation prohibits the use of arbitration clauses (eg Brazil). The justification is that in these relationships, consumers and workers are the weaker parties and the justice system is designed in a manner such that they can effectively access a forum to claim their rights.

[143] This was not explicitly stated in the decision but it could be inferred from the power given to the arbitrator to decide the procedure allowed within the arbitration clause.

[144] See PA Lacovara, 'Class Action Arbitrations—the Challenge for the Business Community' (2008) 24 *Arbitration International* 541, 543–44.

[145] *JSC Surgutneftegaz v President and Fellows of Harvard College*, 2007 WL 3019234 (SDNY 11 October 2007).

[146] Lacovara (n 144) 548.

[147] *Stolt-Nielsen SA v Animalfeeds Int'l Corp*, 435 F Supp 2d 382 (SDNY 2006).

[148] *Bazzle* (n 141).

The second case concerned a doctor suing a health insurance company for denying or delaying reimbursements of medical services fees.[149] In the same manner as the above-mentioned case, the arbitral tribunal issued a Class Construction Award allowing for class arbitration, but when challenged, the award was set aside based on the 'manifest disregard' doctrine, since the judge concluded that the New York law applicable at the time at which the arbitration clause was signed was settled in forbidding class arbitration when the arbitration clause was silent.[150] The judge's decision was reversed on appeal. The justification for reversal was that a court could only vacate an award under the 'manifest disregard' doctrine when the error amounts to an 'egregious impropriety' and not only 'an erroneous interpretation of the law'.[151]

With these decisions it became clear, at least in the United States, that the decision to entertain arbitration in a class form when arbitration clauses are silent is a matter for arbitrators to decide; moreover, courts will back up this decision, even when the applicable law provides otherwise.[152]

Since arbitration was a way identified by these companies to avoid class actions and the perils that followed it, with these decisions and the new landscape in class treatment in arbitration companies had to scramble to find other ways to prevent class disputes. An important parallel development to the class arbitration was the treatment of class action waivers by courts.

B. Class Action Waivers

Class action waivers began appearing in contracts in the 1990s after trade journal articles started encouraging their use.[153] Due to the high litigation costs that are present in the United States, in many instances the class action was the only available means of redress for parties with low-value claims; it has been a widely used procedure. While it is true that in some instances the class action mechanism has been abused, creating unnecessary social costs within the US legal system, it is, to some extent, the only way in which weaker parties can pursue some of their rights.

With this problem in mind, some of the US courts started deploying the 'unconscionability doctrine' to address this problem. In general, to be unconscionable a contractual term has to be both substantively and procedurally unconscionable.[154]

---

[149] See *Cheng v Oxford Health Plans, Inc,* 2005 WL 5359732 (NY Sup Ct 2006) and *Cheng v Oxford Health Plans, Inc,* 45 App Div 3d 356 (NY App Div 2007).

[150] *Cheng* (2006) (n 149).

[151] *Cheng* (2007) (n 149).

[152] Unless of course there is an 'egregious impropriety', which would be an extremely high standard to reach. In practice, arbitrators would have to acknowledge that the applicable law would forbid class treatment and still move forward with the procedure.

[153] JM Glover, 'Beyond Unconscionability: Class Action Waivers and Mandatory Arbitration Agreements' (2006) 59 *Vanderbilt Law Review* 1735, 1746.

[154] RA Hillman, 'Debunking Some Myths About Unconscionability: a New Framework for UCC Section 2–302' (1981–1982) 67 *Cornell Law Review* 1, 2–3.

The doctrine is applicable to class action waivers and to arbitration clauses, since the FAA § 2[155] provides that courts must enforce arbitration agreements 'save upon such grounds as exist at law or in equity for the revocation of any contract',[156] which is mainly a state matter.[157]

Most courts have upheld class action waivers against unconscionability claims, but some have refused to enforce them.[158] Such refusal is important because a nationwide class can be certified in these states.[159]

Even though there is a theoretical possibility of avoiding class action waivers and arbitration clauses on unconscionability grounds, most courts in the United States are enforcing them as a practical matter, with two recent Supreme Court decisions enforcing arbitration clauses and class action waivers outwith and within the arbitral process.[160]

In this scenario, class arbitration will be a creature of consent. Parties who do not wish to engage in class arbitration will spell this out in their contracts, denying the possibility for the use of the mechanism.[161] Otherwise, parties will either accept the possibility of class arbitration by remaining silent in their contracts or will expressly provide in their contract for the design of the mechanism.

C. The Types of Class Arbitration

The development and practice of class arbitration created two main models: the hybrid model and the provider-created model.

i. The Hybrid Model

This model was created, at least in California, in the *Keating v Superior Court* decision.[162] In the decision, the court stated:

> Whether ... an order would be justified in a case of this sort is a question appropriately left to the discretion of the trial court. In making that determination, the trial court would be called upon to consider, not only the factors normally relevant to class certification, but the special characteristics of arbitration as well, including the impact upon an arbitration proceeding of whatever court supervision might be required, and the

---

[155] Federal Arbitration Act, ch 213, § 1, 43 Stat 883 (1925).
[156] 9 USC § 2 (2014).
[157] PJ Kreher and PD Robertson, 'Substance, Process, and the Future of Class Arbitration' (2004) 9 *Harvard Negotiation Law Review* 409, 425.
[158] Enforcing class action waivers, the US Courts of Appeals for the Third, Fourth, Fifth and Seventh Circuits and many District Courts; refusing to enforce class action waivers, US Court of Appeals for the Ninth Circuit and state courts in California and Illinois. See Glover (n 153) 1751–52.
[159] ibid 1754.
[160] See *Oxford Health Plans LLC v Sutter*, 133 S Ct 2064 (2013); *American Express Co v Italian Colors Restaurant*, 133 S Ct 2304 (2013).
[161] Kreher and Robertson (n 157) 423.
[162] See CJ Buckner, 'Due Process in Class Arbitration' (2006) 58 *Florida Law Review* 185, 226–27.

availability of consolidation as an alternative means of assuring fairness. Whether class-wide proceedings would prejudice the legitimate interests of the party which drafted the adhesion agreement must also be considered, and that party should be given the option of remaining in court rather than submitting to class wide arbitration.[163]

In this model, courts are an important part of the class arbitration mechanism; they retain jurisdiction and decide upon various other aspects during the development of the procedure, such as class certification, notice, discovery, settlements and issues of adequate representation.[164]

ii. The Provider-created Model

The provider-created model is based on the involvement of arbitral institutions and the rules they have promulgated to guide the class arbitration procedure. Two known arbitral institutions that have developed a system of class arbitration are the AAA and JAMS,[165] both headquartered in the United States.[166] The rules they have created are patterned on the American class action system.[167] For example, the JAMS rules[168] provide that

> An action may be maintained as a class action if the prerequisites of subdivision (a) are satisfied, in addition to the criteria set forth in the Federal Rules of Civil Procedure, Rule 23(b).[169]

The same is true of the AAA Supplementary Rules for Class Arbitration. To allow a member of a class to represent all others, the arbitrator has to ensure that the following conditions are met:

(1) the class is so numerous that joinder of separate arbitrations on behalf of all members is impracticable;
(2) there are questions of law or fact common to the class;
(3) the claims or defenses of the representative parties are typical of the claims or defenses of the class;
(4) the representative parties will fairly and adequately protect the interests of the class;
(5) counsel selected to represent the class will fairly and adequately protect the interests of the class; and
(6) each class member has entered into an agreement containing an arbitration clause which is substantially similar to that signed by the class representative(s) and each of the other class members.[170]

---

[163] *Keating* (n 136) 1209–10.
[164] Buckner (n 162) 228.
[165] See adr.org and jamsadr.com.
[166] For a European example, see DIS-Supplementary Rules for Corporate Law Disputes 09 (SRCoLD).
[167] Buckner (n 162) 239.
[168] JAMS Class Action Procedures.
[169] JAMS Class Action Procedures, r 3(b).
[170] AAA Supplementary Rules for Class Arbitration, r 4(a).

Also, under the rules class arbitration can only be maintained if

> the questions of law or fact common to the members of the class predominate over any questions affecting only individual members, and ... a class arbitration is superior to other available methods for the fair and efficient adjudication of the controversy.[171]

These requirements are clearly modelled on the class action requirements in the US class action system, and these models of class arbitration will, to a certain extent, mirror what is done in class actions and have similar effects. For this reason, the questions involving conflicts of interest and the funding of the claim are similar. The important question, though, is not how class arbitration is similar to the class action, but how it differs, and how this difference might operate in favour of an enforceable international class dispute resolution system.

D. Class Arbitration Outside the United States

Class arbitration can be an interesting option for an aggregate dispute resolution system for securities disputes, especially in the context of disputes involving issuers and investors.

The possibility of using class arbitration in many jurisdictions is still not clear. As a starting point, arbitration is based on the will of the parties to submit their dispute to a private third party instead of bringing the dispute to court. Theoretically, absent this consent, there are no grounds for a decision from an arbitrator to bind an unsuspecting third party.[172] The arbitration agreement, constituting more than just the expression of consent of the parties, is what legally gives the arbitrator the power to decide the dispute, that is, as the required source of the arbitral tribunal's jurisdiction.[173] It is this notion of consent that will give the arbitral award binding power in relation to those that, in one way or another, have agreed to be part of the arbitration, guaranteeing the binding effect of the decision.

Since consent is the only basis for a tribunal's jurisdiction, the important question in class arbitration is how consent is achieved and whether the means of acknowledging consent within the legal system in which the arbitral tribunal's decision will be enforced can be flexible, as it is within the class action procedure.

The possibility of class arbitration is a function of the type of dispute that is under discussion and the source of the legal relationships that need to be decided.

---

[171] AAA Supplementary Rules for Class Arbitration, r 4(b).

[172] A Redfern and M Hunter, *Law and Practice of International Commercial Arbitration* (Sweet & Maxwell 2004) 9 ('the arbitration agreement fulfils several important functions. The most important of these in the present context is that it shows that the parties have consented to resolve their disputes by arbitration. This element of consent is essential').

[173] ibid 10 ('Arbitrators do not hold public office and are not vested with pre-existing jurisdictional powers, which they acquire only by virtue of the parties' consent'); see also JF Poudret and S Besson, *Comparative Law of International Arbitration* (Sweet & Maxwell 2007) 6–7.

With consent as the legitimating basis of the arbitral procedure, as long as consent is present, class arbitrations should theoretically be possible.[174]

E. Class Arbitration and the European Union

Class arbitration is viewed with scepticism in the European Union[175] and the hurdles that must be overcome to enable it are similar to those related to class actions. The due process and public policy concerns that have already been discussed are also applicable in the context of class arbitration in the EU Member States.[176] To become a possibility, the design of class arbitration in European jurisdictions for securities transactions has to be made in a manner where due process is guaranteed through a mechanism of effective notice, in addition to being a possibility only where the public policy aspect of securities laws does not prohibit the arbitrability of the disputes.

The positive aspects of a class arbitration system in the European Union are twofold: first, access to justice is improved and secondly, mass-type disputes would be resolved similarly across the board, avoiding the problem that multiple and possibly different judgments could arise out of the same fact pattern. Allowing a class action system for securities disputes in the EU context, in connection with a choice-of-law provision, would facilitate the creation of an internal securities market due to the homogenisation of the rights attached to the same securities. In the current scenario this is not the case; the liability regime is dependent on the location of the investor's account.[177]

VIII. Concluding Remarks

This chapter surveyed some of the most discussed aggregate litigation systems that are available today, showing important differences between them. As established in the previous chapter, one of the most important aspects in an aggregate litigation system is the one of incentives; ensuring that the persons who will steer the litigation have adequate incentives to do so is crucial for the success of the system.

In this context, some of the systems discussed are highly inappropriate for a privately based enforcement regime, which should be the aim for the development of an adequate transnational system of dispute resolution for securities transactions.

---

[174] For a more in-depth discussion on class and collective arbitration outside the US, see SI Strong, 'From Class to Collective' (n 137).

[175] P Billiet (ed), *Class Arbitration in the European Union* (Maklu 2013) 233–235.

[176] P Billiet and L Lozano, 'General Reflections on the Recognition and Enforcement of Foreign Class Arbitral Awards in Europe' in P Billiet (ed), *Class Arbitration in the European Union* (Maklu 2013) 24–27.

[177] See Ch 10.

Here the examples are the representative action system, where the incentives lie in the public character of consumer associations and public bodies, and the German system, where lawyers bearing the burden of most of the work will only benefit from their clients' fees, thus allowing for the possibility of this mechanism only where clients have a considerable stake in the matter. In terms of access, as these systems provide different avenues in addition to individual litigation, this is a step forward, but it is still not enough to constitute an efficient mechanism.

The Dutch settlement system seems to be moving in the right direction; even though lawyers are not able to work on a contingency fee basis, the use of outside funders who can do so allows a third party to have a significant stake in the matter, providing incentives for the process to be pushed forward while at the same time aligning its interests with those of the plaintiffs.

As proposed in Chapter 5, class arbitration seems to be an interesting option to create a transnational dispute resolution system for transnational securities transactions due to the overarching effects of an award and the possibility of designing it specifically for securties disputes.

The main point that should be taken from this chapter and the previous one is that a proper system of incentives is crucial for the design of an efficient aggregate litigation system.

10

Transnational Aspects of Dispute Resolution

The purpose of law is to provide stability and certainty in social relations, giving space for the planning and improvement of economic output by diminishing duplicative protection costs that parties would have to incur to protect their assets. Legal systems may be more or less reliable, but legal certainty is what they strive for as otherwise they would be virtually useless, becoming a simple forum for discussion with no mechanism for the enforcement and resolution of real-world problems.

When faced with transnational disputes, legal systems may then become ineffective systems with no real functionality. The problem arises out of the relationship between transnational transactions and the policy choices made in different legal systems. Since each jurisdiction is imbued with its own sovereignty, having power to decide which cases it wishes to entertain and what decisions should be enforceable in its own land, a legal system may not recognise a decision or may not apply a law to a transaction that would have been applied if the case had been litigated elsewhere.

In the securities context this matter is even more evident due to the regulatory nature of securities law and its mandatory character, enhancing the uncertainties that may arise out of transnational transactions. For example, an investor that invests overseas through a foreign broker-dealer or has securities of a foreigner issuer may have a very hard time litigating effectively in his own country for a variety of reasons: his court may not have jurisdiction over the dispute, the decision that may arise out of a local procedure may not be enforceable overseas where the broker-dealer has its assets, and even if it is, the costs of engaging in such transnational litigation might be too significant.[1] Due to the uncertainty of the outcomes and the costs involved, it would only be worthwhile for an investor to pursue this path if there was a lot at stake.

---

[1] One interesting example is Case C-168/02 *Kronhofer v Maier* [2004] ECR I-06009, where Mr Kronhofer, an Austrian resident, transferred money to an investment account in Germany after he was convinced by defendants to invest in a call option contract on the London Stock Exchange relating to shares. He lost a great deal of the money invested and sued to recover in an Austrian court; the matter was referred to the CJEU which decided that 'the expression "place where the harmful event occurred" does not refer to the place where the claimant is domiciled or where "his assets are concentrated" by reason only of the fact the he has suffered financial damage there resulting from the loss of part of his assets which arose and was incurred in another Contracting State'.

This state of affairs limits immensely the transactions that can be made, having a negative effect both on investors who would want to have a wider option of investments and to capital seekers, who have a more limited pool of resources available.

The objective of this chapter is to identify the private international law issues related to liability in transnational securities transactions and justify the choices made in Chapter 5. To achieve this, the chapter is divided into five sections: jurisdiction and enforcement, applicable law, the public policy question, implications for securities disputes and concluding remarks.

I. Jurisdiction and Enforcement

Any analysis of cross-border legal problems should start from a local perspective. By simply understanding the legal mechanisms available locally, it will be possible to extend the analysis to the transnational realm. Connections among different legal systems are made through jurisdictional analysis. Jurisdiction can be understood both from internal and external perspectives. The internal perspective relates to the rules with which a court must comply to exercise decision-making power within its legal system, while the external perspective relates to the requirements that have to be complied with in a given forum in order to recognise that a foreign court had jurisdiction, and therefore that its judgment will be enforceable.[2]

A. Jurisdiction

Jurisdiction is the power of a court to hear cases. With jurisdiction, a court can entertain a lawsuit, decide it and enforce the judgment. If a court decides without having jurisdiction, a higher court will overturn the decision. The jurisdictional rules of a legal system define the scope of the court's power. This characteristic is part of the wider political system, which can translate not only the determination of the role of courts in that particular legal system, but also how that political system defines its importance, from its own perspective, to the outside world. Broader jurisdictional grounds may invade centres of interest of other nations, including local courts, in the external relations considerations of the country.

Even though courts have the power to decide based on the jurisdictional rules that their legal system gives them, this power is only enforceable in the specific territory of the state to which this court belongs and over which it has physical control. A judicial decision that is not complied with will require officers of the law to collect assets or perform any other action that is necessary to oblige the losing

---

[2] See R Michaels, 'Some Fundamental Jurisdictional Conceptions as Applied in Judgment Conventions' (2006) 123 Duke Law School Legal Studies Research Paper Series 1, 7–11.

party to comply. An American court cannot directly enforce one of its decisions in Brazil by using American officers without causing a serious international political incident.

Rules of jurisdiction vary. They are the expression of institutional choice in respect of dispute resolution in a state, while at the same time they are an exercise of that state's sovereignty. Limits to jurisdictional rules can be found in constitutions, the most important being linked to the idea of due process, which, taken out of context, does not mean much since due process is a concept that can also vary substantially depending on the legal system being discussed.[3] From the plaintiff and defendant's perspective, jurisdiction rules are important as they shape the means of accessing the dispute resolution system of a state and the matter being brought to litigation. Jurisdiction rules define who can sue and who can be sued in a given legal system and protect 'the defendant against the burden of litigating in a distant or inconvenient forum'.[4]

On the other hand, jurisdiction rules are also important to mediate the relationship between different courts and sovereigns. On many occasions, conflict situations may allow more than one court the possibility of deciding the dispute.[5] Jurisdiction rules may therefore also be concerned with solving the conflict that may arise out of this conundrum.

This is an important inquiry for most countries as long as they are interested in engaging in international commercial relationships and have their legal system recognised as a trustworthy place in which the disputes that may arise out of these transactions can be resolved. In the securities context this is even more relevant as the public policy aspect of securities regulation creates even more barriers to the solution of problems arising out of transnational transactions.

Policy concerns arising from jurisdictional rules can therefore be translated into two main groups: the relationship between courts and parties to the disputes, which translates into the fairness of the system to the defendant, and the relationship between the forum state and other states.[6]

---

[3] For example, due process in the US means both the idea of substantive due process and procedural due process; even in the US, these concepts may be seen as not having any specific meaning; Frank Easterbrook wrote in 1982 that the 'Court makes no pretence that its judgments have any basis other than the Justices' view of desirable policy. This is fundamentally the method of substantive due process' (FH Easterbrook, 'Substance and Due Process' [1982] *The Supreme Court Review* 85, 125). In Brazil the notion of due process is more significantly linked to the procedural side, encompassing the right to be heard, the right to a 'natural judge' and the right not to be convicted based on illegal evidence, among others (GF Mendes and PGG Branco, *Curso de Direito Constitucional* (7th edn, Saraiva 2012) 641).

[4] *World-Wide Volkswagen v Woodson*, 444 US 286, 292 (1980).

[5] Some areas that are prone to lead to jurisdictional conflicts are antitrust, securities regulation and insolvency when the dispute is related to global business networks. See HL Buxbaum, 'National Jurisdiction and Global Business Networks' (2010) 17 *Indiana Journal of Global Legal Studies* 165.

[6] Ralf Michaels in fact uses the vertical/horizontal dichotomy to classify the different paradigms from which the American system and the civil law systems think about jurisdiction. Nonetheless, the division is useful to categorise the questions that need to be discussed concerning jurisdiction. See R Michaels, 'Two Paradigms of Jurisdiction' (2006) 27 *Michigan Journal of International Law* 1003, 1027.

i. The Relationship Between Courts and Parties to the Disputes

The first dimension of jurisdiction is linked to the possibility for a court to exercise jurisdiction over a defendant. The focus of concern is vertical as it does not include any considerations in respect of foreign sovereigns, being limited to the court–party relationship. The approach is diverse when comparing the American legal system to the civil law system.

In civil law systems, the approach to jurisdiction is usually based on the defendant's domicile[7] but might also be established in the place of contract performance[8] or in the place where a tort has been committed.[9] When disputes regarding *in rem* rights over immovable property are concerned, jurisdiction is exclusively established at the place where the property is situated.[10] The jurisdiction analysis tends to be straightforward as a given court will either have or will not have jurisdiction; there will be no fairness or reasonableness inquiries as to whether the forum is a proper one for the dispute.

In the American legal system the vertical jurisdictional analysis has a higher level of complexity, as there are many different doctrines through which a court may accept jurisdiction over a defendant in order to decide a dispute. While jurisdiction is a matter for the states, its outer limits are drawn by the Due Process clause of the US Constitution,[11] which has generated confusing jurisprudence on the matter.[12] While American states have the right to limit jurisdiction further, the practice has been to follow the guidelines set out by constitutional standards.[13]

Jurisdiction can be general or specific. General jurisdiction is broader than in the civil law system, because 'personal jurisdiction by service of process' and 'doing business' jurisdiction can also be used, in addition to a defendant's domicile or residence, to establish the court's power over a defendant, legalising the lawsuit.

'Personal jurisdiction by service of process' attaches if a person is served with process while being temporarily in the forum state[14] as long as it does not violate 'traditional notions of fair play and substantial justice'.[15] The mere service of process while the person is in the forum state is sufficient for that state to have jurisdiction over the person regardless of the matter at stake.

---

[7] Regulation (EU) 1215/2012 on jurisdiction and the recognition and enforcement of judgments in civil and commercial matters [2012] OJ L351/1 (Brussels I Reg Recast), art 4; Brazilian Law 13.105/2015 (Brazilian Civil Procedure Code), art 21, I.

[8] Brussels I Reg Recast, art 7(1).

[9] Brussels I Reg Recast, art 7(2); Brazilian Civil Procedure Code, art 53, IV, a).

[10] Brussels I Reg Recast, art 24(1); Brazilian Civil Procedure Code, art 47.

[11] Fourteenth amendment.

[12] L Silberman, 'The Impact of Jurisdictional Rules and Recognition Practice on International Business Transactions: The US Regime' (2004) 26 *Houston Journal of International Law* 327, 329–31.

[13] SB Burbank, 'Jurisdiction to Adjudicate: End of the Century or Beginning of the Millennium?' (1999) 7 *Tulane Journal of International and Comparative Law* 111, 113.

[14] See *Burnham v Superior Court of California*, 495 US 604 (1990).

[15] *International Shoe Co v Washington*, 326 US 310, 316 (1945).

If the defendant is not situated in the state then the 'doing business' basis of jurisdiction can apply.[16] 'Doing business' jurisdiction can be exercised when corporations are carrying on a continuous and systematic, even if limited, part of their business in the territory of that forum.[17] This is a highly criticised doctrine, both within and beyond the American legal system,[18] as it does not provide much certainty in practice as to what the standard really is in order to attribute American courts with general jurisdiction,[19] weakening the rule-of-law principle. The problem becomes even more acute when potential foreign defendants are concerned with the possible consequences of transacting with US parties as being caught in a lawsuit in a foreign country without expecting it beforehand may be unfair,[20] diminishing the incentives of a foreigner to do business in the United States.[21]

Different legal systems therefore have different rules shaping the exercise of jurisdiction in respect of a given dispute; even if the rules were the same, without a set of rules to coordinate the exercise of jurisdiction, more than one court might be capable of being the forum in respect of the same dispute, opening the possibility for irreconcilable decisions. The second inquiry in the analysis of jurisdiction concerns the availability of mechanisms that may be used to solve this problem.

ii. The Relationship Between the Forum Court and Other Courts

The second aspect of jurisdiction, referred to by Professor Ralf Michaels as its horizontal aspect,[22] reflects the preferences of the legal system in considering the relationship between jurisdiction and other legal systems.

The relationship between the forum court and other courts can either be integrated through an overarching system or or its rules can be established unilaterally. Integrated systems can be created either through a quasi-federalist method such as the European Union or through less complex but nonetheless complicated structures, such as international treaties. Unilateral systems, on the other hand, can either deal with the relationship with foreign courts on a case-by-case basis, as is the approach in the American system, or have hard and fast rules that do not take into consideration the relationship with foreign courts, as is the approach in the Brazilian system.

As transnational transactions increase, these types of rules become even more important. Jurisdictional rules that clearly provide where lawsuits can be pursued

---

[16] 'Subsequent cases have derived from the *International Shoe* standard the general rule that a State may dispense with in-forum personal service on nonresident defendants in suits arising out of their activities in the State' (*Burnham* (n 14) 618.

[17] *Perkins v Benguet Consolidated Mining Co*, 342 US 437, 445–446 (1952).

[18] For an in-depth discussion of the doctrine, see M Twitchell, 'Why We Keep Doing Business with Doing-Business Jurisdiction' (2001) *University of Chicago Legal Forum* 171.

[19] See ibid 182–94.

[20] See ibid 197–202.

[21] On the other hand, a point to be made is that if a business wants to engage in 'doing business' in the US it should expect to be subject to any kind of jurisdiction that may be exercised over it. In any event, it is the type of decision that is harder to make when the rules are not clear.

[22] Michaels (n 6) 1027.

in these situations go a long way to facilitate them. The avoidance of parallel litigation and of multiple decisions is important to bring legal certainty to a given transaction, especially when there is nothing more than the legal system to be relied upon by the parties.[23]

Integrated Jurisdiction Systems: the EU Example

A good example of an integrated jurisdiction system is that of the European Union. The development of the European system for jurisdiction and enforcement of foreign judgments began with the enactment of the Brussels Convention[24] in 1968, a treaty made between Belgium, Germany, France, Italy, Luxembourg and the Netherlands, implementing the provisions of article 220 of the Treaty Establishing the European Economic Community (EEC); the Convention was a legal document and did not form part of the EEC legislation.[25] The objective of the Brussels Convention was to 'facilitate recognition and to introduce an expeditious procedure for securing the enforcement of judgments'.[26]

The Brussels Convention was created in the context of European integration and was a consequence of the understanding that for cross-border trade to be efficient, the recognition of judgments should be easy. For this it would be important to establish common jurisdictional rules, as it would then become impossible to justify the denial of recognition and enforcement on the basis of exorbitant jurisdiction.[27]

With the entry into force of the Treaty of Amsterdam in 1997, matters of civil jurisdiction came under the competence of the European Union, allowing for the creation of rules through the European Union's legislative process[28] and thus making the enactment, in 2001, of the Brussels I Regulation[29] possible.

The Brussels I Regulation established jurisdiction and enforcement rules for countries that are part of the European Union. The general rule of the Brussels I regime was that a defendant could be sued in his domicile,[30] but there were other specific grounds which provided that the defendant could be sued in the court of

---

[23] The importance of legal certainty and legal mechanisms becomes even more acute in financial markets and financial systems, which are essentially a legal construct. See K Pistor, 'A Legal Theory of Finance' (2013) Columbia Public Law Research Paper No 13–348.

[24] Convention of 27 September 1968 on Jurisdiction and the Enforcement of Judgments in Civil and Commercial Matters [1972] OJ L299/32 (Brussels Convention).

[25] The European Community obtained power to legislate on Civil Jurisdiction matters only after the Treaty of Amsterdam. See T Kruger, *Civil Jurisdiction Rules of the EU and Their Impact on Third States* (Oxford University Press 2008) 2.

[26] Brussels Convention, Preamble. On the importance of private international law for the integration of Europe, see L Gillies, 'Creation of Subsidiary Jurisdiction Rules in the Recast of Brussels I: Back to the Drawing Board?' (2012) 8 *Journal of Private International Law* 489, 494–98.

[27] Kruger (n 25) 12.

[28] ibid 15. See also A Dickinson, 'European Private International Law: Embracing New Horizons or Mourning the Past?' (2005) 1 *Journal of Private International Law* 197.

[29] Regulation (EC) 44/2001 on jurisdiction and the recognition and enforcement of judgments in civil and commercial matters [2001] OJ L12/1 (Brussels I Reg).

[30] Brussels I Reg, art 2.

another Member State or that some Member State courts would have exclusive jurisdiction.[31] The mechanism to avoid parallel proceedings and disputes among different courts was based on articles 27–30 of the Regulation, establishing that the court first seized should be the one to decide if it had jurisdiction or not, and all the other courts had a duty to stay their proceedings until a decision was reached.[32] If the court first seized decided that it had jurisdiction, the other courts had a duty under European law to decline jurisdiction in favour of the court first seized.[33] As a general matter, the Brussels I regime was applicable when the defendant was domiciled in a Member State of the European Union;[34] if the defendant was domiciled outside the European Union, the applicable rules of jurisdiction would be those of his national legal system.[35]

The mechanism provided certainty and efficiency to the functioning of the EU legal system. A single court alone was able to decide whether it had jurisdiction; on this basis, long conflicts as to the place that would be the most appropriate for the resolution of the dispute were avoided. The design of the system fulfilled the need for legal certainty and efficiency as it coordinated the functioning and exercise of the judicial function among the courts of different EU Member States.

Despite the advantages that the Brussels I regime provided to the organisation of different legal regimes and their interaction, the system was not without its flaws. An important area of concern was the improper use of the mechanism, which caused delays in respect of the resolution of the dispute. For example, even when the parties had made a choice-of-court agreement but the lawsuit had been initiated in a different court, the court identified in the agreement had to wait until the court first seized had decided on its lack of jurisdiction.[36] This caused delays, especially when inefficient courts were first seized.[37]

In 2009 a Green Paper[38] was released discussing the problems of the Brussels I Regulation and possible avenues for its improvement. At the end of 2012 the European Parliament and the Council of the European Union adopted the Brussels I Recast,[39] which came into force on 10 January 2015. The Brussels I Recast changed the logic of jurisdictional conflict rules when choice-of-court agreements are at stake, shifting the power to decide on jurisdiction to the court designated in the

---

[31] See Brussels I Reg, arts 2–7.
[32] Brussels I Reg, art 27(1).
[33] Brussels I Reg, art 27(2).
[34] Brussels I Reg, art 2(1).
[35] Brussels I Reg, art 4(1). See also Kruger (n 25) 59.
[36] See Case C-116/02 *Gasser v MISAT* [2003] ECR I-14693 (the court second seized has to suspend the proceedings until the court first seized has accepted or declined jurisdiction) and Case C-159/02 *Turner v Grovit* [2004] ECR I-03565 (the CJEU decided that anti-suit injunctions, mechanisms that could help to give teeth to choice-of-court agreements, are incompatible with the Brussels Regulation).
[37] In the literature, this is known as the 'Italian torpedo' problem.
[38] Green Paper on the Review of Council Regulation (EC) No 44/2001 on Jurisdiction and the Recognition and Enforcement of Judgments in Civil and Commercial Matters COM (2009) 175 Final.
[39] Regulation (EU) 1215/2012 on jurisdiction and the recognition and enforcement of judgments in civil and commercial matters [2012] OJ L351/1 (Brussels I Recast).

agreement,[40] thus solving the problem of the strategic use of courts to cause delay in litigation to which a choice-of-court agreement is relevant.

The Brussels regime, while designed mainly with the integration of Europe in mind, is also applicable in some cases involving parties from third states. Thus, in cases where the claimant is not domiciled in an EU Member State but is suing someone who is, the jurisdictional rules applicable are those found in Brussels I.[41] The logic is extended to the doctrine of *forum non conveniens*,[42] which cannot be applied when the defendant is domiciled in an EU Member State.[43]

The jurisdiction regime in the European context is quite different from that of the United States. The European rules are much more mechanical than the American ones, stripping courts of the scope to engage political considerations as to comity and convenience when deciding whether to entertain a dispute or not. The design of the system is a child of the needs of European integration, which emerged as an economic matter and has evolved in many different areas.[44] In the commercial and financial transaction areas, the development of a strong legal infrastructure for dispute resolution is essential and the Brussels regime goes a long way in providing for this, at least when considering the space within the European Union.

Unilateral Jurisdiction Systems

Unilateral systems are based only on the rules of the forum to mediate conflicts of jurisdiction between different legal systems. The rules and doctrines that are used in unilateral systems can either give the courts room in accepting jurisdiction to decide a case or can be highly specific, offering no possibility of discretion.

The US system is of the first type and it is an extremely complex one;[45] its jurisdictional relationship with other forums is mainly limited through the doctrines of *forum non conveniens* and 'jurisdiction to prescribe'.

Forum non conveniens is a doctrine dating back to the 1940s in the United States[46] that allows courts to decline jurisdiction when the case could be tried more conveniently in another forum.[47] The test was laid down in two decisions: *Gulf Oil Corp v Gilbert*[48] and *Koster v (American) Lumbermens Mutual Casualty Co*.[49] The

---

[40] Brussels I Recast, art 31(3).

[41] See Case C-412/98 *Josi v UGIC* [2000] ECR I-05925.

[42] A doctrine also available in the UK.

[43] See Case C-281/02 *Owusu v Jackson* [2005] ECR I-01383.

[44] For a brief overview of European integration, see P Craig and G Búrca, *EU Law: Text, Cases and Materials* (Oxford University Press 2011) 1–30; for an overview of the development of European private international law, see S Bariatti, *Cases and Materials on EU Private International Law* (Hart Publishing 2011) 1–61.

[45] For an overview, see A Colangelo, 'What is Extraterritorial Jurisdiction?' (2014) 99 *Cornell Law Review* 1303.

[46] SB Burbank, 'Jurisdictional Conflict and Jurisdictional Equilibration: Paths to a Via Media?' (2004) 26 *Houston Journal of International Law* 385, 393.

[47] M Davies, 'Time to Change the Federal Forum Non Conveniens Analysis' (2002) 77 *Tulane Law Review* 309, 311.

[48] *Gulf Oil Corp v Gilbert*, 330 US 501 (1947).

[49] *Koster v (American) Lumbermens Mutual Casualty Co*, 330 US 518 (1947).

courts must apply a test in deciding whether to decline jurisdiction, considering both private and public interests. The private interests to be taken into consideration include the relative ease of access to sources of proof and other practical problems that would make the trial of the case easier, as well as the enforceability of the judgment.[50] Public interest, on the other hand, concerns administrative difficulties that courts may face and the burdens that may be imposed in a community that is not related to the lawsuit, such as jury duty.[51] The approach followed in the United States is based on the notion that its courts should not waste energy in deciding disputes in which there is no relevant interest. One caveat is that the doctrine can only be applied if there is an alternative forum 'available', which means that the defendant must be 'amenable to process'.[52] Therefore, through this doctrine, US courts can decline to exercise their jurisdiction when they believe there is a more convenient forum for the dispute.

The other mechanism that is used by US courts to mediate possible disputes with other courts and sovereigns is the doctrine of 'jurisdiction to prescribe'. The analysis made under this doctrine is geared to answer the question of when the United States can apply its own laws; it becomes especially important in cases with a relevant foreign component occurring outside the United States.[53] Three landmark cases of the doctrine are *Laker Airways Ltd v Sabena, Belgian World Airlines,*[54] *Hartford Fire Insurance Co v California*[55] and *F Hoffmann-La Roche Ltd v Empagran.*[56] In *Laker*, the US District Court for the District of Columbia, while there was a parallel case running in London in respect of the same subject matter, confirmed what had been decided in *United States v Aluminum Co of America*[57] and was clear in stating that 'a country can regulate conduct occurring outside its territory which causes harmful results within its territory'.[58] In addition, the *Laker* decision to grant 'jurisdiction to prescribe' was also based on the conduct of Laker and the appellants, who had airline routes in the United States.[59] *Hartford* took 'jurisdiction to prescribe' a step further. The relevant activity that was under dispute took place in the United Kingdom and had been engaged in by UK corporations and subjects doing business outside of the United States, under an extensive UK

---

[50] *See Gulf Oil Corp* (n 48) 508.

[51] ibid 508–09.

[52] *Piper Aircraft v Reyno*, 454 US 235, 254 fn22 (1981).

[53] The bases of jurisdiction to prescribe are related to the legitimate stake of the state in the matter, which in the US can be nationality, conduct on the territory or substantial effects in the territory, at least in accordance with the Restatement (Third) of the Foreign Relations Law of the United States. See EM Fox, 'Modernization of Effects Jurisdiction: From Hands-off to Hands-linked' (2009) 42 *International Law and Politics* 159, 162–64.

[54] *Laker Airways Ltd v Sabena, Belgian World Airlines*, 731 F 2d 909 (1984).

[55] *Hartford Fire Insurance Co v California*, 509 US 764 (1993).

[56] *F Hoffmann-La Roche Ltd v Empagran*, 542 US 155 (2004).

[57] *United States v Aluminum Co of America*, 148 F 2d 416 (2d Cir 1945).

[58] *Laker Airways Ltd* (n 54) 922.

[59] ibid 924 ('In addition to the protection of American consumers' and creditors' interests, the United States has a substantial interest in regulating the conduct of business within the United States. The landing rights granted to appellants are permits to do business in this country. Foreign airlines fly in the United States on the prerequisite of obeying United States law').

regulatory framework that did not prohibit it.[60] In effect, 'jurisdiction to prescribe' was upheld due to the substantive effects that the conduct of UK corporations had on the US market and on the lack of an obligation imposed by the UK regulatory system to behave in the way they did.[61] Despite the increasingly global US regulatory aspirational trend that was established with *Hartford*, *F Hoffman-La Roche* began to delineate the limits of the US jurisdiction to prescribe. Even though this was a global case also involving American parties, the Americans settled their disputes and the case that went all the way to the US Supreme Court involved only the provision of remedies to foreign plaintiffs in respect of conduct that had been executed abroad and effects that were felt outside the United States. The decision in this case was that in this type of situation US laws would not be applicable.[62]

The rule in the securities context, which was decided in *Morrison v National Australia Bank*,[63] is similar. The case at stake in *Morrison* was a foreign-cubed class action, where foreign investors sued a foreign issuer for a transaction that occurred in the context of a foreign exchange. From a conduct and effects test, the US Supreme Court moved to a focus standard, where 'the focus of the Exchange Act is not upon the place where the deception originated, but upon purchases and sales of securities in the United States',[64] making the place of the transaction the important connection factor for the applicability of US law.

'Jurisdiction to prescribe' is therefore a doctrine that is used to delineate and justify the applicability of US laws when foreign elements are present. It is a doctrine within the doctrine of international comity, which is wider in scope and used for the enforcement of foreign judgments.[65]

It is important to underline the notion that in the US system, while considerations as to jurisdiction and foreign courts are, at times, taken from the perspective of what might happen in other courts and how appropriate it would be to extend US laws outside US territory, they are generally made locally, from the perspective of the US court and only valid within the US legal system; this is contrary to the European system, which has an overarching set of rules that include more than one national legal system.

Brazil, unlike to the United States, presents a more rigid system for dealing with foreign jurisdictions. The Brazilian Civil Procedure Code establishes that Brazilian courts have jurisdiction to resolve the dispute if the defendant is domiciled in

---

[60] See *Hartford Fire Insurance Co* (n 55) 819.

[61] ibid 798–99. This second question on the lack of obligation is a matter of comity and not one of jurisdiction to prescribe.

[62] *F. Hoffmann-La Roche Ltd* (n 56) 164 ('The price-fixing conduct significantly and adversely affects both customers outside the United States and customers within the United States, but the adverse foreign effect is independent of any adverse domestic effect. In these circumstances, we find that the FTAIA exception does not apply').

[63] *Morrison v National Australia Bank*, 561 US 247 (2010).

[64] ibid 265.

[65] For an overview on the US comity doctrine, see DE Childress, 'Comity as Conflict: Resituating International Comity as Conflict of Laws' (2010–2011) 44 *UC Davis Law Review* 11, 47–59; JR Paul, 'The Transformation of International Comity' (2008) 71 *Law and Contemporary Problems* 19.

Brazil, if the obligation has to be performed in Brazil, or if the lawsuit arises out of facts or acts that happened in Brazil;[66] nevertheless, in these cases, decisions that are made in a foreign forum may be recognised in Brazil as jurisdiction is not exclusive.[67] This jurisdictional power is excluded when there is an express choice of a foreign forum to resolve the dispute.[68]

Another important observation to be made is that, even though there is a provision for concurrent jurisdiction in Brazil, the Brazilian Civil Procedure Code is explicit in stating that a lawsuit in a foreign forum does not create *lis pendens* for Brazilian courts, allowing them to hear a dispute even though the dispute is already being litigated in a foreign court.[69]

In the context of a global world, the Brazilian system is adequate, as it gives parties the possibility of choosing where to litigate their dispute.

B. Recognition and Enforcement of Foreign Judgments

The recognition and enforcement of judgments is the external side of jurisdiction. Recognition and enforcement of foreign judgments is the acceptance of the laws and the exercise of power by another legal system. Recognition and enforcement is also a highly local political question that is decided by each legal system: some are more open to foreign judgments, accepting anything that does not go against their public policy, while others deny recognition and enforcement to all foreign judgments.[70]

The enforcement of foreign judicial decisions is a policy choice that a country must make. By accepting foreign judgments a legal system recognises that other courts also have the power to decide certain matters. Absent treaties or other types of integrated jurisdictional mechanisms, the decision to enforce a foreign judgment is made exclusively within the enforcing legal system.

---

[66] Brazilian Civil Procedure Code, art 21.

[67] Cases in which Brazilian courts have exclusive jurisdiction are regulated by article 23 of the Brazilian Civil Procedure Code: this includes matters related to immovable property in Brazil and succession regarding property situated in Brazil.

[68] Brazilian Civil Procedure Code, art 25. Before the new Civil Procedure Code, the choice of a foreign court would not preclude the Brazilian judiciary from hearing the matter. See *World Company Dance Show v Patrícia Chélida de Lima Santos* (STJ, 4th Chamber, REsp 1168547 / RJ) (2010) ('A cláusula de eleição de foro existente em contrato de prestação de serviços no exterior, portanto, não afasta a jurisdição brasileira'); *American Home Assurance Company v Braspetro Oil Services Company* (STJ, 4th Chamber, REsp 251438 / RJ) (2000) ('a competência concorrente do juiz brasileiro não pode ser afastada pela vontade das partes'; 'válida a eleição de um foro estrangeiro, permanece a concorrência, isto é, a autoridade brasileira não estará impedida de apreciar a matéria'). See also *RS Components Limited v RS do Brasil Comércio Importação Exportação Ltda* (STJ, 3rd Chamber, REsp 804306 / SP) (2008).

[69] Brazilian Civil Procedure Code, art 24.

[70] An example of a more liberal country would be the US, and an example of a more closed country would be the Netherlands. See R Michaels, 'Recognition and Enforcement of Foreign Judgments', Max Planck Encyclopedia of Public International Law, opil.ouplaw.com/view/10.1093/law:epil/9780199231690/law-9780199231690-e1848?rskey=dHgRET&result=1&prd=EPIL, 3.

As the recognition of a foreign judgment would imply the recognition of the exercise of power of a foreign state, countries are prone to recognise external judgments only to the extent that they can benefit from such a position. This becomes increasingly important as a country starts to engage in transnational commerce and its subjects develop the need for a legal infrastructure to dispose of any controversies with foreign counterparties. Two of the main objectives underpinning a legal system's recognition and enforcement of foreign judgments regime is the aim of attracting more business or of ensuring the enforceability of its own judgments in the courts of a foreign country, guaranteeing that its citizens may have legal redress mechanisms against outsiders.

As a unilateral approach to this question was not very effective for the purposes of creating a sustainable and robust transnational legal infrastructure, countries started to enter into bilateral treaties and even attempted to establish some multilateral ones to provide for the recognition and enforcement of foreign judgments. One of the most successful examples is the Brussels regime in the European Union.

i. Integrated Recognition and Enforcement Systems: the EU Example

The Brussels regime for jurisdiction and enforcement was born out of necessity. It was a result of the integration efforts that Europe was making and it established a comprehensive system to accommodate and coordinate the functioning of diverse legal systems. Jurisdiction rules were enacted to guarantee that no two courts would have jurisdiction over the same dispute, avoiding unnecessary conflicts between courts of different Member States.

However, ensuring that no two courts would entertain the same dispute was not enough. For an efficient legal infrastructure that could resolve disputes in an efficient manner, more was required; this amounted to provisions on the recognition and enforcement of foreign judgments. Not only would a litigant know with certainty that only one court would be able to decide a case without worrying that other courts might entertain the same dispute, but the decision coming from that court would, moreover, be enforceable in any other country under the same regime.[71]

Under the Brussels regime, the grounds for refusal of recognition are limited. They include only the public policy exception, the existence of a judgment given with a default of appearance if the defendant was not served with process, the impossibility of reconciling the judgment for which recognition is being sought with an earlier judgment given between the same parties in the Member State addressed, in another Member State or in a third state involving the same cause of action and between the same parties, preclusion and lack of jurisdiction on matters of insurance, consumer contracts, individual contracts of employment and exclusive jurisdiction.[72]

---

[71] Brussels I Reg Recast, art 45(3) prohibits raising the public policy exception regarding jurisdiction.
[72] See Brussels I Reg Recast, arts 45–46.

Thus, as the European Union adopts a strict standard for non-recognition, if the procedure leading to the judgment is undertaken properly, in compliance with the minimum requirements for due process and if the exercise of jurisdiction is established in accordance with what it is provided for in the Brussels I Regulation Recast, denial of recognition and enforcement will be highly unlikely.[73]

This design creates a system that brings certainty to litigating parties. By guaranteeing the enforcement of judgments, the system enables reliance on the infrastructure of the legal system. Of course, the functioning of a system like this one presupposes trust in the judicial systems of other countries.[74] Decisions that do not fall within the framework of the regime could cause distrust and, if persistent, lead to the political deconstruction of the system.

Another aspect of the system design is how simple it is to recognise and enforce a judgment. The cheaper and faster it is, the better for the robustness and efficiency of the legal system. On this front, the way in which the Brussels regime formerly operated left grounds for improvement. As it was, judgments had to go through a process of declaration of enforceability to be enforceable in a Member State country other than the one issuing the decision.[75] This is known as the *exequatur* procedure and its costs were considerable for the average investor.[76] This procedure was considered to be an obstacle to the free circulation of judgments, creating costs and delays that harmed the EU internal market.[77] The problem has already been addressed by the Brussels I Recast, which retires the *exequatur* procedure. Today a judgment of another Member State shall be enforced in the same condition as judgments made in the country in which enforcement is sought,[78] subject to the usual grounds of non-recognition.[79]

The new Brussels regime diminishes the hurdles for legal protection in the European environment. It is an interesting development within the European Union as it approximates the different legal systems that exist even further under the umbrella of the EU legal system. Despite some of its obvious advantages, some view these changes with scepticism and identify some dangers.[80] Only time will tell whether the changes have been good ones.

---

[73] See Case C-7/98 *Krombach v Bamberski* [2000] ECR I-1395; Case C-38/98 *Renault v Maxicar SpA* [2000] ECR I-02973.

[74] U Magnus and M Peter, *Brussels I Regulation* (2nd edn, Sellier 2012) 7–8.

[75] See Brussels I Reg, art 38.

[76] This procedure does not apply in relation to uncontested claims and claims under €2,000. See Regulation (EC) 805/2004 creating a European Enforcement Order for Uncontested Claims [2004] OJ L143/15; Regulation (EC) 861/2007 establishing a European Small Claims Procedure [2007] OJ L199/1.

[77] See Commission, 'Proposal for a Regulation of the European Parliament and of the Council on jurisdiction and the recognition and enforcement of judgments in civil and commercial matters' COM (2010) 748 final, explanatory memorandum, 3–4.

[78] Brussels I Recast, recital 26; art 41(1).

[79] Public policy exception, judgment in default with no service and a judgment that is irreconcilable with a judgment given between the same parties in the Member State enforcing the judgment. See Brussels I Recast, art 45.

[80] See LJ Timmer, 'Abolition of *Exequatur* under the Brussels I Regulation: Ill Conceived and Premature?' (2013) 9 *Journal of Private International Law* 129.

ii. Unilateral Recognition Systems

Absent treaties, states are free to design recognition systems as they see fit. At a general level, different recognition and enforcement systems are designed in a similar manner, involving tests of finality of the judgment, personal jurisdiction by the court rendering the decision, service of process, due process and a public policy exception, sometimes also having a reciprocity requirement[81] and engaging comity considerations.[82]

Even though the designs are, in general, similar, the application of recognition and enforcement rules always reflects the particular preferences and requirements of compliance with civil procedure of the country in which enforcement is being sought. For example, service of process on a foreign territory in a US-based dispute according to US standards (eg, by delivery of the documents through a private person or by mail) may preclude the recognition of the judgment in foreign courts.[83] The question is one of whether the decision will harm the sovereignty or the public interest of the state where recognition or enforcement is sought.[84]

The specific rules in Brazil for the recognition and enforcement of foreign judgments fall neatly within this pattern. To be recognised, the foreign decision has to be proffered by an authority with jurisdiction, service of process has to be performed or the absence of a party in a default judgment has to be legally verified, the judgment must be final and duly authenticated by the Brazilian Consul and translated by a sworn translator,[85] and it can be denied if it offends sovereignty or the public order.[86]

The system for recognition and enforcement in the United States is more peculiar: there is no overarching rule that is applicable all over the country, but the rules of each state govern recognition on the state's territory, even in federal courts.[87] While the rules for recognition and enforcement are state specific, they have been harmonised to a certain extent due to the Uniform Foreign Money-Judgments Recognition Act[88] enacted by many US states.[89] The remaining states apply the

---

[81] S Baumgartner, 'Understanding the Obstacles to the Recognition and Enforcement of US Judgments Abroad' (2013) 45 *New York University Journal of International Law & Politics* 965, 971.

[82] Comity is 'neither a matter of absolute obligation … nor of mere courtesy and good will … But it is the recognition which one nation allows within its territory to the legislative, executive or judicial acts of another nation' (*Hilton v Guyot*, 159 US 113, 163–164 (1895)).

[83] Baumgartner (n 81) 972.

[84] ibid 998.

[85] Resolution STJ 9 [2005] art 5.

[86] ibid, art 6.

[87] The existence of a federal common law for recognition and enforcement of foreign judgments was eliminated in *Erie Railroad Co v Tompkins*, 304 US 64 (1938). See also JC Martinez, 'Recognizing and Enforcing Foreign Nation Judgments: the United States and Europe Compared and Contrasted—a Call for Revised Legislation in Florida' (1995) 4 *Journal of Transnational Law & Policy* 49; Y Zeynalova, 'The Law on Recognition and Enforcement of Foreign Judgments: Is It Broken and How Do We Fix It?' (2013) 31 *Berkeley Journal of International Law* 155.

[88] Uniform Foreign Money-Judgments Recognition Act (Uniform Law Commission) www.uniformlaws.org/shared/docs/foreign%20money%20judgments%20recognition/ufmjra%20final%20act.pdf (Foreign Money-Judgments Recognition Act).

[89] The act has been enacted by Alaska, California, Colorado, Connecticut, Delaware, District of Columbia, Florida, Georgia, Hawaii, Idaho, Illinois, Iowa, Maine, Maryland, Massachusetts, Michigan,

common law according to the Restatement (Third) of Foreign Relations of the United States.[90] Also, as soon as the decision is recognised, it becomes domesticated and the same protection afforded by the Full Faith and Credit clause is also given to the foreign judgment.[91]

For the Uniform Foreign Money-Judgments Recognition Act, requirements are similar to the ones mentioned above: recognition is not given if the judgment is not conclusive, if notice was not given to the defendant, if the judgment was obtained by fraud, if the basis for the decision or the claim is against public policy, if the judgment conflicts with another final and conclusive judgment, if the proceeding in the foreign court was against an agreement by the parties or, in the event of jurisdiction based on personal service, if the court where the judgment was made was highly inconvenient.[92] Enforcement is executed according to the procedure for enforcing another US state judgment.[93] In addition to these requirements, some states also require reciprocity.[94]

In the United Kingdom the doctrine that was developed was more prone to the recognition of foreign judgments. The idea was that what was enforced was not the foreign judgment, but the obligation that it produced between the parties. As long as the court rendering the decision had competent jurisdiction over the defendant, the foreign judgment would be enforced.[95]

The lack of an overarching international system of jurisdiction and recognition and enforcement of foreign judgments could be cured by a global convention on jurisdiction.

C. An Attempt at a Global Convention on Jurisdiction

Many of the problems arising from different legal systems having jurisdiction over the same dispute and the lack of certainty for recognition and enforcement of foreign judgments could be solved by a global treaty on jurisdiction; even though there has been an attempt to create one, so far this has not become a reality.

The Judgments Project at the Hague Conference on Private International Law was such an attempt; it had the goal of creating a global treaty for jurisdiction and the recognition and enforcement of foreign judgments, a true double convention.[96] The work was initiated in 1992 and in 1999 a draft of a mixed convention

---

Minnesota, Missouri, Montana, Nevada, New Jersey, New Mexico, New York, North Carolina, North Dakota, Ohio, Oklahoma, Oregon, Pennsylvania, Texas, US Virgin Islands, Virginia, Washington.
[90] Zeynalova (n 87) 156.
[91] ibid 155.
[92] Foreign Money-Judgments Recognition Act, s 4.
[93] Foreign Money-Judgments Recognition Act, s 3.
[94] Zeynalova (n 87) 158. The reciprocity requirement became known in *Hilton* (n 82).
[95] See Michaels (n 70).
[96] See HCCH, 'The Judgments Project', www.hcch.net/en/projects/legislative-projects/judgments.

was published.[97] Despite the effort put into the project, negotiations fell apart due to the different approaches that delegations from the United States and delegations from Europe had in understanding the concept of jurisdiction,[98] leading to the conclusion of a far more limited convention on Choice of Courts,[99] which so far has not entered into force.[100] This is a convention that basically allows parties to choose courts to decide their disputes, avoiding legal uncertainty that may arise from the unacceptability of this kind of choice in some jurisdictions.

Even though the Judgments Project was not successful, in 2012 the Hague Conference on Private International Law decided to resume working towards a future instrument on cross-border litigation.[101]

D. Arbitration

The transnational aspect of judicial disputes is permeated by the efficiency problems of the legal infrastructure for dispute resolution. This is in part an explanation for the creation and growth of international arbitration in recent years.[102] Arbitration allows the parties to choose a mechanism for dispute resolution outside the court structure that is nonetheless enforceable in courts. This is possible due to the NY Convention,[103] an international treaty in force in 156 countries,[104] which gives binding effect to international arbitration clauses and to agreements to arbitrate a dispute.

The number of countries in which the NY Convention is applicable makes it a truly global infrastructure for dispute resolution, avoiding many of the problems that may arise out of the use of choice-of-court agreements, since these do not provide the same legal certainty to the parties as arbitration. This is mainly because of the different approaches for foreign judgments recognition and enforcement, such as the reciprocity requirement, and the insecurity of whether a court will decline jurisdiction when faced with a choice-of-court provision.

---

[97] A mixed convention would be one that includes not only required and excluded bases for jurisdiction, but also permitted ones, which would not be recognisable outside the country establishing jurisdiction based on them.

[98] See Michaels (n 6) 1009–11.

[99] The Hague Convention on Choice of Court Agreements (concluded 30 June 2005) (Hague Conference on Private International Law) (Hague Convention on Choice of Courts).

[100] See HCCH, 'Status Table: Convention of 30 June 2005 on Choice of Court Agreements', www.hcch.net/en/instruments/conventions/status-table/?cid=98.

[101] HCCH, 'Conclusions and Recommendations adopted by the Council' (Council on General Affairs and Policy of the Conference 17–20 April 2012), assets.hcch.net/upload/wop/gap2012concl_en.pdf.

[102] G Born, *International Commercial Arbitration* (Kluwer Law International 2009) 65–66.

[103] Convention on the Recognition and Enforcement of Foreign Arbitral Awards (entered into force 7 June 1959) 330 UNTS 38 (NY Convention).

[104] See UNCITRAL, 'Status: Convention on the Recognition and Enforcement of Foreign Arbitral Awards (New York, 1958)', www.uncitral.org/uncitral/en/uncitral_texts/arbitration/NYConvention_status.html.

By choosing arbitration, the parties can avoid such problems since the NY Convention provides that agreements to arbitrate and arbitral awards must be recognised by a Contracting State.[105]

E. Jurisdiction and Enforcement Aspects of Aggregate Litigation

The involvement of parties of different jurisdictions may create difficulties in respect of a court's exercise of jurisdiction over all of them, especially in cases where the aggregate litigation mechanism is an opt-out one. With opt-in mechanisms, all plaintiffs who will be bound will have given their consent, as they will be the parties initiating the case.[106]

In respect of the opt-out procedure, the matter is more complicated. How can a court have jurisdiction over plaintiffs that have not initiated the lawsuit and are not domiciled in the state in which the court is located? The approach of the Amsterdam Court in certifying the *Shell* and *Converium* settlements under the Dutch Act on Collective Settlement of Mass Damages procedure is enlightening.[107]

Since this was a settlement procedure, the Dutch court treated the applicant parties, the representative of the class and those who would otherwise be defendants in a normal proceeding as the plaintiffs, and the interested parties, the members of the class, as defendants.[108] By doing this, the court established jurisdiction in respect of investors domiciled in the Netherlands, according to Article 2 of the Brussels I Regulation[109] and, having established this, extended jurisdiction to those who were domiciled in other Members States through article 6.1, which provides a basis for jurisdiction if 'the claims are so closely connected that it is expedient to hear and determine them together to avoid the risk of irreconcilable judgments resulting from separate proceedings'. In respect of the other foreign interested parties, the Dutch court used the open-ended provisions of article 3(a) of the Dutch Code of Civil Procedure, which states that Dutch courts have jurisdiction 'if either the petitioner or, where there are more petitioners, one of them, or one of the interested parties mentioned in the petition has his domicile or habitual residence in the Netherlands'.

The important aspect, though, is not whether the Dutch court could have had established jurisdiction, but if jurisdiction established in this manner could have

---

[105] See NY Convention, arts II and III.

[106] In the EU, jurisdiction would be determined per Brussels I Reg Recast, arts 25 and 26.

[107] See *Shell Petroleum NV Settlement*, LJN: BI 5744, NIPR 2010, 71 (Court of Appeal Amsterdam 29 May 2009); *Converium Settlement*, NJ 2010, 683, NIPR 2011, 85 (Court of Appeal Amsterdam 12 November 2010); *Converium Settlement*, no. 200.070.039/01, LJN: BV1026 (Court of Appeal Amsterdam 17 January 2012).

[108] See HV Lith, *The Dutch Collective Settlements Act and Private International Law* (Erasmus School of Law 2010) 36–40 (criticising this approach as leading to multiple forums if more aggregate litigation mechanisms become available in Europe).

[109] In the *Converium* (n 107) settlements, the court also used the basis of article 5.1 to establish jurisdiction, the place where the obligation has to be performed, since the monies would be distributed by a foundation established in the Netherlands.

been seen as a problem for the recognition and enforcement of the settlement/ judgment in other countries. On this matter, Professor Halfmeier expressed his concern that it was not clear whether such an approach would be allowed under Brussels I; clarification is required via the intervention of the Court of Justice of the European Union (CJEU).[110] In the international context, absent a treaty, the matter would be left to the recognising state.

In respect of enforcement, the most pressing aspects that can be a barrier for recognition and enforcement, in addition to the issue of the jurisdiction of the court seized, is the question of proper notice and the adequate representation of the parties; these considerations will be analysed in Section III below.

II. Applicable Law

The question of applicable law is tied to the question of where the dispute is decided. The forum court will apply its own choice-of-law rules to decide the proper law to be applied to the dispute. International treaties and efforts in harmonisation are some of the avenues that have been pursued to reduce the number of different laws that could be applicable in a given dispute depending on the jurisdiction in which it is decided;[111] notwithstanding these efforts, uncertainty as to the applicable law in transnational securities transactions still exists and may represent a legal risk.

As set out previously in this book, there are three different types of disputes arising out of securities transactions: the issuer–investor, the financial intermediary–investor and finally, the information intermediary–investor dispute. The question as to which law will apply depends on what kind of dispute is at stake, the legal relationship between the parties and the forum of the dispute. As many financial disputes involve more than one type of cause of action, for example a dispute based on securities laws and on the contractual relationship, these questions can become quite complex.

Absent treaties on applicable law, the determination of what law applies will fall to the forum deciding the dispute. Even if choice-of-law provisions are used, their applicability may depend on where the lawsuit is being pursued as some legal systems do allow for the use of choice of law, while in others the matter is not so clear.[112] Moreover, public policy considerations may play a role in the law

---

[110] A Halfmeier, 'Recognition of a WCAM Settlement in Germany' [2012] *Nederland International Privaatrecht* 176, 178.

[111] An important objective of conflict-of-laws rules is to provide uniformity of decision regardless of the court in which the matter is decided. See CMV Clarkson and J Hill, *The Conflict of Laws* (4th edn, Oxford University Press 2011) 18–19.

[112] In Brazil, the wording of the law is not clear and the judicial decisions on the matter have not been friendly to choice of law. See AS Aguiar, 'The Law Applicable to International Trade Transactions with Brazilian Parties: a Comparative Study of the Brazilian Law, the CISG, and the American Law about Contract Formation' (LLM, University of Toronto 2011) 4–7; D Stringer, 'Choice of Law and Choice of Forum in Brazilian International Commercial Contracts: Party Autonomy, International Jurisdiction, and the Emerging Third Way' (2005–2006) 44 *Columbia Journal of Transnational Law* 959.

applicable to the dispute.[113] From an ex ante perspective, it might be impossible to know which law will be applicable in a securities transaction involving parties who are situated in multiple jurisdictions,[114] creating serious legal uncertainty that can discourage transactions.[115]

In the European Union the legal infrastructure has been going through a process of harmonisation, or at least of conflict avoidance, due to the efforts to establish a single market and the development of the underlying political structures required to make it work. This is done either through EU-wide legislation harmonising a specific field of law and binding on all EU Member States, or legislation providing for solutions on applicable law in a transnational dispute, such as the Rome Regulations, which aim to discourage the use of forum shopping in the EU context, based on the determination of the substantive law applicable to a given dispute.[116]

In the securities field, this transformation has been particularly intense. In the past few years the regulatory regime has become a full-blown one, operating mainly at the EU level and leaving little, regulation-policy wise, for the national regulators.[117]

The breadth of subject matters covered by EU securities regulation is quite broad, as was seen in the discussion in Chapter 4. The important issue for this chapter is that the rules have been harmonised; these harmonised rules are applicable throughout the European Union, whether they concern the duties of the issuer to provide information or the suitability test that the financial intermediary has to perform to sell securities to investors. Notwithstanding some small differences in implementation in Member States, the general legal framework is the same in respect of the standard of behaviour for securities transactions across the EU area. The difference that is important for applicable law analysis is that liability for non-compliance with EU securities law is regulated nationally.[118]

---

[113] See Section III.

[114] JS Rogers, 'Conflict of Laws for Transactions in Securities Held Through Intermediaries' (2006) 39 *Cornell International Law Journal* 285, 292.

[115] See B Crawford, 'The Hague "Prima" Convention: Choice of Law to Govern Recognition of Dispositions of Book-Based Securities in Cross Border Transactions' (2003) 38 *Canada Business Law Review* 157, 163.

[116] If the substantive rules of law are harmonised, conflict-of-laws rules become unnecessary. Even though the regulatory framework is becoming increasingly harmonised, the liability scheme for breach of securities law is still mainly based on national law.

[117] N Moloney, *EU Securities and Financial Markets Regulation* (3rd edn, Oxford University Press 2014) 21.

[118] See Directive 2004/109/EC on the harmonisation of transparency requirements in relation to information about issuers whose securities are admitted to trading on a regulated market [2004] OJ L390/38, art 7; Directive 2004/39/EC on markets in financial instruments [2004] OJ L145/1, art 25(1); Regulation (EU) 600/2014 on markets in financial instruments [2014] OJ L173/84, arts 24, 25 and 26. These instruments do not have any provisions on civil liability for non-compliance with its rules, meaning that the forum state law and private international law regime constitute the framework for the imposition of liability. See also D Busch, 'Why MiFID Matter to Private Law—the Example of MiFID's Impact on an Asset Manager's Civil Liability' (2012) 7 *Capital Markets Law Journal* 386.

The two broad areas of applicable law that are related to liability aspects of securities transactions are contract and tort. This section also analyses questions related to applicable law in arbitration and in aggregate litigation procedures.

A. Contract

Applicable law in contracts is mainly based on private autonomy, that is, the freedom of the parties to select the law applicable to their relationship.[119] Absent choice, most systems have rules leading to a given applicable law, usually taking into consideration the relationship of the contract to a particular system and the most closely connected law.

Even though private autonomy plays an important role in choice of law, its acceptance is not universal; many countries either do not accept it or impose limitations on its use. Brazil, for example, does not accept a choice-of-law clause in disputes to be decided by courts due to the Introductory Law to the Brazilian Law Norms,[120] which in its article 9 provides that 'to qualify and regulate obligations, the applicable law will be the one of where the obligations have been constituted';[121] if the dispute is to be submitted to arbitration, then choice of law is allowed.[122]

The United States on the other hand, while it is not as closed as Brazil, does not take a consistent position on the choice-of-law question due to the state law nature of the matter, to the extent that the party autonomy doctrine in the United States has been considered 'chaotic'.[123] The Restatement (Second) of Conflict of Laws is an influential secondary source in the United States but is not followed by all courts;[124] it allows for choice when the parties could have resolved the issue by an explicit provision in their agreement.[125] However, it limits the choice if the issue being addressed could not be resolved by an explicit provision in the agreement and at the same time, the chosen state has no substantial relationship to the parties or the transaction, or if applying the law would be 'contrary to a fundamental policy of a state which has a materially greater interest' than the chosen state and where, in the absence of choice, the applicable law[126] would be that of the place that 'has the most significant relationship to the transaction and the parties'.[127]

---

[119] S Symeonides, 'Party Autonomy in Rome I and II from a Comparative Perspective' in K Boele-Woelki, T Einhorn, D Girsberger and S Symeonides (eds), *Convergence and Divergence in Private International Law—Liber Amicorum Kurt Siehr* (Eleven International Publishing 2010) 514–15.

[120] In the event it is not clear where the obligation was constituted, the offeror's place of residence is deemed to be such place. See Brazilian Decree-Law 4.657/1942, art 9 § 2.

[121] See also Aguiar (n 112) 4–7.

[122] Brazilian Law 9.307/96, art 2 § 1.

[123] M Zhang, 'Party Autonomy and Beyond: an International Perspective of Contractual Choice of Law' (2006) 20 *Emory International Law Review* 527, 533.

[124] See S Symeonides, 'Choice of Law in the American Courts in 2009: Twenty-Third Annual Survey' (2010) 58 *American Journal of Comparative Law* 1.

[125] Restatement (Second) of Conflict of Laws § 187(1).

[126] Restatement (Second) of Conflict of Laws §187(2).

[127] Restatement (Second) of Conflict of Laws §188.

In the European Union the approach of the Rome I Regulation to applicable law is based on private autonomy, allowing the parties to decide which law should be applicable to their contractual relationship;[128] this decision cannot displace laws that cannot be derogated from by agreement if the parties are either in the same country for national matters[129] or within one or more EU Member States for Community law purposes.[130]

If no choice is made, article 4 defines the applicable law, which will be the one of the place where the seller or the service provider has residence.[131] In the securities context, contracts with multilateral systems, designed for buying and selling financial interests made in accordance with non-discretionary rules and governed by a single law, will be governed by that law.[132] If the applicable law cannot be established by this analysis, it will be the law of the habitual residence of the party that has to provide the characteristic performance of the contract.[133] Finally, if it is clear that the contract is manifestly more closely connected with a country other than that established by the previous analysis, the law of the most closely connected country will be applicable.[134]

Another aspect of contractual conflict-of-laws provisions that may be relevant in securities transactions, in respect of financial intermediary–investor disputes, is the status of the investor; he might be deemed to fall within some dimension of the 'weaker party' doctrine, that is, within the consumer category, either because of lack of information or because of a lack of bargaining power.[135] If this is the case, private autonomy is limited even further. In the European context, if a professional[136] is transacting with a consumer,[137] the applicable law will be the one of the habitual residence of the consumer if the professional pursues his commercial or professional activities in the place where the consumer has his habitual residence or if the activities are directed to that country.[138] A choice of law can still be made if it does not deprive the consumer of the protection afforded by the law of the country of his habitual residence.[139] In Brazil, which already has limits on choice of law, the rights granted to persons with consumer status are high as any choice that might prejudice the consumer in comparison with the applicable Brazilian regime

---

[128] Regulation (EC) 593/2008 on the law applicable to contractual obligations [2008] OJ L177/6 (Rome I Reg) art 3(1).

[129] Rome I Reg, art 3(3).

[130] Rome I Reg, art 3(4).

[131] Rome I Reg, art 4(1)(a) and (b).

[132] Rome I Reg, art 4(1)(h).

[133] Rome I Reg, art 4(2).

[134] Rome I Reg, art 4(3).

[135] HW Micklitz, J Stuyck and E Terryn, *Cases, Materials and Text on Consumer Law* (Hart Publishing 2010).

[136] A professional is a 'person acting in the exercise of his trade or profession'. Rome I Reg, art. 6(1).

[137] A consumer is 'natural person for a purpose which can be regarded as being outside his trade or profession'. Rome I Reg, art. 6(1).

[138] Rome I Reg, art 6(1)(a) and (b).

[139] Rome I Reg, art 6.2.

is not allowed.[140] Finally, the United States does not have a specific regime for consumers; the general connection to the contract requirement for limitation of choice of law and public policy considerations are applicable to curtail the effects of the choice of law.[141] A problem with the US approach arises from the use of such a broad standard; it becomes unclear what the standards for consumer protection and applicable law are.[142]

B. Tort

In respect of matters of tort, applicable law is also an important issue as an action in a country may have effects in another country, for example in respect of the price of the security being traded elsewhere. The main approaches to tort choice of law are either based on the place where the harm occurred, the place of conduct or another type of interest analysis, engaging relevant connecting factors.

In Brazil there is no distinction between extra-contractual and contractual choice-of-law regulation, as both are governed by article 9 of Decree-Law 4.657/1942, which states, as mentioned above, that 'to qualify and regulate obligations, the applicable law will be the one of where the obligations have been constituted'. The text of the law does not clarify whether the *lex loci delicti* or the *lex loci damni* principle applies.

In the United States the theories and doctrines for applicable law in tort are diverse and provide a highly complex landscape, moving from a single-point-of-contact analysis (the *lex loci delicti*) to considerations about the underlying policies of the states involved in the dispute.[143] Comparing different policies and factors to determine the applicable law in a cross-border tort dispute undermines legal certainty as it is never clear what the decision of the court will be; moreover, it obliges the judge to engage in a complicated analysis.[144] Even though certainty is not absolute in the United States at this moment, the different approaches have converged to provide for similar results as most of the time the law applicable to a given tort dispute will be the law of the state favouring the plaintiff.[145]

In Europe, due to the needs of European integration, the system of applicable law in non-contractual obligations is clearer and more systematised than in Brazil and the United States, having been regulated by the Rome II Regulation.[146] The

---

[140] Brazilian Consumer Defence Code, art 51 I. A textual reading of the provision does not imply that choice of law is forbidden, but since mandatory arbitration clauses are not allowed in consumer transactions (art 51 VII), the use of choice of law would also be severely limited.

[141] See G Ruhl, 'Consumer Protection in Choice of Law' (2011) 44 *Cornell International Law Journal* 569, 587–92.

[142] See JJ Healy, 'Consumer Protection Choice of Law: European Lessons for the United States' (2009) 19 *Duke Journal of Comparative & International Law* 535.

[143] S Symeonides, 'Choice of Law in Cross-Border Torts: Why Plaintiffs Win, and Should' (2009) 61 *Hastings Law Journal* 337, 346–48.

[144] ibid 403.

[145] 86% to be more precise. See ibid 389–92.

[146] Regulation (EC) 864/2007 on the law applicable to non-contractual obligations [2007] OJ L199/ 40 (Rome II Reg).

general rule is that the applicable law will be the *lex loci damni*, according to article 4(1).[147] In some situations, such as car accidents, the location in which the damage occurred is easy to ascertain, but in others, such as negligent or fraudulent misrepresentation,[148] this may be more complicated, undermining legal certainty.[149] The general rule is displaced if the persons involved have their habitual residence in the same country; in this case, the law of that country will be applicable.[150] Finally, when it is clear from the circumstances of the case that the tort is 'manifestly more closely connected' with another country, the law of that country will apply.[151]

Another important characteristic of the European regime for applicable law for non-contractual obligations is that the parties may choose by agreement which law they want to apply to their dispute after the event giving rise to the damage has occurred,[152] or if both parties are pursuing a commercial activity, they can agree on the applicable law before the event happens.[153]

C. Applicable Law in Arbitration

The nature of the securities dispute will determine whether it may be prone to arbitration. Both the financial intermediary–investor and the issuer–investor disputes are theoretically capable of being submitted to arbitration due to the legal link that an investor has with its financial intermediary and the corporation in which it has invested, while it is more difficult for the disputes with informational intermediaries to be submitted to arbitration.[154]

Applicable law in arbitration is a complex issue. The initial assessment starts with the law applicable to the arbitration agreement, which might be different from the applicable law of the substantive part of the contract. This is a consequence of the severability presumption of the arbitration agreement, which is considered in its own right as a separate contract and not as part of the underlying contract.[155]

In the securities context, this consideration is especially important due to the public policy aspects that securities regulation has and that have to be considered in light of arbitration. Disputes involving securities may be non-arbitrable in some jurisdictions; therefore, the law that will be applied to the arbitration agreement is important for the success of the dispute resolution process.

[147] 'Unless otherwise provided for in this Regulation, the law applicable to a non-contractual obligation arising out of a tort/delict shall be the law of the country in which the damage occurs irrespective of the country in which the event giving rise to the damage occurred and irrespective of the country or countries in which the indirect consequences of that event occur'.

[148] A Dickinson, *The Rome II Regulation: the Law Applicable to Non-contractual Obligations* (Oxford University Press 2008) 328–29.

[149] ibid 318–19.

[150] Rome II Reg, art 4(2).

[151] Rome II Reg, art 4(3).

[152] Rome II Reg, art 14(1)(a).

[153] Rome II Reg, art 14(1)(b).

[154] This would be possible if information intermediaries agreed to be part of the arbitration procedure, as explained in Ch 5.

[155] See Born (n 102) 311–53.

To this question a single correct answer is still missing. There is no consistent approach to non-arbitrability across the globe.[156] The NY Convention provides that recognition and enforcement of an arbitral award may be refused if 'The subject matter of the difference is not capable of settlement by arbitration under the law of that country',[157] giving the country in which the enforcement of an arbitral award is sought the possibility of protecting areas of its legal system that it believes should not be submitted to arbitration. This is an important consideration regarding the possible enforcement forums of the arbitral award but it does not provide an answer as to which law should apply to define the non-arbitrability standard at the dispute-resolution stage. Some of the approaches provide for the application of the law of the arbitral seat, the law of the forum in which enforcement may be sought or the law governing the arbitration agreement.[158] The best approach, however, would be one which engages the performance of an analysis similar to that which is done in relation to the public policy exception, regarding the law of the country to which the dispute is most closely connected to.[159]

The second question concerns the law applicable to the substantive part of the dispute, in the absence of agreement by the parties. National arbitral statutes differ in their approach and they may provide that arbitrators have to apply the conflict-of-laws rules of the arbitral seat, those with the closest connection to the case, those that they deem to be 'applicable' or 'appropriate' or just disregard conflict-of-laws analysis and apply directly the substantive law that they deem 'applicable' or 'appropriate'.[160]

Generally, absent agreement of the parties, the approach to be taken is dependent on the law of the arbitral seat. This is an effect of article V(1)(d) of the NY Convention, which allows refusal of recognition and enforcement of an arbitral award if it is not in accordance with the laws of the country in which the arbitration took place. The problem is the public policy aspect of securities regulation, which will be further analysed in Section III. In some specific cases, even if the dispute is arbitrable, it might only be properly resolved if it is done under the laws of the country where it will be enforced, otherwise the award may be denied recognition. Securities law is an area that falls neatly within these concerns.

D. Applicable Law in Aggregate Litigation with Transnational Elements

Applicable law questions in aggregate litigation with transnational elements can be a cause of concern, being also tied to questions of jurisdiction; this is the

---

[156] See ibid 516–35.
[157] Art V(2)a.
[158] Born (n 102) 520–23.
[159] ibid 525–26.
[160] ibid 2114–17.

case even in the EU context, which has a more harmonised system of private international law.

In tort-like cases, which involve issuer–investor and information intermediary–investor types of disputes, and where the *lex loci damni* principle usually applies—as it does in Europe by virtue of article 4 of the Rome II Regulation—there will be as many different laws as there are countries in which parties have been harmed.

The problem with this approach is that it also has effects on jurisdiction. In *Roche v Primus*[161] the CJEU decided that, despite Roche BV in the Netherlands together with eight other companies in the Roche group situated in other countries having violated a European patent, since the Munich Convention establishes that violations have to be examined under the national law of each state in which the patent has been granted, decisions could not be irreconcilable for the purposes of article 8(1) of Brussels I Recast.

The situation in a securities case would be slightly different as there would only be one provider of information that is false or misleading; however, given the *lex loci damni* principle in Rome II, the logic would be the same and there would be as many applicable laws as jurisdictions in which persons have been harmed since liability in securities cases is to be established according to national law, which could preclude the use of article 8(1) of Brussels I Recast for jurisdiction purposes. The difference that exists in securities cases can be its salvation for aggregate litigation purposes; since the person issuing the statement is a single party, there is a possibility to engage the closest connection test for the purposes of determining the applicable law as provided for in article 4(3) of Rome II, thus enabling the use of article 8(1) Brussels I Recast for jurisdiction purposes, and therefore allowing for a European-wide aggregate litigation mechanism.

Transnationally, in the absence of a treaty regulating the matter, the only choice left for dealing with the different applicable laws is to allow for choice of law to regulate the relationship between issuers and investors; this solution could also be applied in the EU context. The argument against this approach is that issuers would then be allowed to choose their laws, undermining investor protection. Nonetheless, this is a system that could possibly work when foreign investors reach the market in which the issuer operates on their own, without the active distribution of securities in the investor's jurisdiction, or if the law chosen is that applicable where the company is listed. This would not only facilitate aggregate litigation, but would also create a fair framework for investors, who, absent such provision, would actually have different rights depending on where they are based, notwithstanding that the securities are the same.

---

[161] Case C-539/03 *Roche v Primus* [2006] ECR I-06535.

III. The Public Policy Question

The public policy provisions of a legal system are those that are applied irrespective of the agreement of the parties, due to their importance to the execution of the forum's policy.[162] They involve sensitive issues in many different areas, ranging from consumer protection[163] to anti-bribery legislation[164] and have as their objective the protection of certain interests that are deemed to be important to the country. What falls within the public policy provisions of a legal system depends on the policy choices that are made by it; for example, the protection afforded to consumers in Brazil is much higher than in the United States.[165]

The approach to public policy and what is accepted or not in a decision may also depend on the national or international character of the dispute. Courts tend to have a different interpretation of what constitutes public policy when the dispute is international, especially in arbitration, as public policy will also involve considerations regarding the public policy of the state of the applicable law and the law of the arbitral seat of the dispute.[166]

A. Public Policy and Securities Disputes

Securities law has an important public policy aspect as it protects investors from fraud and other inequitable acts in securities transactions, creating confidence and allowing for stronger securities markets.[167] A question with which academics have been struggling is when mandatory laws[168] of a foreign country are applicable to a cross-border transaction.[169] An example in the securities field is useful for the purposes of understanding this problem. An English company decides to sell

---

[162] D Donovan and A Greenawalt, '*Mitsubishi* after Twenty Years: Mandatory Rules Before Courts and International Arbitrators' in L Mistelis and J Dew (eds), *Pervasive Problems in International Arbitration* (Kluwer Law International 2006) 13; JR Nuss, 'Public Policy Invoked as a Ground for Contesting the Enforcement of an Arbitral Award, or for Seeking its Annulment' (2013) 7 *Dispute Resolution International* 119.

[163] In the EU context, for example, see Case C-240/98 *Oceano Editorial v Roció Quintero* [2000] ECR I-04941 (allowing courts to make preliminary assessments on the unfairness of a choice-of-court clause for jurisdiction purposes).

[164] See Donovan and Greenawalt (n 162).

[165] Compulsory arbitration in Brazil in consumer relations is forbidden by law, being allowed only in very few cases, while, in the US, arbitration is generally allowed. Compare Brazilian Consumer Defence Code, art. 51 VII with *AT&T Mobility v Concepcion*, 536 US 321 (2011). For a case in which consumer arbitration in Brazil was accepted, see *CZ6 Empreendimentos Comerciais Ltda v Lúcio Maciel* (TJRJ, 15th Chamber, Civil Appeal n. 2008.001.30250) (2008).

[166] Nuss (n 162) 127.

[167] See Ch 4.

[168] For an overview of the term, see HC Grigoleit, 'Mandatory Law: Fundamental Principles' in J Basedow, K Hopt and R Zimmermann (eds), *Max Planck Encyclopaedia of European Private Law* (Oxford University Press 2011).

[169] For an overview on different theories, see TG Guedj, 'The Theory of the Lois de Police, a Functional Trend in Continental Private International Law—A Comparative Analysis with Modern

securities to an American company. The English company is regulated by English securities laws in respect of its establishment and operation, as well as in respect of the duties it owes to its clients, in addition to the applicable anti-fraud provisions. The United States, on the other hand, has its own laws on the selling of securities and the determination of the applicable standards to identify what constitutes fraud in a securities transaction. If there were a choice-of-law provision choosing English law to govern the transaction, would US law be imposed when the US company sued, or would the parties' choice be enforceable?

The real problem mainly arises when the dispute has to be decided or where the judgment has to be enforced in the forum of the law not chosen in the contract; in the example, this would be the US courts.[170] The court considering whether to recognise a decision or a choice of law that does not take account of its domestic policies and laws will have to balance the importance of such policies with the promotion of international harmony; a given rule of law will become a public policy provision that can be used to justify the public policy exception when the court considers that the domestic public policy at stake is more important than these international considerations.[171]

Even though public policy provisions have a mandatory dimension, they may be relativised, depending on the interest in consideration. An interesting example is the interaction of the anti-waiver provisions of US securities law with the choice-of-law and arbitration/forum selection agreements in overseas investment contracts. In *Roby v Corporation of Lloyd's*[172] the Second Circuit decided that notwithstanding the choice of English law and of English forum and the clear inapplicability of US securities law in that forum,[173] the choice of forum and choice of law should be upheld in the US courts unless the agreement was unreasonable under the circumstances.[174] The unreasonable-agreement concept can be translated into 'fraud or overreaching', 'inconvenience or unfairness of the selected forum', deprivation of a remedy under chosen law or the contravention of a public policy of the forum state.[175]

In respect of the public policy aspect, in which US securities legislation is recognised as 'protecting American investors from injury by demanding "full and fair disclosure" from issuers' and 'deterring exploitation of American investors',[176] the court said that it would only 'be contravened if the applicable foreign law failed

---

American Theories' (1991) 39 *American Journal of Comparative Law* 661; see also RJ Weintraub, 'The Extraterritorial Application of Antitrust and Securities Law: an Inquiry into the Utility of a "Choice-of-Law" Approach' (1992) 70 *Texas Law Review* 1799.

[170] In the UK courts, this would be easily solvable, as the problem would concern a UK company with a UK choice-of-law on the contract: Rome I would be applicable. See Dicey, Morris and Collins, *The Conflict of Laws* (15th edn, Sweet and Maxwell 2012) 2103.

[171] Guedj (n 169) 666.

[172] *Roby v Corporation of Lloyd's*, 996 F 2d 1353 (1993).

[173] ibid 1362 ('neither an English court nor an English arbitrator would apply the United States securities laws, because English conflict of law rules do not permit recognition of foreign tort or statutory law').

[174] ibid 1363.

[175] ibid.

[176] ibid 1364.

adequately to deter issuers from exploiting American investors'.[177] The court's next step was to recognise that English law provided similar remedies as US securities law,[178] protecting investors from fraud and misrepresentation,[179] while at the same time accepting that, for the purposes of disclosure requirements, the transaction fell within Regulation D,[180] and that nonetheless English law provided Lloyd's 'adequate inducement to disclose material information'.[181] While recognising that the application of US securities law would give the plaintiffs a higher chance of victory, the Second Circuit established that 'ample and just remedies' were available under English law and therefore that the US public policy on securities legislation was protected.[182] The same approach has been taken by the Fifth,[183] Eighth[184] and Ninth Circuits.[185]

Public policy provisions, therefore, have at their core rules from which parties cannot contract out, due to policy interests of a country. They matter for private international law because they may allow a country to deny the recognition and enforcement of a foreign decision on the basis that the decision is against the public policy of the country; moreover, they might allow it to keep specific substantive matters exclusively within the jurisdiction of national courts. As has been shown, they can be relativised in certain jurisdictions as long as the contracting out does not lead to the complete forfeiture of the protection that the party would enjoy under the rules that have been contracted out, even though the level of protection may be lower.

B. Public Policy and Notice in Aggregate Litigation

The public policy aspects of aggregate litigation are related to the right to a fair trial, recognised in many Constitutions and international treaties.[186] As a background matter, it is important to note that fundamental rights of this type are not absolute; they may be subject to limitations when these are justified by a legitimate aim and proportional measure to achieve this aim.[187]

Regarding aggregate litigation, the main issue related to a fair trial is notice. This is only a problem in opt-out procedures, since in opt-in procedures the plaintiff will actively consent to engage in litigation. The purpose of notice, as a general matter, is to inform a party that there is a legal proceeding (the outcome of which

---

[177] ibid.
[178] Even though while in the US reliance would not have to be proved and controlling persons would also be liable for misrepresentation, this would not be the case in English law; ibid 1365.
[179] ibid.
[180] The US Securities Regulation that exempts issuers from disclosure requirements.
[181] *Roby* (n 172) 1366.
[182] ibid.
[183] *Haynsworth v The Corp*, 121 F 3d 956 (5th Cir 1997).
[184] *Bonny v Society of Lloyd's*, 3 F 3d 156 (8th Cir 1993).
[185] *Richards v Lloyd's of London*, 135 F 3d 1289 (9th Cir 1998).
[186] The Due Process clause in the US Constitution, art 5, LIV of the Brazilian Constitution, art 6 of the European Convention on Human Rights, art 47 of the Charter of Fundamental Rights of the European Union, art 8 of the American Convention on Human Rights, among others.
[187] *Lithgow and Others v the United Kingdom* (1986) Series A no 102 para 194 ('[A] limitation will not be compatible with [a fair trial] if it does not pursue a legitimate aim and if there is not a reasonable

will bind him) in course, in order to allow the person to mount a defence. Its existence therefore becomes crucial to bind plaintiffs in an opt-out procedure. As if they were defendants, proper notice should be sufficient grounds to guarantee that a trial, or settlement, was not unfair; as argued by Professor Feintman, this is more a matter of estoppel than of positive consent.[188] The fundamental right to a fair trial should not be seen as having been breached if the party has knowledge about the procedure and has not opted out or become actively involved in the process.

There are many international instruments that allow for service of process from one jurisdiction to another, such as the Hague Service Convention of 1965 and Regulation (EC) 1393/2007.[189] Given that these are legally permitted mechanisms, notice through them should be sufficient to bring absent plaintiffs to the legal dispute, binding them in respect of the outcome, having given them the opportunity to opt out or to become involved in the lawsuit. To this extent, if notice is properly given, the only remaining objection to aggregate litigation in a foreign country would be the aggregate character of the lawsuit, which becomes a weak argument per se absent a fair trial violation.

A problem with the normal legal ways of giving notice is that they may be costly. In this respect, the approach initially taken by the Amsterdam court in the *Dexia* case was to request notification by ordinary post, contrary to the requirement of a registered letter per Regulation (EC) 1393/2007;[190] it justified this determination by saying that the parties may raise any objections at the recognition and enforcement phase.[191] Since this approach was clearly prone to problems of recognition of the settlement agreement, the Amsterdam court started following the guidelines of Regulation (EC) 1393/2007 in subsequent cases.[192]

The preceding discussion assumed that the address of the persons to be notified was known but in many situations this would not be the case, which could complicate matters tremendously. For example, in the EU context, Regulation (EC) 1393/2007 does not apply when the address of the person to be served is unknown,[193] which may impede the recognition of the judgment in other Member States.[194] In fact, as there are no international mechanisms regulating opting out of aggregate litigation in courts, it becomes impossible to guarantee that foreign class members

---

relationship of proportionality between the means employed and the aim sought to be achieved'); Case C-394/07 *Gambazzi v DaimlerChrysler* [2009] ECR I-02563 para 29 ('It should, however, be borne in mind that fundamental rights, such as respect for the right of the defence, do not constitute unfettered prerogatives and may be subject to restrictions. However, such restrictions must in fact correspond to the objectives of public interest pursued by the measure in question and must not constitute, with regard to the aim pursued, a manifest or disproportionate breach of the rights thus guaranteed').

[188] R Feintman, 'Recognition, Enforcement and Collective Judgments' in A Nuyts and NE Hatzimihail (eds), *Cross-Border Class Actions: The European Way* (Seillier European Law Publishers 2014) 107–08.

[189] Regulation (EC) 1393/2007 on the service in the Member States of judicial and extrajudicial documents in civil or commercial matters [2007] OJ L324/79.

[190] Art 14.

[191] Lith (n 108) 70–71.

[192] ibid.

[193] Art 1(2).

[194] Art 34(2).

will be bound (even when notice by newspapers is widely used, as was the case in the *Shell* Dutch settlement),[195] thus undermining the legal certainty of the decision at a transnational level.

As the methods for notice under different national laws can become a problem for aggregate litigation, a solution based on arbitration as a method of dispute resolution may facilitate the matter. Arbitration laws allow for notice of process through the means agreed by the parties,[196] pre-empting some of the burdensome methods of notice required by national legislation. For example, email could be established as a means of notice for aggregate litigation purposes in issuer–investor disputes, allowing for the development of an efficient opt-out dispute resolution mechanism.

C. Public Policy and Arbitrability of Securities Disputes

Arbitrability is directly related to the public policy provisions of the forum. While matters that are non-arbitrable under a given legal system are matters of importance as far as public policy is concerned, not all matters with public policy importance are non-arbitrable. The consumer dispute example in Brazil discussed above is a matter that falls within the non-arbitrable public policy category. An arbitral award arising out of a consumer dispute with a Brazilian customer based on a compulsory arbitration clause would not be enforceable according to Brazilian law.[197] Within the EU context, arbitrability in consumer disputes is not per se illegal, but courts do have the power to assess the unfairness of the arbitral clause according to the factual circumstances.[198] On the other hand, US antitrust law, clearly a matter of public policy, falls within the arbitrable category. Previously, it was more common that any issues under national mandatory law were excluded from arbitration; this position is no longer as prevalent.[199] Some legal systems are changing, allowing public policy matters to be decided by arbitration but requiring the applicability of those laws in the arbitration procedure as a prerequisite of an enforceable award.[200] Mandatory laws embodying public policy concerns can, therefore, be arbitrable. Accordingly, it is important to establish to what extent securities laws and claims arising out of them can be submitted to arbitration.

---

[195] Lith (n 108) 74.

[196] See *Queensland Cotton Corporation Ltd v Agropastoril Jotabasso Ltda* (STJ, Special Chamber, SEC 6753/EX) (2013). For a discussion on the matter, see Born (n 102) 1748–58.

[197] Brazilian Consumer Defence Code, art 51, VII.

[198] See Case C-168/05 *Mostaza Claro v Centro Móvil* [2006] ECR I-10421 (allowing the annulment of an arbitration award based on an unfair term in the consumer context, even if not pleaded in the proceedings) and Case C-40/08 *Asturcom Telecomunicaciones v Cristina Rodríguez* [2009] ECR I-09579 (giving the court that has to enforce an arbitral award made in the absence of the consumer, the power to assess of its own motion whether the arbitration clause was unfair, if that is possible according to national law).

[199] P Viscasilas, 'Arbitrability of (Intra-) Corporate Disputes' in LA Mistelis and SL Brekoulakis (eds), *Arbitrability: International & Comparative Perspectives* (Wolters Kluwer 2009) 285.

[200] ibid.

In the United States securities transactions are clearly arbitrable, both in issuer–investor and financial intermediary–investor disputes.[201] This was not always the case. In 1953 the US Supreme Court decided in *Wilko v Swan*[202] that the provisions of the FAA could not displace the provisions of the Securities Act of 1933 due to the language in Section 14, which provided that 'any condition, stipulation, or provision binding any person acquiring any security to waive compliance with any provision of this subchapter or of the rules and regulations of the Commission shall be void'. Even though this seemed the best approach due to the objectives of the Securities Act, which in part was created to protect investors and give them rights of redress, the situation was reversed in *Scherk v Alberto Culver*[203] and *Mitsubishi v Soler Chrysler-Plymouth Inc*.[204] The first case involved the Securities and Exchange Act anti-fraud provision. The US Supreme Court differentiated the case from *Wilko v Swan* due to its international aspect, allowing arbitration in securities cases that involved disputes with parties from different countries,[205] while the second extended this rationale to antitrust claims and consolidated the arbitrability of rights that fall within public policy.

In civil law countries it is not clear whether securities disputes, especially of the investor–issuer type, are arbitrable. In Brazil the set-up of the financial market and the existence of the Câmara de Arbitragem de Mercado, coupled with the differentiated corporate governance levels that are available in BM&FBovespa and require arbitration of intra-corporate disputes,[206] indicate that securities disputes can be arbitrable.[207] The arbitration clauses in the corporate charter of the companies listed in the relevant segments indicate that disputes arising out of the rules enacted by the CVM, which regulates information disclosure and fraud, have to be resolved through arbitration.[208]

Therefore, even though securities laws have a relevant public policy dimension, recent developments in the field show that there might be space to soften the mandatory aspects involved, as long as the final regulatory aim of a strong market, based on some degree of investor protection, is maintained.

---

[201] *See* I Bantekas, 'Arbitrability in Finance and Banking' in LA Mistelis and SL Brekoulakis (eds), *Arbitrability: International & Comparative Perspectives* (Wolters Kluwer 2009) 297–300.

[202] *Wilko v Swan*, 346 US 427 (1953).

[203] *Scherk v Alberto Culver*, 417 US 506 (1974).

[204] *Mitsubishi v Soler Chrysler-Plymouth Inc*, 473 US 614 (1985).

[205] *Scherck* (n 203) 517 ('Alberto-Culver's contract to purchase the business entities belonging to Scherk was a truly international agreement. … The exception to the clear provisions of the Arbitration Act carved out by Wilko is simply inapposite to a case such as the one before us').

[206] Novo Mercado, Nível 2, Bovespa Mais and Bovespa Mais Nível 2.

[207] See BM&FBOVESPA, 'O que são Segmentos de Listagem', www.bmfbovespa.com.br/pt_br/listagem/acoes/segmentos-de-listagem/sobre-segmentos-de-listagem/.

[208] eg Estatuto Social Consolidado Somos Educação SA, http://ri.somoseducacao.com.br/pt-br/governanca/Documents/Estatuto%20Social_23072015_SOMOS.pdf, art 48, and Estatuto Social Brasil Brokers Participações SA, www.mzweb.com.br/brbrokers/web/conteudo_pt.asp?idioma=0&conta=28&tipo=12126, art 37.

D. Public Policy and Arbitration Based on Corporate Charters

In the investor–issuer dispute, the question of the arbitrability of intra-corporation disputes is an important one.[209] Arbitration through corporate charter provisions can be a viable alternative for creating a mass dispute resolution system.

Whether arbitration based on corporate charter provisions is allowed varies greatly depending on the jurisdiction under analysis. While in Spain and Brazil arbitration is accepted as a means of solving disputes based on corporate charters, in the United States the question is still hotly debated.

In Brazil and Spain the arbitration law is clear in allowing for arbitration agreements in corporate charters. The Brazilian Corporation Law states that

> the corporate charter may establish that the disputes between shareholders and the company, or the controlling shareholders and minority shareholders, may be solved through arbitration, within the specified terms.[210]

This paragraph was added by Brazilian Law 10.303/2001 in 2001, which changed relevant provisions of the Brazilian Corporate Law and of the Brazilian Law 6.385/76, the law regulating the securities market and the CVM.

The Spanish Arbitration Law has a provision of the same nature, which states that 'corporations may submit to arbitration the conflicts arising out of them'.[211] This provision in Spanish law is new, having been added in 2011 through Spanish Law 11/2011, and enacted with the objective of modernising arbitration in Spain. In its Preamble, it was clear the intent of the drafters was to 'clarify … the existing doubts related to corporate charter arbitration in corporations'.[212]

In Brazil corporate charter arbitration is not only a possibility, but it has been institutionalised through the BM&Bovespa Listing Requirements for its two highest corporate governance levels.[213] The arbitration requirement is attached to a specific arbitral institution, the Câmara de Arbitragem de Mercado.[214] Therefore, corporate charter arbitration is seen in Brazil as being better than the use of courts for these cases. There are some criticisms to be made in respect of this current scenario in Brazil[215] but legally corporate charter arbitration is a possibility.

In the United States this subject is not as simple and despite the possibility of using corporate charter arbitration,[216] its use in public companies is a disputed

---

[209] It is true that those who have sold a security based on misleading information do not have a link to the company when the suit is brought, but nonetheless they did have a link at the moment when the sale was made.

[210] Brazilian Law 6.404/76 (Brazilian Corporate Law), art 109 § 3 (trans by the author).

[211] Spanish Law 60/2003, art 11 *bis* 1.

[212] Spanish Law 11/2011, Preamble, II (trans by the author).

[213] See BM&FBOVESPA (n 207).

[214] ibid.

[215] For example, the confidentiality surrounding the financial markets arbitration system in Brazil. See E Bezerra, 'Especialista critica arbitragem em mercado de capitais' (*Consultor Jurídico*, 30 May 2013), www.conjur.com.br/2013-mai-30/arbitragem-retrocesso-mercado-capitais-professora-gv.

[216] This is a discussion that has gone as far back as 1988, see JC Coffee, 'No Exit?: Opting Out, the Contractual Theory of the Corporation, and the Special Case of Remedies' (1988) 53 *Brooklyn Law*

matter. There has been resistance from various sectors, public and private, since the first attempts to use arbitration clauses in corporate charters of public companies. On the public side, in 1990, a Pennsylvania corporation tried to include arbitration clauses in its charter and bylaws, but the SEC decided to decline to accelerate the effectiveness of the company's registration statement, pushing it to exclude those provisions.[217] On the private side, the NYSE regulatory arm changed its arbitration regulation rules to ban arbitration of class and derivatives claims.[218]

Despite the pro-arbitration policy in the United States, recent developments have reaffirmed the negative stance taken in respect of intra-corporate arbitration for public companies. In January 2012 the Carlyle Group was preparing an initial public offering (IPO) and tried to include an arbitration provision in their corporate charter;[219] they were soon discouraged from doing so after consulting with the SEC and other interested parties.[220] It is also important to note that while the SEC and investor protection groups are fierce in combating arbitration clauses in American public companies, the same is not true for foreign companies trading in the United States. There are many foreign companies that do have an arbitration clause in their corporate charter and are currently traded in the US securities market.[221] This is interesting because foreign companies have to comply with the same requirements as American ones in order to trade their shares in the United States, and the perils that American investors might face from an arbitration clause are virtually the same, regardless of whether the companies are American or foreign.[222]

In any event, this is more of a political than a legal dispute. Legally speaking, in the American legal system, corporate arbitration has already been accepted as being possible.[223] Under this legal framework the arbitrability of securities disputes arising out of shareholder–company relationships is a possibility, despite the resistance of the SEC in accepting these provisions in the corporate charters of American companies.

Review 919. At that time it already seemed that this was a path where American law would lead due to the pre-emptive character of the FAA (ibid 954). See also *Perry v Thomas*, 107 S Ct 2520 (1987).

[217] C Ravanides, 'Arbitration Clauses in Public Company Charters: an Expansion of the ADR Elysian Fields or a Descent into Hades?' (2007) 18 *The American Review of International Arbitration* 371, 375.

[218] See FINRA Customer Code, arts 12204 and 12205.

[219] S Davidoff, 'Carlyle Readies an Unfriendly I.P.O. for Shareholders' (*NYT Dealbook*, 18 January 2012) dealbook.nytimes.com/2012/01/18/carlyle-readies-an-unfriendly-i-p-o-for-shareholders/.

[220] K Roose, 'Carlyle Drops Arbitration Clause from I.P.O. Plans' (*NYT Dealbook*, 3 February 2012) dealbook.nytimes.com/2012/02/03/carlyle-drops-arbitration-clause-from-i-p-o-plans/.

[221] Ravanides (n 217) 389–407.

[222] Except when exemptions for cross-border offerings are applicable. See CFR § 230.800–230.802.

[223] See Ravanides (n 217) 414–26.

IV. Implications for Securities Disputes

The efficiency of law in transnational transactions depends on the mechanisms available to apply and enforce legal rules in the jurisdictions where the parties to a dispute are situated or have assets. The analysis that has to be made involves jurisdiction, the applicable law to the dispute and the possibility of recognition and enforcement of the judgment. Having identified the general aspects of private international law in the systems under analysis, I will now analyse their implications in the securities field for each type of dispute.

A. Investor–Issuer Disputes

Transnational investor–issuer disputes can be categorised in the following way: if the transaction is exchange based it can either be an investment from the investor in a foreign exchange or it can be made through the depositary receipt system of a foreign share in a local exchange; otherwise, it is an open-market transaction with a foreign counterparty.

i. Exchange-based

Securities that are listed on a stock exchange have a strong tie to the laws and regulations of the country in which the stock exchange is located. Listing requirements will have to be complied with, prospectus disclosure, transparency requirements and accounting information will all have to be satisfied in accordance with what is required by that legal system.[224] As a general matter, listed securities and the obligations arising out of securities laws are governed by the law of the country in which the exchange is located, as this is considered as the relevant market for the transactions in such securities;[225] however, private international law rules may allow for a lawsuit in a different country, as well as a different applicable law regarding liability than that of the place of the exchange.

Foreign Exchange

An example can be provided. A national from country A buys securities being traded on an exchange located in country B. It will normally be the case that the issuer could be sued in the courts of his domicile. Beyond domicile, the question of

---

[224] In the EU regime the information requirements for listing and public trading of securities will be those of the place where the issuer is registered, which will then be used for listing in another country within the EU passport regime. See WG Ringe and A Hellgardt, 'The International Dimension of Issuer Liability—Liability and Choice of Law from a Transatlantic Perspective' (2011) 31 *Oxford Journal of Legal Studies* 23, 30–31 and Directive 2003/71/EC, art 17.

[225] G Wegen and C Lindemann, 'The Law Applicable to Public Offerings in Continental Europe' in HV Houtte (ed), *The Laws of Cross-Border Securities Transactions* (Sweet & Maxwell 1999) 153–59.

jurisdiction becomes more complicated since plenty of disagreement remains as to the characterisation of damages arising out of securities fraud.[226] In the European Union there is no clear answer to the matter. Following the logic of *Kronhofer*,[227] to establish jurisdiction the approach would be to consider the place where the investor's account is situated as the place where the harmful event occurred; the court in this case excluded the domicile of the claimant or where his assets were concentrated for jurisdiction purposes. Another approach would be to specify the place where the damage occurred[228] as the exchange where securities are bought and sold, since this would be the place in which the first impact is felt[229] and the place where the event giving rise to it (the transaction with securities) is located. In Brazil, establishing jurisdiction would be unlikely as there is no clear basis for it if the transaction is done outside Brazil (foreign exchange) unless the defendant has established legal presence in the country or accepted Brazilian jurisdiction.[230] In the United States, under the *Morrison* decision,[231] foreign issuers would hardly be subject to jurisdiction unless their securities were traded in a US exchange or sold in the United States.[232] These considerations show that investors who invest in foreign exchanges would probably have to sue in a foreign dispute resolution system to recover if fraud was ever perpetrated.

As to the applicable law, in the European Union the logic should follow *Kronhofer*,[233] which identifies the applicable law as that of the place of the investor's investment account, since both Brussels I and Rome II use the *lex damni* standard to assess jurisdiction and applicable law in tort.[234] This would cause a problem since it would subject an issuer to liability according to as many laws as there are securities owners with accounts in different jurisdictions. Instead of using this approach, one which provides for the identification of the place of the exchange as the place where the damage occurred would be a better option.[235] This could be done in the Rome II context with the application of the close connection test of article 4(3). In Brazil it is not clear whether its law would be applicable but an affirmative answer is unlikely. Since the transaction is done in a foreign exchange and there are no clear private international law rules for such a situation, it is likely that the applicable law would be that applicable where the harmful act was

---

[226] Ringe and Hellgardt (n 224) 34.

[227] *Kronhofer* (n 1).

[228] See Case C-21/76 *Bier v Mines de Potasse d'Alsace* [1976] ECR 01735. This case established that the expression 'place where the harmful event occurred', for jurisdiction purposes, applies both to the place where the damage occurred (*lex loci damni*) and the place of the event giving rise to it (*lex loci delicti*).

[229] P Huber, *Rome II Regulation: Pocket Commentary* (Sellier European Law Publ. 2011) 84–85.

[230] Brazilian Civil Procedure Code, art 21, single para and art 22, III.

[231] *Morrison* (n 63).

[232] One problem would be the exact definition of 'a sale of any other security in the United States' (see *Morrison* (n 63) 273).

[233] *Kronhofer* (n 1).

[234] According to *Mines de Potasse d'Alsace* (n 228), jurisdiction can also be established with the *lex loci delicti* standard.

[235] This approach would guarantee one applicable law for each market, equating securities rights with the specific regulation of the market in which it is being traded. A criticism at the EU level is that,

perpetrated (foreign exchange or issuer domicile), as they are the strongest connecting factors and could be deemed where the 'obligation was constituted'. In the United States, applicable law would not be an issue; it is likely that US courts would either apply US law for securities liability or would dismiss the case for failure to state a claim through a 'jurisdiction to prescribe' analysis, not engaging in a private international law analysis due to the public policy character of the matter.[236]

Recognition and enforcement would be an issue if jurisdiction were established in a forum different from where the company being sued has its assets. In any event, the lawsuit would by itself be a complicated one, as the investor would most likely have to use a foreign forum to litigate; the preferable forum would be where the issuer's assets are available, as long as it has jurisdiction.

The overall discussion in this section demonstrates that investors who wish to invest directly in foreign exchanges do not face an easy enforcement regime, unless some mechanism in the foreign forum in which the issuer will be subject to jurisdiction offers such a system; this would include, for example, the class action scheme in the United States.

Depositary Receipt[237]

The example here is the following: a national from country A buys securities traded on an exchange in country A, representing securities traded on an exchange in country B. This means that the securities are anchored in country A, where the investor is situated. Therefore, the courts of the investor's country provide the first option for the lawsuit. The question then is whether a lawsuit in country B, where the issuer is located, will be possible. As a general matter, this would constitute a proper basis of jurisdiction, both in the European Union and Brazil.[238] In the United States, it is not completely clear what would be the case since this would be deemed to be a foreign transaction, even though it would be tied to an American issuer. In the *Morrison* decision there is language suggesting that a transaction of this kind would fall outside the scope of US securities laws, therefore precluding the exercise by courts of 'jurisdiction to prescribe'.[239] Another recent decision confirmed this trend, when it was decided that US securities laws do not apply to transactions in foreign exchanges when the securities are cross-listed in the United

---

with the rules on best execution, an investor that gives an order will not know in advance which liability regime would apply to him. See Ringe and Hellgardt (n 224) 53–54.

[236] ibid 38–39.

[237] A depositary receipt is '[a] negotiable financial instrument issued by a bank to represent a foreign company's publicly traded securities. A depository receipt trades on a local stock exchange, but a custodian bank in the foreign country holds the actual shares. Depository receipts can be sponsored or unsponsored depending on whether the company that issued the shares enters into an agreement with the custodian bank that issues the depository receipt.' Investopedia, 'Depositary Receipt' (*Investopedia*), http://www.investopedia.com/terms/d/depositaryreceipt.asp.

[238] Brussels I Reg Recast, art 4(1); Brazilian Civil Procedure Code, art 21; for the US, see the discussion above in this chapter.

[239] *Morrison* (n 63) 266 ('we think that the focus of the Exchange Act is not upon the place where the deception originated, but upon purchases and sales of securities in the United States').

States, even if the buyer is American.[240] It seems that any transaction executed on a foreign exchange would not be subject to US laws; nevertheless, it is still necessary to confirm if this is the case when the issuer is American.

As to the applicable law, even though the depositary receipt will be governed by the laws of the investor's country and at the same time, the share that it represents will be governed by the laws of the issuer's country, it is not always clear which law will apply where the investor is harmed as a result of the issuer's fraud or misrepresentation. If the investor is suing in his country, it seems clear that his own law would apply, since the securities would be subject to that legal system. What is not clear is what law would apply if the dispute were litigated in the issuer's forum based on a depositary receipt transacted outside of it. In the EU context, the applicable law would be that applicable where the damage occurred,[241] bringing us back to the uncertainties discussed in the foreign-exchange section. In the United States the applicability of its laws would depend on whether US courts exercised jurisdiction to prescribe or not; in Brazil there would be some uncertainty as to which law would be applicable due to the underdevelopment of its private international law, however it is possible to envisage a convincing argument mounted on the violation of Brazilian securities laws coupled with the general liability standard.

Therefore, for securities regulation to be effective, recognition and enforcement of the judgment would be important, as the likely place for the dispute to be resolved would be the investor's forum, under that forum's law. This would require the enforcing forum to accept the investor's country's securities laws and not raise any public policy considerations if the company does not have sufficient assets in the investor's forum.

Another aspect that may create a difference in this analysis is whether the depositary receipt is sponsored, with the participation of the issuer, or unsponsored, where only the depositary bank is responsible for the securities. Unsponsored depositary receipts do not involve the issuer but only involve financial intermediaries that coordinate the programme in the foreign country. In this case it is unlikely that the issuer will be subject to foreign securities laws, and even if it is, it is unlikely that a judgment made in such circumstances would be enforced.

ii. Open Market

Securities can also be transacted outside exchanges, through direct purchase agreements on the secondary market or through public offerings. As there is no exchange tying the regulatory obligations of the transaction, the private international law analysis becomes more complicated than exchange-based ones, since the centre of gravity disappears and different mandatory laws may be required depending on where the issuer and the buyer of securities are located and how the securities are marketed.

---

[240] *City of Pontiac v UBS AG*, No 12-4355-cv (2nd Cir, May 2014).
[241] Rome II Reg, art 4(1).

The first aspect concerns where the lawsuit should be brought. In this case, the issuer's forum is an obvious choice for legal purposes as any decision arising out of that judgment will be enforceable, even though it may be inconvenient for the investor. The investor's forum can also be a second choice, depending on the fulfilment of the requirements necessary for the court to exercise jurisdiction.[242]

On the applicable law question, two approaches can be used: the law of the market in which the transaction took place and the effects test. In the first approach, the applicable law would depend on who initiated the transaction as the law of the other party would be the applicable one since the first party went to the market of the second; in the second approach, the law of the investor, or, in the EU case, following the *Kronhofer*[243] logic, where his investment account is situated, would always be the applicable one.[244] Of course, this would assume that the transaction did not constitute a public offering falling within the regulatory purview of the country in which the investor is situated; in this case, the transaction would be submitted to national mandatory law and subject to its liability standards. In any event, the approach to applicable law in non-exchange situations will be linked to the concept of the 'market' in which the transaction was executed.[245]

Finally, recognition would be required in the issuer's forum (or where the assets are located) if the dispute were pursued in the investor's forum; this could be complicated depending on whether the issuer's forum considers its securities laws to be mandatory and, if it does, whether it accepts a judgment made in a foreign country to have precedence over its public policy matters.

B. Investor–Financial Intermediary Disputes

The transnational factor in a dispute with a financial intermediary only arises if the investor is transacting with a foreign financial intermediary. The private international law analysis will depend on who took the initiative to search for the counterparty and where the transactions finally took place, as these transactions are based on contracts and regulated by the legal provisions of the place where the intermediary is located.

---

[242] As the requirement that the transaction occurred in the country, for a Brazilian law example, or that the forum has personal jurisdiction over the defendant and is a convenient one, for a US example. In the EU, if the issuer were domiciled in another Member State, jurisdiction could be established under the tort heading of the Brussels I Recast, which gives jurisdiction to the place 'where the harmful event occurred' (Brussels I Recast, art 7(2)), which would raise the problems discussed above in this chapter.

[243] *Kronhofer* (n 1).

[244] Wegen and Lindemann (n 225) 161–62.

[245] See Huber (n 229) 84–85. In the EU, as explained above, the situation is not so clear due to the fact that the standard of the applicable law is of 'the place in which the damage occurs' (Rome II, art 4(3)).

i. Investor Acts Towards Financial Intermediary

When the investor reaches out to a foreign financial intermediary to enter into a financial services contract, all of the transaction's aspects are strongly tied to the financial intermediary's forum, weakening the grounds to either start a lawsuit in another country or to apply the law of such country to the contract. Under the Brussels regime this would not be possible as there are no specific grounds for it. In the EU regime, the place of performance of an obligation, which gives jurisdictional basis in contractual relations, is deemed to be where the services are provided; in the case of financial services, this would be the place where the financial intermediary is situated.[246] In Brazil, either the obligation would have to be executed in Brazil or the fact or act considered as the basis for the lawsuit would have taken place in Brazil;[247] there are two interpretations of this provision: the act or fact is the securities transaction at stake, which would preclude Brazilian jurisdiction since the order would be placed and executed in a foreign country, or the fact or act that is the basis of the lawsuit is considered to be the contract between investor and financial intermediary, which would have to be deemed constituted in Brazil to allow the lawsuit to be heard in its courts.[248] In the United States, jurisdiction would be available only if the foreign financial intermediary had sufficient 'minimum contacts', assuming that the case would not be dismissed on the basis of *forum non conveniens*.

A caveat in the Brazilian system concerns whether the investor can be considered a consumer, since a consumer is any 'physical or legal person that buys or uses a product or service as the final user'.[249] If this is the case, then jurisdiction is available under article 22, II of the Brazilian Civil Procedure Code. The jurisprudence in Brazil is still not clear on the subject but a recent decision has allowed choice of foreign law in a contract, recognising a US judgment and displacing Brazilian law, even though the party resisting enforcement requested the application of the Brazilian Consumer Code.[250] Despite this being a case concerning the determination of applicable law, the logic of the analysis could also be extended for jurisdictional purposes, avoiding the jurisdictional basis of the Brazilian Consumer Defence Code.

---

[246] Brussels I Reg Recast, art 7(1)(b).

[247] Brazilian Civil Procedure Code, art 21, II and III.

[248] The obligation is deemed constituted where the offeror resides. See Brazilian Decree-Law 4.657/1942, art 9, § 2°. In an insurance case decided by the Rio de Janeiro Tribunal, the offeror was always deemed to be the insurer. See N Araujo, *Direito Internacional Privado: Teoria e Prática Brasileira* (5th edn, Renovar 2011) 425–26.

[249] Brazilian Consumer Defence Code, art 2.

[250] *General Electric Company v Varig SA* (STJ, Special Chamber, SEC 646/US) (2008) ('Deveras eleito o direito aplicável à espécie em manifestação de vontade livre (GTA) referido *pactum, mutadis mutandis*, faz as vezes de "compromisso" insuperável pela alegação de aplicação em contrato internacional do Código de defesa do Consumidor – CDC, lei interna, sob o argumento de apenação inversa investiria contra a ordem pública'). In this case, it is important to note that the party resisting enforcement and asking for the application of the Brazilian Consumer Code was Varig, which was an airline company in Brazil. The court did not appreciate this request due to the fact that this was an enforcement procedure, therefore it was prohibited from engaging the merits of the decision being enforced, even though consumer law is considered to be a matter of public policy in Brazil.

On the applicable law question, the answer would depend on the rules of the forum. In the European Union, in the absence of an agreement, the applicable law would be that of the financial intermediary's forum,[251] while in Brazil it would be the law of the investor since he would be the offeror,[252] unless the courts have a different interpretation of 'offeror'.[253] In the United States, with its 'most significant relationship' standard for applicable law, the law most likely to be applied would also be the one of the financial intermediary.

If jurisdiction is established in the investor's forum, then recognition and enforcement will be an issue. In this case, since there is a contractual relationship, the public policy aspect that might preclude recognition is less prevalent, therefore being easier for the investor to enforce a favourable decision obtained through his courts.

ii. Financial Intermediary Acts Towards Investor

In the situation where the financial intermediary is the one reaching out to the investor to offer financial services, the relationship can more easily be characterised as one in which consumer regulation applies.[254]

Both in the European Union and in Brazil the characterisation of the investor as a consumer opens the door of the domestic forum to resolve disputes,[255] while in the United States this characterisation is not legally relevant for the purposes of this work. It is important to note that in the European Union, if the defendant is not domiciled in another Member State, jurisdiction is established according to the jurisdiction laws of the state in which the investor is domiciled.[256]

The applicable law will also change, becoming the one where the investor has his habitual residence, both in the European Union and in Brazil,[257] even though choice is expressly allowed in the EU regime, as long as it does not deprive the investor of the protection that he would have under the otherwise applicable law.[258]

Then, if the lawsuit is entertained in the investor's forum, recognition and enforcement of the decision will be necessary; this can be problematic if the financial intermediary's forum does not recognise the decision of the investor's forum or if there was a choice-of-forum or arbitration provision that was not respected.

---

[251] Rome I, art 4(1)(b).

[252] Brazilian Decree-Law 4.657/1942, art 9, § 2°.

[253] See n 248.

[254] In the EU this is clear both in the jurisdiction and the applicable law context as the financial intermediary would be directing his activities to the Member State where the consumer is domiciled. See Brussels I Reg Recast, art 17(1)(c) and Rome I, art 6(1)(b). For a more detailed analysis of the EU context, see GP Calliess, *Rome Regulations: Commentary on the European Rules on the Conflict of Laws* (Kluwer Law International 2011).

[255] Brussels I Reg Recast, art 18 and Brazilian Consumer Defence Code, art 101.

[256] Brussels I Reg Recast, arts 6, 17(1) and 18.

[257] Rome I, art 6(1); Brazilian Decree-Law 4.657/1942, art 9, § 2°.

[258] Rome I, Article 6(2).

C. Investor–Informational Intermediary Disputes

In this scenario the investor would act based on information provided by a foreign informational intermediary. As there is no direct link between investors and informational intermediaries, such as CRAs and accounting firms, the private international law analysis is based on tort standards.

Jurisdiction can commonly be established where the defendant is domiciled, but sometimes also where the harmful event occurred. In the EU context, the harmful event can be understood to be both the place where the event giving rise to it was perpetrated and also the place where the damage arose,[259] which, in this situation, would imply the relevant securities market.[260] In Brazil it would not be possible to start a lawsuit against a foreign informational intermediary due to the lack of proper jurisdictional basis, unless the defendant were to accept Brazilian jurisdiction.[261] In the United States, even though jurisdiction could be based on the effects that the act caused,[262] it would most likely not survive a minimum contacts test.[263]

The applicable law question in the European Union is a complicated one, as the standard is where the 'damage occurs',[264] giving rise to different possibilities such as the place where the assets were located just before the transfer or the branch of the bank where the account is held.[265] In this case though, the most likely result is the use of the 'closest connection' escape clause[266] and the application of the law of the market for which the rating was intended. In Brazil there is no clear rule for applicable law in this case, but it is likely to be the applicable law of where the informational intermediary is located since the applicable law should be that of the place where the obligation was constituted (in this case, by applying the *lex loci delicti* standard). Another position would be to defend the applicability of Brazilian law since the harm would be felt in Brazil (*lex damni*), but this seems to be a weaker position than the previous one, as the connecting factor is not as strong. As mentioned before, in the United States the applicable law analysis is more convoluted, usually favouring the plaintiff.

Recognition and enforcement may be necessary when the informational intermediary is sued outside its jurisdiction. Public policy could play a role if the jurisdiction that has to enforce the judgment finds either that the forum country had no jurisdiction or that the applicable law is against its public policy.

---

[259] See *Mines de Potasse d'Alsace* (n 228); Case C-51/97 *Réunion Européennee SA v Spliethoff's Becrachtingskantoor BV* [1998] ECR I-6534, para 28.
[260] What exactly the relevant market is has not been made clear under EU law.
[261] Brazilian Civil Procedure Code, art 22, III.
[262] See Restatement (Second) of Conflict of Laws § 37 ('A state has a natural interest in the effects of an act within its territory even though the act itself was done elsewhere').
[263] *International Shoe* (n 15).
[264] Rome II, art 4(1).
[265] See Dickinson (n 148) 327–30; Huber (n 229) 76–83.
[266] Rome II, Art 4(3).

V. Concluding Remarks on the Transnational Aspects of Securities Disputes

This chapter has shown that the transnational infrastructure for dispute resolution in transnational securities transactions stands on weak ground. Not only might the investor face problems in solving a securities dispute in his own country, he may also encounter problems regarding the law that would be applicable to his transaction.

The lack of clear guidance in EU private international law in respect of securities transactions and pure economic loss situations, the discretionary aspect of the American system of private international law, and the underdevelopment of the Brazilian private international law system pose clear problems of legal certainty for investors wishing to invest in foreign markets. In these situations, the safest approach is litigation in the place where the defendant is situated, which is an unrealistic proposition for small and medium retail investors.

A reliable option, at least for issuer–investor and, to a lesser extent, informational intermediary–investor disputes, as long as public policy questions do not stand in the way, is the use of arbitration for the resolution of disputes, especially if coupled with aggregate litigation mechanisms, as discussed in the previous chapters. This would resolve both the jurisdiction and applicable law issues, while at the same time providing a mechanism to deal with low-value claims.

Regarding financial intermediary–investor disputes, an aggregate dispute resolution system is unlikely due to the personal character of the transaction and therefore enhancing the effectiveness of low-cost alternative dispute resolution systems is a better option to improve access to justice.

The objective of this discussion is not investor protection per se, as the capital markets regimes analysed in this work do present a strong level of investor protection for the national market, but rather the task of making it easier for a foreign investor to be protected by foreign regimes, increasing the possibility of reliance on legal mechanisms for cross-border transactions.

If this is accomplished, capital markets will find a road paved for foreign investor confidence, opening the possibility for stronger integration without losing the regulatory safeguards that national jurisdictions have developed in order to protect their investors from foreign predatory practices. Chapter 5 presented a roadmap of possible solutions to overcome these problems.

BIBLIOGRAPHY

Aguiar AS, 'The Law Applicable to International Trade Transactions with Brazilian Parties: a Comparative Study of the Brazilian Law, the CISG, and the American Law about Contract Formation' (LLM, University of Toronto 2011)

Akerlof GA, 'The Market for "Lemons": Quality Uncertainty and the Market Mechanism' (1970) 84 *The Quarterly Journal of Economics* 488

Albert J, *Study on the Transparency of Costs of Civil Judicial Proceedings in the European Union—Final Report—Annex 48—Spain* (European Commission 2007)

Al-Shawaf HT, 'Bargaining for Salvation: How Alternative Auditor Liability Regimes Can Save the Capital Markets' [2012] *University of Illinois Law Review* 502

Alter K, 'The European Court's Political Power Across Time and Space' (2009) Northwestern Law & Econ Research Paper No 09-03

Andreotti T, 'The Legitimacy and Accountability of the IASB as an International Standard Setter' in Cafaggi F and Miller G (eds), *Private Regulation and Enforcement in Financial Institutions* (Edward Elgar 2013)

Andrews N, 'Multi-Party Proceedings in England: Representative and Group Actions' (2001) 11 *Duke Journal of Comparative & International Law* 249

Araujo N, Direito Internacional Privado: Teoria e Prática Brasileira (5th edn, Renovar 2011)

Armour J, Hansmann H and Kraakman R, 'Agency Problems and Legal Strategies' in Kraakman R, Armour J and Enriques L (eds), *The Anatomy of Corporate Law: a Comparative and Functional Approach* (2nd edn, Oxford University Press 2009)

Arnett GW, *Global Securities Markets: Navigating the World's Exchanges and OTC Markets* (John Wiley & Sons, Inc 2011)

Aroca, Juan Monero, Colomer, Juan Luis Gómez and Vilar, Silvia Barona, *Derecho Jurisdiccional II—Proceso Civil* (Tirant Lo Blanch 2004)

Ásgeirsson H, 'Integration of European Securities Markets' [2004] *Monetary Bulletin—The Central Bank of Iceland* 50

Ashenfelter O and Iyengar R (eds), *Economics of Commercial Arbitration and Dispute Resolution* (Edward Elgar 2009)

Atiyah PS, *The Rise and Fall of Freedom of Contract* (Clarendon Press 1979)

Baker J, 'From Lovedays to ADR: Arbitration and Dispute Resolution in England 1066–1800' [2006] *Transnational Dispute Management* 1

Baldwin R, Cave M and Lodge M, *Understanding Regulation: Theory, Strategy, and Practice* (2nd edn, Oxford University Press 2012)

Bantekas I, 'Arbitrability in Finance and Banking' in Mistelis LA and Brekoulakis SL (eds), *Arbitrability: International & Comparative Perspectives* (Wolters Kluwer 2009)

Bariatti S, *Cases and materials on EU Private International Law* (Hart Publishing 2011)

Barkow RE, 'Insulating Agencies: Avoiding Capture through Institutional Design' (2010) 89 *Texas Law Review* 15

Bassett DL, 'Constructing Class Action Reality' [2006] *Brigham Young University Law Review* 1415

Baumgartner S, 'Understanding the Obstacles to the Recognition and Enforcement of US Judgments Abroad' (2013) 45 *New York University Journal of International Law & Politics* 965

Becker GS and Stigler GJ, 'Law Enforcement, Malfeasance, and Compensation of Enforcers' (1974) 3 *Journal of Legal Studies* 1

Benston GJ, 'The Value of the SEC's Accounting Disclosure Requirements' (1969) 44 *The Accounting Review* 515

Berg AJ, *The New York Arbitration Convention of 1958* (Kluwer Law and Taxation 1981)

Bernstein L, 'Opting Out of the Legal System: Extralegal Contractual Relations in the Diamond Industry' (1992) 21 *Journal of Legal Studies* 115

—— , 'Private Commercial Law in the Cotton Industry: Creating Cooperation through Rules, Norms, and Institutions' (2000–2001) 99 Michigan Law Review 1724

Billiet P (ed), *Class Arbitration in the European Union* (Maklu 2013)

—— and Lozano L, 'General Reflections on the Recognition and Enforcement of Foreign Class Arbitral Awards in Europe' in Billiet P (ed), *Class Arbitration in the European Union* (Maklu 2013)

Bingham T, *The Rule of Law* (Allen Lane 2010)

Bó ED, 'Regulatory Capture: a Review' (2006) 22 *Oxford Review of Economic Policy* 203

Bone RG and Evans DS, 'Class Certification and the Substantive Merits' (2001–2002) 51 *Duke Law Journal* 1521

Borkowski A, *Borkowski's Textbook on Roman Law* (Oxford University Press 2010)

Born G, *International Commercial Arbitration* (Kluwer Law International 2009)

Brazil-David R, 'An Examination of the Law and Practice of International Commercial Arbitration in Brazil' (2011) 27 *Arbitration International* 57

Brownsword R, 'The Theoretical Foundations of European Private Law: A Time to Stand and Stare' in Brownsword R, Hans-W Micklitz, Leone Niglia and Stephen Weatherill (eds), *The Foundations of European Private Law* (Hart Publishing 2011)

Buckner CJ, 'Due Process in Class Arbitration' (2006) 58 *Florida Law Review* 185

Buell S, 'What is Securities Fraud?' (2011) 61 *Duke Law Journal* 511

Burbank SB, 'Jurisdiction to Adjudicate: End of the Century or Beginning of the Millennium?' (1999) 7 *Tulane Journal of International and Comparative Law* 111

—— , 'Jurisdictional Conflict and Jurisdictional Equilibration: Paths to a Via Media?' (2004) 26 *Houston Journal of International Law* 385

—— , 'The Class Action Fairness Act of 2005 in Historical Context: a Preliminary View' (2008) 156 *University of Pennsylvania Law Review* 1439

Burch EC, 'Procedural Justice in Nonclass Aggregation' (2009) 44 *Wake Forest Law Review* 1

—— , 'Litigating Together: Social, Moral, and Legal Obligations' (2011) 91 *Boston University Law Review* 87

—— , 'Financiers as Monitors in Aggregate Litigation' (2012) 87 *New York University Law Review* 1273

Burk, J, 'The Origins of Federal Securities Regulation: A Case Study in the Social Control of Finance' (1985) 63 *Social Forces* 1010

Busch D, 'Why MiFID Matters to Private Law—The Example of MiFID's Impact on an Asset Manager's Civil Liability' (2012) 7 *Capital Markets Law Journal* 386

Buxbaum HL, 'Multinantional Class Actions Under Federal Securities Law: Managing Jurisdictional Conflict' (2007–2008) 46 *Columbia Journal of Transnational Law* 14

—— , 'National Jurisdiction and Global Business Networks' (2010) 17 *Indiana Journal of Global Legal Studies* 165

Cable V, 'The Diminished Nation-State: a Study in the Loss of Economic Power' (1995) 124 *Daedalus* 23

Cafaggi F, 'Rethinking Private Regulation in the European Regulatory Space' (2006) EUI Working Papers 13

Calamari J and Perillo J, *The Law of Contracts* (4th edn, West Group 1998)

Calixto N and Marins VA, 'Eficácia da Sentença e Coisa Julgada Perante Terceiros' (1989) 25 *Revista da Faculdade de Direito da UFPR* 93

Calliess GP, *Rome Regulations: Commentary on the European Rules on the Conflict of Laws* (Kluwer Law International 2011)

Carbonell F, 'Reasoning by Consequences: Applying Different Argumentation Structures to the Analysis of Consequentialist Reasoning in Judicial Decisions' in Dahlman C and Feteris E (eds), *Legal Argumentation Theory: Cross-Disciplinary Perspectives*, vol 102 (Springer 2013)

Carneiro RL, 'A Theory of the Origin of the State: Traditional Theories of State Origins are Considered and Rejected in Favor of a New Ecological Hypothesis' in Hall JA (ed), *The State: Critical Concepts*, vol I (Routlegde 1994)

Cavanagh ED, 'Issue Preclusion in Complex Litigation' (2009–2010) 29 *The Review of Litigation* 859

Chalmers D, Davies G and Monti G, *European Union Law* (2nd edn, Cambridge University Press 2010)

Chasin ACM, *Uma Simples Formalidade: estudo sobre a experiência dos Juizados Especiais Cíveis em São Paulo* (LLM, USP 2007)

Cherednychenko O, 'European Securities Regulation, Private Law and the Investment Firm-Client Relationship' [2009] *European Review of Private Law* 925

Chiapello E and Medjad K, 'An Unprecedented Privatisation of Mandatory Standard-Setting: the Case of European Accounting Policy' (2009) 20 *Critical Perspectives on Accounting* 448

Childress DE, 'Comity as Conflict: Resituating International Comity as Conflict of Laws' (2010–2011) 44 *UC Davis Law Review* 11

Chisholm AM, *An Introduction to International Capital Markets* (2nd edn, John Wiley & Sons 2009)

Chiu IHY, *Regulatory convergence in EU securities regulation* (Kluwer Law International 2008)

Choi SJ, 'Do the Merits Matter Less After the Private Securities Litigation Reform Act?' (2006) 23 *The Journal of Law, Economics, & Organization* 598

—— and Thompson RB, 'Securities Litigation and Its Lawyers: Changes During the First Decade After PSLRA' (2006) 06-26 NYU Law and Economics Research Paper Series 1

——, Fisch JE and Pritchard AC, 'Do Institutions Matter? The Impact of the Lead Plaintiff Provision of the Private Securities Litigation Reform Act' (2005) 83 *Washington University Law Quarterly* 869

Clarkson CMV and Hill J, *The Conflict of Laws* (4th edn, Oxford University Press 2011)

Coffee JC, 'Rescuing the Private Attorney General: Why the Model of the Lawyer as a Bounty Hunter Is Not Working' (1983) 42 *Maryland Law Review* 215

——, 'Market Failure and the Economic Case for a Mandatory Disclosure System' (1984) 70 *Virginia Law Review* 717

——, 'Understanding the Plaintiff's Attorney: the Implications of Economic Theory for Private Enforcement of Law Through Class and Derivative Actions' (1986) 86 *Columbia Law Review* 669

——, 'The Regulation of Entrepeneurial Litigation: Balancing Fairness and Efficiency in the Large Class Action' (1987) 54 *University of Chicago Law Review* 877

——, 'No Exit?: Opting Out, the Contractual Theory of the Corporation, and the Special Case of Remedies' (1988) 53 *Brooklyn Law Review* 919

——, 'Class Wars: the Dillemma of the Mass Tort Class Action' (1995) 95 *Columbia Law Review* 1351

——, 'Class Action Accountability: Reconciling Exit, Voice and Loyalty in Representative Litigation' (2000) 100 *Columbia Law Review* 370

——, 'Law and the Market: the Impact of Enforcement' (2007) 156 *University of Pennsylvania Law Review* 229

Coglianese C and Mendelson E, 'Meta-Regulation and Self-Regulation' in Baldwin R, Cave M and Lodge M (eds), *The Oxford Handbook of Regulation* (Oxford University Press 2010)

Colangelo A, 'What is Extraterritorial Jurisdiction?' (2014) 99 *Cornell Law Review* 1303.

Cooter R and Rubinfeld DL, 'Economic Analysis of Legal Disputes and Their Resolution' (1989) XXVII *Journal of Economic Literature* 1067

—— and Ulen T, *Law and Economics* (6th edn, Addison Wesley 2016)

Cornes R and Sandler T, *The Theory of Externalities, Public Goods and Club Goods* (Cambridge University Press 1996)

Couture WG, 'Mixed Statements: the Safe Harbor's Rocky Shore' (2011) 39 *Securities Regulation Law Journal* 257

Craig P and Búrca GD, *EU Law, Text, Cases, and Materials* (Oxford University Press 2011)

Crawford B, 'The Hague "Prima" Convention: Choice of Law to Govern Recognition of Dispositions of Book-Based Securities in Cross Border Transactions' (2003) 38 *Canada Business Law Review* 157

Cunningham GM and Harris JE, 'Enron and Arthur Andersen: the Case of the Crooked E and Fallen A' (2006) 3 *Global Perspectives on Accounting Education* 27

David TR, Corley JP and Delawalla AA, 'Heightened Pleading Requirements, Due Diligence, Reliance, Loss Causation, and Truth-on-the-Market—Available Defenses to Claims under Sections 11 and 12 of the Securities Act of 1933' (2009) 11 *Transactions Tennessee Journal of Business Law* 53

Davies M, 'Time to Change the Federal Forum Non Conveniens Analysis' (2002) 77 *Tulane Law Review* 309

Deaking S, 'The Evolution of Theory and Method in Law and Finance' in Moloney N, Ferran E and Payne J (eds), *The Oxford Handbook of Financial Regulation* (Oxford University Press 2015)

Demsetz H, 'Towards a Theory of Property Rights' (1967) 57 *American Economic Review, Papers and Proceedings* 347

Diamond D and Verrecchia R, 'Disclosure, Liquidity, and the Cost of Capital' (1991) 46 *The Journal of Finance* 1325

Dicey, Morris and Collins, *The Conflict of Laws* (15th edn, Sweet and Maxwell 2012)

Dicey AV, *The Law of the Constitution* (Oxford University Press 2013)

Dickinson A, 'European Private International Law: Embracing New Horizons or Mourning the Past?' (2005) 1 *Journal of Private International Law* 197

——, *The Rome II Regulation: the Law Applicable to Non-contractual Obligations* (Oxford University Press 2008)

Didier F, *Curso de Direito Processual Civil*, vol 2 (5th edn, Juspodivm 2010)

—— and Zaneti H, *Curso de Direito Processual Civil—Processo Coletivo*, vol 4 (Juspodivm 2011)

——, Braga PS and Oliveira RA, *Curso de Direito Processual Civil—Teoria da Prova, Direito Probatório, Decisão, Precedente, Coisa Julgada e Tutela Provisória*, vol 2 (11th edn, Juspodivm 2016)

Dinamarco CR, 'Relativizar a Coisa Julgada Material' (2001) 55/56 *Revista da Procuradoria Geral do Estado de São Paulo* 31

Doherty JW, Reville RT and Zakaras L (eds), *Confidentiality, Transparency, and the US Civil Justice System* (Oxford University Press 2012)

Doidge C, Karolyi GA and Stulz RM, 'Why Are Foreign Firms Listed in the US Worth More?' (2004) 71 *Journal of Financial Economics* 205

Donovan D and Greenawalt A, '*Mitsubishi* after Twenty Years: Mandatory Rules Before Courts and International Arbitrators' in Mistelis L and Dew J (eds), *Pervasive Problems in International Arbitration* (Kluwer Law International 2006)

Drahozal CR, 'Federal Arbitration Act Preemption' (2004) 79 *Indiana Law Journal* 393

Easterbrook FH, 'Substance and Due Process' [1982] *The Supreme Court Review* 85

—— and Fischel DR, 'Mandatory Disclosure and the Protection of Investors' (1984) 70 *Virginia Law Review* 669

El-Agraa A, 'The Theory of Economic Integration' in El-Agraa A (ed), *The European Union: Economics and Policies* (9th edn, Cambridge University Press 2011)

Ellis N, Fairchild L and D'Souza F, 'Is Imposing Liability on Credit Ratings Agencies a Good Idea?: Credit Rating Agency Reform in the Aftermath of the Global Financial Crisis' (2011–2012) 17 *Stanford Journal of Law, Business and Finance* 175

Enriques L and Gilotta S, 'Disclosure and Financial Market Regulation' in Moloney N, Ferran E and Payne J (eds), *The Oxford Handbook of Financial Regulation* (Oxford University Press 2015)

Epstein RA (ed) *Economics of Property Law* (Edward Elgar 2007)

Erichson H, 'Beyond the Class Action: Lawyer Loyalty and Client Autonomy in Non-class Collective Representation' [2003] *University of Chicago Legal Forum* 519

Fairgrieve D and Howells G, 'Collective Redress Procedures: European Debates' in Fairgrieve D and Lein E (eds), *Extraterritoriality and Collective Redress* (Oxford University Press 2012)

Fama EF, 'Efficient Capital Markets: a Review of Theory and Empirical Work' (1970) 25 *The Journal of Finance* 383

Fentiman R, *International Commercial Litigation* (Oxford University Press 2010)

——, 'Recognition, Enforcement and Collective Judgments' in Nuyts A and Hatzimihail NE (eds), *Cross-Border Class Actions: The European Way* (Seillier European Law Publishers 2014)

Ferejohn JA and Kramer LD, 'Independent Judges, Dependent Judiciary: Institutionalizing Judicial Restraint' (2002) 77 *New York University Law Review* 962

Field BC, 'The Evolution of Property Rights' (1989) 42 *Kyklos* 319

Fleckner AM, 'FASB and IASB: Dependence Despite Independence' (2008) 3 *Virginia Law & Business Review* 275

Flesher DL, Previts GJ and Samson WD, 'Auditing in the United States: a Historical Perspective' (2005) 41 *Abacus* 21

Ford T, 'The History and Development of Old Rule 23 and the Development of Amended Rule 23' (1966) 32 *Antitrust Law Journal* 254

Fox EM, 'Modernization of Effects Jurisdiction: From Hands-off to Hands-linked' (2009) 42 *International Law and Politics* 159

Fox MB, 'Demystifying Causation in Fraud-on-the-Market Actions' (2005) 60 *The Business Lawyer* 507

——, Durnev A, Morck R and Yeung BY, 'Law, Share Price Accuracy, and Economic Performance: the New Evidence' (2003) 102 *Michigan Law Review* 331

Frank R, *Microeconomics and Behavior* (McGraw-Hill Irwin 2010)

Fukuyama F, *State-Building: Governance and World Order in the 21st Century* (Cornell University Press 2004)

Garner BA, *Black's Law Dictionary* (9th edn, West 2009)

Gaspari E, *A Ditadura Envergonhada*, vol 1 (Companhia das Letras 2002)

——, *A Ditadura Escancarada*, vol 2 (Companhia das Letras 2002)

——, *A Ditadura Derrotada*, vol 3 (Companhia das Letras 2003)

——, *A Ditadura Encurralada*, vol 4 (Companhia das Letras 2004)

Georgosouli A, 'The Debate over the Economic Rationale for Investor Protection Regulation: a Critical Appraisal' (2007) 15 *Journal of Financial Regulation and Compliance* 236

Gidi A, 'Class Actions in Brazil: a Model for Civil Law Countries' (2003) 51 *The American Journal of Comparative Law* 311

Gilles M and Friedman GB, 'Exploding the Class Action Agency Costs Myth: the Social Utility of Entrepreneurial Lawyers' (2006–2007) 155 *University of Pennsylvania Law Review* 103

Gillies L, 'Creation of Subsidiary Jurisdiction Rules in the Recast of Brussels I: Back to the Drawing Board?' (2012) 8 *Journal of Private International Law* 489

Gilson RJ and Kraakman R, 'The Mechanisms of Market Efficiency Twenty Years Later: The Hindsight Bias', 446 Harvard Law School John M Olin Center for Law, Economics and Business Discussion Paper Series 1

—— and Kraakman R, 'The Mechanisms of Market Efficiency' (1984) 70 *Virginia Law Review* 549

Glover JM, 'Beyond Unconscionability: Class Action Waivers and Mandatory Arbitration Agreements' (2006) 59 *Vanderbilt Law Review* 1735

Goetz CJ and Scott RE, 'Enforcing Promises: An Examination of the Basis of Contract' (1980) 89 *Yale Law Journal* 1261

Gordon JN and Kornhauser LA, 'Efficient Markets, Costly Information, and Securities Research' (1985) 60 *New York University Law Journal* 761

Grigoleit HC, 'Mandatory Law: Fundamental Principles' in Basedow J, Hopt K and Zimmermann R (eds), *Max Planck Encyclopaedia of European Private Law* (Oxford University Press 2011)

Gross JI, 'The End of Mandatory Securities Arbitration?' (2010) 30 *Pace Law Review* 1174

Grossman S and Hart OD, 'Disclosure Laws and Takeover Bids' (1980) 35 *The Journal of Finance* 323

—— and Stiglitz J, 'On the Impossibility of Informationally Efficient Markets' (1980) 70 *The American Economic Review* 393

Grundmann S, 'The Bankinter Case on MIFID Regulation and Contract Law' (2013) 9 *European Review of Contract Law* 267

Gu L and Hackbarth D, 'Governance and Equity Prices: Does Transparency Matter?' [2013] *Review of Finance* 1

Guedj TG, 'The Theory of the Lois de Police, a Functional Trend in Continental Private International Law—A Comparative Analysis with Modern American Theories' (1991) 39 *American Journal of Comparative Law* 661

Gutmann A, 'Democracy' in Goodin RE, Pettit P and Pogge T (eds), *A Companion to Contemporary Political Philosophy*, vol 2 (Blackwell Publishing 2007)

Haar B, 'Civil Liability of Credit Rating Agencies—Regulatory All-or-Nothing Approaches between Immunity and Over-Deterrence' 2013-02 University of Olso Faculty of Law Legal Studies Research Paper Series 1

Hail L and Leuz C, 'International Differences in the Cost of Equity Capital: Do Legal Institutions and Securities Regulation Matter?' (2006) 44 *Journal of Accounting Research* 485

Halfmeier A, 'Recognition of a WCAM Settlement in Germany' [2012] *Nederland International Privaatrecht* 176

Hampton J, 'Democracy and the Rule of Law' in Shapiro I (ed), *The Rule of Law: Nomos XXXVI* (New York University Press 1994)

Hardin G, 'The Tragedy of the Commons' (1968) 162 *Science* 1243

Hart HLA, *The Concept of Law* (Oxford University Press 1994)

Hazard GC, Gedid JL and Sowle S, 'An Historical Analysis of the Binding Effect of Class Suits' (1998) 146 *University of Pennsylvania Law Review* 1849

Healy JJ, 'Consumer Protection Choice of Law: European Lessons for the United States' (2009) 19 *Duke Journal of Comparative & International Law* 535

Healy PM and Palepu KG, 'Information Asymmetry, Corporate Disclosure, and the Capital Markets: A Review of the Empirical Disclosure Literature' (2001) 21 *Journal of Accounting and Economics* 405

Heller MA, 'The Tragedy of the Anticommons: Property in the Transition from Marx to Markets' (1988) 111 *Harvard Law Review* 621

Hensler DR, *Class Action Dilemmas: Pursuing Public Goals for Private Gains* (RAND Institute for Civil Justice, 1999)

—— and Rowe TD, 'Beyond "It Just Ain't Worth It": Alternative Strategies for Damages Class Action Reform' (2001) 64 *Law and Contemporary Problems* 137

Hermans R and Tjeenk JBL, 'International Class Action Settlements in the Netherlands since *Converium*' in Dodds-Smith I and Brown A (eds), *The International Comparative Guide to: Class & Group Actions 2013* (5th edn, Global Legal Group Ltd 2012)

Hill CA, 'Regulating the Rating Agencies' (2004) 82 *Washington University Law Quarterly* 43

Hillman RA, 'Debunking Some Myths About Unconscionability: a New Framework for UCC Section 2–302' (1981–1982) 67 *Cornell Law Review* 1

Hirschman AO, *Exit, Voice, and Loyalty: Responses to Decline in Firms* (Harvard University Press 1970)

Hodges C, *The Reform of Class and Representative Actions in European Legal Systems* (Hart Publishing 2008)

——, 'Objectives, Mechanisms and Policy Choices in Collective Enforcement and Redress' in Steele J and Boom WH (eds), *Mass Justice: Challenges of Representation and Distribution* (Edward Elgar 2011)

——, 'Public and Private Enforcement: The Practical Implications for Policy Architecture' in Brownsword R, Hans-W Micklitz, Leone Niglia and Stephen Weatherill (eds), *The Foundations of European Private Law* (Hart Publishing 2011)

——, Vogenauer S and Tulibacka M (eds), *The Costs and Funding of Civil Litigation: a Comparative Perspective* (Hart Publishing 2010)

Huber P, *Rome II Regulation: Pocket Commentary* (Sellier European Law Pub 2011)

Humphrey C, Benau MAG and Barbadillo ER, 'El Debate de la Responsabilidad Civil de la Auditoría en España: la Construcción del Discurso sobre la Limitación de Responsabilidades por las Corporaciones Profesionales' (2003) XXXII *Revista Española de Financiación y Contabilidad* 1091

International Monetary Fund, 'The Liberalization and Management of Capital Flows: an Institutional View' (2012)

International T, *Global Corruption Report 2007* (Cambridge University Press 2007)

Issacharoff S, 'Governance and Legitimacy in the Law of Class Actions' [1999] *Supreme Court Review* 337

—— and Samuel I, 'New Frontiers of Consumer Protection: the Interplay Between Private and Public Enforcement' in Cafaggi F and Micklitz HW (eds), *New Frontiers of Consumer Protection: the Interplay Between Private and Public Enforcement* (Intersentia 2009)

Harkins JG, 'Federal Rule 23—The Early Years' (1997) 39 *Arizona Law Review* 705

Jackson HE and Roe MJ, *Public and Private Enforcement of Securities Laws: Resource-Based Evidence* (Harvard Law School 2009)

Jensen MC and Meckling WH, 'Theory of the Firm: Managerial Behavior, Agency Costs and Ownership Structure' (1976) 3 *Journal of Financial Economics* 305

Johnson JJ, 'Securities Class Actions in State Court' (2011 Lewis & Clark Law School Legal Research Paper Series No 17)

Kahan M, 'Securities Laws and the Social Costs of "Inaccurate" Stock Prices' (1992) 41 *Duke Law Journal* 977

King RG and Levine R, 'Finance and Growth: Schumpeter Might be Right' (1993) 108 *The Quarterly Journal of Economics* 717

Kreher PJ and Robertson PD, 'Substance, Process, and the Future of Class Arbitration' (2004) 9 *Harvard Negotiation Law Review* 409

Kripke H, 'The SEC, the Accountants, Some Myths and Some Realities' (1970) 45 *New York University Law Review* 1151

Kritzer HM, *Risks, Reputations, and Rewards: Contingency Fee Legal Practice in the United States* (Stanford Law and Politics 2004)

Kroszner RS, 'The Role of Private Regulation in Maintaining Global Financial Stability' (1999) 18 *Cato Journal* 355

Kruger T, *Civil Jurisdiciton Rules of the EU and Their Impact on Third States* (Oxford University Press 2008)

Laby AB, 'Selling Advice and Creating Expectations: Why Brokers Should be Fiduciaries' (2012) 87 *Washington Law Review* 707

Lacovara PA, 'Class Action Arbitrations—the Challenge for the Business Community' (2008) 24 *Arbitration International* 541

Landes WM and Posner RA, 'The Private Enforcement of Law' (1975) 4 *Journal of Legal Studies* 1

Langevoort DC, 'Basic at Twenty: Rethinking Fraud on the Market' [2009] *Wisconsin Law Review* 151

LaPorta R, Lopez-de-Silanes F and Shleifer A, 'Corporate Ownership around the World' (1999) 54 *The Journal of Finance* 471

——, Lopez-de-Silanes F and Shleifer A, 'What Works in Securities Law?' (2006) 61 *The Journal of Finance* 1

——, Lopez-de-Silanes F, Shleifer A and Vishny R, 'Legal Determinants of External Finance' (1997) 52 *The Journal of Finance* 1131

——, Lopez-de-Silanes F, Shleifer A and Vishny R, 'Investor Protection and Corporate Valuation' (2002) 57 *The Journal of Finance* 1147

Larkins C, 'Judicial Independence and Democratization: a Theoretical and Conceptual Analaysis' (1996) 44 *The American Journal of Comparative Law* 605

Law J and Smullen J, *A Dictionary of Finance and Banking* (Oxford University Press 2008)

Layton A, 'Collective Redress: Policy Objectives and Practical Problems' in Fairgrieve D and Lein E (eds), *Extraterritoriality and Collective Redress* (Oxford University Press 2012)

Lemos M, 'Aggregate Litigation Goes Public: Representative Suits by State Attorneys General' (2012) 126 *Harvard Law Review* 486

—— and Minzner M, 'For-Profit Public Enforcement' (2014) 127 *Harvard Law Review* 853

Levine R and Zervos S, 'Stock Markets, Banks and Economic Growth' (1998) 88 *The American Economic Review* 537

Lewis M, *Flash Boys: A Wall Street Revolt* (WW Norton & Company Inc 2014)

Lith HV, *The Dutch Collective Settlements Act and Private International Law* (Erasmus School of Law 2010)

López JJM, 'Las Acciones de Clase en el Derecho Español' (2001) 3 *InDret* 1

López SC, 'La Cobertura Actual de La Cosa Juzgada' (2009) 20 *Revista Jurídica de la Universidad Autónoma de Madrid* 67

LoPucki LM, 'The Future of Court System Transparency' in Doherty JW, Reville RT and Zakaras L (eds), *Confidentiality, Transparency, and the US Civil Justice System* (Oxford University Press 2012)

MacCormick N, *Rhetoric and The Rule of Law: A Theory of Legal Reasoning* (Oxford University Press 2005)

Macey JR and Miller G, 'The Plaintiffs' Attorney's Role in Class Action and Derivative Litigation: Economic Analysis and Recommendations for Reform' (1991) 58 *University of Chicago Law Review* 1

Mackenzie R, Romano C and Shany Y, *The Manual on International Courts and Tribunals* (Oxford University Press 2010)

MacNeil I, 'Enforcement and Sanctioning' in Moloney N, Ferran E and Payne J (eds), *The Oxford Handbook of Financial Regulation* (Oxford 2015)

Magnus U and Peter M, *Brussels I Regulation* (2nd edn, Sellier 2012)

Mahoney PG, 'Precaution Costs and the Law of Fraud in Impersonal Markets' (1992) 78 *Virginia Law Review* 623

Manne HG, *Insider Trading and the Stock Market* (The Free Press 1966)

Martinez JC, 'Recognizing and Enforcing Foreign Nation Judgments: the United States and Europe Compared and Contrasted—a Call for Revised Legislation in Florida' (1995) 4 *Journal of Transnational Law & Policy* 49

McCormick R, *Legal Risk in the Financial Markets* (2nd edn, Oxford University Press 2010)

Mendes GF and Branco PGG, *Curso de Direito Constitucional* (7th edn, Saraiva 2012)

Merchán JFM, 'La Constitución de 1812 y el Arbitraje' (2012) 14 *Revista del Club Español del Arbitraje* 33

Michaels R, 'Some Fundamental Jurisdictional Conceptions as Applied in Judgment Conventions' (2006) 123 Duke Law School Legal Studies Research Paper Series 1

——, 'Two Paradigms of Jurisdiction' (2006) 27 *Michigan Journal of International Law* 1003

Micklitz HW, *The Many Concepts of Social Justice in European Private Law* (Edward Elgar 2011)

——, Stuyck J and Terryn E, *Cases, Materials and Text on Consumer Law* (Hart Publishing 2010)

Miller G, 'Some Agency Problems in Settlements' (1987) 16 *Journal of Legal Studies* 189

——, 'Conflicts of Interest in Class Action Litigation: an Inquiry into the Appropriate Standard' [2003] *University of Chicago Legal Forum* 581

——, 'Compensation and Deterrence in Consumer Class Actions in the US and Europe' in Cafaggi F and Micklitz HW (eds), *New Frontiers of Consumer Protection: the Interplay Between Private and Public Enforcement* (Intersentia 2009)

Moloney N, *EC Securities Regulation* (2nd edn, Oxford University Press 2008)

——, *How to Protect Investors: Lessons from the EC and the UK* (Cambridge University Press 2010)

——, *EU Securities and Financial Markets Regulation* (3rd edn, Oxford University Press 2014)

Molot J, 'Litigation Finance: a Market Solution to a Procedural Problem' (2010–2011) 99 *Georgetown Law Journal* 65

Moran M, 'The Mutually Constitutive Nature of Public and Private Law' in Robertson A and Wu TH (eds), *The Goals of Private Law* (Hart Publishing 2009)

Mulheron R, *The Class Action in Common Legal Systems* (Hart Publishing 2004)

Muñoz DR, *The Law of Transnational Securitization* (Oxford University Press 2010)

Nacimiento P, 'Article V(1)(a)' in Port N, Otto D, Nacimiento P and Kronke H (eds), *Recognition and Enforcement of Foreign Arbitral Awards: a Global Commentary on the New York Convention* (Wolters Kluwer Law and Business 2010)

Nagareda R, 'Class Certification in the Age of Aggregate Proof' (2009) 84 *New York University Law Review* 97

——, *The Law of Class Actions and Other Aggregate Litigation* (Foundation Press 2009)

Nagy T, 'Credit Rating Agencies and the First Amendment: Applying Constitutional Journalistic Protections to Subprime Mortgage Litigation' (2009) 94 *Minnesota Law Review* 140

Neves DAA, *Manual de Direito Processual Civil* (8th edn, Juspodivm 2016)

Nuss JR, 'Public Policy Invoked as a Ground for Contesting the Enforcement of an Arbitral Award, or for Seeking its Annulment' (2013) 7 *Dispute Resolution International* 119

Nussbaum A, 'Treaties on Commercial Arbitration: a Test of International Private-Law Legislation' (1942) 56 *Harvard Law Review* 219

Olson M, *The Logic of Collective Action: Public Goods and the Theory of Groups* (Harvard University Press 1971)

Ostrom E, *Governing the Commons: The Evolution of Institutions for Collective Action* (Cambridge University Press 1990)

Pace NM and Zakaras L, *Where the Money Goes: Understanding Litigation Expenditures for Producing Electronic Discovery* (Rand Institute for Civil Justice 2012)

Paradise J, Tisdale A, Hall R and Kokkoli E, 'Evaluating Oversight of Human Drugs and Medical Devices: a Case Study of the FDA and Implications for Nanobiotechnology' (2009) 37 *Journal of Law, Medicine & Ethics* 598

Partnoy F, 'The Siskel and Ebert of Financial Markets?: Two Thumbs Down for the Credit Rating Agencies' (1999) 77 *Washington University Law Quarterly* 619

Paul JR, 'The Transformation of International Comity' (2008) 71 *Law and Contemporary Problems* 19

Paulsson J, 'Ethics, Elitism, Eligibility' (1997) 14 *Journal of International Arbitration* 13

Pierson C, *The Modern State* (Routledge 2011)

Pinho HDB, 'A Tutela Coletiva no Brasil e a Sistemática dos Novos Direitos' (2007) 15 *Revista Diálogo Jurídico* 1

Pistor K, 'A Legal Theory of Finance' (2013) Columbia Public Law Research Paper No 13–348

Poorter ID, 'Auditor's Liability towards Third Parties within the EU: A Comparative Study between the United Kingdom, the Netherlands, Germany and Belgium' (2008) 3 *Journal of International Commercial Law and Technology* 68

Poudret JF and Besson S, *Comparative Law of International Arbitration* (Sweet & Maxwell 2007)

Pritchard AC, 'The SEC at 70: Time for Retirement?' (2005) 80 *Notre Dame Law Review* 1073

Ravanides C, 'Arbitration Clauses in Public Company Charters: an Expansion of the ADR Elysian Fields or a Descent into Hades?' (2007) 18 *The American Review of International Arbitration* 371

Ravdin G, 'One Step Forward, Two Steps Back: Arguing for a Transatlantic Investor Protection Regime' (2012) 50 *Columbia Journal of Transnational Law* 490

Redfern A and Hunter M, *Law and Practice of International Commercial Arbitration* (Sweet & Maxwell 2004)

Redish MH, 'Class Actions and the Democratic Difficulty: Rethinking the Intersection of Private Litigation and Public Goals' [2003] *University of Chicago Legal Forum* 71

Reisman WM and Richardson B, 'Tribunals and Courts: An Interpretation of the Architecture of International Commercial Arbitration' in Berg AJ (ed), *Arbitration—The Next Fifty Years* (Kluwer Law International 2012)

Ringe WG and Hellgardt A, 'The International Dimension of Issuer Liability—Liability and Choice of Law from a Transatlantic Perspective' (2011) 31 *Oxford Journal of Legal Studies* 23

Robertson A, 'Introduction: Goals, Rights and Obligations' in Robertson A and Wu TH (eds), *The Goals of Private Law* (Hart Publishing 2009)

Rogers JS, 'Conflict of Laws for Transactions in Securities Held Through Intermediaries' (2006) 39 *Cornell International Law Journal* 285

Rose AM, 'The Multienforcer Approach to Securities Fraud Deterrence: a Critical Analysis' (2010) 158 *University of Pennsylvania Law Review* 2173

Rosenn K, 'The Protection of Judicial Independence in Latin America' (1987) 19 *The University of Miami Inter-American Law Review* 1

Rubenstein WB, 'On What a "Private Attorney General" Is—And Why it Matters' (2004) 57 *Vanderbilt Law Review* 2129

Ruhl G, 'Consumer Protection in Choice of Law' (2011) 44 *Cornell International Law Journal* 569

Santos AO and Gimenez IDP, *Derecho Procesal Civil: El Proceso de Declaracion* (3rd edn, Editorial Universitaria Ramon Areces 2004)

Scarso A, 'The Liability of Credit Rating Agencies in a Comparative Perspective' (2013) 4 *Journal of European Tort Law* 163

Schramm D, Geisinger E and Pinsolle P, 'Article II' in Port N, Otto D, Nacimiento P and Kronke H (eds), *Recognition and Enforcement of Foreign Arbitral Awards: a Global Commentary on the New York Convention* (Wolters Kluwer Law and Business 2010)

Schwarcz SL, 'Enron and the Use and Abuse of Special Purpose Entities in Corporate Structures' (2001–2002) 70 *University of Cincinnati Law Review* 1309

Scott HS, *International Finance: Transactions, Policy, and Regulation* (Foundation Press 2010)

Sebok A, 'The Inauthentic Claim' (2011) 64 *Vanderbilt Law Review* 61

Seligman J, 'The Historical Need for a Mandatory Corporate Disclosure System' (1983) 9 *The Journal of Corporation Law* 1

Shavell S, 'The Fundamental Divergence Between the Private and the Social Motive to Use the Legal System' (1997) 26 *Journal of Legal Studies* 575

Sheppard A, 'Res Judicata and Estoppel' in Cremades B and Lew J (eds), *Parallel State and Arbitral Procedures in International Arbitration* (ICC 2005)

Shleifer A and Wolfenzon D, 'Investor Protection and Equity Markets' (2002) 66 *Journal of Financial Economics* 3

Silberman L, 'The Impact of Jurisdictional Rules and Recognition Practice on International Business Transactions: The US Regime' (2004) 26 *Houston Journal of International Law* 327

——, 'Preclusion Doctrine' in Chase OG and HHershkoff H (eds), *Civil Litigation in Comparative Context* (Thomson West 2007)

Silver C, ' "We're Scared to Death": Class Certification and Blackmail' (2003) 78 *New York University Law Review* 1357

——, 'Ethics and Innovation' (2011) 79 *George Washington Law Review* 754

Skinner Q, 'The State' in Goodin R and Pettit P (eds), *Contemporary Political Philosophy: An Anthology* (Blackwell Publishing 2006)

Soto H, *The Mystery of Capital: Why Capitalism Triumphs in the West and Fails Everywhere Else* (Bantam Press 2000)

Spence M, 'Signaling in Retrospect and the Informational Structure of Markets' (2002) 92 *The American Economic Review* 434

Steele J and Boon WH, 'Mass Justice and its Challenges' in Steele J and Boon WH (eds), *Mass Justice: Challenges of Representation and Distribution* (Edward Elgar 2011)

Steinberg M and Kirby B, 'The Assault on Section 11 of the Securities Act: a Study in Judicial Activism' (2010) 63 *Rutgers Law Review* 1

Stigler GJ, 'Public Regulation of the Securities Markets' (1964) 37 *The Journal of Business* 117

Stoll HR, 'Market Microstructure' in Constantinides GM, Harris M and Stulz RM (eds), *Handbook of the Economics of Finance*, vol 1A (Elsevier 2003)

Stout LA, 'The Unimportance of Being Efficient: An Economic Analysis of Stock Market Pricing and Securities Regulation' (1988) 87 *Michigan Law Review* 613

Stringer D, 'Choice of Law and Choice of Forum in Brazilian International Commercial Contracts: Party Autonomy, International Jurisdiction, and the Emerging Third Way' (2005–2006) 44 *Columbia Journal of Transnational Law* 959

Strong SI, 'Enforcing Class Arbitration in the International Sphere: Due Process and Public Policy Concerns' (2008) 30 *University of Pennsylvania Journal of International Law* 1

——, 'From Class to Collective: The De-Americanization of Class Arbitration' (2010) 26 *Arbitration International* 493

Sylla R, 'An Historical Primer on the Business of Credit Rating Agencies' (Prepared for the Conference The Role of Credit Reporting Systems in the International Economy, 2001)

Symeonides S, 'Choice of Law in Cross-Border Torts: Why Plaintiffs Win, and Should' (2009) 61 *Hastings Law Journal* 337

——, 'Choice of Law in the American Courts in 2009: Twenty-Third Annual Survey' (2010) 58 *American Journal of Comparative Law* 1

——, 'Party Autonomy in Rome I and II from a Comparative Perspective' in Boele-Woelki K, Einhorn, T, Girsberger, D and Symeonides, S (eds), *Convergence and Divergence in Private International Law—Liber Amicorum Kurt Siehr* (Eleven International Publishing 2010)

Szalai IS, 'The Federal Arbitration Act and the Jurisdiction of the Federal Courts' (2007) 12 *Harvard Negotiation Law Review* 319

Talamini E, 'A dimensão coletiva dos direitos individuais homogêneos: ações coletivas e os mecanismos previstos no Código de Processo Civil de 2015' in Zaneti H (ed), *Coleção Repercussões do Novo CPC—Processo Coletivo*, vol 8 (Juspodivm 2016)

Talisse RB, 'Democracy' in Gaus G and D'Agostino F (eds), *The Routledge Companion to Social and Political Philosophy* (Routledge 2013)

Talley EL, 'Cataclysmic Liability Risk among Big Four Auditors' (2006) 106 *Columbia Law Review* 1641

Teubner G, *Law as an Autopoietic System* (Blackwell Publishers 1993)

Theodoro H, *Curso de Direito Processual Civil—Teoria Geral do Direito Processual Civil e Processo de Conhecimento*, vol 1 (Forense 2012)

Thompson F and Pollitt DH, 'Impeachment of Federal Judges: an Historical Overview' (1970–1971) 49 *North Carolina Law Review* 87

Timmer LJ, 'Abolition of *Exequatur* under the Brussels I Regulation: Ill Conceived and Premature?' (2013) 9 *Journal of Private International Law* 129

Twitchell M, 'Why We Keep Doing Business with Doing-Business Jurisdiction' (2001) *University of Chicago Legal Forum* 171

Vanberg G, 'Establishing and Maintaining Judicial Independence' in Whittington K, Kelemen D and Caldeira G (eds), *The Oxford Handbook of Law and Politics* (Oxford University Press 2008)

Velden J and Stefanelli J, *The Effect in the European Community of Judgments in Civil and Commercial Matters: Recognition, Res Judicata and Abuse of Process* (British Institute of International and Comparative Law 2008)

Viscasilas P, 'Arbitrability of (Intra-) Corporate Disputes' in Mistelis LA and Brekoulakis SL (eds), *Arbitrability: International & Comparative Perspectives* (Wolters Kluwer 2009)

Weber M, *The Theory of Social and Economic Organization* (The Free Press 1947)

——, *Economy and Society* (University of California Press 1978)

——, *From Max Weber: Essays in Sociology* (Routledge 1991)

Wegen G and Lindemann C, 'The Law Applicable to Public Offerings in Continental Europe' in Houtte HV (ed), *The Laws of Cross-Border Securities Transactions* (Sweet & Maxwell 1999)

Weintraub RJ, 'The Extraterritorial Application of Antitrust and Securities Law: an Inquiry into the Utility of a "Choice-of-Law" Approach' (1992) 70 *Texas Law Review* 1799

Willging TE, Hooper LL and Niemic RJ, *Empirical Study of Class Actions in Four Federal District Courts: Final Report to the Advisory Committee on Civil Rules* (Federal Judicial Center 1996)

Wolff RP, *In Defense of Anarchism* (Harper & Row 1998)

Wolff TB, 'Preclusion in Class Action Litigation' (2005) 105 *Columbia Law Review* 717

Wurgler J, 'Financial Markets and the Allocation of Capital' (2000) 58 *Journal of Financial Economics* 187

Yeazell SC, 'Group Litigation and Social Context: Toward a History of the Class Action' (1977) 77 *Columbia Law Review* 866

——, 'The Past and Future of Defendant and Settlement Classes in Collective Litigation' (1997) 39 *Arizona Law Review* 687

Zeff SA, 'How the US Accounting Profession Got Where It Is Today: Part I' (2003) 17 *Accounting Horizons* 189

——, 'How the US Accounting Profession Got Where It Is Today: Part II' (2003) 17 *Accounting Horizons* 267

Zeynalova Y, 'The Law on Recognition and Enforcement of Foreign Judgments: Is It Broken and How Do We Fix It?' (2013) 31 *Berkeley Journal of International Law* 155

Zhang M, 'Party Autonomy and Beyond: an International Perspective of Contractual Choice of Law' (2006) 20 *Emory International Law Review* 527

INDEX

NB – Page numbers in **bold** denote information in tables, and those in *italics* denote information in figures

access to justice, 79, 81, 85, 112, 117
    collective redress, 134, 135, 144–45, 158, 176–79, 185
    costs of engaging in a dispute resolution procedure, 113–14, **114**
    European Union, 133
        collective redress, 176–79, 185
    financial intermediary-investor disputes, 85–86, 228
    financial ombudsman service, 120–22
    informational intermediary-investor disputes, 89
    public policy conflicts, 97–98
    self-regulation model for dispute resolution, 123
    small claims courts for dispute resolution, 118–20
    small investors, 95
accountability of decision makers, 107
    balance between accountability and independence, 116
    issuer-investor disputes, 84–85
    judicial accountability, 108–09
    private decision makers, 109–10
    public officials, 108–09
aggregate litigation:
    access to justice, 135, 144–45, 158
        access to justice for small investors, 95
    applicable law, 210–11
    arbitration 117
        access to justice for small investors, 95
        arbitrability, 91–92
        arbitral institutions, 94–95
        arbitration clauses, 92–94
        class arbitration, 160–61
        European Union, 96
        issuer-investor disputes, 83–85
        seat of arbitration, 91–92
    class arbitration, 160–61
    conflicts between group members, 138–39
    conflicts between plaintiffs and lawyer:
        contingency fee arrangements, 137
        fixed sum agreements, 138
        hourly fee arrangements, 138

        role of lawyer, 137
        settlement possibilities, 137
    conflicts in an opt-out procedure, 140–44
    ethical limitations:
        attorney/client relations, 144–45
        champerty and maintenance rules, 144
        rules on client solicitation, 144
    financial intermediary-investor disputes, 159, 160
    incentives of parties, 158
    informational intermediary-investor disputes, 159, 160
    issuer-investor disputes, 159–60
    models of aggregate litigation 162, 185–86
        Capital Market Model Claims Act (D) 2005, 175–76
        class action model (USA), 162–70
        Collective Settlement of Mass Damages Act (NL), 173–74
        collective redress (EU), 176–79
        Group Litigation Orders (UK), 174–75
        representative actions, 170–73
    preclusion principles:
        arbitration, 156–57
        causes of action, 147–48
        claim preclusion, 149
        concept, 145
        exceptions to the mutuality requirement, 151–56
        fairness in legal proceedings and, 146
        issue preclusion, 149–51, 151–52
        judgement on the merits, 148
        jurisdiction, 145–46
        mutuality principle, 146–47, 151–56
        res judicata, 149–51
        right to a fair trial, 146–47
    public policy:
        notice in aggregate litigation, 214–16
    system design 134–35, 158–61
        access to justice, 135, 144–45, 158
        agents, 136
        conflicts included, 137–44
        ethical limitations, 144–45

jurisdiction and enforcement, 203–04
   opt-in mechanisms, 136
   opt-out mechanisms, 136
   preclusion principles, 145–58
   third-party financiers, 139–40
applicable law, 3, 89, 90–94
   choice of law provisions, 204
   contract law, 206–08
   European Union, 205–06
   informational intermediary-investor
      disputes, 89–90
   public policy considerations, 204–05
   tort law, 208–09
   transnational dispute resolution, 204–06
      aggregate litigation, 210–11
      arbitration, 209–10
      contract law, 206–08
      tort law, 208–09
arbitrability, 210
   aggregate litigation, 91–92
   foreign investors suing overseas, 95–96
   public policy and, 185, 216–19
arbitral awards:
   binding nature, 184
   enforcement, 83–84, 101, 103–06, 210
   New York Convention, 83–84, 101,
      103–06, 210
   preclusive effects, 156–57, 161
arbitration:
   aggregate litigation through arbitration 117
   access to justice for small investors, 95
   arbitrability, 91–92
   arbitral institutions, 94–95
   arbitration clauses, 92–94
   European Union, 96
   issuer-investor disputes, 83–85
   seat of arbitration, 91–92
   applicable law, 209–10
   Geneva Convention for the Execution of
      Foreign Arbitral Awards 1927, 104
   Geneva Protocol on Arbitral Clauses
      1923, 103–04
   ICC Draft Convention, 104
   institutional framework 99–100
      consent jurisdictional basis, 101–06
      legal basis, 100–06
   International Chamber of Commerce, 104
   issuer-investor disputes:
      accountability of decision makers, 84–85
      implementation aspects, 85
      independence of decision-makers, 84
      prohibition of opt-out aggregate
         litigation, 83–84
      rule of law, 84–85
      system design, 84–85
      transnational aspects, 84
   national legal frameworks for arbitration:
      Brazil, 102–03

Spain, 102
   United States, 102
New York Convention on International
   Commercial Arbitration 1958, 105
   private arbitration model, 126–27
   state-supervised model:
      fees paid, 125
      qualification of arbitrators, 125
      selection of arbitrators, 125
      United States, 124–25
   transnational aspects of dispute
      resolution, 202–03
   UN Economic and Social Council
      1955, 104
arbitration clauses, 92
   corporate charter clauses, 92–93
   depositary agreement clauses, 94
   informational intermediary services contract
      clauses, 93
auditors' liability:
   Brazil, 77
   compensation, 73–74
   European Union, 77
   issuance of securities, 46–47, *48*, 49–50
   pleading requirements, 76
   United States, 76

Brazil, 9, 25
   arbitration, 102–03
      arbitration clauses, 85
      corporate charters, 218
   BM&F Bovespa, 39, 127
   Câmara de Arbitragem do Mercado, 127, 217
   causes of action, 148
   client solicitation, 144
   Comissão de Valores Mobiliários, 63–64
   consumer protection, 212, 216
   contract law, 206, 207–08
   disclosure duties, 63
      disclosure liability standards, 66
   disclosure of material facts, 64
   financial intermediaries' liability, 70–71
   financial intermediary-investor
      disputes, 225–26
   informational intermediaries' liability, 77
   informational intermediary-investor
      disputes, 227
   issuance of securities, 63–64
   issuer-investor disputes:
      depositary receipt disputes, 222–23
      foreign exchange disputes, 221
   issuers liability 63–66
      disclosure liability standards, 66
   legal certainty, 221–22, 228
   national legal frameworks for
      arbitration, 102–03
   number of securities transactions, 3–4
   preclusion principles:

exceptions to the mutuality requirement, 153, 154–55
  res judicata, 150
prejudicial issues, 158
recognition and enforcement of foreign judgments, 200
regulating agency, 63
representative actions, 170–73
res judicata, 147, 150
self-regulation model for dispute resolution, 123
small claims courts for dispute resolution, 86, 119
system design, 84
tort law, 208
transnational transactions, 49
unilateral jurisdiction systems, 196–97
unilateral recognition systems, 200
US system compared, 64
broker-dealers liability, 67–68
Brussels Regime (EU), 192–94, 198–99
  aggregate litigation, 96, 211
  financial intermediary-investor disputes, 225
  lex damni standard, 221
  preclusion, 149–50

Capital Market Model Claims Act (D) 2005, 175–76
causes of action, 147
  Brazil, 148
  preclusion, 145–46, 147–48, 149
  Spain, 148
  United States, 51–58, 147
champerty and maintenance rules, 82, 144
Charter of Fundamental Rights of the European Union:
  right to a fair trial, 146–47
choice of court:
  Hague Convention, 202
choice of forum, 213
choice of law, 3, 204, 211, 213
  contract law, 206–08
  tort law, 208–09
  see also applicable law
class action model of aggregate litigation (USA):
  background, 162–64
  certification, 166
    process, 167
    settlements, 167
  Federal Rules of Civil Procedure, 166
  prerequisites:
    adequate representation, 165–66
    commonality requirement, 165
    numerosity requirement, 165
    typicality requirement, 165
  Private Securities Litigation Reform Act 1995, 168–69
  securities litigation, 168–70

Securities Litigation Uniform Standards Act 1998, 169
  types, 165–66
class action waivers, 181–82
class arbitration, 159–61, 179
  background, 179–81
  class action waivers, 181–82
  European Union, 185
  other jurisdictions, 184–85
  United States:
    class action waivers, 181–82
    hybrid model, 182–83
    provide-created model, 183–84
class certification, 57, 166–67, 182–83
collective redress, 176–79
  Brazil, 154
  issuer-investor dispute resolution, 81–82
  preclusion 145–46
    causes of action, 148
  see also aggregate litigation; arbitration; class action model of aggregate litigation; class arbitration; representative actions
Collective Settlement of Mass Damages Act (NL), 173–74
commercial arbitration, *see* New York Convention
comity considerations, 106, 194, 196, 200
compensation, 21, 42, 44, 72–74
  aggregate litigation, 129, 135, 138, 158, 178
conflict of laws:
  comity as, 196
  see also applicable law
Consumer Credit Act 2006 (UK):
  financial ombudsman scheme, 120–21
consumer protection, 97, 120–21, 176, 208
contract law, 206
  Brazil, 206, 207–08
  economic organisation of private matters 18
    property law compared, 19
  European Union, 207
  United States, 206, 208
corporate charters, 64
  arbitration clauses, 83–85, 89, 92–94, 159
  Brazil, 217
  Spain, 218
  United States, 218–19
  public policy considerations, 218–20
costs of engaging in a dispute resolution procedure, 113
  costs of access, **114**, 114
  costs of evidence, 115
  costs of legal representation, 115
  small claims courts for dispute resolution, 120
courts
  parties' relationship with:
    civil law systems, 190
    doing business basis of jurisdiction, 191

personal jurisdiction by service of
process, 190
transnational dispute resolution, 190–91
United States, 190
credit rating agencies:
issuing securities, 47, *48*
liability for transnational security
transactions 49–50
compensation, 72–73
European Union, 75
gross negligence, 75–76
intention, 75
knowing or reckless failure of duty, 75
misrepresentation, 75–76
United States, 74–75
cross-border transactions, *see* transnational
aspects of dispute resolution

damages, 5, 45
Brazil, 65
calculation methods, 66
European Union, 62
United States, 53–54, 57
see also settlements
democracy:
institutionalisation of, 16–17
legitimate power, exercise of, 15
deterrence, 21, 42–44, 117
aggregate litigation, 135–37
disclosure liability standards, 66
disclosure of information, 6
Brazil, 63–64
mandatory disclosure systems:
criticisms of, 32–33
defence of, 33–36
quality of information, 33
self-induced disclosure theory, 34
dispute resolution mechanisms:
role, 21
public and private enforcement, 21–22
opt-out dispute resolution mechanisms, 216
see also aggregate litigation; arbitration
dispute resolution systems, 79, 187–88, 228
applicable law 204–06
aggregate litigation, 210–11
arbitration, 209–10
contract law, 206–08
tort law, 208–09
arbitration, 202–03
costs of engaging in a dispute resolution
procedure 113
costs of access, **114**, 114
costs of evidence, 115
costs of legal representation, 115
costs of maintaining dispute resolution
systems, 113
current framework, 80
access to foreign systems, 80–81

jurisdiction, 80
financial intermediary-investor disputes,
85–88, 224–26
informational intermediary-investor disputes,
88–90, 227
institutional framework 99–100
access to justice, 112
consent jurisdictional basis, 101–06
decision makers independence and
accountability, 106–10
direct jurisdictional basis, 100
economic aspects, 112–15, 116–17
implications, 115–17
legal basis, 100–06
legal reasoning, 110–12
transparency, 112, 116
international models:
international courts, 128–29
international arbitral institutions, 130
European cross-border mechanisms,
130–31, 133
issuer-investor disputes, 81–85, 220–24
jurisdiction, 188–97
jurisdiction and enforcement of aggregate
litigation, 203–04
national models:
arbitration, 124–27
Financial Ombudsman Service model,
120–22, 132
self-regulation model, 123
small claims court model, 118–20
public policy provisions 212
arbitrability of securities disputes, 216–17
arbitration based on corporate
charters, 218–20
notices in aggregate litigation, 214–16
securities disputes, 212–14
recognition and enforcement of foreign
judgments, 197–201
Judgements Project, 201–02
Dodd-Frank Act 2010 (USA):
broker-dealers' liability, 67–68
information intermediaries' liability, 75
doing business basis of jurisdiction, 190–91
due diligence, 66, 89, 92

ecological theory of state creation:
environmental circumscription, 12
resource concentration, 12–13
social circumscription, 12–13
enforcement, 3, 21–22, 38–39
see also private enforcement; recognition and
enforcement of foreign judgments
estoppel, 152, 215
European Convention on Human Rights:
right to a fair trial, 146–47, 214
European Union, 1, 9, 36, 49–50
aggregate litigation 176–77

access to justice, 177–78
  aggregate litigation through arbitration, 96
  contingency fees, 178
  ethical limitations, 177–78
  external funding, 177
  opt-in system, 177–78
  private parties and, 178–79
  procedural fairness, 178
class arbitration, 185
cross-border disputes, 130–31
Fin-net, 130–31, 133
financial intermediaries' liability 68
  appropriateness standard, 68–69
  eligible counterparties, 69
  execution-only service, 69
  harmonisation, 70
  suitability requirement, 68
  US system compared, 70
Financial Service Action Plan 1998, 36
information intermediaries' liability, 77
issuers' liability, 58–60
  French domestic law, 62
  German domestic law, 62
  harmonisation efforts, 62–63
  Spanish domestic law, 60–62
  UK domestic law, 62
securities regulation:
  maximum harmonisation approach, 36
  minimum harmonisation approach, 36
  mutual recognition principle, 36
single market, 36–37
Treaty on the Functioning of the European
    Union, 36
  see also Brussels Regime
exequatur procedure, 199
  double-*exequatur*, 105

false or misleading information, 50–51, 53–54,
    55–56, 58, 66–67, 72
  aggregate litigation, 134, 139, 152, 159–60
  Germany, 175
  informational intermediary-investor disputes,
    88–89, 160
  issuer-investor disputes, 81, 159
  Rome II Regulation, 211
Fin-net (EU), 97, 130–33
Financial Conduct Authority (UK):
  financial ombudsman scheme, 121–22
Financial Industry Regulatory Authority
    (FINRA) (USA), 39, 124–25
  cost of access to dispute resolution
    procedures, **114**
  financial intermediaries' liability, 67
financial intermediaries' liability, 66
  Brazil, 70–71
  broker-dealers, 67–68
  European Union, 68
    appropriateness standard, 68–69

    eligible counterparties, 69
    execution-only service, 69
    harmonisation, 70
    suitability requirement, 68
    US system compared, 70
  investment advisers, 67
  United States:
    Dodd-Frank Act 2010, 67–68
    European Union compared, 70
    FINRA rules, 67
    Investment Advisers Act 1940, 66–67
financial intermediary-investor disputes, 47,
    224, 228
  access to justice, 85–86
  development of a network of dispute
    resolution systems, 86–87, 96–97
  financial intermediaries seeking out
    investors, 86, 87
  financial intermediary acts towards
    investors, 226
  implementation aspects, 87–88
  investor acts towards financial
    intermediaries, 225–26
  investors seeking out financial
    intermediaries, 86–87
  language difficulties, 87
financial markets:
  allocation of economic resources, 26–27
  costs of transactions, 26
  definition, 25
  developing rules and institutions, 26
  price accuracy:
    consequences of inaccuracy, 29–31
    corporate governance failures, 30–31
    incorporation of information into
      prices, 28–29
    market liquidity, 30
    mechanics, 27–29
    non-optimal capital allocation, 29
    role, 25–26
Financial Ombudsman Service model (UK) for
    dispute resolution, 86, 120–22, 132
Financial Services and Markets Act 2000
    (UK), 62
  financial ombudsman scheme, 120–22
formation of the modern state:
  ecological theory of state, 12–13
  exercise of legitimate power, 13–15
  democracy, 15
  rule of law, 15–16
forum non conveniens:
  unilateral jurisdiction systems, 194–95, 225
fraud-on-the-market doctrine, 57–58
freedom of contract, 20
funding of dispute resolutions systems:
  class actions, 184
  European Union, 177
  Financial Ombudsman Service, 120

Netherlands, 174
small claims courts for dispute resolution, 118
United States, 184

Geneva Convention for the Execution of Foreign
Arbitral Awards 1927, 104
Geneva Protocol on Arbitral Clauses
1923, 103–04
Germany:
Capital Market Model Claims Act (D)
2005, 175–76
globalisation
impact on financial transactions, 1–3, 85, 97
Group Litigation Orders (UK), 174–75

heightened pleading requirements, 52, 55–57

imperfect markets, 20
see also price (in)accuracy
independence of decision makers, 107
balance between accountability and
independence, 116
issuer-investor disputes, 84
judicial independence, 107–09
private decision makers, 109–10
informational intermediaries' liability:
auditors liability, 76–77
compensation, 73–74
pleading requirements, 76
compensation:
auditing firms, 73–74
credit rating agencies, 72–73
credit rating agencies' liability, 74–75
compensation, 72–73
gross negligence, 75–76
intention, 75
knowing or reckless failure of duty, 75
misrepresentation, 75–76
disclosure duties, 33
liability regimes 71–72
Australia, 75–76
Dodd-Frank Act 2010, 75
European Union, 75
United States, 74–75
informational intermediary-investor
disputes, 47
access to justice, 89
applicable law, 89–90, 227
extent of harm caused, 89
false/misleading information, 88
jurisdiction, 227
recognition and enforcement of
judgements, 227
scope of different laws, 89
integrated jurisdiction systems:
forum court and other courts, relationship
between, 191, 192–94
international arbitral institutions, 130

International Centre for Settlement of
Investment Disputes (ICSID), 130
International Chamber of Commerce (ICC), 104
cost of dispute resolution, **114**
International Court of Justice, 126, 128
international courts:
International Court of Justice, 126, 128
International Tribunal for the Law of the
Sea, 128–29
International Tribunal for the Law of the
Sea, 128–29
investment advisers' liability, 66–68
Investment Advisers Act 1940:
financial intermediaries' liability, 66–67
issuer-investor disputes, 47
aggregate litigation, 82–84, 117
arbitration:
accountability of decision makers, 84–85
implementation aspects, 85
independence of decision-makers, 84
prohibition of opt-out aggregate
litigation, 83–84
rule of law, 84–85
system design, 84–85
dispute resolution 81–82
accountability of decision makers, 84–85
aggregate litigation, 82–84, 117
arbitration, 83–85
independence of decision-makers, 84
prohibition of opt-out aggregate
litigation, 83–84
rule of law, 84–85
system design, 84–85
transnational aspects of dispute
resolution 220
depositary receipt transactions, 222–23
exchange-based transactions, 220–23
foreign-exchange-based
transactions, 220–22
open market transactions, 223–24
issuers' liability, 50–51
Brazil:
Civil Code, 64–65
measure of damages, 65
European Union:
EU law, 58–60
French domestic law, 62
German domestic law, 62
harmonisation efforts, 62–63
Spanish domestic law, 60–62
UK domestic law, 62
United States:
Private Securities Litigation Reform Act
1995 (USA), 55–57
Securities Act 1933, 51–54
Securities and Exchange Act 1934
(USA), 54–57
issuing securities, 46, *48*

auditing firms, 46–47
audits, 46
Brazil, 63–64
credit rating firms, 47
distribution of prospectuses, 47
placing securities on the market, 47
registration statements, 47

joint and several liability, 66
issuers, 52, 55–56
judgment on the merits:
preclusion principles, 146, 148
judiciary, 100
class certification, 167
independence and accountability, 107–09
international courts, 128–29
legal reasoning, 110–11
remuneration, 22, 110
jurisdiction, 80
aggregate litigation, 145–46, 203–04
doing business basis of jurisdiction, 191
preclusion principles, 145–46
transnational dispute resolution 188–89
courts and parties, relationship
between, 190–91
forum courts and other courts, relationship
between, 191–97
integrated jurisdiction systems, 192–94
unilateral jurisdiction systems, 194–97
unilateral jurisdiction systems, 191
jurisdiction to prescribe, 194–96

legal institutions:
economic importance, 17–22
legal reasoning, 110–11
transparency, 112, 116
legal representation costs, 115
legal uncertainty, 6, 62–63, 66, 97–98, 106, 163–
64, 202, 204–05
legitimate power, exercise of, 13–15
democracy, 15
rule of law, 15–16
liability regimes, 45–46
financial intermediaries, 66
Brazil, 70–71
European Union, 68–70
United States, 66–68, 70
informational intermediaries, 71–74
Australia, 75
Brazil, 77
European Union, 75, 77
United States, 74–75, 76
issuers 50–51
Brazil, 63–65
European Union, 58–63
United States, 51–58
types of disputes, 47, 77–78
loss causation, 53, 56–57

mandatory disclosure systems, 32–36
Markets in Financial Instruments Directive 2004
(MiFID) (EU), 40, 70
misleading information, *see* false or misleading
information
mutuality principle:
claim preclusion, 149
exceptions to the mutuality requirement:
Brazil, 153, 154–55
Spain, 153, 155–56
United States, 151–52
issue preclusion, 149–51
exceptions to the mutuality
requirement, 151–52
preclusion principles:
Brazil, 147
European Union, 146–47
right to a fair trial, 146–47
United States, 146
unfairness in collateral estoppel, 152

national mandatory law, 4, 216, 224
negligence, 62, 64, 75–76
Netherlands:
Collective Settlement of Mass Damages Act
(NL), 173–74
New York Convention, 84, 88, 91–92, 96, 156–
57, 202–03, 210
Conference on International Commercial
Arbitration 1958, 105–06
New York Stock Exchange, 39, 219
non-contractual obligations, 209

opt-out procedures:
aggregate litigation design:
conflicts in an opt-out procedure,
138, 140–44
opt-out mechanisms, 136
issuer-investor disputes, 82
prohibition of opt-out aggregate
litigation, 83–84
notice in aggregate litigation, 214–16
preclusion principles, 145, 151–56
prohibition of opt-out aggregate
litigation, 83–84

party autonomy doctrine, 206
Permanent Court of Arbitration (PCA), 130
personal jurisdiction by service of process, 190
preclusion principles:
aggregate litigation design, 145–58
arbitration, 156–57
causes of action, 147–48
claim preclusion, 149
concept, 145
exceptions to the mutuality requirement:
Brazil, 153, 154–55
Spain, 153, 155–56

United States, 151–52
issue preclusion, 149–51, 151–52
judgement on the merits, 148
jurisdiction, 145–46
  fairness in legal proceedings and, 146
mutuality principle, 146–47, 151–56
res judicata, 149–51
right to a fair trial, 146–47
price (in)accuracy:
  consequences of inaccuracy:
    corporate governance failures, 30–31
    market liquidity, 30
    non-optimal capital allocation, 29
  incorporation of information into
    prices, 28–29
  mechanics, 27–29
Private Securities Litigation Reform Act 1995
    (USA), 55–57
  heightened pleading standards, 56
  impact, 56–57
  joint and several liability, 56
  proportionate liability, 56
  safe-harbour, 55–56
private enforcement, 7–8, 21
  advantages, 43
  importance of, 37–44
  public enforcement compared, 41–44
  standards, 40–41
private regulation, 39
  see also Financial Industry Regulatory
    Authority
property rights, 18–19
  economic organisation of private matters, 18
    avoidance of disputes on use of
      resources, 18
    incentives to invest, 18
    overuse of resources, 18
  proportionate liability, 52, 55–56
prospectuses:
  European Union, 50, 59–60
  France, 62
  Germany, 62
  issuance of securities, 47, *48*, 63–64
  prospectus disclosure, 220
  prospectus liability, 61–62
  Spain, 61
  UK, 62
  United States, 53
public enforcement, 21–22
  enforcers, 41
    remuneration, 41–42
  goals, 42
  government agencies, 41
  justifications for, 43–44
  non-compliance, 42–43
  private enforcement compared, 41–44
public goods nature of information, 33–34
public policy provisions, 212

arbitrability of securities disputes, 185, 216–17
arbitration based on corporate
    charters, 218–20
  notices in aggregate litigation, 214–16
  securities disputes, 212–14

recognition and enforcement of foreign
    judgments:
  Brussels Regime, 198–99
  grounds for refusal of recognition, 198–99
  integrated recognition and enforcement
    systems, 198–99
  Judgements Project, 201–02
  transnational aspects of dispute resolution,
    197–202
  unilateral recognition systems 200
    Brazil, 200
    United Kingdom, 201
    United States, 200–01
registration statements:
  credit-rating agencies' liability, 75
  issuance of securities, 47, *48*, 52–53
regulation, *see* securities regulation
reliance, 56, 75
  fraud-on-the-market theory, 57–58
  registration statements, on, 52, 53
  statutory audit, on, 76
remuneration:
  arbitrators, 114, 126
  judges, 22, 27, 110, 120, 128
  public and private enforcers, 41–42
representative actions:
  Brazil, 170–71, 173
  Spain, 171–73
res judicata, 147, 149–55, 157, 165
  preclusion principles, 149–51
Restatement (Second) of Conflict of Laws
    (USA), 206, 227
Restatement (Second) of Judgments (USA),
    147, 151
Restatement (Third) of Foreign Relations of the
    United States (USA), 195, 200–01
right to a fair trial, 83–84, 146–47, 214–15
Rome I Regulation (EU), 207, 208
Rome II Regulation (EU), 208–09, 211, 221
rule of law, 1, 14–15, 22, 106–07, 116–17
  judiciary, role of, 17, 108–09
  legal reasoning, 111
  legitimate power, exercise of, 15–16

safe harbour, 55–56
securities:
  advantages, 24, 25
  definition, 24
  regulation:
    disclosure duties, 32–36
  role, 24
Securities Act 1933 (USA), 51–52

damages, 53
grounds for recovery, 52–54
identification of defendants, 54
joint and several liability, 52
knowledge of untrue or misleading
statement, 53
loss causation, 53
proportionate liability, 52
reliance, 53
Section 11, 52–53
Section 12, 53–54
statutory defences, 52–53
Securities and Exchange Act 1934 (USA), 54
damages, 57
forbidden behaviour, 55
fraud-on-market doctrine, 57–58
heightened pleading standards, 56
identification of defendants, 57
joint and several liability, 56
Private Securities Litigation Reform Act
1995, 55–57
proportionate liability, 56
recognition of rights, 55
safe-harbour, 55–56
Securities and Exchange Commission
(USA), 39
securities regulation, 3–4
disclosure duties, 32–36
mandatory disclosure system:
criticisms of, 32–33
defence of, 33–36
private enforcement, 39–40
public regulation, 39
regulatory regime, 37
enforcement, 38–39
design of the system, 38
public/private, 39–40
self-regulation model for dispute resolution, 123
settlement procedures, 87, 95, 104, 129, 133,
137–38, 140, 177, 210, 215–16
class settlements, 112, 167, 173–74,
183, 203–04
share price accuracy, *see* price (in)accuracy
small claims courts for dispute resolution:
access to justice, 120
Brazil, 119
costs, 120
criticisms, 120
funding, 118
jurisdictional scope, 118
procedure, 119
quality of justice, 120
structure, 119–20
Spain:
arbitration, 102, 218
auditors' liability, 76–77
disclosure liability standards, 66
domestic securities disputes, 60–61

exceptions to the mutuality requirement,
153, 155–56
national legal frameworks for arbitration, 102
preclusion principles:
mutuality requirement, 153, 155–56
res judicata, 153
representative actions, 171–73
states, *see* ecological theory of state; formation of
the modern state

technology:
impact on financial transactions, 2, 5, 33, 84
third parties, 144–45
aggregate litigation costs, 81
arbitration:
consent jurisdictional basis, 101
liability regimes, 77
res judicata, 147, 153
tort law, 208
Brazil, 208
European Union, 208–09
United States, 208
transnational aspects of dispute resolution,
187–88, 228
applicable law 204–06
aggregate litigation, 210–11
arbitration, 209–10
contract law, 206–08
tort law, 208–09
arbitration, 202–03
implications for securities disputes:
financial intermediary-investor
disputes, 224–26
informational intermediary-investor
disputes, 227
issuer-investor disputes, 220–24
jurisdiction, 188–97
jurisdiction and enforcement of aggregate
litigation, 203–04
public policy provisions 212
arbitrability of securities disputes, 216–17
arbitration based on corporate
charters, 218–20
notices in aggregate litigation, 214–16
securities disputes, 212–14
recognition and enforcement of foreign
judgments, 197–201
Judgements Project, 201–02
transnational transactions:
Brazil, 49
European Union, 50
United States, 49–50
transparency, 85, 220
dispute resolution systems, 112, 116
Financial Ombudsman Service, 122
private arbitration, 127
self-regulation model for dispute
resolution, 123

uncertainty, *see* legal uncertainty
unconscionability:
  class action waivers, 181–82
unilateral jurisdiction systems, 191
  Brazil, 196–97
  forum non conveniens, 194–95
  jurisdiction to prescribe, 194–96
  United Kingdom, 195–96
  United States, 194–96
United Kingdom, 195–96
  auditors' liability, 76
  Financial Ombudsman Service, 86, 120–22
  Group Litigation Orders (UK), 174–75
  liability regimes, 62
  recognition and enforcement of foreign
    judgments, 201
  unilateral jurisdiction systems, 195–96
  unilateral recognition systems, 201
United Nations:
  international arbitration:
    UN Economic and Social Council
      1955, 104
  International Court of Justice, 128
United States, 9
  class action model of aggregate
    litigation 162
    background, 162–64
    certification, 166–67
    prerequisites, 165–66
    securities litigation and, 168–70
    types, 165–66
  class arbitration 179
    background, 179–81

class action waivers, 181–82
  hybrid model, 182–83
  provide-created model, 183–84
financial intermediaries' liability, 66
  Dodd-Frank Act 2010, 67–68
  European Union compared, 70
  FINRA rules, 67
  Investment Advisers Act 1940, 66–67
information intermediaries' liability, 76
issuers' liability:
  Private Securities Litigation Reform Act
    1995 (USA), 55–57
  Securities Act 1933, 51–54
  Securities and Exchange Act 1934
    (USA), 54–57
national legal frameworks for arbitration, 102
opt-out procedure, 140–41
preclusion principles:
  exceptions to the mutuality
    requirement, 151–52
  mutuality requirement, 151–52
  res judicata, 150–51
Private Securities Litigation Reform Act
  1995, 55–57
recognition and enforcement of foreign
  judgments, 200–01
Securities and Exchange Act 1934, 54–58
Securities Act 1933, 51–54
transnational transactions, 49–50
unilateral jurisdiction systems, 194–96

World Trade Organization, 106
  Dispute Settlement Body, 129